POLICING INTIMACY

POLICING INTIMACY

Law, Sexuality, and the Color Line in Twentieth-Century Hemispheric American Literature

Jenna Grace Sciuto

University Press of Mississippi / Jackson

The University Press of Mississippi is the scholarly publishing agency of
the Mississippi Institutions of Higher Learning: Alcorn State University,
Delta State University, Jackson State University, Mississippi State University,
Mississippi University for Women, Mississippi Valley State University,
University of Mississippi, and University of Southern Mississippi.

www.upress.state.ms.us

The University Press of Mississippi is a member
of the Association of University Presses.

Copyright © 2021 by University Press of Mississippi
All rights reserved

First printing 2021
∞

*Portions of chapters 1 and 4 appear in *Faulkner and the Black Literatures of the Americas* from the University Press of Mississippi, edited by Jay Watson and James G. Thomas, Jr. Sections of the introduction and chapter 1 appear in *ARIEL: A Review of International English Literature*, Volume 47, Issue 4, October 2016, pages 1–23. Copyright © 2016 Johns Hopkins University Press and the University of Calgary.

Library of Congress Cataloging-in-Publication Data available

LCCN 2021006483
ISBN 9781496833440 (hardback)
ISBN 9781496833457 (trade paperback)
ISBN 9781496833464 (epub single)
ISBN 9781496833471 (epub institutional)
ISBN 9781496833488 (pdf single)
ISBN 9781496833495 (pdf institutional)

British Library Cataloging-in-Publication Data available

*Frank, Joanne, and Kimi, this one is for you.
And for Joan, who taught me to wonder.*

CONTENTS

ACKNOWLEDGMENTS ... IX

INTRODUCTION ... 3

CHAPTER 1.
"We Will Have to Wait"
Racial Hierarchies, Plantation Intimacy, and Sexual Policing in William Faulkner's Mississippi ... 21

CHAPTER 2.
"There Is No In-Between"
Community, Sexuality, and the Shifting Construction of Race in Ernest Gaines's Louisiana ... 47

CHAPTER 3.
"They Were Starting Something"
Race, Gender, and Failed Revolution in Ernest Gaines's Of Love and Dust ... 74

CHAPTER 4.
"For Fear of a Scandal"
Sexual Control, Racism, and the Public Nature of Private Relations in Marie Chauvet's Twentieth-Century Haiti ... 99

CHAPTER 5.
"We Are Trawling in Silences Here"
Race, Sexuality, and Unnarratable Histories in Literary Depictions of Dominican Dictatorship ... 134

CODA
Looking Back in Resistance, Looking to the Present ... 166

NOTES ... 176

WORKS CITED ... 216

INDEX ... 234

ACKNOWLEDGMENTS

I have so many individuals and institutions to thank for helping to make this project possible. Thank you to Elizabeth Maddock Dillon, Kimberly Juanita Brown, and Nicole N. Aljoe for sharing your brilliance, guidance, and unending support over the years. Elizabeth, thanks for the ever-accumulating sage advice and insightful feedback. Kimberly, I am so grateful for our strategizing sessions, and I don't know where I would be without your kindness and wisdom. Nicole, I deeply appreciate everything you have done for me. I am so thankful for your friendship and mentorship. And more specifically, thank you for introducing me to *The Brief Wondrous Life of Oscar Wao* and its deconstruction of hypermasculinity in the Introduction to Postcolonial Literature course for which I worked as your teaching assistant at Northeastern University. To my colleague and friend John T. Matthews, thank you for your generosity, feedback, and encouragement, as well as for that ride to West Point and the June Bugs inclusion! I have learned so much from you.

Along with Nicole and Jack, a number of colleagues and friends assisted with this project through reading chapter drafts and providing invaluable feedback. I am eternally grateful for the insights of Matthew Dischinger, Amber Engelson, Zack Finch, Taylor Hagood, Maria Hebert-Leiter, Amy King, and James Pihakis, as well as the reviewer of the manuscript who helped with the framing of the final chapters. Maria, thanks in particular for your insights into Cajun culture. In addition to Zack and Amber, I am indebted to the other members of my faculty writing group, Caren Beilin, Hannah Noel, and Victoria Papa, for their brilliance. Caren, thanks for leading me to push further on the disruptive aspects of both love and literature. Zack, thank you for encouraging me to explicate the relationship between the form and content of the novels more directly, and for all your generous feedback—particularly in the final stretch. A hearty thank-you also to my graduate school writing group: Elizabeth Hopwood and Lana Cook! Erich T. Nunn, thanks for your guidance and for connecting me with like-minded scholars. You and Matt have helped me to find a space within southern studies to share my work and ideas, and I am grateful. Richard Lawrence and John Guevremont, thank you for sharing your knowledge and love of literature with me all those years ago at Mount St. Charles Academy.

I'd like to acknowledge my colleagues at the Massachusetts College of Liberal Arts, including Mark Miller for his support and continuous advocacy, Jennifer Dermady, David Langston, and many others in my department and across campus. Thank you to my current and former students (looking at you, Bryanna Bradley!). With each semester, I learn so much from you. Shun Y. Kiang, Rebecca Nisetich, and Zakiya Adair, I look forward to many future collaborations. And thank you to my fellow officers of the William Faulkner Society.

I'm thankful for the wisdom and fellowship of all those involved with the National Endowment for the Humanities Summer Institute, "Ernest J. Gaines and the Southern Experience"—especially the director of the Ernest J. Gaines Center, Cheylon Woods, for her deep knowledge of the archives, Matthew Teutsch for the slew of great resources, and Katharine Henry for generously sharing her scans. I am grateful to have received the 2016 and 2018 Faculty Incentive Awards for Junior Faculty from the Massachusetts College of Liberal Arts that supported much of the travel required by this project, the Lillian Gary Taylor Visiting Fellowship in American Literature that enabled me to work with the William Faulkner Collection at the University of Virginia, and the AAUW American Fellowship Summer/Short-Term Research Publication Grant that allowed me to write full-time when it was most needed in the summer of 2018. Thank you to the Faulkner Society for the John W. Hunt Memorial Scholarship, which supported me in presenting the paper that laid the foundation for this project at the "Faulkner and the Black Literatures of the Americas" Conference in 2013. Thank you to the librarians, curators, and archivists at UVA's Albert and Shirley Small Special Collections Library, the Harry Ransom Center at the University of Texas at Austin, and the John Carter Brown Library at Brown University for all of your knowledge and assistance. John B. Padgett, thank you for the creation of your incomparable website, William Faulkner on the Web, and for allowing me to reprint two of the essential genealogies. Thanks to Stephen Railton for involving me in the Digital Yoknapatawpha project as a collaborating teacher. Lastly, although not directly connected to this project, I was grateful to participate in the National Endowment for the Humanities Summer Institute, "José Martí and the Immigrant Communities of Florida in Cuban Independence and the Dawn of the American Century," at the University of Tampa in the summer of 2019. James López and Denis Rey, thanks for the opportunity, and to all the participants, I learned so much from you that I cannot wait to bring into my future projects.

Undying gratitude to my amazing support system without whom I could not have imagined making it out of graduate school, including my family—Frank, Joanne, and Kimi (and Brent and Zooey!)—as well as my incredible friends, including Emily Artiano, Jenn Chan, Betsy DiPardo, Katie Gardner, Liz Hartung, Ben Kamber, Dayne Wahl, and many more. I feel lucky that I have you in my life every day. Maggie the cat, you are the perfect writing buddy. And finally, to my grandmother Joan, who passed on during the writing of this book, thank you for sharing your passion for learning with me. You are forever my role model and my ideal of a strong, independent, intellectually curious woman.

POLICING INTIMACY

INTRODUCTION

Sexual control of colonized bodies in the French American colonies, such as Haiti and Louisiana, can be traced back to the 1685 Code Noir, a colonial policy relying on surveillance and the regulation of behavior to instate hierarchies of race, class, gender, and sexuality. According to the code, which was applied throughout King Louis XIV's French colonial empire, if a free man had children with an enslaved woman, he was to be fined two thousand pounds of sugar, and if the woman was his own property, she and her child were to be sent to work at the local hospital, remaining perpetually enslaved (Riddell 323). If the offending father married the woman within the rites of the church, however, she and her offspring were freed and the children became legitimate (Riddell 323). While the Code Noir was not always observed, it was an attempt to regulate the social conditions of slavery—in particular, the status of the enslaved population, the interactions between the enslavers and the enslaved, and the punishments applied if either group should not adhere to the code. Through this policy, control over sexuality became an official, national project in the colonies: official since it was authorized by those in power, and national because it occurred broadly at the level of government, laws, and court proceedings.

Attempts to control interracial sexual relations were transmitted from the French colonial period of the Code Noir to later decades in distinct but still recognizable forms. For example, Claire Clamont, narrator of Marie Chauvet's novella *Love*, directly experiences the obsession with and unrelenting observation of the behavior of others rampant in her unnamed Haitian town in 1939, which can be directly connected back to this history.[1] A shift occurred in the postindependence period from European pan-Caribbean racial laws like the Code Noir to national forms and systems, illustrated by the repressive reign of a totalitarian dictator in the novella and the policing of individuals' intimate behavior by the collective community. In this way, the Code Noir's emphasis on surveillance and the regulation of sexuality, both in terms of preference and activity, has echoed in wider contexts across the centuries and throughout the hemisphere.

Policing Intimacy analyzes literary depictions of sexual policing of the color line across multiple spaces with diverse colonial histories that resulted in the construction of societies, cultures, and identity categories grounded in different ideological and legal systems. The four connected spaces include Mississippi through William Faulkner's work, Louisiana through Ernest Gaines's novels, Haiti through the work of Marie Chauvet and Edwidge Danticat, and the Dominican Republic through writing by Julia Alvarez, Junot Díaz, and Nelly Rosario. I begin my exploration with representations of the late 1930s and early 1940s—the end of the plantation economy in the US South and the post–US occupation years in Haiti and the Dominican Republic (DR). I then expand outward to the latter half of the twentieth century, the 1950s through 1980s, to focus on the dictatorial regimes of François Duvalier in Haiti and Rafael Leónidas Trujillo Molina in the DR, as well as immigration from Hispaniola to the US. This literature reflects how, despite the different constructions of race in these regions, the policing of sexuality by communities remained in vestigial forms. In these novels, we see how, by the 1930s and 1940s, national forms of control had supplanted the sweeping pan-Caribbean racial codes, functioning both at the level of unofficial plantation rules governing interpersonal behavior and as repressive regulation imposed by dictators and their supporters.

Thus, I consider the residual effects of British, French, and Spanish colonialisms by reading the early twentieth-century period in terms of a post-/neocoloniality connecting US democracy and foreign policy, such as military occupations, to Caribbean dictatorships.[2] Ultimately, through linking these disparate spaces, I argue that the policing of sexual activity was used to ensure the continuity of hierarchical structures of race, class, gender, and sexual preference, including the elevated position of Whiteness, across varying societies in the hemispheric south. This literature reveals that support for the status quo is resurgent in periods of historical transition when adherence to lingering colonial ideologies begins to break down. For instance, after slavery was abolished in the US, the fears surrounding the blurring of the groups constructed as Black and White led White people to fasten "on the taboo of sex between black men and white women with newfound urgency" (Hodes, *White Women, Black Men* 147), fixating on a color line, in an attempt to control the bonds of love and family, in addition to material effects, such as lines of inheritance.[3]

Sexuality, thus, reveals itself to be a specific expression of White supremacist neocolonial relations throughout the US South and Greater Caribbean. Sexual legislation is directly linked to the preservation of Whiteness as a source of power, privilege, and protected capital—a central motivation for this regulation linking circum-Caribbean societies. It becomes clear through an intersectional lens that racialized, queer, and gendered bodies are policed more ardently than those identities topping the social hierarchies. Patterns are discernable, as a result of systemic inequality and large-scale historical events, revealing the ways in which private relations can reflect national occurrences and the intimate can be brought under public scrutiny. As Ann Laura Stoler succinctly states, "Matters of the intimate are critical sites for the consolidation of colonial power" (4).[4] However, on an individual level, love, or deep bonds of affection, has revolutionary power to challenge existing hierarchies.[5] Love as resistance to the confining social formations runs throughout the novels explored here, revealing what literature gives access to that the study of history can obscure. Acknowledging and recognizing the widespread effects of colonial ideologies and hierarchies across the circum-Caribbean can in turn bring to light permutations of resistance to the violent discriminations of the status quo.[6]

WAVES OF HISTORICAL UPHEAVAL ACROSS TIME AND SPACE

In terms of the logic of periodization, this project focuses on waves of historical upheaval and moments of transition running throughout the twentieth century when the hierarchical mentalities and policing of sexuality become even more entrenched. Each historical moment functions as a node linking the spaces explored here with some points of overlap between time and place. Chapter 1 analyzes the depiction of Mississippi in the 1930s and 1940s in Faulkner's *Go Down, Moses* (1942) and *Requiem for a Nun* (1951), along with examples from the immediate post-Emancipation era, also portrayed in *Go Down, Moses*, as well as in *Absalom, Absalom!* (1936). I examine the two periods together to emphasize the similarities and differences between these times of transition: Reconstruction (1863–1877), following the Civil War, was a period of change in the South, and similarly, the 1930s–1940s represented the final years of the plantation economy and the shift to a more modern capitalist system, with technological advances finally resulting in the dissolution of the plantation economy in the 1940s (Mandle 93). The 1930s and 1940s were also an important period in the fiction of another US southern writer, Ernest Gaines, and his portrayals of plantation culture in rural Louisiana. Louisiana has a distinct colonial history as a former French and Spanish colony where assimilation was not replaced by segregation until after the Louisiana Purchase in 1803 (Ladd xiv). The transition away from the plantation economy similarly positioned these decades as an era of change in Louisiana during which White Cajun farmers, with the aid of tractors, began to take over land that had previously been worked by Black sharecroppers.

The points of connection highlighted in this project progress linearly in time, replicating the artifice of order typical of historical studies, while moving spatially south to consider examples located to the south of the US South—"to the south of this capitalized South" (Glissant 30). The racialized policing common to the US writers examined here also plays a role in Marie Chauvet's fiction. Chapter 4 analyzes her novella *Love*, the first story of the triptych *Love, Anger, Madness* (1968), which, like Gaines's work, was written in the 1960s to critique the societal adherence to hierarchical structures in the 1930s and 1940s and the accompanying racism, colorism, classism, and sexism. *Love* is set in post–American occupation Haiti (1934–1957), while also evoking the dictatorship of François Duvalier (1957–1971). Through casting an earlier era in terms of the present period, Gaines and Chauvet illustrate the cyclical nature of these histories in order to dramatize the social changes still needed. Additionally, authors writing after the collapse of the Duvalier dynasty, such as Haitian American writer Edwidge Danticat, have been able to illustrate more overtly the regime's widespread violence, which disproportionately affected young girls and women. Chapter 5 likewise draws connections between the 1930s and the 1960s through the reign of another infamous twentieth-century dictator, Rafael Leónidas Trujillo Molina, who ruled the Dominican Republic from 1930 to 1961. Literary representations of Trujillo's dictatorship reveal that the entwinement of colorism and sexual violence was central to his regime, portraying his obsession with Whiteness, alongside his predatorial behavior. Writing in the 1990s and 2000s about Trujillo's reign, Julia Alvarez, Junot Díaz, and Nelly Rosario reveal how the control over sexuality—and particularly over women, girls, and marginalized bodies—plays out during a dictator's regime.

Further, my work contributes to a discussion of how the present-day issues of the hemisphere can be linked back to the policing of gendered and racialized bodies in the US South and the Greater Caribbean, explored briefly in the coda. For example, in the US, the prison industrial complex—especially in the shape of privatized prisons and detention centers for undocumented immigrants—may be seen as a logical continuation of the regulation engrained by early slave laws like the Code Noir. In a comparable way, the current policies against Haitians and Dominicans of Haitian descent in the Dominican Republic may be connected back to the way Haitians were racialized differently than Dominicans during the early twentieth-century US occupations of both nations or the anti-Haitianism of Trujillo's government particularly after the 1937 Haitian massacre. The major work of decolonization is to liberate people and spaces from the exploitative structures of colonialism. *Policing Intimacy* underscores the necessity of this multifaceted work: a recognition of the colonial continuities running from the past into our present moment and connecting the diverse terrains of Mississippi, Louisiana, Haiti, and the Dominican Republic, as depicted in literature.

METHODOLOGIES: WHERE HEMISPHERIC AMERICAN LITERATURE MEETS CRITICAL MIXED RACE STUDIES

By bringing into conversation novels from these diverse but interrelated spaces, *Policing Intimacy* emphasizes the United States' relation to the crucial legacies of formerly colonized nations, pushing American literary studies toward a deeper reckoning with hemispheric currents.[7] I recognize the complex power dynamics that exist between the US and the Caribbean without privileging one over the other. Putting these spaces in conversation with each other resists constructions of the US South or the Caribbean as a monolith, as well as narratives of American, southern, or Haitian exceptionalism.[8] This book examines depictions of the sexual policing of the color line in literature from spaces with distinct constructions of race and colonial histories.[9] Indeed, understandings of colonialism, "the conquest and control of other people's land and goods" (Loomba 2), are contingent on circumstance and locality. I leave space to differentiate between British, French, and Spanish colonialisms and their accompanying racial ideologies, in addition to the neocolonial practices of the United States in the twentieth century.

Scholars have noted the similarities shared between the US South and the Caribbean, including the history of plantation slavery, the experience of occupation, and a warm climate.[10] In other words, the factors that supposedly make the South "exceptional within the context of the United States thus make it acutely familiar within broader categories of Americanness and postcoloniality" (Smith and Cohn 3).[11] This project links distinct geographic points of the circum-Caribbean to illustrate that while the differences are significant, in many ways, "the South and the Caribbean flow into each other culturally, economically, and socially" (Sullivan-González and Wilson xii). I draw on recent work in hemispheric theory, multilingual American studies, and critical mixed race studies to consider the historical interplay of the legacies of the British, French, and Spanish empires in the US South and the Caribbean and their impact running through the twentieth century.[12] The book builds on groundbreaking work in the field of hemispheric American studies, which has charted "new literary and cultural geographies by decentering the U.S. nation and excavating the intricate and complex politics, histories, and discourses of spatial encounter that occur throughout the hemisphere but tend to be obscured in U.S. nation-based inquiries" (Levander and Levine 3). The framing of the chapters develops beyond the limited structure of the nation-state to draw connections between particular literatures across the invented entity known as the Americas.[13]

Policing Intimacy also interacts with the recently formulated critical mixed race studies, a field dedicated to the study of multiracial identities and experiences. Critical mixed race studies not only "stresses that racial categories and racial designations are 'unstable' and 'decentered' complexes of sociocultural meanings that are continuously being created, inhabited, contested, transformed, and destroyed" in a way that interrogates essentialism and hierarchy, but also underscores the interconnection of race with class, gender, sexuality, and other identity categories (Daniel et al. 8).[14] *Policing Intimacy* engages with this field through both the emphasis on interracial intimacy and multiracial identities, as well as the intersectional focus on the linked nature of social identities. Drawing on the foundational work of Kimberlé Crenshaw, Patricia Hill Collins, and bell hooks, as well as more recent work by Anna Carastathis and Brittney C. Cooper, this book explores the complex ways "racism and sexism are interlocking systems of domination which uphold and sustain one another" (hooks 59).[15] To avoid privileging one category of oppression above others, "intersectionality theorists argue that oppression is produced through the interaction of multiple, decentered, and mutually constitutive axes" (Carastathis 56) that should be considered simultaneously as they are experienced. Therefore, *Policing Intimacy* analyzes the control over sexuality resulting from the construction of a color line—particularly between groups designated as Black and those labeled White or light (Creoles of Color, *Mulâtres-Aristocrates*, etc.)—but with attention paid to other identity categories, including gender, class, color, and ethnicity, which are dependent on the specific societies and cultures in which they are grounded.[16]

As a scholar inscribed within my own location as a heterosexual, White-passing multiracial, cisgender woman from the northeastern United States, I am keenly aware of the limitations to writing about histories, spaces, and cultures from a single viewpoint.[17] In order to address these inherent biases and the unevenness of any single perspective, I ground my discussions sociohistorically in literary representations, historical accounts, law, and the archive. With an eye firmly to the intricacies of each locality, I hope to consider literature from Mississippi and Louisiana alongside that from Haiti and the Dominican Republic without forcing comparisons, inscribing unidirectional lines of influence, or privileging the cultural production of the United States. Patterns, similarities, and parallels are identifiable in the literatures considered here, yet at the same time, recognizing the differences and the specificities of the distinct spaces, cultures, and histories is essential to avoid collapsing them into each other.[18] *Policing Intimacy* draws on colonial documents, such as early law systems like the 1685 French Code Noir instated in Haiti, the 1724 Code Noir in Louisiana, and the 1865 Black Code in Mississippi, in tandem with examples drawn from literature to humanize the effects of legal histories and leave space for local particularities. By no means do I intend this study to be comprehensive, but as an opening to a broader conversation about the relationship between sexual policing and the residue of colonial structures in societies across the hemispheric south, enduring in our present period.[19] The recognition of these effects is the first step toward addressing them.

CASE STUDY: CHARLES BON'S FLUID NATIONAL, RACIAL, AND SEXUAL IDENTITY

An example from William Faulkner's *Absalom, Absalom!* elucidates the divergent colonial histories and constructions of race in different spaces, the stakes for the sexual policing of lines of color, as well as an alternative to the preservation of colonial ideologies in the twentieth century. In addition to revealing the multiple overlapping constructions of race in the times and places in which he is situated, Charles Bon represents the contrasting ideological investments of the narrators, along with the potential for a more nuanced understanding of national, racial, and sexual identities through his own indefiniteness. The narrators of *Absalom, Absalom!* present vastly dissimilar portraits of Charles Bon and disagree as to basic facts of his identity, including his origins, race, and sexuality.[20] Miss Rosa describes him as an "unseen male caller" or "a gallant '*dream*,'" perhaps because of her own status as spinster and wronged fiancée (Gerend 24). Jason Compson envisions Bon as a "cynical or fatalistic European charged with the seduction of the South" (Ladd 148). In the final telling of Bon's origins in the novel, Quentin and Shreve identify him as the son Thomas Sutpen had on a sugar plantation in Haiti with his first wife, Eulalia, whom he abandoned after the discovery of her Black ancestry. Through this association, Quentin and Shreve connect the novel to a story of Caribbean plantation life and the sexual subordination of enslaved people, and they thus position Bon as a Black Creole. Such an understanding reveals Faulkner's multiplicitous portrayal of Bon and the potential that he represents for a more variegated racial system had his *métissage*, or national, racial, and sexual fluidity, been accepted by the broader community.[21] This fluidity ties together a number of the spaces to be explored in this project: Haiti, where he is born into the *Mulâtres-Aristocrates*, or the biracial propertied class that succeeded the White French aristocracy after the revolution; Louisiana, where he could be accepted as a member of the Creole of Color elite; and Mississippi, where he is considered Black under a binary system. Bon illustrates not only that race is socially constructed, but also that racial structures differ from society to society as a result of social and cultural differences, as well as colonial and legal histories.

Although Bon is the offspring of both the enslavers and the enslaved, as a member of the *Mulâtres-Aristocrates* in Haiti, he is positioned on a level analogous to that of the White plantation heirs, Henry and Judith Sutpen, in the United States.[22] Due to the influence of French and Spanish colonialisms, Haiti developed a three-tiered social structure with the *Mulâtres-Aristocrates*, an elite, light-skinned biracial class, functioning as a separate racial group.[23] Similarly, in Louisiana, Bon's light skin and high class may have positioned him as a Creole of Color, a privileged position in jeopardy following the Louisiana Purchase.[24] Nevertheless, after his arrival in Mississippi, Bon is aligned with enslaved people and their violent inheritance, according to the binaristic conception of race in that space, which he seems to avoid by passing as White.[25] This alignment ultimately results in his death. The conflicting positions Bon inhabits illustrate the multiplicity not only of his lineage but also his experiences, caused by different cultural conceptions of race in Haiti, Louisiana, and Mississippi. The multiple roles assigned to Bon are confirmation of the narrators' contradictory conceptions of him, which, as I have argued elsewhere, are grounded in their own ideological investments: he is both sophisticated White brother/lover in Jason's colonial-era version and banished Black brother/rapist in Quentin and Shreve's neocolonial reconfiguration.[26] Accordingly, the love stories between Quentin/Henry and Shreve/Bon exist at the same time that Bon is portrayed by Quentin and Shreve as the mythical Black rapist of the southern Radical mentality popular between 1889 and 1915 (Godden, *Fictions of Labor* 23).[27] Given the layered nature of the narrative and the constant reiterations of the Sutpen story with revised evidence, an understanding of Bon as European suitor and as mythical Black rapist operate simultaneously in the text. In this way, each internal teller's version of Bon can be seen to reflect larger hemispheric interests and positionings of Blackness.

Alongside the geographic and cultural differences, as well as colonial investments he represents, Bon also symbolizes the possibility of a more nuanced racial system—an opportunity left open by the potential acceptance of his national, racial, and sexual fluidity. Along with his shifting nationality and racial identity, Bon cannot be easily contained by binaristic understandings of gender or heteronormative conceptions of sexuality. Jason Compson portrays Bon as a decadent European "crossing the campus on foot in the slightly Frenchified cloak and hat" or "reclining in a flowered, almost feminized gown, in a sunny window in his chambers" with "some tangible effluvium of knowledge, surfeit: of actions done and satiations plumbed and pleasures exhausted and even forgotten" (76).[28] In addition to Bon's French and feminine appearance, he is also presented as so experienced and worldly as to be able to seduce both Judith and Henry, his naïve siblings from the country, through his mannerisms and appearance. An analysis of Bon's sexuality requires more space, and I return to him in chapter 1; however, I mention him here to suggest that as racial and sexual Other, Bon's actions are policed more severely in Mississippi, resulting in his death. In Quentin and Shreve's version, Bon reveals his biracial ancestry to Henry, encouraging his brother to shoot him to prevent him from being "the n*** that's going to sleep with [his] sister" (286).[29] While the potential for sex between Bon and Judith is positioned as a reason for his death, his inclusion within the family structure and lines of inheritance as the eldest son would be even more disruptive. As illustrated through Bon's example, the preservation of Whiteness as protected capital often serves as a motivation for sexual policing of the color line. Bon's death highlights the stakes for interracial love and sex, family formations, and ultimately lines of inheritance.

SEXUALITY, RACE, AND LAW

More specifically, according to Siobhan Somerville, sexuality is "a historically and culturally contingent category of identity," which, while "at times linked directly to one's sexual activities, more often describes a complex ideological position, into which one is interpellated based partly on the culture's mapping of bodies and desires and partly on one's response to that interpellation" (6). By sexuality, I refer not only to the preferences of individuals in terms of intimate partners and society's interpellation of them, but also a broader recognition of themselves as sexual beings with erotic impulses and feelings. Eve Kosofsky Sedgwick argues that categories "presented in a culture as symmetrical binary oppositions—heterosexual/homosexual, in this case—actually subsist in a more unsettled and dynamic tacit relation according to which, first, term B is not symmetrical with but subordinated to term A"

(*Epistemology of the Closet* 9–10). To combat such power dynamics in specific cultural framings of sexuality, I value a more fluid conceptualization of both sexuality and gender, beyond reductive binaristic framings, as exemplified through the example of Faulkner's Charles Bon. Understandings of gender roles and relations, as well as sexuality, are contingent on social and cultural differences and prove fluid both within and between societies.

Moreover, while throughout the literature considered in this book race is presented for the most part as a natural, organic feature of life, constructed socially, it holds different meanings across societies that can shift over time, demonstrated by Charles Bon. Ian Haney López defines race in the US as "the historically contingent social systems of meaning that attach to elements of morphology and ancestry" (*White by Law* 10). Thus, while race, described by Ann Laura Stoler as a "central colonial sorting technique," is conceptualized in a binary frame in many regions throughout the US, including Mississippi, in other societies, such as Haiti, race is viewed as a spectrum (2). Whether subscribing to a binaristic or spectrum-based understanding of race, the texts I analyze focus primarily on individuals of European and African descent positioned as Black, White, or biracial. Given the presence of other socially constructed racial groups in these spaces during the twentieth century, I encourage future scholarship exploring the representation of sexual policing of Indigenous, Latinx, and Asian American individuals in multilingual literature from across the Americas.[30] This will help open up an understanding of the relationship between racial construction, colonial ideologies, and sexual policing in the hemisphere more broadly.

In addition to demonstrating shifting constructions of sexuality, gender, and race, the example of Charles Bon illustrates the fact that particular bodies—queer, gendered, racialized—are policed more fervently to maintain colonial hierarchies, the protected position of Whiteness, and the status quo.[31] Since their conceptualization in US society, sexuality and race have been entwined, as the "classifications of bodies as either 'homosexual' or 'heterosexual' emerged at the same time that the United States was aggressively constructing and policing the boundary between 'black' and 'white' bodies" through institutionalized segregation (Somerville 3).[32] As will become apparent through an exploration of other examples, there exists a gendered dimension to the policies of sexual control, which continue to affect girls and women in a disproportionate way. The vulnerability of women, alongside people of color and the LGBTQIA+ community, is a thread running throughout this literature.[33] Across the hemisphere and throughout different historical moments, women are consistently left open to sexual violation and control—whether in the plantation literature of William Faulkner and Ernest

Gaines, or the representations of dictatorship in Marie Chauvet, Edwidge Danticat, Julia Alvarez, Junot Díaz, and Nelly Rosario. Indeed, sexuality may be seen to express neocolonial relations across the various spaces considered here.[34] This is evident from the antimiscegenation laws widespread in the United States to the predatorial sexuality condoned and even promoted by two of the Western Hemisphere's most notorious dictators, François Duvalier of Haiti and Rafael Trujillo of the Dominican Republic, and the individualized systems of surveillance in each space.[35] The lingering effects of previous policies and legal systems remain, influencing gender expectations, stereotypes, and sexualized conceptions of race throughout the twentieth century and into the present period, as revealed in literature spanning the circum-Caribbean.

Additionally, across the societies explored here, law plays a key role in the social construction of race.[36] More specifically, "U.S. racial identity is a constructed legal fiction" (Holloway 5). The legal system in Mississippi understood race as a binary between Black and White, illustrated in the 1865 Black Code, as opposed to the three-tiered system demonstrated by the 1685 Code Noir in Saint-Domingue (Haiti) and the 1724 Code Noir in Louisiana. The third Spanish Code, Código Negro Carolino (1784), in Santo Domingo (today's Dominican Republic) allowed for more movement between racial categories than either the Black Code or Code Noir. Law itself is not a monolith but has been described in a US context as "a complex, incoherent system of practices" (Haney López, *White by Law* 80) from legal systems to court cases that work to influence behaviors, as well as the broader ideologies of a given society. For example, different facets of law were responsible for the elevated position of Creoles of Color in early Louisiana society: legally the society was separated into Whites, free people of color, and enslaved people (Domínguez 24). Free individuals of color in Louisiana "inserted themselves into the legal system to protect and enhance their rights as free people" (Aslakson 7), manipulating "different aspects of the plural legal traditions of the city to maximize their fortunes in individual lawsuits" (Aslakson 8). Law shapes race, and although race is socially constructed, it has concrete effects on the material realities of individuals and broader groups.

When the color line was "fundamentally eroticized in the early twentieth century" in the US (Somerville 35), large-scale systems, such as the Jim Crow laws throughout the South, were mobilized alongside the smaller-scale acts of individual policing in communities. Both aspects worked together "not only to demand constant adherence to the fictions of racial identity but also to police sexual mobility" (Somerville 35). This interplay between the individual and society demonstrates that sexual policing of the color line occurred on various levels, including but not limited to official laws and policies, like the Mississippi Black Code, the Code Noir for the French colonies, and the Códigos Negros for the Spanish. Self-regulation through the ubiquitous controlling gaze of the community, gossip, and other networks of control—such as the "everyday forms of terror" implemented by two of Hispaniola's ruthless twentieth-century dictators, François Duvalier and Rafael Trujillo—functioned on another level (Derby, *The Dictator's Seduction* 2). The private interactions of communities were made public in an attempt to extend influence into the intimate sphere of relations. Taking various forms, from legal policies to the regulatory eyes of the community, attempts to control sexuality and interpersonal interactions survived and thrived after the demise of colonial systems, illustrating the shared past and present of racialized sexual policing across circum-Caribbean societies.

THE ARCHIVE OF AUTHORS: REFLECTING COLONIAL CONTINUITIES

Policing Intimacy draws on a diverse archive of authors to elucidate important patterns found when examining the regulation of sexuality, reflecting the ongoing coloniality linking the US to the Caribbean. This collection of writers spans time periods, languages, and styles, as well as the contexts of race, gender, class, and canon. However, their work is linked through their direct engagement with the inheritance of plantation policings of sexuality and race throughout the hemisphere and across the century. White southern modernist William Faulkner, whose fiction career spanned from 1926 with *Soldiers' Pay* to 1962 with *The Reivers*, is situated solidly within the canon of US literature. However, Black southern writer Ernest Gaines, who began his career with *Catherine Carmier* in 1964 and released his last novella *The Tragedy of Brady Sims* in 2017 before his death in 2019, is a more recent addition to the US canon and is typically confined to studies of African American literature. Faulkner descended from slaveowners, while Gaines spent his youth as a sharecropper living in the former slave quarters on a plantation in Pointe Coupee Parish. While Faulkner is known for his experimental aesthetics, Gaines is more straightforward in style, engaging with orality and storytelling. However, both write in English about the twentieth-century US South and its colonial past with a critical eye to the reverberations of slavery primarily for a US-based audience, and both elucidate the impact of sexual policing in the twentieth century on individuals and communities.[37]

In contrast, Haitian writer Marie Chauvet, herself a member of the *Mulâtres-Aristocrates*, was writing in French during the oppressive regime of dictator François Duvalier and publishing her work primarily in France in the 1950s and 1960s, before electing to live in exile in New York after the publication of *Love, Anger, Madness* in 1968 (Chancy, *Framing Silence* 149). Warned that the triptych, which uses both content and form as a veiled critique, would "provoke serious reprisals" from Duvalier's repressive regime, Chauvet persuaded her French publisher, Gallimard, to retract it (Bell par. 1).[38] In recent generations, Chauvet's work has received more serious treatment by scholars, such as Haitian Canadian writer and scholar Myriam Chancy, who refers to her as the writer "now, with good reason, considered Haiti's foremost woman writer" (50).[39] Contemporary Haitian American writer Edwidge Danticat, who began her career as a novelist with *Breath, Eyes, Memory* in 1994, may be seen as inheriting the aesthetically strategic, politically engaged legacy of Marie Chauvet. Danticat commemorates the traumatic events of history, such as the massacre of Haitians on the Dominican border in 1937, and as a result of her historical references is able to speak to multiple audiences—simultaneously "writing for the benefit of her community" (Charters), as well as to educate the wider world.[40]

Like Danticat, the Dominican American writers that conclude the book are part of a later generation publishing from the 1990s to today. Julia Alvarez, Junot Díaz, and Nelly Rosario primarily publish in English, with the inclusion of Spanish words and phrases using formal techniques such as lacuna, fragmentation, and polyvocality to engage with history. The question of audience is complex here. When Julia Alvarez, who began publishing in 1991, wrote *In the Time of the Butterflies*, the history of Rafael Trujillo's dictatorship was all but unknown in the US. In the novel's postscript, she directly describes her hope that the book "deepens North Americans' understanding of the nightmare you [Dominicans] endured and the heavy losses you suffered" (324). While she describes having had an Anglophone readership in mind when writing, her use of the pronoun "you," seemingly a direct address to Dominicans, reveals a more complicated relationship to audience. In this way, Alvarez gestures toward a multivocal readership, deconstructing the idea of audience as linked directly to nation state. Junot Díaz—whose first collection of short stories, *Drown*, was published in 1996—also educates primarily English-speaking readers about this traumatic episode in Dominican history in *The Brief Wondrous Life of Oscar Wao* through the inclusion of heavy historical footnotes and fictionalized experiences based on real accounts. Nelly Rosario relies less on historical contextualization in *Song of the*

Water Saints. Her debut novel, published in 2002, focuses on the individual experiences of four generations of Dominican women spanning the events of the twentieth century, including occupation, dictatorship, and immigration to the US, while consistently regulating "capital H" History that centers large-scale Western historical events to the background. Thus, the diverse writers collected here share the historically engaged project of depicting the abusive relations that result from continued adherence to hierarchical social structures and colonial ideologies in the twentieth century, from the US South to the Caribbean, as well as the resistance to these forms of control.

Taken together, the novels considered here demonstrate the negative effects of the systematized sexual control over gendered and racialized subjects. However, the connections between them help to highlight not only patterns of subjection but also of resistance, gesturing toward the erosion of boundaries. Resistance to the status quo is found in the broader projects of each writer: for instance, in Faulkner questioning the racist social fictions of his time, Gaines flipping the script and focusing on Black and Creole of Color communities in Louisiana, and Chauvet publishing a thinly veiled critical piece under dictatorship, as well as in contemporary writers memorializing these important histories and writing back to official representations. The novels themselves reveal other possibilities, alternatives to the replication of destructive colonial hierarchies, such as the acceptance of racial and sexual fluidity exemplified in Bon's story.

Through a consideration of these diverse texts, this project brings to light the remnants of the colonial systems that held fast in the hemispheric American South into the twentieth century to make evident both a shared global colonial inheritance as well as the examples of collective resistance that continue to challenge those structures of dominance through inspiring new ways of interacting. We see consensual interracial relationships depicted between Roth Edmonds and his unnamed biracial relative, and between Hubert Beauchamp and the nameless biracial cook in Faulkner's *Go Down, Moses*. Additionally, the novels contain positive portrayals of interracial friendships, like that between Jules Raynard and Jane Pittman in Gaines's *The Autobiography of Jane Pittman*; same-sex friendships, such as that between Claire Clamont and Jane Bavière in Chauvet's *Love*; and interclass relationships, for instance, those shared between the Mirabal sisters and their cellmates in Alvarez's *In the Time of the Butterflies*. These authors challenge, rather than passively embed, colonial relations in the post-/neocolonial era through depicting characters that recognize the humanity of each other across lines of difference. Love and emotional connections, in the form of consensual interracial relationships and same-sex friendships, have the potential to defy colonial hierarchies through the relatively egalitarian footing on which the involved parties are situated, modeling of another mode of interaction.

BOUNDARY-CROSSING LOVE'S RESISTANCE TO HIERARCHIES

Thus, while interracial and nonheteronormative sexuality has subversive potential in the challenge to colonial social formations, I also position love, or deep emotional bonds beyond physical intimacy, as containing a disruptive component to the status quo. Boundary-crossing love can threaten the rigid hierarchal social systems in place through its "political and racial implications" (Hebert-Leiter 105). As sexual intimacy can result in children (i.e., future citizens) and disrupt family formations (whether recognized by the state or not), love and broader emotional attachments have the potential for the same via state structures like marriage and lines of inheritance. Indeed, the regulation of intimacy first centered on sex, for instance in Virginia in the 1660s, before shifting to control over marriage (Kennedy 216–17). Early slave codes and later the various iterations of antimiscegenation laws specific to Mississippi and Louisiana attempted to regulate sexual contact or corporeal acts between individuals, yet sex was never the sole target: love and marriage were also policed. As mentioned previously, Whiteness held power and privilege in relation to social hierarchies and thus needed to be protected—particularly for its association with social and economic capital. The protection of this capital led to an investment in physical acts, but also the regulation of love and the deep familial bonds, greater kinship ties, and at times monetary legacies that accompanied it. As a form of resistance, boundary-crossing love works on the individual level and is not reliant on managing others' behavior on a large scale; however, it also holds the potential to spread in influence.

On individual and collective scales, love has the power to break down injurious preoccupations with difference and constitute, or at least anticipate, progressive futures. Characters, such as Marcus Payne and Louise Bonbon in *Of Love and Dust* and Tonton Mathurin and Agnès Grandupré in *Love*, are able to put aside racial and class prejudices to relate to each other as individuals. Others, such as Charles Bon and Judith, and perhaps the Sutpen family more broadly, are not given the chance; nevertheless, the novel gestures toward the recuperation of Bon as a way out of the cycles of hatred and violence. Love—whether platonic, familial, or erotic—can be revolutionary when running counter to societal structures, which may explain the deep fixation on the policing of sexuality and also individual relationships and family formations. For those invested in the status quo, the stakes for these laws and unspoken rules of the community are high in their attempts to control not only sexuality, but also through that love, family connections, and lines of inheritance.

More explicitly, in Ernest Gaines's *Of Love and Dust* the love between Marcus, a multiracial convict laborer, and Louise, the White Cajun wife of the overseer, breaks the unspoken rules of social relations on their Louisiana plantation. In an early draft of the novel, Gaines allowed the couple to get away, before his publisher encouraged him to revise in the more realistic direction of a failed escape.[41] Shortly after their flight in the unpublished draft, narrator Jim reflects on the role of love: "I love those two people, I love them very much. And I love these here [the Black community in the quarters]. That's why I'm here; that's why I'm here. I'm no brave man—God knows I'm not. But I'm a man, and man must do, and man must surely love. 'Love is everything; dust [Gaines's symbol for death] is what's left'" (Gaines Papers 3.27, 380).[42] Here, Jim describes his love for Marcus and Louise, as well as the community they put in danger through their escape. Jim's multifaceted love in response to Marcus and Louise's love is the counterpoint to regulation and death—one that he positions as essential to his existence as a man. While some forms of love and societal expectations about what it should look like are socially constructed, love is disruptive enough to defy monolithic understandings, existing nebulously beyond the reach of analysis. Literature may be taken as a form of history that is engaged with the intricacies of interpersonal relationships and interactions and that reveals the subjective, erotic, and relational intensities at play through its depths. Indeed, literature as an artform is unruly enough to honor the disruptive concept of love. However, the realities of regulation during Gaines's historical moment restrict this disruption and in the published version of the novel, the dust wins. Nonetheless, the escape attempt itself is a moment of opposition to the status quo.

As this example demonstrates, I utilize the literary archives, in addition to historical documents, to deepen my engagement with the novels analyzed. In opposition to William Faulkner and Julia Alverez, Ernest Gaines is an author who extensively revises his work, writing a wealth of comments and alterations on his handwritten and later typewritten manuscript pages, and thus, chapters 2 and 3 rely more heavily on the literary archives.[43] However, while I ground this work in colonial histories and the archive, I simultaneously allow the aesthetic affordances of literature to open up the discussion, adding the rich layers of fictionalized personal accounts that underscore the impact of the political on the individual (and vice versa). In this way, literary fiction is the ideal object of analysis for this type of historically engaged work. This book exists at the intersection of the literary and the historical.

LITERATURE AND HISTORY

A final constructed border that I wish to interrogate is that separating literature from history.[44] Literature is often thought of as separate from the work of history: more fanciful, whimsical, less based in the concrete reality of the everyday. However, literature, particularly historically grounded texts, can elucidate or reflect aspects of reality, and also offer alternatives to official histories and one-sided versions of major events. The literary is on the side of the singular, the human: it particularizes personal stories of large-scale occurrences and can simultaneously construct and free individuals from constructions. We know that "history [is] told by the victors, for the victors—and all too often, the scholars of history tow the line" (Bond 2). Literature can function as a corrective to the limited scope of history. If history is told by the victors, then only when we hear from everyone else can we hope to recount the events that came before with any accuracy. I read the novels in this project in a similar way to historical texts, more frequently positioned as realist, as a way to achieve a more multiplicitous understanding of the dynamics of the past.

Thus, I focus on the relationship between history and literature because I believe that fiction is an effective way to capture the layers and resonances present in stories of the past. Texts written to look back at a past era, whether in the field of history or literature, are necessarily affected by the time in which they are written. There is no such thing as pure history: it is always mediated. Certain aspects are brought into focus, and others are left out. Fiction provides some distance from the pressures of reality, and I believe it is in these spaces that contextual truths about the past can emerge. Experimental formal techniques, such as fragmentation, deferred revelation, and polyvocality are used to represent stories, experiences, and even traumas that may not otherwise be captured. There are narratives that can never be recuperated, and space must be left for their absent-presence, the perceived substance of a gap.[45] In Sadiya Hartman's words, the intent of literature and criticism can be to "imagine what cannot be verified" ("Venus in Two Acts" 12).[46] In doing so, literature's emphasis on multiplicity, its focus on gaps, silences, and absences, can represent the incomplete nature of history and its archives. There are always more stories to tell, other perspectives to consider. Novels written with these factors in mind are as close as we can come to a necessarily imperfect understanding of history. The aesthetics of Faulkner, Gaines, Chauvet, Danticat, Alvarez, Díaz, and Rosario—ranging from experimental approaches to more realist representations—connect to their conceptions of history, encapsulating a variety of voices, stories, and experiences. These novels illustrate the value of literature in representing the past and the ways that readers in the present are implicated in these histories.

Chapter 1

"WE WILL HAVE TO WAIT"

Racial Hierarchies, Plantation Intimacy, and Sexual Policing in William Faulkner's Mississippi

The relationships between William Faulkner's characters demonstrate the various ways in which sexuality was policed across lines of race, color, class, and gender while also presenting alternatives to the preservation of colonial hierarchies in the form of consensual interracial relationships and more fluid conceptions of identity. For instance, in Faulkner's *Absalom, Absalom!*, Henry Sutpen, White male heir to Thomas Sutpen's self-made plantation, shoots and kills his dear friend Charles Bon, for whom he had repudiated his inheritance. While Bon's race is never known in the novel, Henry believes Bon to have traces of Black ancestry, and he feels it necessary to shoot his friend, later revealed to be his half-brother, to prevent Bon from marrying Judith Sutpen, their sister. Faulkner places this depiction of the sexual policing of the color line in 1865, the same year that the Mississippi Black Code—an early system of laws that in part served the same function—went into effect. According to the Mississippi Black Code, "all freedmen, free Negroes, and mulattoes" were allowed to intermarry with one another "in the same manner and under the same regulations that are provided by law for white persons" (Mississippi Legislature).[1] And beyond that, freedmen and women—Black and biracial—who have lived together as husband and wife "shall be taken and held in law as legally married" (Mississippi Legislature). However, in the same section, the code specified that "it shall not be lawful for any freedman, free Negro, or mulatto to intermarry with any white person; nor for any white person to intermarry with any freedman, free Negro, or mulatto; and any person who shall so intermarry shall be deemed guilty of felony and, on conviction thereof, shall be confined in the state penitentiary for life" (Mississippi Legislature). Both Henry Sutpen's actions and the early systems of law in the state of Mississippi exemplify a belief in the necessity of segregation over assimilation, particularly in the immediate postbellum period.

Through the regulation of the interpersonal, the Mississippi Black Code and later iterations strove to control familial configurations and all that accompanied them, including children, inheritance, property, and land. In this direct way, the state of Mississippi attempted to create race through the terms used and the categories referenced by its legal system, including "freedman," "free Negro," "mulatto," and "white person." For example, the code is very specific about who counts as Black: "those shall be deemed freedmen, free Negroes, and mulattoes who are of pure Negro blood; and those descended from a Negro to the third generation inclusive, though one ancestor of each generation may have been a white person" (Mississippi Legislature). Further, these laws provided a legal basis for the policing of sexuality and interracial sex under the guise of defending White womanhood (while women of color were systematically exploited), family units, and lines of inheritance against a racialized Other. This policing became entrenched in society and, as seen in a number of William Faulkner's late novels, worked not only to control the sexuality of others and regulate family units but also to uphold colonial society and in particular the privileges accompanying Whiteness.

Sexual policing, or the regulation of who sleeps with whom and who marries whom in relation to race, color, class, and gender, was integral to maintaining the restrictive hierarchical social structures central to plantation society, as portrayed in *Absalom, Absalom!*; *Go Down, Moses*; and a number of Faulkner's other works. One method of upholding the color line was to control the interactions between individuals from different racial groups. As Randall Kennedy, Harvard Law School professor and legal scholar, has stated, the regulation of interracial intimacy had the effect of both pitting White people against people of color and also setting men against women within racial groups and between them (221). In this way, the regulation of sexuality depicted in the novels allowed the beneficiaries of colonialism to control the intersection of race and sexuality and to maintain colonial hierarchies and mentalities in post-/neocolonial societies as adherence to them began to wane. Ultimately, however, through the inclusion of alternative ways of interacting, Faulkner challenges the widespread reliance on these systems of regulation.

More specifically, as Faulkner's *Absalom, Absalom!*; *Go Down, Moses*; and *Requiem for a Nun* reveal, sexuality in particular can be seen as an expression of the neocolonial relationship in the postbellum US South, reproducing the conditions of slavery after the loss of the Civil War. In other words, the sexual policing of the color line, along with the other engrained facets of plantation society—such as the exploitation of women of color, damaging stereotypes such as the myth of the Black rapist, and the resulting lynch culture—worked to preserve hierarchical ideologies and colonial mentalities in the South from the post-Emancipation period into the twentieth century. Policing efforts crossed class lines: upper-class White men were invested in keeping the same social structures in place with themselves on top, and lower-class Whites violently enforced segregation to retain their positions above people of color (Alexander 22).[2] Although White men seem to have positioned themselves above the color line in the South through their widespread sexual violation of Black and biracial women, they were heavily invested in prohibiting sexual contact between White women and Black or biracial men since White women were assigned the role of maintaining the purity of family lines. I examine the preoccupation with shielding White women from interracial sex—frequently used as justification for the lynching of Black and biracial men—before expanding outward to consider the related preservation of White, upper-class family units and acceptable lines of descent and inheritance.

In this chapter, I will analyze the 1930s and 1940s, as depicted in Faulkner's *Go Down, Moses* (1942) and *Requiem for a Nun* (1951), alongside examples from the immediate post-Emancipation era, also represented in *Go Down, Moses*, as well as in *Absalom, Absalom!* (1936). An examination of these texts together emphasizes the vestigial connections between the antebellum and postbellum periods and the ways in which the past remains present in Mississippi plantation culture, connecting to other circum-Caribbean spaces that share this inheritance of racial and sexual policing. While slavery was abolished in the United States in 1865, the arduous conditions of many African Americans' lives continued in a different form as a result of various factors from White supremacy and limited job mobility to the violence of lynch culture. Enslaved people were technically freed from their subjugated status after the Civil War; however, policies such as sharecropping,[3] the convict lease system,[4] the Black Code,[5] and the Jim Crow laws,[6] replicated the racist structures of slavery during the neocolonial era. Significant change to the economic system of the plantation was not seen until the post–World War II period (Mandle 84). Therefore, in addition to the decades following the Civil War, the 1930s–1940s was similarly an era of turmoil in the US South. This period encompassed the final years of the plantation economy that continued to survive "through the second half of the nineteenth century and about a third of the twentieth century" (Mandle 21). The economic system was accompanied by social ideologies governing the hierarchical relations among White people, the formerly enslaved population, Indigenous peoples, and other racial groups. During such times of turmoil, the maintenance of the ideological color line became more important in an attempt to preserve the status quo: hierarchical relations between individuals and Whiteness as a source of both power and protected capital.

Why is literature the appropriate medium to explore the relationship between intimacy and broader social structures? What does literature, and specifically Faulkner's work, lend to an exploration of the impact of systems of law and colonial hierarchies on sexuality? Faulkner situates readers, along with Isaac McCaslin in *Go Down, Moses* and Quentin and Shreve in *Absalom, Absalom!*, in the position of a forensic explorer investigating the sexual violations and other inhumane acts of previous generations. As a result of the connections running through the novels' various time periods, the characters in the present, and by extension the readers, are also implicated in these histories, illustrating the continuity of colonial mentalities. Further, through this positioning, as well as his experimental aesthetics—including the use of deferred revelation, fragmentation, and stream of consciousness—Faulkner's prose activates readers in a way that a straightforward historical account would not accomplish. The difficult readerly experience of the dense prose and frequent shifts in time mirror the effort needed to piece together an account of the past that official records intend to cover up. In other words, the structure of the novels themselves mimic the experience of unfolding the layers of history, blurring the border between literature and history. The novels portray different iterations of intersectional relationships, including patterns, substitutions, reversals, and variations. Interpersonal interactions are never static, as the messiness involved in parsing out Faulkner's interconnecting stories reveals. However, through an exploration of the patterns, I attempt to bring a clarity often purposely withheld by Faulkner's aesthetic to these intersections. In this way, the form and content of the novels work together to emphasize the significance of these intimate, shifting familial histories and elucidate their connection to large-scale events, such as the Civil War, Reconstruction, and the end of the plantation economy. Faulkner locates resistance to the status quo within these depictions of substitutions and reversals.

Although the Black Code attempted to prevent interracial interactions and plantation ledgers tried to reduce human beings to numbers on a paper, neither could erase the reality of interracial contact occurring on the plantation and the resulting entwined multiracial families and sometimes entire shadow families, such as those produced by Faulkner's great-grandfather Colonel William C. Falkner or Faulkner's fictional patriarchs, such as Thomas Sutpen in *Absalom, Absalom!*[7] Written from the perspective of the post-Reconstruction US South reflecting on the experience of a single family—the Sutpens—throughout the antebellum, Civil War, and Reconstruction periods,

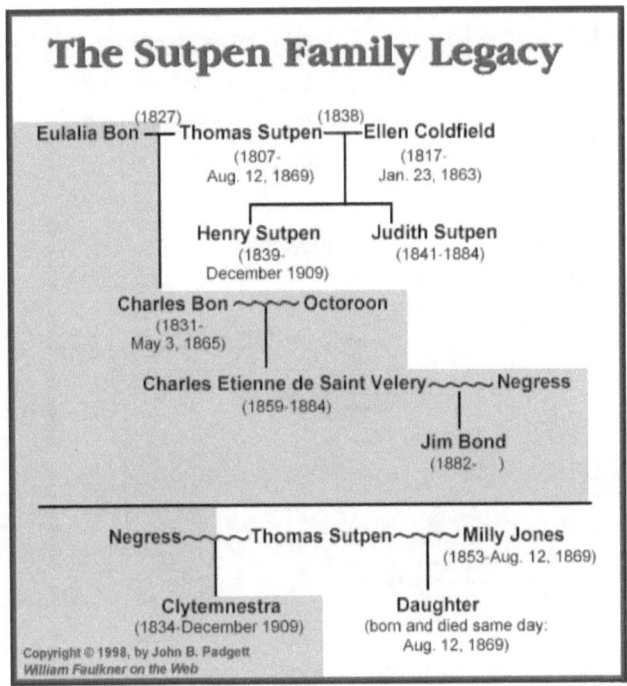

Figure 1.1: Genealogy of *Absalom, Absalom!* This figure was created by John B. Padgett in 1998 for William Faulkner on the Web. Through the use of white and gray backgrounds, it visually represents the racial distinctions between Sutpen's relationships. This includes his first nullified marriage and later shadow family with an unnamed "negress," as well as the legally legitimate white family he forms with Ellen and his exploitation of young Milly Jones. Figure 1.1 highlights the novel's problematic language, such as "negress" and "octoroon," terms that reify colonial hierarchies of color, and also emphasizes the high number of unnamed women of color in the novel. Copyright © 1995–2008 by John B. Padgett.

Absalom, Absalom! is a fictional representation of the struggles of the White southern plantocracy during this period of transition. In addition to the family unit Thomas Sutpen forms with Ellen, his White wife from a respected local family, he also fathers a daughter, Clytie, with an unnamed enslaved Haitian woman. Additionally, he had a son, Charles Bon, with his first wife, Eulalia, whom he put aside due to her alleged Black ancestry. Constructed by multiple narrators, the final version of the story, which includes Bon's supposed biracial Haitian lineage, is deferred until the end of the novel. Nevertheless, the Sutpen family tree has both White branches—occupied by Ellen Sutpen and her children, Henry and Judith—as well as Black or biracial branches, such as Eulalia and Charles Bon's branch and also that of Clytie and her unnamed mother.[8] Miss Rosa emphasizes the enmeshed web of family relations toward the beginning of the novel, when she states: "I was

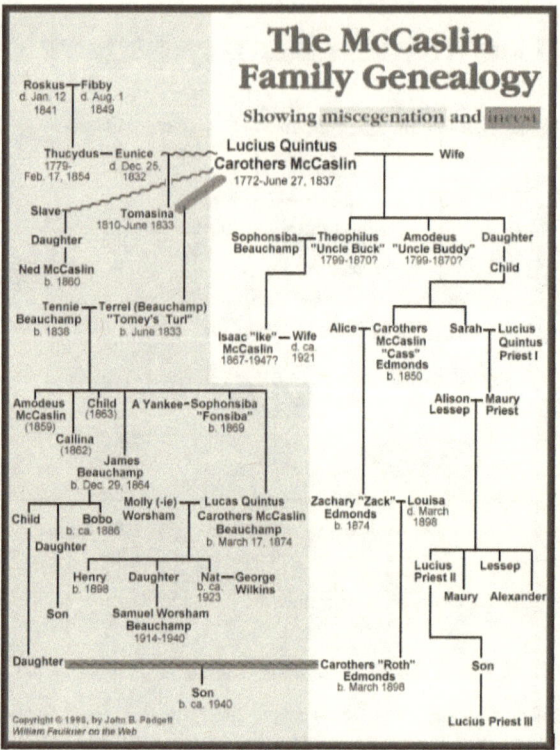

Figure 1.2: Genealogy of *Go Down, Moses*. This figure was created by John Padgett also in 1998 and details more explicitly the fact that the gray background denotes an interracial family through the key at the top. The original figure uses red highlighting to represent visually the disruptive instances of incest, which notably cross racial lines in both cases. The figures display a binaristic understanding of race in line with the one-drop rule. Copyright © 1995–2008 by John B. Padgett.

not there to see the two Sutpen faces this time—once on Judith and once on the negro girl beside her—looking down through the square entrance to the loft" (*Absalom, Absalom!* 22). In the case of the Sutpens, only the White branch is considered legitimate in terms of inheritance and lines of descent, preserving Whiteness as a source of social power and capital.

To the example of the Sutpens, I would add the McCaslin family, central to Faulkner's *Go Down, Moses*, as an emblematic enmeshed family. *Go Down, Moses* is a novel made up of seven interrelated stories detailing the relations between a number of interconnected multiracial families—the McCaslins, the Edmondses, and the Beauchamps—in the antebellum, postbellum, and twentieth-century US South. While the aesthetics differ from story to story, polyvocality and the focus on multiple characters and experiences run throughout with greater emphasis placed on the lives of the male—and most frequently White male—relatives. The seven unnamed female characters in figure 1.2, including the wives and mistresses of the main characters, demonstrate this—compared with the three unnamed males. The patriarch of the McCaslin family, Lucius Quintus Carothers McCaslin, had sexual relations with multiple enslaved people on his plantation, including the unnamed enslaved woman who is the grandmother of Ned McCaslin and Eunice, with whom he fathers Tomasina (see figure 1.2). Old Carothers McCaslin simultaneously violates the bans placed on interracial sex and incest in his plantation society through fathering Terrel with his own daughter, Tomasina, in the 1830s.[9] Old Carothers's secret is discerned from the ledgers generations later by his grandson, Isaac McCaslin, and is the catalyst behind Isaac's renunciation of his plantation inheritance. Old Carothers's singular act of interracial sex and incest is repeated generations later by his great-great-great-grandson, Carothers Roth Edmonds (see figure 1.2), who fathers a son with an unnamed female descendant of Tomey's Terrell or Turl. According to the woman, however, Edmonds is unaware of their familial connection, and their relationship is consensual. Roth refuses parental acknowledgement of the child in the 1940s.

Readers can discern a pattern here: White men of the plantocracy and its descendants knowingly (or unknowingly in Roth's case) committing incest and having interracial sex—whether coerced as presumably in the case of Tomasina, whose mother commits suicide as a result of the coupling, or not as in Roth's example. This pattern centers the exploitative behavior of White men and highlights the continuity of these dynamics in the twentieth-century South, although the contextual specifics change: for instance, under the system of slavery, Eunice's and Tomasina's children are considered property, as opposed to family members.[10] *Miscegenation*, described by Marlene Daut as "the utterly unfortunate term" (45), originated in the North during the Civil War in place of "amalgamation" when Democrats attempted to worry voters that Lincoln supported interracial marriage (Wallenstein 51). The term refers to sexual relationships or marriages between people of distinct races, as well as "laws that long banned marriages between a person defined as white and someone of another racial identity" (Wallenstein 51). The ban against "miscegenation" in particular is essential to the politics of colonialism, which draw their power from the intersectional hierarchies of race, class, and gender. As the two family trees (figures 1.1 and 1.2) demonstrate, White men considered themselves above the ban, which they used to regulate the behavior of those below them on the hierarchies.

The longevity and widespread establishment of these laws speak to their centrality in shaping understandings of race in the United States. In the three centuries between the 1660s and 1960s, forty-one colonies or states enacted racial laws policing sex and/or marriage (Kennedy 18). Further, laws against interracial marriages remained on the books in Mississippi throughout the early twentieth-century period examined in this chapter and up until the early 1970s. In the words of Rachel Moran: "Antimiscegenation laws have played an integral role in defining racial identity and enforcing racial hierarchy" (17). The first marriage law in Mississippi legalized solely the unions of White people in 1822 (Mississippi Department of Archives and History 2), and the first legal ban on the marriage between Whites and Blacks accompanied the Black Code in 1865 and included a penalty of imprisonment for life (Wallenstein 82).[11] The color line in Mississippi was redefined in 1890 following Reconstruction, and anyone of one-eighth Black ethnicity, as opposed to one-fourth, was considered Black (Wallenstein 93).[12] In 1917, Mississippi officially adopted the one-drop statute, positioning anyone with any degree of African ancestry as Black in the eyes of the law (Sweet 318). Nevertheless, when the case of a Virginia couple, Richard Loving, a White man, and Mildred Jeter, a multiracial woman, was brought before the US Supreme Court in 1967, Chief Justice Earl Warren's ruling rendered antimiscegenation laws invalid and unenforceable (Kennedy 274) and Virginia's one-drop rule unconstitutional (A. Morrison 241).[13]

Just as the Black Code could not effectively control the behavior of Mississippi residents, the antimiscegenation laws, while they could prevent legal unions, did not erase the reality of interracial contact. In addition to White men's widespread sexual exploitation of women of color, interracial sex between White women and men of color occurred during slavery, according to Joel Williamson, although it is not often highlighted in history books (385). This pattern of relations, however, happened less frequently than was the case with White men and women of color, in part because maternity was more visible than paternity and, as a result of plantation hierarchies, "women were generally dependent, and the sanctions that could be brought against them very severe" (Williamson 385). The fear of losing control over White women's sexuality led to the Cult of Southern Womanhood through which White men attempted to keep White women submissive and place them above the exploitative interracial sex that was rampant between White men and enslaved women (Godden, *Fictions of Labor* 23). As a result of the Cult of Southern Womanhood, White women were the repositories of White civilization that southern White men would place on pedestals before running off to gratify their lascivious passions elsewhere (Jordan 148). Therefore, there existed a conceptual split between Black and White gender roles in the colonial period, which reveals a "sexual hierarchy in operation that holds certain female bodies in higher regard than others" (Crenshaw, "Mapping the Margins" 1269) and speaks to the simultaneous and overlapping forms of oppression experienced by women of color.

White women were stereotyped as domesticated and desexualized, and Black women were seen as savage and hypersexual—a purposeful stereotype that had the effect of assuaging White men's guilt over sexual abuse; that is, it isn't rape if they wanted it (Abrahams 230). In this way, the rape of enslaved women was institutionalized by White enslavers as a means of keeping the enslaved women in line and emasculating the enslaved men through the latter's inability to prevent this violation. This abuse also gratified the planters' lusts and made such desires economically beneficial by producing more enslaved people, more property (Angela Davis 183). Thus, Whiteness was equated with not only social power but also capital accumulation: Whiteness under plantation slavery was accompanied by economic benefits, such as the extracted labor, resources, and reproductive lives of people of color in the hemispheric south. Jennifer Morgan states that women's "reproductive lives were at the heart of the entire venture of racial slavery" (4), and due to inherited beliefs about race and gender, enslavers expected their wealth, as well as that of colonial empires, to result from the reproductivity of African women (8). According to Adrienne Davis, the "political economy of slavery systematically expropriated black women's sexuality and reproductive capacity for white pleasure and profit" (105), which created "value for the slaveholding class. Enslaved black women gave birth to white wealth" (117). The sexuality and reproductive labor of enslaved women directly translated to White capital accumulation, which underscores the zealous attachment to the plantation status quo via racial and sexual policing.

Indeed, *Absalom, Absalom!* illustrates the accepted and encouraged nature of the sexual abuse of Black women in southern society or, in other words, the "production of a fundamental familiar violence, of multiple subjections, the tolerance for and necessity of them within the spaces and the forms of intimacy" that can only be described as "monstrous" (C. Sharpe 2). While Thomas Sutpen's sexual relationships with his enslaved people are never directly discussed, the existence of Judith's half-sister Clytie gestures toward the untold story of the exploitation and impregnation of enslaved women. The differing statuses of Judith and Clytie illustrate the divergent positions granted to White and Black women under slavery. Similarly, the only unnamed characters in the Sutpen family genealogy, in addition to Milly Jones's newborn daughter, are women of color (figure 1.1). These women are described as either "Octoroon[s]" or "Negress[es]," terms which Werner Sollors has referred to as "the calculus of color," given the colonial connotations of racial categorization that they evoke (118). Writing in the postbellum US South, Faulkner was not free from the lingering impact of colonial ideologies of race and gender on his work. Faulkner's novel, nevertheless, leaves space for what is left out of official histories, such as the names and perspectives of women of color, although without attempting to recuperate them. The gaps in the storytelling are central to *Absalom, Absalom!* and often speak as loudly as what is said.[14]

In addition to the equation of Whiteness with social power and protected capital, scholars such as Aliyyah Abdur-Rahman have also linked Whiteness to heteronormativity. According to Abdur-Rahman, slavery itself and the sexual violence accompanying it "established whiteness as the requisite racial category for heteronormative qualification" (226). White womanhood gained meaning only in relation to the experiences of enslaved women (Abdur-Rahman 226). White women were charged with the responsibility of producing heirs to the plantation and future enslavers, while the routine rape of enslaved women necessitated the matrilineal descent of slavery (Abdur-Rahman 228). Since White enslavers, like Thomas Sutpen and Old Carothers McCaslin, were socially sanctioned to impregnate both enslaved women and their White wives, the status of the mother established the position of the child. Consequently, Whiteness was determined and shaped by the aberrant sexual practices of slavery. While the interracial sex common on plantations would seem to threaten to blur the lines between the White and Black races through the biracial offspring produced, the one-drop rule negated this threat by positioning every individual with even a drop of "Black blood" as Black and thus enslaved—as property as opposed to people.[15]

As a result of the high stakes for Whiteness, in terms of social and economic power, the regulation of sexuality was taken more seriously when White women were involved. *Absalom, Absalom!*'s Charles Bon illustrates this in the immediate postbellum period: his relations were heavily policed due to their interracial component—and also same-sex if we include his connection to his half-brother, Henry Sutpen. Bon's sexual proclivities—including his support of a biracial mistress and their child and his general philandering, having "already acquired a name for prowess among women" (78)—were not under scrutiny when he was believed to be a White man.[16] However, in Quentin and Shreve's version of the story, Bon is revealed to be biracial and is shot in order to prevent his marriage to the White plantation daughter, Judith Sutpen. The racial identity of Charles Bon, whom the Sutpen family viewed as a wealthy New Orleanian but actually hailed from the "little lost island" of Haiti, would have been of the utmost importance in the Radical era that followed Reconstruction (1889–1915), from which

Quentin and Shreve construct Bon's story (202).[17] As a result of their fixation on the color line during that period, Quentin and Shreve make Bon's race the principal mystery of the story and speculate that he is not a flamboyant White Creole with ties to European culture but in fact had inherited a trace of African ancestry on his Haitian mother's side (202).[18] A focus on Bon opens the novel to a hemispheric reading of racial differences: Bon's race is constructed differently in Haiti, where he is a member of the elite *Mulâtres-Aristocrates*; Louisiana, where he may be positioned as a Creole of Color when he isn't passing for White; and Mississippi, where the one-drop rule would position him as Black.[19] Bon's sexual proclivities are accepted in Mississippi when he is thought to be White; however, when he is considered Black, his actions are policed by the community, both reaffirming colonial relations and resulting in his death.

In addition to his unstable racial and national identities, philandering, and attempted bigamy—having already formed a family unit in New Orleans—Bon's connection to Henry links him to the emergent figure of the homosexual. Bon is associated with queer sexuality during the late nineteenth century, a time when alternative sexual identities, such as auto-monosexualists, pedophiles, and homosexuals, were constructed and recognized by society (Abdur-Rahman 225). To consider Bon's friendship with Henry on Eve Sedgwick's "continuum of male 'homosocial desire'" (*Between Men* 1) connects it to "a cultural system in which male-male desire became widely intelligible primarily by being routed through nonexistent desire involving a woman" (*Epistemology of the Closet* 15). Judith can be seen as an empty vessel linking the men and providing a socially acceptable outlet for their feelings for each other. Jason Compson supports this view of the homosocial desire between Henry and Bon, stating: "Bon not only loved Judith after his fashion but he loved Henry too and I believe in a deeper sense than merely after his fashion . . . seeing perhaps in the sister merely the shadow, the woman vessel with which to consummate the love whose actual object was the youth" (85–86). The desire between the two men is here routed through their sister Judith, who functions as a "woman vessel" through which they can express their love.

As far as the narrators of *Absalom, Absalom!*, and consequently the readers, are aware, the relationship between Henry and Bon is never physically consummated. Nevertheless, the relationship between the two men has the potential for creativity and resistance in its alternativeness. In the mutuality found in his relationship with Henry, Bon pursues what Michael Bibler calls a "horizontal model of egalitarian social relations" and disrupts the colonial hierarchies of race, class, and gender central to the plantation South (6). While relations between White men and Black women were accepted in the

South (and Bibler argues even relations between White men of the planter class [18]), egalitarian relationships between Black and White men were not, since they threatened core racial plantation hierarchies. This threat of racial egalitarianism proves to be too much for Henry. He accepts that bigamy and incest may occur between his sister and half-brother but cannot consent to the interracial component, due to the centrality of the color line and colonial hierarchies to the South's plantation culture. While neither were allowed to flourish, Bon's relationships with both Henry and Judith challenge the fixation on difference in the antebellum South.

In Quentin and Shreve's multivalent portrayal of Bon and his fluid national, racial, and sexual identity, he seems to encompass what Valérie Loichot, borrowing from Édouard Glissant's Antillean discourse, refers to as *métissage* (Loichot 117).[20] Bon's uncertain racial heritage, coupled with his sexual fluidity, makes him a fitting example of a *métis*.[21] Indeed, Bon clears room for new social, racial, and sexual forms in the segregated South with his Caribbean-infused fluidity (Loichot 130).[22] As a social *métis*, Bon lives like an elite White Creole in New Orleans, yet is (perhaps) technically Black, a mutability that identifies him also as a racial *métis*. If Quentin and Shreve's version of events is to be believed, then Bon has Black ancestry on his mother's side and for all intents and purposes is passing.[23] Faulkner tells the reader this account is "probably true enough" (268), and Barbara Ladd states that it "probably comes as close to fact as any other detail concerning Bon, which is to say not very close at all" (141). Through living as a White man regardless of his Black ancestry, Bon disrupts the Black/White binary accepted as law in Mississippi.[24] Moreover, Bon is a sexual *métis*. In his attraction to and love for both Henry and Judith, Bon is bi- or pansexual by nature, an additional characteristic of his shifting sexuality alongside his philandering, attempted incest and bigamy, interracial and homosocial desires, and even cross-dressing, described in the introduction. In the 1860s, this fluidity, however, results in the destruction of Bon's racialized and sexualized body. Bon's story illustrates that racialized, gendered, and queer bodies were more ardently policed to maintain the hierarchies in place, as well as the high stakes for those seeking to preserve their privileged positions.

Nevertheless, in Glissant's model of generalized *métissage*, "the category of métis disappears altogether," becoming the norm as opposed to the exception (Loichot 156). Perhaps this generalized *métissage* in which racial hierarchies lose their significance is not far from what Faulkner envisioned at the end of *Absalom, Absalom!* through both Shreve's fantasy of racial amalgamation and Quentin and Shreve's acceptance of Bon (whether intentional or not) by merging with him and Henry: "not two of them there and then either but four of them riding two horses through the iron darkness" (237). At the same time that Quentin and Shreve follow Henry in fearing the racial and sexual subversions Bon embodies, they become one with him as they reconstruct his story. In this way, the early twentieth-century narrators leave room for the possibility of Bon's acceptance and recuperation by later generations. His story provides an alternative to the reiterations of the tragedies that result from continued adherence to outmoded colonial ideologies, contesting the predominance of regulation and restriction as the only narrative available.

Therefore, focus on Bon's fluid nationality, race, and sexuality challenges Quentin and Shreve's portrayal of him and the reductive colonial stereotypes on which they rely. For instance, as a result of his fatalism and nonnormative sexuality, Charles Bon subverts the figure of the biracial "revenger" (676) to which scholars such as Melvin Seiden link him, as well as the stereotype of the Black rapist with which Quentin and Shreve associate him. Biracial blood relatives were barred from White southern family trees, and "mulattoes" were not only seen as the offspring of "unnatural" relationships but also as "the rapists and criminals of the present time," as Charles Carroll argues in *The Negro a Beast* in 1900 (Fredrickson 277). In the words of one southern woman, Mrs. L. H. Harris, writing to the *Independent* in 1899, the Black rapist of the neocolonial period was "'nearly always a mulatto,' with 'enough white blood in him to replace native humility and cowardice with Caucasian audacity'" (Fredrickson 277). In the US South, White racists associated biracial men with violent sexual tendencies, due to the "mixture of blood" and the combined characteristics of both White and Black men, emphasizing the racial and sexual hierarchies.

In Quentin and Shreve's version, Henry shoots Bon to prevent him from being "the n*** that's going to sleep with [his] sister," aligning Bon even more precisely with the figure of the Black rapist (286). Bon's words as imagined by the White narrators connect him to the myth of the Black rapist, yet all other aspects of his life and identity subvert this pairing. Jason Compson's portrayal of Bon as a cosmopolitan dandy, "lounging before them in the outlandish and almost feminine garments," differs from the hypersexual beast rapist stereotype, who cannot control his sexual urges (76). Similarly, Bon does not have a solid corporeal dimension and is described as a shadowy specter by Miss Rosa—"For all I was allowed to know, we had no corpse... [only] the abstraction which we nailed into a box"—which contrasts directly with the brutal, bodily virility of the Black rapist stereotype (123). Further, no rape occurs, and Bon is the victim and not the propagator of the violence that claims his life. The novel subverts Bon's alignment with the figure of the Black rapist in the same way that it destabilizes his association with the "biracial revenger." Nevertheless, through his death at Henry's hands for the protection of his White sister's sexual honor in the final telling of his story, Bon becomes both lynched rapist and abandoned Black lover/brother for the White collective, which includes not only the Sutpens, but also Quentin and Shreve, due to reverberations of the trauma that ripple out through the generations.[25]

Racial ambiguity is common to Faulkner's accused rapists in other texts as well, presenting variations of this figure and demonstrating a progressive thread running through his novels.[26] Lee Goodwin is lynched for Temple Drake's rape and Tommy's murder in *Sanctuary* (1931), although both acts are committed by his bootlegging partner, Popeye. Goodwin is a poor White man; however, he is described throughout the novel as Black: "Goodwin said, jerking up his black head, his gaunt, brown, faintly harried face" (115) and later "Goodwin's black head and gaunt brown face" (281). *Light in August*'s (1932) Joe Christmas is positioned as a Black rapist by his southern White community in the 1930s. In contrast, Christmas's racial background is unknown, and he had an ongoing consensual sexual relationship with Joanna Burden, the White woman he is suspected of raping.[27] Further, while never accused of rape, Lucas Beauchamp of *Go Down, Moses* may be considered racially ambiguous as a financially successful biracial man who carries himself as if he were a White man. In *Intruder in the Dust* (1948), Lucas is falsely suspected of murder in the 1940s and almost lynched by a White mob. Through his depictions of the figure of the racially ambiguous accused rapist, Faulkner inverts the stereotype of the Black rapist and simultaneously calls attention to the detrimental impact of lynch culture.[28]

Bon is shot to prevent "miscegenation" with the White plantation mistress, Goodwin is burned due to accusations of rape and murder, and Christmas is killed for supposedly raping Joanna Burden. These examples demonstrate that the racialized violence of lynch culture is directly connected to gender and sexuality, underscoring the point that sexuality is a particular expression of the neocolonial relationship in the South. The alleged sexual violation of White women by Black men, the myth of the Black rapist, was commonly used as a pretext for lynching and also as a means of shifting attention from the very real White male rapists who continued to prey upon Black women after Emancipation. After Reconstruction, lynching became an increasingly customary practice in the postbellum South and reached epidemic proportions in the 1890s; Stewart E. Tolnay and E. M. Beck have calculated that 2,462 Black Americans were lynched between 1882 and 1930 (Adams 87). Further, lynching attempted to contain sexualized and racialized bodies and was often accompanied by sexualized violence, as depicted in *Light in August* when Joe Christmas is castrated and lynched. In *Sanctuary*, Lee Goodwin is lynched and the novel implies also sexually violated by the mob before his death. One of Goodwin's lynchers states in reference to Horace Benbow, "Do to the lawyer what we did to him. What he did to her. Only we never used a cob. We made him wish we had used a cob" (296). Therefore, lynching can be seen as a form of sexualized violence given the nature of the assault, which frequently included castration and dismemberment, along with other forms of torture, and may be seen as an inheritance from the institution of slavery that granted White males complete control over Black male and female bodies.[29]

Thus, there is a connection between the overthrow of slavery, the deteriorating mastery of White men, and consequently the racial and sexual order (Hale 232), resulting in the fervent protection of Whiteness as both a source of capital and social power. As Jacquelyn Dowd Hall and Grace Elizabeth Hale have argued, it was not a coincidence that the myth of the Black rapist and the resulting lynching of Black men occurred concurrently with the southern women's rights movement, since the myth exaggerates women's dependence on men at a time when women were fighting for increased independence (Hale 23). In other words, the myth of the Black rapist created a scenario in which White women, for example Judith Sutpen, Temple Drake, and Joanna Burden, were reliant on White men for protection (or retaliation) in the eyes of their communities. Lynching was a practice that attempted to maintain the plantation hierarchies not only of race but also of gender in the neocolonial era through the use of women's susceptibility to sexual violation as a pretext.[30] Lynch culture and the racist social fictions sustaining it illustrate bell hooks's assertion that "racism and sexism are interlocking systems of dominance which uphold and sustain one another" (59). The reality of Black women's vulnerability to rape by White men was ignored, yet the invented threat of the Black rapist for White women was emphasized to the point that it was the rationale for the torture and death of Black men. In addition to distracting from the real violation of Black women by White men and creating an excuse for violence against Black men, lynching served to reinforce the subordinate position of White women to White men through using the sexual vulnerability of White women as an unfounded excuse for racial violence.

In this way, the protection of White womanhood became an obsession not out of an antiquated chivalry but as a way to uphold plantation hierarchies and the cumulative value of Whiteness in the postbellum era. Also factored into this fixation is the role of White women in the family unit. White women were charged with producing heirs and White lines of descent—another reason their sexuality was of particular importance. Through regulating sexuality, the plantocracy could attempt to control emotional bonds, resulting family configurations, and thus broader plantation social formations. For instance, in *Go Down, Moses*, Isaac McCaslin is clearly more distressed by his discovery that the mistress of his cousin Roth Edmonds is biracial and that the two produced a child out of wedlock together than he is by the fact that the relationship was incestuous. Isaac discerns the unnamed woman's racial heritage after she mentions that her aunt took in washing to help support her large family: "'Took in what?' he said. 'Took in washing?' He sprang, still seated even, flinging himself backward onto one arm, awry-haired, glaring. Now he understood what it was she had brought into the tent with her . . . He cried, not loud, in a voice of amazement, pity, and outrage: 'You're a n***!'" (344). In this passage, Isaac "sprang," "flinging himself," while "glaring" and crying out. The verbs used demonstrate the extent to which Isaac is disturbed by this revelation, as displayed by his movements. His declaration, "You're a n***!," speaks to the ingrained racism and enduring effects of the one-drop rule in the mid-twentieth century. Although he positions himself as progressive, through distancing himself from the sexual crimes of his grandfather Old Carothers McCaslin and disavowing his plantation inheritance, Isaac is unable to accept interracial relationships in the 1940s. He tells the woman: "We will have to wait" (346).[31]

However, while on the surface Roth's relationship appears to be an echo of the exploitative, incestuous relations between Old Carothers, Eunice, and Tomasina, this is an example of repetition with a difference. Roth's lover has agency in their coupling, as well as deep feelings for him. The reader does not know much about their time together beyond that they cohabitated in New Mexico and a child resulted from the union: "We were there six weeks, where I could at least sleep in the same apartment where I cooked for him and looked after his clothes—" (341). While he may shirk her as a result of her racial status, there is also evidence that Roth is generally unable to settle down as a family man. The woman puts this to Isaac directly, stating, "He's not a man yet. You spoiled him" (343). Roth is a forty-something bachelor spoiled by his comfortable upbringing and inheritance, who does not value the family unit he inadvertently formed, asking Isaac if he hasn't discovered that "women and children are one thing there's never any scarcity of?" (323). Regardless of the more traditional place in which they end up, Roth and the woman's atypical domestic situation out west challenged the plantation hierarchies he had been raised to value. As noted above, interracial relationships and multiracial families were still illegal in some states, such as Mississippi, in the 1940s as a result of antimiscegenation laws.[32] Many communities viewed these relationships as unacceptable, as demonstrated by Isaac's distraught reaction to hearing the woman takes in washing, which codes her as Black (344). While he ultimately abandons the woman and their child, for a time Roth subverts the South's colonial ideologies through openly cohabitating with her—albeit in another state—demonstrating the revolutionary potential of love and the ways in which sexuality was regulated in the attempt to also control love and family formations.

The examples of Roth's relationship, Bon's potential pairing, and even Christmas's coupling depict consensual interracial interactions (well, possibly as the racial identities of Bon and Christmas can never be recovered), which, like Bon's fluidity, constitute a threat to the colonial relations in the South and the racial segregation upon which they rest. For all of his seemingly progressive views on race and inheritance, Isaac McCaslin unwittingly becomes an agent of the sexual policing of the color line, perhaps in order to assuage this threat. Isaac gives the girl a "thick sheaf of banknotes" on behalf of Roth in place of the acknowledgment of their interracial child and their twofold familial connection (339). In a way, Isaac's action echoes Old Carothers's attempt to bequeath to his slave Thucydus Roskus ten acres of plantation land, and later the land's cash equivalent of $200, as compensation for violating and impregnating, first, Eunice, Thucydus's wife, and then Tomasina, the daughter whom McCaslin sires with Eunice. Ironically, it was this act by Old Carothers that led Isaac to relinquish his inheritance—a deed that according to Roth's mistress directly contributed to Roth's immaturity and perhaps also his dismissal of the woman and Isaac's resulting attempt at policing. The substitution of money or property for affection or a rightful place in the family tree thus continues in the twentieth century, evidence of how slavery's disruption of intimate relations and familial connections lingered in the neocolonial US South due to the persistence of colonial ideologies.

Thus, incest and interracial sex on a plantation complicate the role of the father and necessitate alternative kinship systems. There is no one relation, no singular form taken by sexual abuse and the resulting family formations, but different entanglements across generations. As Kimberly Juanita Brown writes, "slavery ruptures a linear trajectory in favor of flux" (17). This should complicate our understanding of what sexual violation looks like and how it affects all those involved. Under the system of slavery, enslaved men are powerless to protect their women, and while some give their lives in attempt, others, as slave narrator Harriet Jacobs mentions, are "poor creatures [who] have been so brutalized by the lash that they will sneak out of the way to give their masters free access to their wives and daughters" (38). Through this choice between death and submissive acceptance, Black men are often depicted as emasculated, such as Thucydus, who is powerless to protect Eunice or Tomasina.

Faulkner subverts this through his portrayal of Lucas Beauchamp in the postbellum era. Lucas is a descendent of Thucydus, although not by blood, due to Old Carothers's exploitation of Eunice. In this example, Lucas does not accept Zack's decision to take Lucas's wife, Molly, into his home after his wife dies. Lucas pulls a razor on a sleeping Zack, demanding his wife back, and luckily is not killed by Zack as a result. Lucas's relationship with Zack and privileged position on the plantation allow him to resist in ways that would have been impossible for those in previous generations. More specifically, Lucas believes that his power to resist results from the elevated status of his "white blood" and his intergenerational connection to Old Carothers (68).[33] While this mindset reaffirms the structures in place, at the same time, the fact that Lucas values his own White heritage in spite of the one-drop rule and the White community's views is also a form of resistance to accepted racial structures. He ultimately insists on the recognition of his humanity; however, this resistance is grounded in the values of a racist and hierarchical society.

In addition to Black men, White women are also impacted by White men's exploitation of Black women's bodies in the plantation South. They are seen as chaste and are associated with reproductive sexuality within the bounds of the family unit. When their husbands desire fetishized sex for the purpose of pleasure, White women are cast aside in deference to enslaved women, over whom the men can exercise unrestricted control.[34] In many cases, White women were constantly reminded of their unfaithful husbands' acts of sexual violence by the existence of their husbands' biracial children. The presence of these children often unleashed from the White wives a ferocious cruelty. For example, in Harriet Jacobs's slave narrative, she tells the story of an enslaved girl, who is dying after the birth of her light-skinned child, and her mistress, who "stood by, and mocked at her like an incarnate fiend" (16). The rape of Black women by White men negatively impacted all involved parties. Old Carothers's nameless wife is notably absent from *Go Down, Moses*. She and her thoughts or actions in response to her husband's abuses and infidelities are never described in the novel. As a woman, she would likely not have written entries into the plantation ledgers, the documents that endure for perusal by the progeny, such as Isaac McCaslin, which may account for this silence.[35] The silencing of the voices of women and people of color from economic records, laws and legal documents, and court proceedings directly contests the comprehensive nature of historical accounts.[36]

Indeed, the perspectives of Black, biracial, and multiracial women, such as Clytie and her unnamed mother or Eunice and Tomasina, are notably absent from these novels. Additionally, the Black men who are often unable to protect their wives and daughters from violation are also silenced. While not told to readers directly, we are better able to piece together the stories of the White women in this configuration—likely due to the preference granted to White narratives in Faulkner's oeuvre overall. The reaction of Old Carothers's unnamed wife to her husband's sex across the color line and incest can never be ascertained; however, that of her daughter-in-law, Sophonsiba Beauchamp (Isaac's mother), may be read as a substitution. Sophonsiba's brother, Hubert Beauchamp, takes on a Black cook and implied lover, whose "nameless illicit hybrid female flesh" excites and disturbs young Isaac, after Sophonsiba's marriage to Theophilus "Uncle Buck" McCaslin (289). The reader is privy to Sophonsiba's extreme response. Isaac remembers "his mother's tearful lamentations," his uncle's assertion that "They're free now! They're folks too just like we are!" and his mother's dramatic ejection of the cook from the family's home (289). Although Sophonsiba is agitated by the actions of her brother, not her husband, her distraught reaction is comparable to the sexual jealousy experienced by many plantation mistresses. Sophonsiba balks at the feeling that she has been replaced in her brother's home, and on a less personal level, she attempts to preserve the family line and uphold the colonial hierarchies in the immediate postbellum period.

As the coupling between Hubert and his Black cook appears consensual, it is important to consider what the stakes are for consensual interracial relationships in the antebellum and postbellum South and what is threatened by this sexual activity. These relationships constitute an even greater threat to the colonial relations in the South and the racial segregation upon which they rest through the egalitarian nature of consensual interactions. If both members of an interracial relationship have a say in their liaison, it diminishes the power and significance of racial differences (i.e., love as revolutionary). Racial differences were central to the hierarchical plantation system, as well as to colonialism more generally, as they helped the plantocracy justify the abuse of the Black bodies they judged to be less than human, less vulnerable to suffering than White bodies. The threat held by consensual interracial relationships in the de-emphasis of racial differences was also a threat to the colonial system in its entirety. This may in part explain the fixation on the color line in the US South, as we see in Sophonsiba's response, particularly during periods in which colonial structures began to break down, such as following the Civil War. Therefore, the sexual policing of the color line by those from different levels of society, such as White women in this example and White men discussed previously, was essential to the functioning of plantation society and the maintenance of the status quo: Whiteness as social, political, and economic power.

Another noteworthy aspect of Sophonsiba's reaction is that she is not only perturbed that the biracial cook takes over her position in her brother's life and their family unit but also by the fact that she is wearing one of Sophonsiba's dresses. Her son, Isaac McCaslin, remembers the day that Sophonsiba threw the cook out of the house: "And he remembered this, he had seen it: an instant, a flash, his mother's soprano 'Even my dress! Even my dress!' loud and outraged in the barren unswept hall; a face young and female and even lighter in color than Tomey's Terrel's for an instant in a closing door; a swirl, a glimpse of the silk gown and the flick and glint of an ear-ring" (289). Sophonsiba is distressed by the material aspects of this usurpation. Although the dress, left behind in the move following her marriage, could not be one she particularly valued, she is outraged that this woman would be wearing her clothes and in her family's home. One way to read this is that Sophonsiba views the cook as performing White, upper-class femininity through wearing the clothing of the former mistress of the home. Sophonsiba, who seems to be threatened by the instability of racial hierarchies, finds this disturbing. After Hubert asserts that they are "folks just like we are," Sophonsiba responds, "That's why! That's why! My mother's house! Defiled! Defiled!" (289). She is again concerned with the material usurpation here, and what it implies about the destabilization of the plantation system and threat to Whiteness as capital. Her exclamation of "That's why!" supports the reading that she is agitated because society no longer recognizes a distinction between her humanity and that of the formerly enslaved population.

Moreover, because she is carrying a carpetbag, the reader is led to associate the cook with carpetbaggers, the ultimate usurpers. This connection to northerners relocating to the South to profit from the upheaval of Reconstruction, in addition to Sophonsiba's focus on the material, precludes any possibility that the unnamed cook may have had an emotional attachment to Hubert or been involved with him for reasons other than the material benefits. This erasure of emotion is echoed later in the novel when Isaac assumes that Roth's mistress must want either money or revenge, to which she replies, "Have you lived so long and forgotten so much that you dont remember anything you ever knew or felt or even heard about love?" (346). However, the portrait of the cook, who never speaks in the novel, is even less developed. Readers lack any direct knowledge of her beyond Isaac's brief glances between his mother's frenetic outbursts. Isaac observes:

The back, the nameless face which he had seen only for a moment, the once-hooped dress ballooning and flapping below a man's overcoat, the worn heavy carpet-bag jouncing and banging against her knee, routed and in retreat true enough and in the empty lane solitary young-looking and forlorn yet withal still exciting and evocative and wearing still the silken banner captured inside the very citadel of respectability ... (290)

The materiality of dress is emphasized again in this passage, "ballooning and flapping," alongside the carpetbag, "jouncing and banging against her knee." The dress is compared with a silk banner stolen from the citadel of "respectability," returning to the significance of the objects for Sophonsiba and her resistance to changing social landscape. The depiction of the dress itself also contains class connotations in the fact that it was "once-hoop," a stereotypical fashion of the plantocracy, evoking images of the hoop-skirts and plug hats, markers of class disdained by the author.[37] According to Isaac, the clothes, house, and material goods—capital accumulation associated with Whiteness—would seem to be the woman's endgame (or so Sophonsiba fears), which is why they are the primary focus of this passage. The readers can never know this woman's emotions or intentions. Not only is all we see of her filtered through Isaac and distorted by his excitement at the "illicit hybrid female flesh," but he also views nothing apart from a quick glimpse of her face. The biracial cook's thoughts and motivations join Mrs. McCaslin's perspective and Clytie's mother's experiences in the imposed silences and weighty absences in Faulkner's account of interracial interactions.

* * *

Thus far, this exploration of sexual policing in Faulkner's later novels reveals three latent motivations linking the post–Civil War period to the 1930s and 1940s: 1) the pseudo-defense of White womanhood—in reality an excuse for the lynching of Black men, 2) the protection of White, upper-class family units, and 3) the preservation of lines of inheritance. To conclude this chapter, I turn to another example from the late 1930s found in Faulkner's *Requiem for a Nun*, which complicates the discussion even further, depicting infanticide as a form of sexual policing, as well as the virality of confining plantation structures that spiral out to impact intersectional hierarchies and social positions. This novel explores the damaged nature of intimate relationships and family units and provides an inverse example of sexual policing to those considered so far in which a Black woman functions as the agent of regulation.

Requiem for a Nun is a sequel to the sensational novel *Sanctuary*, in which a young coed at the University of Mississippi, Temple Drake, is abducted, raped by the impotent Popeye (whose given name we learn in *Requiem for a Nun* is Vitelli) with a corncob, and held in a Memphis brothel until she is needed to testify that her rape and the murder of Tommy (both committed by Popeye) were in actuality performed by his fellow bootlegger, Lee Goodwin (*Requiem for a Nun* 114). *Requiem for a Nun* catches up with Temple Drake eight years after these events. She is the wife of Gowan Stevens, whose reckless driving under the influence of alcohol left her susceptible to the abduction in the first place, and has two children, a son named Bucky and a six-month-old girl, who like scores of female characters before her is left unnamed.[38] *Requiem for a Nun* is a hybrid of a play and a novel. It follows the early history of Jefferson, particularly surrounding the old jail building, in segments written in prose that alternate with three acts centering on the story of Temple Drake, or Mrs. Gowan Stevens, and her family. This form highlights the relationship between the history of the town and the previous experiences of our characters, as well as the centrality of the past to both. The events of this plotline open with the conviction of Nancy Mannigoe, a former sex worker employed by Temple and Gowan as a nurse for their children, for the murder of the youngest Stevens child. *Requiem for a Nun* registers the long-term effects of Temple's own sexual abuse and abduction in the earlier *Sanctuary* plotline, implicitly linking these traumatic events with Temple's seeming inability to perform the expected role of wife and mother.[39]

Requiem for a Nun makes visceral for the reader the relationship between the events of the past and the present. Gavin Stevens, Gowan's uncle and Nancy's attorney, implores Temple to come forward with the truth of her past, stating: "Mrs Gowan Stevens is not even fighting in this class. This is Temple Drake's" (73). Gavin makes a distinction between Temple Drake and the experiences to which she was subjected in *Sanctuary* and Mrs. Gowan Stevens, noting that this is Temple's fight. Following Gavin's lead, Temple refers to her own split identity, which I read as the fragmentation of her subjectivity resulting from her experience of trauma. She replies, "Temple Drake is dead," to which Gavin responds with one of Faulkner's most quoted lines "The past is never dead. It's not even past" (73). Just as the twentieth-century US South cannot escape the effects of slavery on sexuality and interpersonal relationships, Temple Drake cannot shake free from her traumatic past depicted in *Sanctuary*.[40] The bodily trauma common to both sexual abuse and slavery helps to perpetuate colonial mentalities through keeping the hierarchies of race, gender, and class in place.[41]

Through a flashback in act II, readers learn Pete, the brother of Red, a young man who raped Temple in the Memphis brothel while Popeye watched in *Sanctuary*, is blackmailing Temple with incriminating letters she had written to Red.[42] No longer about the letters, the situation turns when Temple plans to forsake her children and husband and run away with Pete.[43] Nancy desperately works to keep the family together and prevent Temple's flight. She first steals the couple's getaway money and jewels and, when that fails to work, appeals to Temple's feelings for her children. Nancy reminds her that Gowan has questioned his paternity of Bucky and will likely not prove a supportive father to him, in the same way that unsavory Pete will probably throw both Temple and the baby out: "To leave one with a man that's willing to believe the child aint got no father, willing to take the other one to a man that dont even want no children—" (150). Temple makes it clear that she plans to leave, "money or no money" and "children or no children" (150). As a result, after Nancy claims to have "tried everything [she] knowed" (151), she smothers the infant with a blanket, seemingly to prevent her from coming to any harm, as well as to reaffirm the ties keeping Temple both in Jefferson and with Bucky and Gowan.

Doreen Fowler reads infanticide as "the central crisis which the novel ceaselessly investigates, casting forward and back for answers, seeking to see and know" (Fowler 140). I argue that Nancy committed this murder in an effort not only to spare the children from abandonment—and perhaps worse at the hands of the criminal, Pete, whom Faulkner describes as having "a definite 'untamed' air to him" and "a hard, ruthless quality, not immoral but unmoral"—but also to attempt to hold together Temple's family unit (137).[44] While Nancy's infanticide is obviously destructive to the family unit through killing a member of the group, there is also a way in which the act can be seen as an effort to preserve kinship systems in the impossible circumstances caused by Temple's abuse and resulting inability to function as a mother. *Requiem* insists that Temple's decision to abandon her husband and children and run away with a criminal does not occur in a vacuum but is directly connected to her own sexual abuse as a White woman in a plantation culture that grants White men authority over female and Black bodies.

In this sense, Nancy's action and the motivation behind it connect her to the historic attempts made by enslaved people to preserve their families in the face of the horrors of slavery, including the breakup of family units and natal alienation.[45] This example is further evidence of the slave system's lingering capacity to alter a society's relationship to sexuality and familial relations in the postbellum period (Abdur-Rahman 224). Acting along the same lines as Sethe in Morrison's *Beloved* (1987), who murders her baby rather than see her subjected to the abuses of slavery, Nancy can only see murder, and more specifically infanticide, as a solution to the problem of damaged interpersonal relationships and the breakup of the family unit that result from the ingrained colonial ideologies and hierarchical relationships remaining in the twentieth-century US South.⁴⁶

While Nancy's infanticide can be read as resistance to the separation of the family unit, her action should also be understood as a form of sexual policing. Like Henry Sutpen before her, in his murder of Bon to prevent him from marrying their White sister, and Isaac McCaslin after her, who cannot bear the thought of Roth Edmonds and his biracial lover and child living together as a family unit, Nancy's infanticide prevents Temple from leaving her husband for White, lower-class gangster Pete. As the other examples of sexual policing described in Faulkner's works typically involve a White man policing the color line to prevent Black or biracial men (like Bon) from sleeping with White women and Black or biracial women from forming families with White plantation heirs (like Roth) in the postbellum era, Nancy's act is a reverse example. Nancy, a lower-class Black woman, polices the sexuality of an upper-class White woman, preventing her from leaving her family for a sexual union with a lower-class White man (48). Nancy's act is complicated. While of course it is problematic to glorify infanticide as a moment of resistance, the act does result in the reversal of hierarchies with Nancy attempting to control the behavior of Temple.

Unlike the other examples I've discussed, the sexual policing at work in *Requiem for a Nun* occurs from the bottom of society upward as opposed to from the top down. Nancy is not a beneficiary of colonial society: she is repeatedly characterized by Gowan and Temple as a "dope-fiend n*** whore" (55). Rather, her policing of sexuality seems to result from her desire to protect the child and preserve Temple's family unit, not from a conscious investment in colonial hierarchies. Further, although Nancy claims her deed is for the children more so than Temple and Gowan, her action still results in the policing of Temple's sexuality, reinscribing the family ties that hold her and her subordinance to her husband.⁴⁷ This example and its variation on the traditional patterns of the sexual policing of the color line common to the US South demonstrate that hierarchies of class are equally active to those of race, gender, and sexuality. Although this chapter is centrally concerned with the policing of sexuality in relation to race and gender, this example shows how resilient colonial mentalities also reify class structures, illustrating the plurality of hierarchical colonial structures.⁴⁸

Along the same lines, the pattern of subjection present in the relations between Old Carothers, Eunice, and Tomasina is reproduced with a difference in the neocolonial period through the relationship between Roth, his unnamed distant relative/lover, and his child—both of whom he forsakes. This dynamic is also repeated in the relations between Thomas Sutpen, Milly Jones, and her unnamed female newborn in *Absalom, Absalom!* (see figure 1.1). Sutpen's original design is destroyed when Henry Sutpen shoots his half-brother Charles Bon and must go into exile as a result, leaving Sutpen without a White male heir to inherit his Hundred. After he insults his fiancée, Miss Rosa, with some version of the offer that if they attempted to have a male child and were successful then he would marry her, Sutpen uses candy and ribbons to seduce fifteen-year-old Milly Sutpen, who is forty-six years his junior. When Milly's child is born female and not male, Sutpen discards her with the words: "Well, Milly; too bad you're not a mare too. Then I could give you a decent stall in the stable," which causes Wash Jones, Milly's grandfather who raised her, to kill Sutpen with a scythe (*Absalom, Absalom!* 229). Some critics, such as Édouard Glissant, have speculated that perhaps Faulkner, "who hides as much as he dares to reveal, had hidden the fact—as Sutpen would have been able to hide it from the whole country, from everyone including Wash Jones—that Sutpen was Milly's father, who, in his madness, decided to trust only his own bloodline to get the male heir he longed for" (135).[49] As the opposite of "miscegenation" (exogamy), incest (endogamy) ensures that a genealogy will not suffer from the "taint" of racial difference. In this case, Sutpen would have relied on endogamy, marrying too far into his tribe or group, as an insurance against the greater risk for his White supremacist mentality, exogamy—marrying too far outside of his group and perhaps inviting in the Other.

In this example, the pattern of subjection common to Old Carothers's sexual relationship with his daughter Tomasina is reproduced but with class brought to the fore, illustrating the intersectional nature of oppressions. Here plantation hierarchies work to dehumanize a poor White girl in a comparable way to routine dehumanization of African American women and men through the system of slavery. Through the example of Milly Jones's exploitation at the hands of Sutpen, as well as what can be read in *Requiem for a Nun* as Nancy's policing of class lines, Faulkner underscores the multiplicity of neocolonial configurations. In the postbellum and twentieth-century South, where these two examples occur, the hierarchical mindsets that lay the foundation for colonial relations spiral out to affect every aspect of society through race, color, gender, sexuality, and class relations. By ending with these examples of poor Whites joining Black characters in common patterns of subjection, I emphasize both the reach and negative consequences of colonial ideologies in the post-/neocolonial era, during which no group in

Faulkner's South, as designated by race, gender, class, nationality, and sexual preference, is left unaffected.

Faulkner's novels do more than just expose the negative impacts of colonialism on all aspects of society. *Absalom, Absalom!*; *Go Down, Moses*; and *Requiem for a Nun*, for example, illustrate the virality of colonial crimes. Throughout the novels, Faulkner hints at other options in addition to the replication of destructive colonial relations, for example Bon's fluid relationship to nationality, race, and sexuality; Lucas Beauchamp's resistance to Zack's authority; and although more controversial, Nancy's act of infanticide.[50] Faulkner's portrayals of consensual interracial relationships, such as those existing between Hubert Beauchamp and his nameless cook, Carothers Roth Edmonds and his unnamed relative, and also Charles Bon, Judith, and Henry Sutpen, have the potential to defy colonial hierarchies. Thus, an examination of the patterns and reversals in the characters' relationships foregrounds the novels' more subversive aspects, which are often obscured beneath the imbricated layers of complex depictions and evocative aesthetics. The clarity granted by positioning these configurations, substitutions, and variations alongside one another is antithetical to the experience of reading Faulkner's prose. However, through examining the relationships in this way, it becomes clear that these novels confront, rather than passively reinscribe, colonial relations and mentalities in the post-/neocolonial South through the inclusion of depictions of resistance to the status quo. Faulkner is able to represent alternative ways of interacting and, as a result, to challenge the patterns of subjection and abuse ubiquitous in earlier eras.

Chapter 2

"THERE IS NO IN-BETWEEN"

Community, Sexuality, and the Shifting Construction of Race in Ernest Gaines's Louisiana

In the plantation culture of rural Louisiana, the policing of sexuality and interracial sex institutionalized by colonial laws, such as the 1724 Code Noir, remained in the twentieth century, working to control the sexuality of others and thus preserve colonial society. Three novels by Black southern writer Ernest J. Gaines deal overtly with interracial relationships across these enduring legal-social structures. *Catherine Carmier* (1964) examines the relationship between a Black man and a Creole of Color woman, *The Autobiography of Miss Jane Pittman* (1973) explores a strained friendship between a White man and a Creole of Color woman, and *Of Love and Dust* (1967) depicts a love rectangle between a White Cajun man, his White wife, a Black woman, and a multiracial man positioned as Black. The patterns of policing are complex in Gaines's work due to the entwinement of the different race and class groups; for instance, the planter class, the Creoles of Color, and the Cajuns will police the sexuality of others in order to retain their relatively privileged statuses in community. On the other hand, the Black community often polices the color line for the protection of individuals: many of the older members have seen the violence resulting from seemingly personal or private interactions spiral out to impact the entire community. Although the reasons behind their actions may differ, the White planter class, the White Cajuns, the Creoles of Color, and the Black community all play a role, resulting in multidirectional self-policing from different levels of society. After examining the history surrounding the racial formation and the policing of sexuality in early Louisianan society, I explore their lingering ramifications in the twentieth century, as depicted in two plantation novels of Ernest Gaines, *Catherine Carmier* and *The Autobiography of Miss Jane Pittman*, before turning to *Of Love and Dust* in the next chapter. Through his emphasis on multiple voices, stories, and perspectives, Gaines examines the effects of entwined legal, social, and cultural structures on interpersonal relationships in twentieth-century Louisiana, taking into account hierarchies of race, color, gender, and class.

The United States and its expanding national boundaries had never been particularly open to amalgamation, as the slave system rested on the belief that African Americans are less than human and not subject to the same rights (Ladd 23). The central difference between racial policies in France and the former French colonies (such as Haiti and the deep US South) and the rest of the US hinged on the fact that the French government pursued a policy of assimilation in its colonies, whereas segregation was key in the formerly English territories of the upper South (where the status of the child followed that of the mother from the early eighteenth century) (Ladd xiv, 21).[1] In particular, the state of Louisiana has a unique colonial history that distinguishes it from the rest of the South, opening up to more hemispheric understandings of space. Thadious Davis describes Louisiana as "a microcosm of multiculturalism within the southern region that was not allowed to become the nation's dominant societal model" (*Southscapes* 20), as a result of the racial and linguistic mixture that took place and the proximity to the Caribbean and Latin and South America (*Southscapes* 8).

A former French and Spanish colony, there existed in Louisiana the potential for a more nuanced, variegated racial system, linking the region to the more multiplicitous structures of the Caribbean. The *Gens des Couleur Libres*, or Creoles of Color, functioned as a separate race, putting the racial categorization in Louisiana at odds with the binary understanding that resulted from the one drop rule in other areas of the US South. After acquiring the Louisiana Territory from France in 1803, however, the US worked to replace the "assimilationist and colonialist policy" with "a segregationist and nationalist policy" (Ladd 23). Upholding the color line became central to the racial hierarchies in Louisiana as White southerners worked to differentiate themselves from the enslaved population. This form of policing remained central to Louisiana's plantation society well into the twentieth century, as this chapter explores, underscoring a shared link between Louisiana and Mississippi (explored in chapter 1), as well as ties to Haiti and the Dominican Republic. The inheritance of plantation policing persists in the current economic, legal, and political infrastructures across these spaces. Ernest Gaines's novels demonstrate that literature elucidates and individualizes this history, while in this case simultaneously emphasizing connections between the twentieth-century US South and Caribbean.

Gaines's *Catherine Carmier* focuses on a Black man and a Creole of Color woman, while *The Autobiography of Miss Jane Pittman* depicts an interracial friendship between a White man and Creole of Color woman and the conflict that results. Taken together, the two novels provide insight into the racial positioning of Creoles of Color on the early twentieth-century plantation and the communities' varied reactions to these boundary-crossing relationships due to the intricacies of race, color, gender, and class. First, I focus on the relationship between Catherine Carmier, a light-skinned Creole of Color, and her Black friend from childhood, Jackson Bradley, in order to illustrate the remnants of the three-tiered system in Louisiana and the lowered stakes for this type of interracial relationship. I then turn to the relationship between Robert Samson Jr., nicknamed Tee Bob, and Mary Agnes LeFabre in *The Autobiography of Miss Jane Pittman*, and what it reveals about the collective community's self-regulation based on unwritten codes. Grounded in evidence from earlier drafts of the novel, I argue that this episode is less about Tee Bob and Mary Agnes and more about the community's engagement with their story and underlying commitment to colonial ideologies. I continue this exploration of interracial relationships in the next chapter through analyzing Gaines's *Of Love and Dust*. This novel's portrayal of the relationships between a White Cajun overseer and a Black housekeeper, as well as the overseer's White Cajun wife and a multiracial convict laborer, requires a more extensive analysis and adds further layers to the discussion.

Before turning to the literature to illuminate this history, I examine the interplay between various factors that led Louisiana to develop a distinctive racial system in the antebellum US South. One such influence was the impact of refugees from its "more prosperous sister" (Domínguez 23) and fellow French colony, Saint-Domingue, which would become Haiti in 1804 following the revolution. A hemispheric frame reveals that the legal and racial systems in New Orleans were in flux when Louisiana transitioned from a French colony to a US territory. Kenneth Aslakson asserts that "a more thorough Anglo-Americanization of the system was deterred by the arrival of St. Domingan refuges (white, black, and of color), which helped fix the fluidity in a direction that was more comparable with the late eighteenth-century St. Domingue norms than with contemporary Anglo-American ones" (2).[2] This was a foundational period for Louisiana. The thousands of multiracial immigrants arriving in waves from Saint-Domingue from 1793 to 1804 added to the region's deep multicultural roots and bolstered the three-tiered social hierarchy in place from the Spanish colonial period: White people, free people of color, and enslaved people (Aslakson 21, 27).[3] In this respect, the racial system of antebellum Louisiana had more in common with racial classification in the Caribbean and Latin America, emphasizing circum-Caribbean connections dating back to the colonial era. The majority of the

New World slave systems, regardless of the colonizers' origins, developed three-tiered structures in which a racially mixed class of a marginal status existed between Blacks and Whites, in opposition to "the rigid, two-tiered structure that drew a single unyielding line between the white and the nonwhite" common to the rest of the United States (Hirsch and Logsdon 189).[4] The three-tiered racial system in Louisiana led to a similar fluidity, which managed to survive the increasing US influence (Diamond and Cottrol 504).

Thus, the colonial history of the region had a substantial impact on the development of Louisiana's social and racial structures. New Orleans and Louisiana were "culturally, demographically, and economically part of the French and Spanish empires during [their] formative years" as much as they were "legally and institutionally part of the United States during the nineteenth and twentieth centuries" (Hirsch and Logsdon 189). Indeed, Louisiana's French and Spanish origins had social, cultural, and legal ramifications on the region. Scholars, such as Vernon Palmer and Leonard Oppenheim, have described the laws of the French and Spanish slave systems as "relatively more 'humane' or less dehumanizing than slavery rules developed by English colonies," due to the connection to Roman law (Palmer 332). Debating the degrees of dehumanization does not seem particularly productive; however, the important point here is that the French laws are more comprehensive. Unlike other slave states, Louisiana had a "Romanist background" for its laws, which led to a more comprehensive system for regulating the rights, obligations, and interactions of both the enslavers and enslaved (Oppenheim 312).[5] The Superior Council of Louisiana adopted the Code Noir, the comprehensive French legislation; however, the state also borrowed heavily from Roman and Spanish laws, such as the *Las Siete Partidas* (Oppenheim 319). Louis XIV first promulgated the Code Noir, "a law affecting social, religious and property relationships between all classes," in 1685 for the French Antilles, and it was applied in Louisiana in 1724 (Palmer 331)—another shared historical tie between Louisiana and the French Caribbean. While the Code Noir was used to establish the control of an enslaver over the enslaved, versions of the Code following the Louisiana Purchase—the Digest of 1808 and the Louisiana Civil Code of 1825—placed certain restrictions on that power (Oppenheim 319). For instance, article 173 of the Civil Code of Louisiana in 1825 states: "The slave is entirely subject to the will of his master, who may correct him and chastise him, though not with unusual vigor so as to maim or mutilate him or expose him to the danger of loss of life, or to cause his death" (as qtd. in F. Burns 307–8). Although not always followed to the letter, the Codes attempt to hold enslavers responsible for the relative well-being of the enslaved population—at least superficially.

LE CODE NOIR
OU
EDIT DU ROY,
SERVANT DE REGLEMENT
Pour

Le Gouvernement & l'Adminiſtration de la Juſtice, Police, Diſcipline & le Commerce des Eſclaves Negres, dans la Province & Colonie de la Loüiſianne.

Donné à Verſailles au mois de Mars 1724.

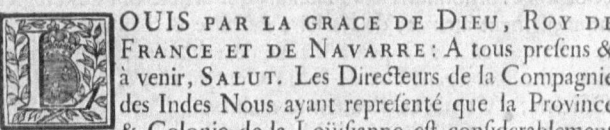OUIS PAR LA GRACE DE DIEU, ROY DE FRANCE ET DE NAVARRE: A tous preſens & à venir, SALUT. Les Directeurs de la Compagnie des Indes Nous ayant repreſenté que la Province & Colonie de la Loüiſianne eſt conſiderablement eſtablie par un grand nombre de nos Sujets, leſquels ſe ſervent d'Eſclaves Negres pour la culture des terres; Nous avons jugé qu'il eſtoit de noſtre authorité & de noſtre Juſtice, pour la conſervation de cette Colonie, d'y eſtablir une loy & des regles certaines, pour y maintenir la diſcipline de l'Egliſe Catholique,

A

Figure 2.1: First page from the 1724 *Le code noir ou Edit du roy.* Courtesy of the John Carter Brown Library at Brown University.

Further, article IX of the 1685 Code Noir contains direct efforts to regulate sexuality—for instance, stating that any enslaver who has a child with an enslaved woman will be fined in sugar (*"seront chacun condamnez à une amende de deux mille livres de sucre"*) and deprived of the woman and child, who will be sent to the hospital to remain enslaved (*"eux soient confisquez au*

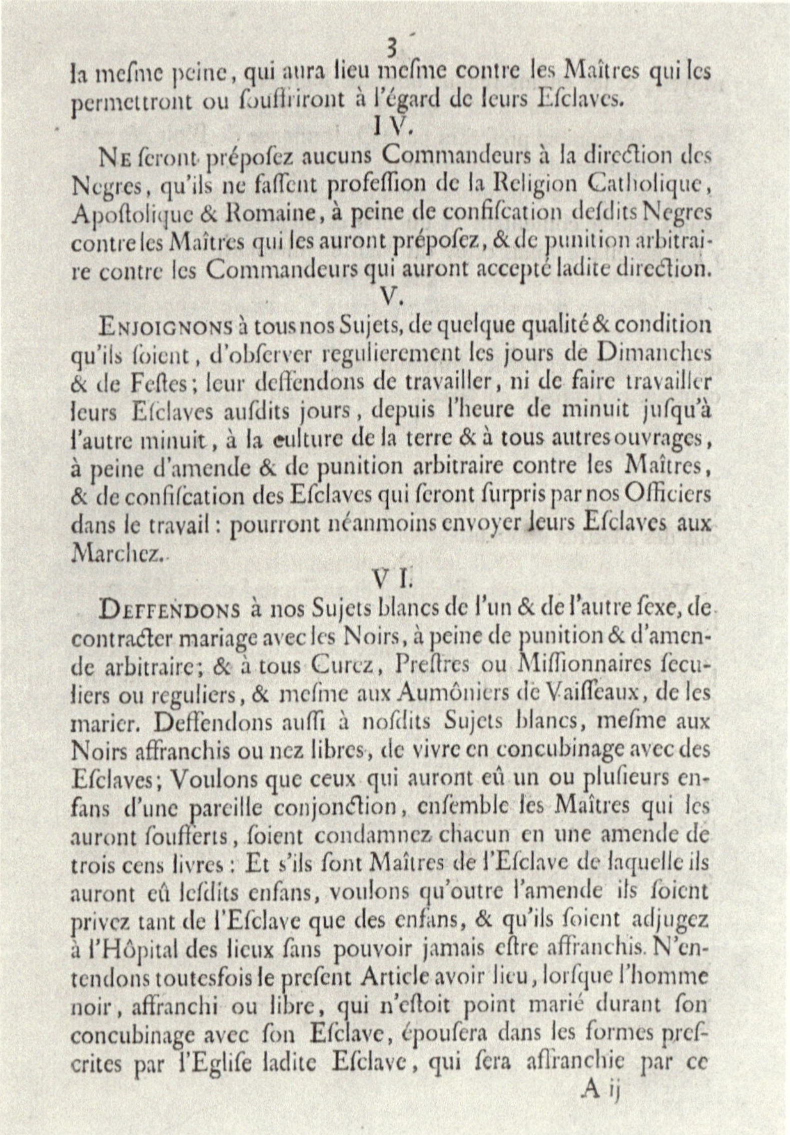

> 3
> la mesme peine, qui aura lieu mesme contre les Maîtres qui les permettront ou souffriront à l'égard de leurs Esclaves.
>
> IV.
> NE seront préposez aucuns Commandeurs à la direction des Negres, qu'ils ne fassent profession de la Religion Catholique, Apostolique & Romaine, à peine de confiscation desdits Negres contre les Maîtres qui les auront préposez, & de punition arbitraire contre les Commandeurs qui auront accepté ladite direction.
>
> V.
> ENJOIGNONS à tous nos Sujets, de quelque qualité & condition qu'ils soient, d'observer regulierement les jours de Dimanches & de Festes; leur deffendons de travailler, ni de faire travailler leurs Esclaves ausdits jours, depuis l'heure de minuit jusqu'à l'autre minuit, à la culture de la terre & à tous autres ouvrages, à peine d'amende & de punition arbitraire contre les Maîtres, & de confiscation des Esclaves qui seront surpris par nos Officiers dans le travail : pourront néanmoins envoyer leurs Esclaves aux Marchez.
>
> VI.
> DEFFENDONS à nos Sujets blancs de l'un & de l'autre sexe, de contracter mariage avec les Noirs, à peine de punition & d'amende arbitraire; & à tous Curez, Prestres ou Missionnaires seculiers ou reguliers, & mesme aux Aumôniers de Vaisseaux, de les marier. Deffendons aussi à nosdits Sujets blancs, mesme aux Noirs affranchis ou nez libres, de vivre en concubinage avec des Esclaves; Voulons que ceux qui auront eû un ou plusieurs enfans d'une pareille conjonction, ensemble les Maîtres qui les auront soufferts, soient condamnez chacun en une amende de trois cens livres : Et s'ils sont Maîtres de l'Esclave de laquelle ils auront eû lesdits enfans, voulons qu'outre l'amende ils soient privez tant de l'Esclave que des enfans, & qu'ils soient adjugez à l'Hôpital des lieux sans pouvoir jamais estre affranchis. N'entendons toutesfois le present Article avoir lieu, lorsque l'homme noir, affranchi ou libre, qui n'estoit point marié durant son concubinage avec son Esclave, épousera dans les formes prescrites par l'Eglise ladite Esclave, qui sera affranchie par ce
> A ij

Figure 2.2: Third page from the 1724 *Le code noir ou Edit du roy*. Courtesy of the John Carter Brown Library at Brown University.

profit de l'Hôpital, sans jamais pouvoir être affranchis") (*Le code noir ou Edit du roy* [1685] 5, transcription mine). Similarly, article VI of the 1724 version of the Code Noir forbids White subjects of either sex, presumably men or women, from marriage to Blacks ("*Défendons à nos Sujets blancs de l'un & de l'autre séxe, de contracter mariage avec les Noirs*"), as well as White and free

Black subjects from living in "concubinage" with enslaved people (*"Défendons aussi à nosdits Sujets blancs, même aux Noirs afranchis, ou nez libres, de vivre en concubinage avec des Esclaves"*) (*Le code noir ou Edit du roy* [1724] 3, transcription mine). If one or several children result, the enslaver and the subject who committed the offense will each need to pay a three hundred livres fine, and as in the 1685 Code, if the enslaved woman belongs to the offender, she and the children will be given to the hospital and can never be freed (*Le code noir ou Edit du roy* [1724] 3, French 89–90). While cohabitation is forbidden, only those unions resulting in children are assigned a material punishment according to the codes, emphasizing the intended regulation of family structures.

While the intent is the same, the 1724 version is more specific, differentiating between marriage and cohabitation, as well as between free Blacks and the enslaved population. Not only are White subjects of both sexes forbidden from marriage to Black subjects, but Whites and free Blacks are also prohibited from cohabitation with the enslaved—these added complexities perhaps speaking to the growing complications of Louisiana's social landscape.[6] Moreover, the codes sought to control not only sexual interactions but also romantic relationships and family formations. Given the expanding size of the multiracial population and the rampant sexual exploitation under the slave system, this aspect of the laws was not always an effective deterrent (Domínguez 26). Nevertheless, I argue that through the 1685 Code Noir and its later iterations, the colonial powers, and later the US government, attempted to control the intimate and sexual interactions between individuals. These laws cast private relations into the public domain—an effect that remained with the Louisiana plantation system into the twentieth century, as explored in Ernest Gaines's novels.

The unofficial rules regulating both sexual and romantic relationships on Gaines's Grover and Samson plantations in the early twentieth century may be seen as the inheritance from the earlier sexual policing of the Code Noir. The Louisiana Civil Codes maintained the policing initiated by the French legal system. For instance, the Digest of 1808 recognized the existence of three sectors of society and attempted to prevent marriage across the boundaries of race and freedom (Domínguez 25). The Civil Code of 1825 also prohibited marriage between enslaved people, free people of color, and White people, but sexual relationships continued, as evidenced by a growing multiracial population (Domínguez 26). A bill passed by the legislature in 1908 attached a punishment to "concubinage" between Black and White individuals (Domínguez 29), returning to the language of the 1724 Code Noir that forces a negative connotation on these relationships. The 1908 bill also illustrates the change from the legal recognition of three races to two: Black and White. Although there were shifts in the number of races acknowledged, interracial marriages were banned by Louisiana law from 1807 to 1972, aside from a brief window during Reconstruction (1870–1894) (Domínguez 57). Indeed, an examination of sexuality reveals the persistence of colonial dynamics in the post-/neocolonial period. The hostility that we see toward the interracial pairings in *Catherine Carmier* and *The Autobiography of Miss Jane Pittman* can be traced to these early laws, the effects of which linger within the culture and communal attitudes generations later.

In addition to the regulation of sexuality and family formations, these legal systems ultimately led to a distinct understanding of race and racial groups in Louisiana. The Code Noir of 1724 set the precedent for Louisiana's legal system to play a role in the region's construction of race. The Code officially created a three-tier racial and social structure with an elite White community and an enslaved Black population at either end and a liminal free biracial class in between who enjoyed the privileges and rights of Whites but lacked the high social standing (Brasseaux 72). Focusing on early New Orleans, Kenneth Aslakson agrees with Ian Haney López that "law constructs race" (*White by Law* 10), arguing that what happens in the courts plays a role in the construction of race for a particular society: race is a process "historically constructed by the choices that individuals make within structural boundaries" (4). As a result, systems of law, including the 1685 Code Noir, 1724 Code Noir, the Digest of 1808, and the Civil Code of 1825, not only regulate the interactions between individuals but also have large-scale impacts, such as how race and other social markers are defined by society. In the antebellum period, Louisiana's system of racial classification was dependent on two criteria: "being legally free or not, and having African blood or not" (Martin 60). As a result of these criteria, the court system in Louisiana supported the existence of a third group distinct from the Black and White races: the biracial, primarily light-skinned *Gens des Couleur Libres* or free Creoles of Color.

Louisiana's Creoles of Color located in New Orleans and the bayou regions were historically endogamous, "until late in the 19th century spoke mostly French . . . [and were] overwhelmingly Catholic . . . Over time, a great many have passed into white groups in other parts of the country, and others have become integrated as blacks" (Kein xiv). This distinct social, racial, and cultural group was granted legal rights and privileges that were off-limits to free Blacks in other states, such as the ability to own all types of property (including enslaved people), to engage in legal contracts, to testify in court against White people, and to sue (Aslakson 5). In this way, the legal system played a role in differentiating Creoles of Color from both the free White and enslaved Black populations. The interactions between this group and both the White and Black races will be the focus of the remainder of this chapter, in which I examine two corresponding examples from the novels of Ernest Gaines.

The three-tiered and binary structures existed alongside each other in the ethnically divided New Orleans until the Jim Crow period (1877 to the 1950s), during which the binary system officially won out (Hirsch and Logsdon 189). Laws once again played a role in the shift in racial categorization from the three-tiered system to the Black and White binaristic model: the black codes following the Civil War institutionalized the monolithic view of nonwhites (Brasseaux et al. 104). Up until the late 1940s and early 1950s, Creoles of Color remained a marginal racial group with the prevailing culture and attitudes supporting this positioning and tensions remaining between Black Louisianans and Creoles of Color (Brasseaux et al. 119). The distinctions began to fade with the advance of the civil rights movements in the 1950s and 1960s (Brasseaux et al. 119). We see this shift in an episode toward the end of Gaines's *The Autobiography of Miss Jane Pittman* when a Creole of Color, "one of the Hebert girls," is chosen to drink from the White people's fountain as part of a civil rights protest (Gaines 246), exemplifying the convergence of the Black and Creole of Color communities in the push toward civil rights.

This chapter focuses on the 1930s and 1940s in rural Louisiana, as depicted in the works of Ernest Gaines. During this period, the Creoles of Color still existed as a distinct racial group, although the shift toward the binary classification system had been initiated after Reconstruction. A tension is observable in both novels between the three-tiered and binary systems of race. Moreover, in the agricultural US South, the 1930s and 1940s were the final decades of the transition from the plantation economy to the modern capitalist system that had begun during Reconstruction (Mandle 68–69). Many of Gaines's novels focus on this period of transition when White Cajun farmers, with the aid of tractors and other agricultural technology, began to take over land from Black sharecroppers. The three-tiered system was complex and not simply composed of three monolithic racial groups. For instance, the Cajuns—the descendants from the Acadians who settled in Louisiana from 1764 to 1767 (T. Davis, "Headlands and Quarters" 5)—are considered socially, culturally, and ethnically distinct from the White planter class. While the Cajuns "inhabit the space between white landowners and Creoles" of Color (Teutsch 117), the legal system of Louisiana never recognized the Cajuns as racially distinct: their Whiteness takes precedent over their lower-class status. Madame Bayonne illustrates this in *Catherine Carmier*, noting that the Cajuns were given the better tracts of land because "white still sticks with white" (73). As a result, the Cajun farmers make more money and can afford to buy better equipment. In the words of Madame Bayonne: "They have wrangled and wrangled until they have gotten everybody else to quit farming" (73). The Cajuns continue working with these advantages until they have pushed the Black sharecroppers off of the land entirely, keeping colonial hierarchies of race in place.

Whereas the Tee Bob episode of *The Autobiography of Miss Jane Pittman* depicts the tragic outcomes that result from a White man falling in love with a Creole of Color, *Catherine Carmier* focuses on a reciprocal relationship between a Black man and Creole of Color woman in the early twentieth century. The policing of sexuality functions differently in this novel from the other two: since the relations between the Black and Creole of Color groups are emphasized without the White communities' direct involvement, the stakes are lowered. This novel, Gaines's first, provides evidence of the shift from a three-tiered to binary racial structure in Louisiana with various societal groups adhering to different models. According to the legal conceptualization of race in Louisiana in the early twentieth century—the setting for this novel—both Catherine and Jackson would have been considered Black.[7] However, less officially, the third racial group, Creoles of Color, was still recognized by some communities, as demonstrated by the restrictions against Jackson and Catherine's love. A tension exists in the novel between the three-tiered racial system recognized by the Black and Creole of Color communities and the simplified binary structure supported by the White Cajun and planter classes. For instance, plantation owner Mack Grover dismisses Creole of Color Robert Carmier's strong work ethic at the same time that he conflates the Creole of Color and Black racial groups together as "n***s": "'His share of the work, yeah,' Mack Grover said. 'But that ain't enough for a n***, no matter how white he is'" (11). Characters in the Black community, however, such as Madame Bayonne, consider Robert's son and Catherine's father, Raoul, to be "neither white nor black" (74), subscribing to the older model of racial relations, dating back to the 1724 Code Noir.

The Creole of Color and Black communities in the novel not only recognize the differences between their groups but also hold fast to prejudices running both ways. Creole of Color Raoul Carmier does not permit his daughter Catherine to interact with darker-skinned boys. As children, Jackson could only visit Catherine when Raoul was not home (15). Similarly, Aunt Charlotte would punish Jackson if she discovered he was spending time at the Carmiers' (38). According to Aunt Charlotte, talking to Catherine and her sister Lillian: "That just's bad's white," later adding "Worser..." (24).

Moreover, Lillian's experience is revealing in juxtaposition to Catherine's: she was not raised on the Grover plantation alongside Black children from the quarters but by her Creole of Color aunts in New Orleans. The aunts taught her to "hate black worse than whites hate it" (48). Lillian, visiting the plantation from her cosmopolitan home before she plans to pass into the White race, recognizes the shift in racial categorizations in postbellum Louisiana. Lillian explains to Catherine: "I can't stand in the middle of the road any longer. Neither can you, and neither can you let Nelson. Daddy and his sisters can't understand this. They want us to be Creoles. Creoles. What a joke. Today you're one way or the other; you're white or you're black. There is no in-between" (48).[8] While Creoles of Color, like Raoul and his sisters, cling to the distinctions of the three-tiered model because of the privileged status it grants them, those in other communities have shifted to a binary way of thinking.

As a result of these reciprocal prejudices on the Grover plantation, the obstacles facing the relationship between Jackson Bradley, who has returned from college in California to live with his aunt in the quarters, and Catherine Carmier, who "was Negro, but with extremely light skin," are brought to the fore (8). Catherine's appearance is described in detail, including her skin, lips, nose, cheekbones, eyes, and hair: "With her thin lips and aquiline nose, with her high cheekbones, dark eyes, and dark hair, Catherine Carmier could have easily passed as Indian" (8). In contrast, Jackson is described only as "six feet tall or better" (17). At the same time that Gaines gives us complex depictions of interracial interactions, he puts his characters in conversation with stereotypes and tropes, such as the exoticization/eroticization of the "tragic mulatto."[9] Like William Faulkner before him and Marie Chauvet concurrently, Gaines often places his characters in relation to the flat figures, only to have them break out of the molds, or in Alvin Aubert's words, "undermin[e] the stereotype through irony" (69).[10] For instance, given the high stakes and tense circumstances, the ending of the story for Catherine is not very tragic—neither she nor her lover ends up dead. While forced to decide between staying to support her father and leaving the plantation with Jackson, ultimately, it is her choice to make. She has the agency to leave or stay. This agency is in direct opposition to the common use of the "tragic mulatto" as a "determinist concept"—a character who is powerless to change her fate (and typically authors using the trope are likewise powerless to steer her away from tragedy) (Sollors 228). After Jackson defeats Raoul, Della foreshadows that Catherine will eventually leave with him, once she has taken care of her father. Catherine herself pleads with her eyes following the fight: "Just have faith in me" (245). The relationship between Catherine and her father is complicated, however, and it will take time for Catherine to feel comfortable leaving him behind. While the ending is ambiguous, if the readers follow Catherine's instructions to Jackson and have a little faith, it seems likely that the couple's love will overcome the prejudices of their families and community, demonstrating the revolutionary potential in loving despite hierarchies.

Moreover, shades of incest are visible in the relationship between Catherine and Raoul, revealing incest to be less of a threat to the plantation hierarchies in the South than interracial sex, and thus not policed as rigorously, as examined in chapter 1. Multiple characters question the nature of Catherine and Raoul's relationship, including Catherine's mom, Della, and lover, Jackson, who thinks it would be better for the two if he wasn't standing between them: "They could have each other all to themselves for the rest of their twisted lives" (161). Although they are very close and Raoul seems to rely too heavily on Catherine, readers are never shown anything beyond affection between the two. Keith Byerman argues that "the Carmier house becomes an incestuous space even without acts of sexual violation" (195), and Jackson is convinced that "she was Raoul's lover" (Gaines 175). While incestuous marriages in a direct line between ascendants and descendants—like Catherine and Raoul's would be—were always outlawed by the civil law of Louisiana, there were shifts in what other relationships were acceptable (Domínguez 58). For instance, the turn toward outlawing first-cousin marriage was difficult for many, as these marriages were "popular, even customary" in Louisiana since the eighteenth century (Domínguez 61). Aristocratic planter families (both White and Creole of Color) believed "it is better to marry a close cousin than to marry someone of much lower social status" (Domínguez 61), which also ensured the inheritance stayed within the family.[11] By way of contrast, interracial marriages were always prohibited, barring the brief window during Reconstruction (Domínguez 61). Thus, communities throughout Louisiana held the prohibition against exogamy of higher importance than that against endogamy. Indeed, the endogamy "encouraged by early Louisiana's legal and social systems" is credited with sustaining "the emerging Creole of Color community of the prairie country" (Brasseaux et al. 14). Marrying inward helped to solidify the Creoles of Color as a racial, social, and cultural group distinct from Black and White, which—along with an entrenched fear of the racial Other—may explain why it is the more accepted of the two common prohibitions.

Since this relationship is between a Black man and Creole of Color woman, the community's role in the policing of sexuality differs from the patterns we will examine next in *The Autobiography of Miss Jane Pittman*. Catherine

Carmier is told from the third-person perspective, highlighting this focus on the collective. Stylistically Gaines's prose has a more realist feel compared with William Faulkner's experimental aesthetics, discussed in the previous chapter. Nevertheless, the aesthetics of the novel foreground a communal voice, in addition to Black and Creole of Color perspectives, aligning the form with the content. The story follows different characters' points of view, depicting the voice of the community; however, it lacks a central narrator like Miss Jane through which to filter everything. The viewpoints brought to the fore are those of Black or Creole of Color characters, which explains the nuanced view of racial differences in opposition to the monolithic view of the two groups held by the White Cajun and planter classes. The reciprocal racial prejudice, or what the White groups would consider to be colorism, between the Black and Creole of Color communities is a lingering effect from the three-tiered racial system. Because half of society—the White planter and Cajun classes—views racial classification through a binary lens, the policing by the community functions differently in this novel, lowering the stakes.

Just as the novel only follows the perspectives of Black and Creole of Color characters, the climax—a physical fight between Raoul and Jackson—solely involves members of those racial groups. Unlike both *The Autobiography of Miss Jane Pittman* and *Of Love and Dust*, the White characters are peripheral to the interracial love plot in *Catherine Carmier*, functioning as instigators, such as the Cajuns who pay two Black men "twenty dollars each if they would let Raoul know that Catherine and Jackson were seeing each other" (225). Here, the Cajuns do not have a vested interest in the relationship but consider it to be an opportunity to drive Raoul from his land. Raoul is well aware of this intention, telling himself: "They would do anything to hurt him, to make him pack up and leave" (227). White people are not directly involved in this interracial love affair, and therefore, the relationship is not policed from all levels of society, as we will see in the next example from *The Autobiography of Miss Jane Pittman* and also in *Of Love and Dust* in the following chapter.[12]

The community's policing of race and sexuality examined in *Catherine Carmier* continues in *The Autobiography of Miss Jane Pittman*, although the relationship policed is inverted with a White man falling for a Creole of Color woman. This episode takes place during the final decades of transition from the plantation economy in the South. While the exact year these events transpire is unclear, they occur after the September 10, 1935 death of beloved Louisiana governor Huey Long. Tee Bob, a White male descendent of the planter family who was "small and delicate all his life" (146), becomes infatuated with Mary Agnes, the new teacher at the plantation school who is a light-skinned Creole of Color. Mary Agnes is described as looking like a Sicilian: "She was medium height, but a little thin . . . She had long black hair, black as any hair I have ever seen, and it used to come way down her back" (166). The amount of detail used to physically describe Mary Agnes, as opposed to Tee Bob, puts this episode in conversation with the fetishization of the "tragic mulatto" figure in literature. Whereas Catherine could have passed as Native American, Mary Agnes could be Sicilian, underscoring the mixed-race appearances of both, their liminality, and their ability to pass for racial groups other than their own. Similarly, as was the case in *Catherine Carmier*, the female Creoles of Color receive full physical descriptions that are lacking from the male characters. However, like Catherine, Mary Agnes survives the episode and has agency: she refuses Tee Bob, even if he does not respect her wishes, and chooses to focus on her job at the school instead of relationships. Gaines is simultaneously invoking and subverting common racial and sexual stereotypes—acknowledging their widespread presence in various forms of cultural production but also challenging their dominance.

At the same time, this relationship is a reversal of many earlier depictions of interracial pairings in southern literature. For instance, there is a pattern in William Faulkner's work in which a White woman has a relationship with a racially ambiguous man, playing into the panic about sexual mobility. In this case, however, Mary Agnes is the multiracial partner, who "comes from a long line of Creoles back there in New Orleans. Her grandmother was one drop from being white herself. Her grandmother had been one of those ladies for white men" (166). This type of arrangement, frequently described in scholarship on antebellum New Orleans as *plaçage*, is not an option for Tee Bob in the twentieth century.[13] His only choice, according to the community, is to sexually exploit Mary Agnes, who in the words of Jimmy Caya is "there for his pleasure, for nothing else" (200). Tee Bob rejects his patriarchal privileges to an extent, and as Matthew Teutsch and Katharine Henry argue, "Tee Bob is a culmination, or close to it, of the region's inability to continue the unwritten rules of the land because he opposes them by loving a mixed-race Creole woman" (518). However, Tee Bob feels entitled to court Mary Agnes, regardless of her viewpoint on the matter. An intersectional lens reveals that Tee Bob is positioned above Mary Agnes in terms of the overlapping hierarchies of race, color, gender, and class, which may explain this expectant attitude. Although against the rules of the plantation system, Tee Bob develops feelings Mary Agnes, returning home from Baton Rouge frequently in order to walk and talk with her.

These walks do not go unnoticed by the community. The couple is literally spied upon and surveyed by everyone from the quarters to the big house. Looking is central to the community's policing of the interracial interactions in this episode: a tool that can be used to regulate the behavior of others. The structure of the plantation is particularly conducive to this form of surveillance. As John Wharton Lowe observes, "The quarters/big house configuration echoes that of early factories, where huge walls were erected to maximize concentration of labor, to protect materials and tools, but above all, to control the labor force, which is accomplished through order and constant surveillance" ("Transcendence in the House of the Dead" 148). In an obvious example of this culture of surveillance, Tee Bob's mother, Amma Dean, sits physically on the back gallery watching Tee Bob through spyglasses. Jane, a formerly enslaved woman and narrator of the novel, states that she "watched a little bit, then she let me watch some" (180).[14] This overt policing, here turned against the heir of the plantation, is also used to regulate the behavior of laborers, as Lowe notes, creating the panoptic effect of constant yet unverifiable surveillance from which no one is spared. As Michel Foucault famously wrote, "Visibility is a trap" (200), which applies to individuals on all rungs of the plantation hierarchies. The White, male heir is subject to the same set of rules concerning interracial interactions as the Black and Creole of Color communities and must also be surveyed and regulated accordingly, illustrating how policing works to sustain colonial mentalities.

To add complexity to this example, the agents of policing are an interracial pair of women, representing the fact that all members of the community have a stake in maintaining the status quo with motivations for doing so ranging widely from the retention of power to the avoidance of retaliatory violence. Just as it matters little who occupies the central tower in Foucault's Panopticon, the power resides in the structure of surveillance on the plantation as well.[15] This allows both a White and a Black woman respectively to watch and attempt to regulate a White man's behavior through the use of a panoptic gaze, which when located in the structure is theorized as raceless, classless, sexless, and so forth. Amma Dean and Jane watch Tee Bob saddle the horse and go down to the quarters to walk Mary Agnes home from school: Tee Bob is on the horse, and Mary Agnes walks beside him. This passive observation of Tee Bob's behavior from a distance aligns with analogous actions as well—for instance, Amma Dean's arrangement of a party with Tee Bob's fiancée, Judy Major, and her family. Through playing their roles in the surveillance mechanism and borrowing power from the structure itself, those from lower social positions can impact (or attempt to impact in this case, since Tee Bob shows little respect for the rules) the actions of individuals above them.

Looking is central to the following scene as well. Jane is sent to inform Tee Bob that Judy Major, his fiancée, has arrived. Jane notes:

> He just turned his head and looked down at Mary Agnes. She told him good day and went into the yard. I was looking up there at him, and I could see how much he wanted her to stay out there. He watched her till she had gone in that house, and he didn't look at her the way you think a white man look at a n*** woman, either. He looked at her with love, and I mean the kind that's way deep inside of you. I have not seen too many men, of any color, look at women that way. After she had closed the door he looked down at me again. His face scared me. I saw in his face he was ready to go against his family, this whole world, for Mary Agnes. (180–81)

Jane seems to function as more of a witness than agent of policing in this scene; nevertheless, she retains what she observes and later attempts in conversation to dissuade Tee Bob from his fixation. I quote from this scene at length in order to demonstrate the complex multidirectional instances of looking—reminiscent of the multidirectional instances of sexual policing—that occur between Tee Bob, Jane, and Mary Agnes. In addition to a panoptic gaze employed by would-be sexual policers, looking can also be a more personal act conveying emotion or desire. This more subjective gaze engages with the erotics of looking and can be used to indicate interest. There is a thin line between looking for pleasure and looking for policing, and often the two are entwined: a pleasure can be derived from policing others. Tee Bob's looking in this scene, however, is an act signaling intent in a way not only observable to Mary Agnes but also to the general community—symbolized by Jane. With the gaze of a Black, female observer, Jane claims to be able to discern his feelings through watching him watch Mary Agnes, reading a much deeper love in his face than she believes most men, of any color, to be capable of.[16] Thus, desire (or, if Jane is to be believed, love) in this scene becomes something that resides in the face and can be observed. Not only are Mary Agnes and Tee Bob watched and scrutinized by the community, but looking itself is an act: a way to reveal emotion or intention to observers.

Among these three, the only character that does not do any looking in this scene is Mary Agnes. This underscores the fact that Mary Agnes, who exists below him on the hierarchies of race, gender, and class, does not have any control over these events or Tee Bob's actions.[17] Tee Bob, on the other hand, is in a position—literally, as he is elevated on a horse—to look at Mary Agnes and watch her as she walks away. He is entitled to cast his White, male gaze on Mary Agnes—"there for his pleasure"—who does not reciprocate his open interest. Tee Bob's unwelcome gaze reveals "the insidious nature of whiteness and subtextually speak[s] to the pain and suffering of Black bodies that have been stereotyped, criminalized, and rendered invisible by the white gaze" (Yancy xxix). Tee Bob does not see Mary Agnes for who she is or respect what she wants: her desires are "rendered invisible" by his gaze. If he would have bothered to ask, Mary Agnes could have told him what she told Jane: "I have no interest in that boy" (178), and later, "But I got no interest in men, black or white. I'm for these children here. That's why I left home" (178). The absoluteness of this statement, Mary Agnes has no interest in men of any race, leaves space for reading queerness into her comments. While she likely intends to imply that she has no romantic interests due to her dedication to her job, it is worth noting that she doesn't say that exactly, but says she is not interested in men of any race. Nevertheless, the "white gaze, given the power of the ocular metaphor in Western culture, is an important site of power and control" (Yancy xxxii), negating Mary Agnes's desires entirely. While Tee Bob resists the rules of plantation culture, at the same time he imposes his wishes on Mary Agnes, negating her own. Tee Bob tells Jimmy Caya that "he loved a n*** woman more than he loved his own life" (181). However, he uses the derogatory language of his period to refer to her—emphasizing the distance between his strong feelings and the propriety of the day—and further, does not respect her enough to factor in her preferences. While Tee Bob's "love" can be seen as resistance to the restrictions dictated by the status quo (similar to that between Catherine and Jackson), he does not factor in Mary Agnes's wishes, and thus, I do not consider this a convincing portrayal of the revolutionary potential of love.

If not love, power and pleasure are complexly entwined in Tee Bob's gaze in this scene. The fact that he literally and figuratively casts his gaze down on one socially beneath him speaks to Tee Bob's position of power. He likely derives pleasure from the looking itself, as a result of the scopophilic instinct, or what Laura Mulvey describes as "pleasure in looking at another person as an erotic object" (843). Tee Bob objectifies her as the focus of his sexual desire as she walks away, and it is also significant that she is walking away here and cannot control what occurs behind her back. Moreover, Mary Agnes misreads Tee Bob's looking: "She had always looked at him like that [a brother or cousin]: like he was more like her; not like he was a white man. She thought he looked at her that same way" (185). If Tee Bob's emotions and intentions were obvious to Jane, perhaps we can view this as a willful misreading, wishful thinking on Mary Agnes's part that Tee Bob reciprocated her warm, familial feelings toward him and nothing more. Further, the language of this passage—"like he was a white man"—suggests that her experiences in a plantation culture have caused Mary Agnes to view White men in a specific way. The particulars of how she views White men are notably absent, since the readers are not granted access into the depths of her subjectivity or past experiences—similar to the absent perspectives of White, Black, and biracial women in Faulkner's works. Nevertheless, she considers Tee Bob as more of an equal or someone "more like her" than like "a white man." Had the expectations for White men under this hierarchical system not skewed Tee Bob's mindset, this could have been an opportunity for two individuals to connect in spite of plantation power structures. Yet, while Mary Agnes does not look at him like he is a White man, Tee Bob cannot help looking at her from that position. Even though he does not fully understand or support the unwritten rules governing the plantation system, Tee Bob was raised as a White man of the planter class, and this unavoidably impacts his worldview.[18] He does not want to simply take Mary Agnes, an accepted entitlement of his social standing, yet this sense that he *could* possess her must infiltrate his understanding of their relationship, even subconsciously, as exemplified by leaving her desires unacknowledged.

Further, looking is not only the province of the novel's central characters: looking is widely used by members of the broader community to observe interactions that they then relay to others. Touching, looking, and speaking are intertwined, and the eyes of the community are attached to its voice. Gaines relies on an assortment of observers to report what they witness about Tee Bob's behavior and seeming infatuation, such as Etienne Boule, who was there when Tee Bob first saw Mary Agnes, and Clamp Brown, who overhears a conversation between the two. As Jane reports to the reader: "Everybody knowed about [Tee Bob's interest in Mary Agnes] now. The ones here in the quarters, the ones at the house up there, the ones on that river. From Bayonne to Baton Rouge they talked about it" (177). Jane's comment emphasizes the fact that individuals from all levels of society are interested, although none view his attention as serious: "Reason he don't show more interest in Frank Major's daughter, Judy, there, he ain't sowed all his wild oats yet. From what I hear, he found something on his daddy's place. One of them high yellow from New Orleans almost white there" (177). This quote is not attributed to any character in particular, but can be read as the voice of the community in general. This polyvocal technique represents the orality common to the culture Gaines depicts and the central role played by "porch talk" in rural Louisiana. Gaines pairs form and content to portray this culture through his focus on multiple perspectives and voices, underscoring that fiction and its aesthetic affordances are a fitting mode to convey these collective histories.

This emphasis on the voice of the community—multiple voices working together to tell the story—is especially evident in early drafts of the novel. Jane is the central narrator in the published version, telling her story in the

> Everybody knowed waht was going on. Them at that house,
> on the river, same like these in the quarters. From Bayonne
> to Baton Rouge, people was talking. "Oh, ho," the White folks
> was saying. "The reason he don't show interest in Paul Memor
> daughter, he ain t sowed all his wild seeds, yet. Well, from
> what the people say, he found some interest on his daddy's
> place. Ha-ha-ha. They say she one of them high yellows from
> New Orleans almost can pass for White." The talk went on
> from Bayonne to Baton Rouge--up and down the river. The old
> school supertindent knowed about it too. Anybody else, he
> woulda got rid of her in a minute--whether anything was going
> on or not; but it was Tee Bob, and that was different. It
> was the naturalis thing for the young owner of a place to sow
> his wild seeds with a black woman before he finally settled
> down to marriage and family with his white sweetheart.
> "If they only knowed."
> "Ha."
> "Go on, Etienne."

Figure 2.3: Excerpt from an unpublished draft of *The Autobiography of Miss Jane Pittman*. From Gaines Papers 5.71, 7, or 5.79, 7 in the new system.

frame narrative to a young Black history teacher. However, *The Autobiography of Miss Jane Pittman* was originally constructed as a polyvocal text with multiple voices from the community, in addition to Jane's, narrating the various episodes. For instance, Etienne Boule primarily narrates the interactions between Tee Bob and Mary Agnes in a number of the drafts with others interrupting to correct or question him:

> It was the naturalis thing for the young owner of a place to sow his wild seeds with a black woman before he finally settled down to marriage and family with his white sweetheart.
> "If they only knowed."
> "Ha."
> "Go on, Etienne." (Gaines Papers 5.71, 208, underlining in original)

Etienne reveals the community's understanding and seeming acceptance of plantation culture's intersecting hierarchies: the exploitation experienced by women of color is described as "the naturalis thing" and depicted through the euphemism to "sow his wild seeds," a phrase mirrored by "ain't sowed all his wild oats yet" in the published version. Marriage and family are positioned as off-limits for the Black woman in this passage, although sex is expected—sex without emotional, familial, or material commitments. The Black woman is positioned as a temporary stand-in to be replaced by the "white sweetheart." Further, the use of multiple voices and narrators demonstrates the broader community's acceptance of these dynamics. Their role in surveying and policing the couple becomes even more pronounced in the drafts: it is a collective effort from all levels of society.[19]

One of the most overt agents of the sexual policing of the color line is Tee Bob's friend from college, Jimmy Caya. Jimmy reminds Tee Bob of the sexual privileges granted to men of his race and class. When that doesn't work, he takes a more dominant stance: "I'll have her run off the place. I'll see to it they run her out of the State" (182). Jimmy explains the rules, "I didn't tell him no more than what my daddy told me . . . What my daddy's daddy told him. What Mr. Paul told Mr. Robert. What Mr. Paul's daddy told him. What your daddy told you. No more than the rules we been living by ever since we been here" (201). In this statement, Jimmy emphasizes the entrenched nature of the rules, which spiral out to affect all families in the plantation South. Jimmy reminds Tee Bob that he learned all this in class from his teacher "over and over and over" (182). The references to family life and school illustrate the role of socialization in institutionalizing this system of abuse: the members of the White planter class are taught their "privileges" in both private and public spaces—from the dinner table to the classroom (182). As a member of the White lower-middle class, Jimmy is not entitled to the same advantages as his friend Tee Bob, which may explain his fervor for upholding colonial hierarchies. Jimmy's motivation is to retain his comparatively privileged position in plantation society above Creoles of Color like Mary Agnes.[20] This conversation with Jimmy leaves an impression on Tee Bob; he cites it directly in his suicide note.[21] Jules Raynard, an upper-class White man and Tee Bob's *parrain*, or godfather, succinctly describes Tee Bob's motivations for his suicide, killing himself with a letter opener[22]: "because she couldn't love him back, because she knowed better, he killed himself" (199).[23]

Indeed, Mary Agnes knows what Tee Bob does not: the community will never let them be together. From her position as a light-skinned Creole of Color, she also polices the color line, dissuading Tee Bob from his pursuit of her. Mary Agnes does not act to preserve her position among the elite Creoles of Color, which she had already lost as a result of her job at the plantation school. Leaving the insular Creole of Color society to teach Black children in the quarters was enough to exile her from that community—a fate Catherine would have likely experienced through marrying Jackson. Mary Agnes polices the color line because she knows both the "rules" and the violence that will occur through failing to uphold them. For similar reasons, narrator Jane Pittman acts as an agent of sexual policing, telling Tee Bob that Mary Agnes is "almost, but not quite [White]" (172). Jane's comment calls to mind Homi Bhabha's notion of colonial mimicry, which he defines as "the desire for a reformed, recognizable Other, *as a subject of difference that is almost the same, but not quite*" and later almost the same, but not White (86).[24] As in the case of the colonial Other, however, the difference carries more weight than the sameness. Having already lost her surrogate son, Ned Douglass, to interracial violence, Jane knows what is at stake in these situations and, like Mary Agnes, acts accordingly to prevent future violence, even if it means keeping the status quo in place.

Echoing the other voices of the community, Jules Raynard reminds his godson that although she could easily pass, Mary Agnes is not White and "love for her, at least in the open, was impossible" (191). Jules's motivations here are more complex. As a White man in a plantation society, he has something to lose as a result of the destabilization of racial hierarchies; however, he also genuinely seems concerned with protecting members of the community with a status below his own. Jules uses Tee Bob's letter to protect Mary Agnes as evidence of her innocence. This multidirectional sexual policing from all levels of society, which includes White men like Jimmy Caya and Jules Raynard, Black and Creole women like Jane and Mary Agnes, demonstrates that the entire community had a hand in keeping this couple apart. Jimmy, in an uncharacteristic moment of insight, states that he didn't kill Tee Bob by himself: "We all killed him" (201). The community itself is responsible for Tee Bob's death, as a result of forcing him to live within their set rules concerning appropriate sexual pairing.

Jules Raynard, the seeming voice of reason in this episode, agrees with Jimmy: "We tried to make him follow a set of rules our people gave us long ago. But these rules just ain't old enough, Jane" (204). Jules is likely referring to the shift from assimilation to segregation that occurred in Louisiana following the Louisiana Purchase and the shift away from an accepted racial fluidity that accompanied it. He mentions that in the past, men like Tee Bob could love women like Mary Agnes but that "somewhere along the way somebody wrote a new set of rules condemning all that. I had to live by them, Robert at that house now had to live by them, and Clarence Caya had to live by them. Clarence Caya told Jimmy to live by them, and Jimmy obeyed. But Tee Bob couldn't obey. That's why we got rid of him. All us. Me, you, the girl—all us" (204). Here, Jules reiterates the widespread multigenerational commitment to the rules, as well as the colonial hierarchies on which they rest.

In addition to the gradual shift in policies toward segregation in Louisiana, Jules may also be referring to the shift after the Civil War when, as Jessica Adams describes, "an acknowledged intimate connection between a white man and a woman of color became problematic, and white men's legal acknowledgment of their mixed-race children became more difficult" (23). Sex across the color line persisted after Emancipation but became less socially acceptable in the Jim Crow era. As the United States' brand of White supremacy, which attempts to dehumanize African Americans, spread throughout Louisiana, rape or paying for sex continued to fit within plantation society, but there was no space for any less exploitative relations or interracial marriages (Long 59), which had been briefly legal in Louisiana in the late nineteenth century (Long 10). Tee Bob's internal conflict exists in the space between the past's way of constructing race in Louisiana, as a three-tiered system with Creoles of Color forming a distinct racial group, and the present's commitment to the binary system. There was no room for fluidity in the new system—just the reduction of the impossible complexities of identity to two stark categories. We see this difference played out overtly when Tee Bob naively asks, "He said you was a n*** . . . I was supposed to look at you like you look at a n***. Do to you what you suppose to do to a n***. You're not a n***, are you, Mary Agnes?" and she replies, "Jimmy is right" (186).²⁵ Tee Bob's mindset is more in line with the outmoded racial system (or the more generous among us may view him as ahead of his time), while Mary Agnes is well aware of the present model, which would position her as Black.

Further, in Jules's mind, history played a central role in Tee Bob's tragic death: not only official accounts of History in terms of the development of the rules and the shift in acceptable interracial interactions but also more personal connections to individual and familial histories. Jules recounts how on the night of Tee Bob's suicide, during his final discussion with Mary Agnes, Tee Bob "was standing over her. To carry her to that car? To choke her? To rape her?—I don't know. But he was standing close enough to see something in her face" (205). This part of the story is entirely speculation: Jules draws these conclusions based on what he knows of the situation. Jules suspects that when "her head and back hit the wall" during their altercation (note the neutral language as opposed to a more active construction like "when he slammed her into the wall"):

The past and the present got all mixed up. That stiff proudness left. Making up for the past left. She *was* the past now. She was grandma now, and he was that Creole gentleman. She was Verda now, and he

was Robert. It showed in her face. It showed in the way she laid down
there on the floor. Helpless; waiting. She knowed how she looked to
him, but she couldn't do nothing about it. (206)

Mary Agnes's helplessness and anticipation of sexual violence is easily read in her face, echoing Tee Bob's look of love described earlier. Tee Bob knows that she is expecting him to rape her like her grandmother expected of the White man and countless other examples throughout plantation history. After reading their relation to this history in her face, Tee Bob is compelled to kill himself, in Jules's words, "for our sins" (206). The community positions him as a problematic Christ figure to assuage its own guilt.[26]

The couple's connection to the weight of plantation history is another aspect that is brought out more directly in earlier drafts of the novel. The link to their historical antecedents is not just something put on them by Jules and Jane, as in the published version, but something they directly reference themselves. Mary Agnes is described as a "plantation whore," sometimes by an angry Tee Bob and sometimes by herself, and Tee Bob is positioned as an enslaver:

> She started packing again. He jecked her around again.
> "I told you don't do that," she said. "I'm no [plantation] whore."
> "I never said that," he said.
> "You never said it, but that's how you feel," she said. (Gaines Papers 5.76, 11–12)

In another draft she is a "n*** wench": "'That'[s] right, I'm a n***,' the girl said. 'I'm a n***, but I'm not your n*** wench" (Gaines Papers 5.71, 217). The difference in language in these early drafts is striking and makes the connection to the history of slavery and the institutionalization of sexual abuse more pronounced. Tee Bob and Mary Agnes are aware of this history, and although Mary Agnes has little agency throughout this episode, she is able to refuse alignment with those historical roles while at the same time accepting her positioning as Black in a binaristic system. Thus, the characters' relationships to these histories are multilayered. On one level the histories are inescapable: the community allows no option but violence and sexual abuse. Yet on another level, there is space for the subversion of the typical narratives of exploitation. Mary Agnes has the power to deny the White planter's advances, and Tee Bob balks at his alignment with the planter figure. Moreover, through connecting Tee Bob and Mary Agnes to the generations that preceded them, in a way their "love story" isn't even their own, underscoring

>   Now
> She put her hand on his hand to calm him down. ~~But~~ he just sat there looking at her like a child. When she thought he was calm, she got up and started packing.
>
>   "Where you think you going, Mary Agnes?" he asked her.
>
>   "New Orleans," she said.
>
>   "You think I'm go'n let you go just like that?"
>
>   "You can't stop me," she told him.
>
>   She went on packing. He sat there watching her a while, then he got up and jecked her arould.
>
>   "Don't do that," she said.
>
>   "You might leave in that car out there, but you not leaving me," he said. "I Offer you Samson, you have my love, and there's all the money you'll ever need. I don't have nothing more to give but my life."
>
>   She started packing again. He jecked her around again.
>
>   "I told you don't do that," she said. "I'm no paantation whore."

Figure 2.4: Excerpt from an unpublished draft of *The Autobiography of Miss Jane Pittman*. From Gaines Papers 5.76, 11–12, or 5.84, 11–12 in the new system.

that this episode is really more about the community—its histories, its rules, its hierarchies—than it is about Tee Bob and Mary Agnes.

    Finally, the actual story of what transpires between Tee Bob and Mary Agnes changes dramatically from draft to draft, proving that the focus of this episode is not on them but on what they bring to light in the community. Tee Bob's motivations for his suicide change significantly from one draft to the next. In some of the drafts, he actually rapes Mary Agnes, and thus, the suicide results more from his guilt at committing the "worse crime [he could] commit—because [he] loved her dearly," as opposed to his dying for the historic sins of his community (Gaines Paper 5.71, 224). The title of this section in one draft is "A Southern White Boy writes a Letter to his Mother after raping a Black Woman," leaving Tee Bob's actions, and Mary Agnes's racial position in a binary system, unambiguous (Gaines Papers 5.71, 219). In another version, Tee Bob, the rapist, believes himself to be the party most deserving of sympathy: "I begged her on my knees. I slapped her, I beat her, I slammed her again the wall. But I'm sure none of this hurt her as much as I hurt myself fouling her body" (Gaines Papers 6.10, 255). Although he has physically abused Mary Agnes, the recipient of his supposed love—slapping her, beating her, slamming her against the wall before raping her—Tee Bob buries her sexual trauma and physical pain beneath the weight of his own guilt and self-pity. Through his negation of Mary Agnes's pain, Tee Bob places himself within the long history of the slave system's institutionalization of racism, which absorbed "the cries of those who suffer by making them sound less than human" (Gilroy 57).[27]

Although he kills himself after recognizing the connection, Tee Bob is deeply entrenched within the mentality of the plantation system that produced him, in spite of his romantic feelings for Mary Agnes. This association runs deeper than he knows, as demonstrated by his statement valuing his pain above hers. No longer simply a Christ figure who dies for the prejudices of the community, Tee Bob is directly implicated in the plantation history and colonial hierarchies out of which he is produced, as the drafts reveal. Many scholars, and indeed Gaines himself, have read Tee Bob in a more favorable light. Gaines stated in an interview that he is "very sympathetic toward Tee Bob, as that innocent person caught up in something he has no control over," going as far as to refer to him as a "victim" (Laney 62). The fact that Tee Bob does not factor in his beloved's wishes—or he would have left her alone—and actually rapes her in the drafts leads to my more negative reading. While still present in the published version, the earlier drafts emphasize the ingrained nature of plantation relations more overtly. Reading the published version through this lens elucidates the imbricated nature of the episode, calling attention to the layering of histories within characters and events. Does reading Tee Bob through this lens detract from the positive message of this episode?

I would argue that it does not and that the friendship between Jules and Jane is the true moment of resistance to colonial hierarchies in this section. While Tee Bob's actions change dramatically from draft to draft, the friendship between these two remains the same throughout. The fact that Gaines is consistent in his portrayal of this relationship confirms my argument that the true focus is not on the seemingly central "love story." Further, the episode is bookended with communal moments between Jules and Jane. It opens with the two sitting in the kitchen sharing a cup of coffee and ends with Jules dropping Jane off at her gate. Jane mentions that she and Jules talk every time he comes to the house, which he has been doing for years: sometimes "just the two of us at that house, sitting back there in the kitchen drinking coffee and talking" (191). The friendship is contained within the rules for interracial relationships. They never sit at the table together, but Jules "always let [her] sit at the table and he sat in a chair by the door" (191). In spite of these restrictions, the friendship between Jules and Jane flourishes, and it is to Jane that Jules shares his final thoughts on Tee Bob's tragic demise. The fact that an upper-class White man described by Jane as a "big man with snow-white hair and a red red face" (191) and a formerly enslaved woman are able to share a friendship represents a partial respite from the endless cycles of racial violence and hatred exemplified by Tee Bob's death. The interracial friendship between Jules and Jane challenges the heavy histories preceding it in a way that the "love story" between Tee Bob and Mary Agnes ultimately fails to do.

Through his layered portrayal of interracial relationships in *Catherine Carmier* and *The Autobiography of Miss Jane Pittman*, Ernest Gaines illustrates the positioning of the Creoles of Color as a racial group distinct from both Black and White, as well as the changes in racial categorization throughout Louisiana's history. Due to the shift from the three-tiered model of racial relations to the binary structure following the Civil War, relations between Blacks and Creoles of Color were more widely accepted, since according to the binary system they would have been considered part of the same race. Relations between Whites and Creoles of Color, however, became less tolerable. Thus, the changes in racial categorization manifest through which interracial relationships are policed by whom and to what extent. The stakes are lowered in *Catherine Carmier*: only the Black and Creole of Color communities are directly involved in the policing and none of the central characters end up dead. However, relationships between Whites and Creoles of Color remain prohibited in this period and are policed by individuals on every rung of society for varying reasons. A future with Mary Agnes is not an option for Tee Bob in the early twentieth century; as heir to the Samson plantation, his private relations are regulated by the public community.

Nevertheless, I'd like to conclude by turning once more to Mary Agnes and what she is left with at the close of the section. While the episode ends unfortunately for Tee Bob, who takes his own life, it is likewise tragic for Mary Agnes. She is forced to leave the plantation behind along with her life's passion (for which she had already sacrificed her family connections and social standing): her work with the school children. Mary Agnes values her work at the school above everything else in her life and, as an early draft reveals, views it as atonement for the insular ways of the Creoles of Color: "To make up for what her people had done her people, she wanted to give her body, her soul, all her strength for these children. Her life, for her life sake, didn't mean anything" (Gaines Papers 6.18, 242).[28] One way to interpret "what her people had done her people" would be the historic ills of the Creoles of Color against the Black population, ranging from the Creoles of Colors owning enslaved people to viewing themselves as a class apart and above. This reading would indicate that Mary Agnes considers the Creoles of Color and the Black community both as "her people," which aligns with the fact that she seems to have accepted the binary system and her positioning as Black in society. Further, given the patriarchal and paternalist undertones to her relations with Tee Bob, which manifest, for instance, in his dismissal of her desires, there is perhaps a silver lining to Mary Agnes's adverse ending: she is free from the imposed affections of a White man in whom she had no interest. Given the time and place, Tee Bob's pursuit of Mary Agnes would never have ended well for her, and although he loses his life in the end, the fact that she holds onto hers should be counted no small stroke of luck.

Chapter 3

"THEY WERE STARTING SOMETHING"

Race, Gender, and Failed Revolution in Ernest Gaines's
Of Love and Dust

"Miss Louise—ran away, Mr. Sidney," I said.
"Run away?" he said. "Run where?"
"I don't know."
"Run with who?" he said.
"Marcus," I said.
"That convict—that boy—that n***?"
"Yes sir." (Gaines Papers 3.27, 382)

This scene is from an unpublished draft of Ernest Gaines's *Of Love and Dust*. Interracial couple Marcus and Louise do not escape together in the published version of the novel. Instead, Marcus stays behind to fight: "Sun said Marcus had all the chance in the world to get away from there, and he couldn't understand why Marcus didn't run. Sun was screaming inside—'Run, boy; run, run, run.' But instead, Marcus jumped on the ground to fight" (275). As a result of this decision, Marcus loses his life: "Then, for a second, everything was too quiet. Then he heard a scream, and he jerked his head to the left. He saw that Marcus had lost the picket and he saw Bonbon raising the blade. He had to shut his eyes, and even though he couldn't see, he heard when the blade hit" (276). Why this difference? What influenced Ernest Gaines to change the ending from the couple's successful escape in an earlier draft to Marcus's death in the published version?

Ernest Gaines is a writer who heavily revises his work, marking up his handwritten and later typewritten pages with a wealth of comments in the margins and in between lines of text.[1] One reason for this particular change may have been the influence of the media. *Of Love and Dust* was published in 1967, the same year the Supreme Court decided the landmark civil rights case *Loving v. Virginia* (Jones 152).[2] In 1958 Richard Loving, a White man, and

Mildred Jeter, a woman who appeared Black but identified as "a descendant of an indigenous nation rather than slaves" (Cashin 2), crossed the border from their home state of Virginia to Washington, DC, in order to get married (Kennedy 273). The couple had been involved since the 1940s, which can in part be attributed to the fact that they lived in Central Point in Caroline County, Virginia, an area that had "historically been a locus of a considerable amount of interracial sex among whites, blacks, and Indians" (Kennedy 273).[3] While interracial interactions had occurred in this region for years, the difference is that Richard Loving wanted his relationship on paper; he wanted it to be official (Cashin 106).[4] Five weeks after they wed, Mildred and Richard were roused from their bed in the middle of the night and arrested (Kennedy 273). They were indicted for violating the state's Racial Integrity Act and sentenced by Judge Leon Bazile to one year in jail, which they avoided by taking the court up on the option to leave Virginia and not return for twenty-five years (Kennedy 273–74). The couple lived in Washington, DC, with their three children for the next five years, and in 1963 Mildred wrote a letter to Attorney General Robert Kennedy detailing their situation (Kennedy 274). The letter was forwarded to the American Civil Liberties Union, and eventually Bernard Cohen and Philip Hirschkop took the Lovings' case to the US Supreme Court (Kennedy 274). In 1967 Chief Justice Warren reversed the decision of the Virginia Supreme Court, negating the legal power of antimiscegenation laws (Kennedy 274). The historic struggle to legitimize interracial marriage may have brought home for Gaines the impossibility of a positive outcome for a couple running away together two decades earlier.

Just as the Lovings' case offers a personal experience against the setting of the civil rights movement, Gaines's novel is more invested in an exploration of individual relations than the larger political moment.[5] In this way, fiction is an incomparable means for bringing to light interpersonal histories against the backdrop of large-scale events, muddling the edge between literature and history through overlap in the projects of both fields. Through its examination of the revolutionary potential of relationships, *Of Love and Dust* is in conversation with the issues raised by the Lovings' case, such as the power of the government to regulate one of the most intimate choices an individual can make—the selection of a partner with whom to build a family. However, as Peter Wallenstein describes, "When people challenged the law as it was applied to them, private relationships could shape public policy" (5). And in this way both Gaines's novel and the Lovings' lives demonstrate that to "love beyond boundaries is the most radical of acts" (Cashin 1). I argue in this chapter that boundary-defying love has the power to combat the dehumanizing effects of plantation hierarchies and the resulting racist

> (382)
>
> "All right," he said.
>
> "Your wife's not here."
>
> "Not here?"
>
> "No sir."
>
> "Something happened to my chap?"
>
> "Miss Louise--ran away, Mr. Sidney," I said.
>
> "Run away?" he said. "Run where?"
>
> "I don't know."
>
> "Run with who?" he said.
>
> "Marcus," I said.
>
> "That convict--that boy--that nigger?"
>
> "Yes sir."
>
> "You know, you talk wrong, Geam," he said. "You know that?"
>
> I just stood there now looking at him. He didn't believe a word I had said--how could he? He glanced toward his house again, then he turned to get his gun to take it inside. I got between him and the door.
>
> "She's gone," I said.
>
> "Get out the way, Geam," he said.

Figure 3.1: Excerpt from an unpublished draft of *Of Love and Dust*. From Gaines Papers 3.27, 382.

mentalities. Just as the "moral panic" over the perceived rise of muggings in England in the 1970s was never about muggings as much as fear of shifting demographics and the "disintegration of the social order" (S. Hall et al. vii–viii), the policing of sexuality is never just about sex. It is about regulating love, deep familial bonds, and greater kinship ties, which contain a threat to the plantation system in its entirety. As *Of Love and Dust* demonstrates, love is a civil right, and revolution can start with the individual.

Ernest Gaines scholar Maria Hebert-Leiter describes the original version of the story in which Marcus and Louise run away together as not a realistic—or even possible—outcome in Louisiana in the 1940s "because white society would not allow a Cajun woman and an African American man, regardless of their sincere feelings for each other, to escape the political and racial implications of their *love*. This *love* threatened the white system of control, and thus, had to be silenced" (105, emphasis added).[6] I view love as a deep emotional bond beyond physical affection and attraction, and sex as the accompanying corporeal encounters. Beginning in the 1660s, sex was the center of regulation; however, as "the racial regulation of intimacy matured, though, authorities generally chose to police marriage more closely than sex" (Kennedy 217). While sex can be revolutionary by going against the accepted rules governing who can interact with whom, boundary-crossing love has a greater potential to be truly world shattering through its "political and racial implications" (Hebert-Leiter 105). A love that is all encompassing is by nature oppositional to hierarchies.

According to Anthony Giddens, passionate love is "marked by an urgency which sets it apart from the routines of everyday life with which, indeed, it tends to come into conflict. The emotional involvement with the other is pervasive—so strong that it may lead the individual, or both individuals, to ignore their ordinary obligations" (37–38). This applies well to the love between Marcus and Louise: both plan to walk away from their commitments on the plantation and escape to a new life together.[7] Through generating in an individual "a preparedness to consider radical options as well as sacrifices . . . from the point of view of social order and duty, it is dangerous" (Giddens 38). This type of love runs antithetical to the status quo—a destabilizing force to plantation structures. In Gaines's novel, the moments when characters from various social positions put aside the hierarchies and relate as individuals contain the greatest potential for change. This change may have roots on an individualized, interpersonal plane but with the capacity to build toward more sweeping social ramifications, demonstrating the important role of the individual in social change. Thus, sexual policing is about imposing order, not just on sex but on love and resulting family and kinship structures, which have the potential to destabilize the status quo.

Of Love and Dust contains multiple relationships and potential pairings that could threaten the structures in place, exemplifying the high stakes for relationships that cross the color line, not only for the couples but also for the broader community. At the start of the novel, Marcus arrives at the plantation after Marshall Hebert bonded him out to be a laborer, seemingly as a favor to Hebert's former longtime housekeeper, Julie Rand. We later learn Marshall intends for Marcus to kill Bonbon, who after killing for Marshall in the past is both blackmailing and stealing from him in the present. Marcus plans to escape the plantation with Bonbon's wife, Louise, and young daughter, Tite, but is ultimately killed by Bonbon, as orchestrated by Marshall. The events take place on the Hebert plantation in 1948, the final years of the transition away from the plantation economy. Yet, characters are still faced with the same unwritten rules regulating interracial pairings examined in chapter 2.[8]

The demise of the older economic system is evident in Gaines's description of the plantation: "The plantation (or what was left of the plantation now) had all its crops far back in the field. The front land was for the sharecroppers. The Cajuns had the front-est and best land, and the colored people (those who were still hanging on) had the middle and worst land" (26). Gaines's depiction also sets the stage for the central conflicts of the novel, existing between the Cajun and Black populations. Perhaps due to the later setting, *Of Love and Dust* is less concerned with the status of the Creoles of Color as a racial group—central to *The Autobiography of Miss Jane Pittman* and *Catherine Carmier*—and more with exploring what happens when sexual (physical) turned romantic (emotional) relationships cross the color line separating Black from White. In what follows, I examine the different treatment the couples in the novel receive at the hands of the community as a result of the hierarchies of race, gender, sexuality, ethnicity, and class, before turning to the relationship between these conflicting hierarchies and Marcus's partial (failed?) rebellion. I end where I began, with the revolutionary power of love and the groundwork that may have been laid for future resistance.

As a result of the rules governing interracial relations, which we can see as the inheritance from earlier legal systems such as the Code Noir and Louisiana Civil Codes explored in chapter 2, some relationships are acceptable and some forbidden, as determined by the race, gender, sexuality, ethnicity, color, and class of the parties involved. The racial structures in Louisiana shifted throughout the centuries from a three-tiered model more common in the Caribbean and the broader hemisphere to a binary system, emphasizing colonial connections between the US South and the Caribbean. The relationships in *Of Love and Dust* complicate the more straightforward episode in *The Autobiography of Miss Jane Pittman* in which a White planter desires a Creole of Color woman, demonstrating the intricacies of individual lives and intimate relations against the backdrop of multilayered histories. *Of Love and Dust* doubles the policing depicted, portraying both the relationship between a White Cajun overseer, Sidney Bonbon, and a Black woman who lives in the quarters, Pauline Guerin, as well as the love between a multiracial convict laborer, Marcus Payne, and the overseer's White wife, Louise Bonbon. The plantation community sanctions the relationship between Bonbon and Pauline by looking the other way, yet, because love, or an emotional bond, is involved and not just sex, the pair is "still subject to the strict rules of their environment despite Bonbon's authority and status as a white male" (Bibler 27). The community attempts to regulate the emotional through policing the physical in this way. It would not be safe for Pauline and Bonbon to ride together with Pauline dressed up, which is why they bring Jim Kelly along with them to Baton Rouge (Gaines 140). Jim notes that the "whites didn't like that [Bonbon's neglect of his wife for Pauline] at all, and the Negros giggled about it" (Gaines 147). The Cajun community would support a sexually exploitative but not romantic relationship between the two.

In a similar way, the unwritten rules dictating plantation life would never permit Marcus to be with Louise in any capacity. The relationship between a multiracial man—of White, Native American, and Black lineage—positioned as Black in the novel and a White woman threatens the racial hierarchies on which the entire system rests.[9] According to the rules, Bonbon would need to follow Marcus and Louise or his own people would kill him because, as Jim states, "This is the South, and the South ain't go'n let no n*** run away with no white woman and let that white husband walk around here scot-free" (224). In exploring the relationship between Marcus and Louise, Gaines investigates the "most delicate and incendiary portions of that code" (Griffin 75), even more so than in the novels explored in the previous chapter, as this interracial pairing involves a White woman. White women were expected to uphold the purity of southern family lines, preserving Whiteness as a form of protected capital with economic, social, and political benefits in plantation society.

Louise's Cajun ethnicity and lower class, however, add more complexity to her relationship with Marcus, who looks down on Cajuns like Bonbon. Yet, as Hebert-Leiter asserts, "Marcus's love for Louise seems to exist beyond his notions of race and class because he does not disparage her ethnic identity as he does her husband's" (104). As with the legal and cultural distinctions between the Black race and the biracial Creoles of Color explored in chapter 2, the social construction of Whiteness occurs intersectionally and involves nuances of class and social positioning. Although Bonbon and Louise are White, they are White Cajuns, which makes them "definitely not black but only marginally white" (Hebert-Leiter 98). The White identity of Cajuns is complicated by their lower-class status—positioned as "white trash" (Costello 103)—and placement between wealthy Whites and African American laborers (Hebert-Leiter 97). In Louisiana specifically, the White planter class topped the racial and ethnic hierarchies, followed by the White Cajuns, who were very invested in maintaining Whiteness as protected capital. Historically, beneath the Cajuns were the Creoles of Color (before the acceptance of a binary racial system slowly eroded their position) and the Black community. In this way, the peripherally White Cajuns, "like both the blacks and the Creoles, are victims of the economic system and ethnic structure of Louisiana" (T. Davis, "Headlands and Quarters" 5), although to a lesser extent as a result of their Whiteness in a racist system. Marcus's acceptance of the individual over the class position when it comes to Louise exemplifies one way out of the dehumanizing status quo: relating to others as individuals, as opposed to rungs of a hierarchy.

However, the plantation is a self-sustaining organism that works to thwart subversions like the feelings Marcus develops for Louise. Individuals on all levels of society are responsible for regulating one another and maintaining the rules governing individual interactions. Sexual policing, a holdover from plantation slavery, operates in large part through the activation of the controlling gaze of the community. Its members see and know everything that occurs on the Panopticon-like plantation, and the pairs of lovers for the most part act accordingly. Marcus feigns looking for Bonbon on the nights that he first visits Louise's home, and rightly so, as his actions are observed and later discussed by Sun Brown. This illustrates John Wharton Lowe's claim that the "endless inventory of patriarchal, legal, penal, servile, and subversive gazes" are "a regular, public feature of contemporary life," turning all public spaces from the plantation to the town into variants of the prison ("Transcendence in the House of the Dead" 151). The watchful gaze sees all, from Pauline and Bonbon traveling to Baton Rouge together to Marcus's late-night visits to the Bonbon residence. Private interactions are subject to the eyes of the community, as will be explored further in the next chapter in relation to a dictatorial regime in Haiti. Remaining from earlier colonial structures spanning the US South and the Caribbean, the policing of the community occurs through the pluralized panoptic gaze of its own members. Each set of eyes observes and reports on the behavior of others, making not only the watchful gaze but gossip and porch talk central to the maintenance of the plantation system. This is how multidirectional policing of personal interactions is accomplished: the private is made public to uphold persistent plantation hierarchies. While the gaze can be an erotic subversive act signaling interest or emotions, Gaines reminds us throughout the book that more frequently it is a tool for policing interracial interactions in an integrated space in service of a destructive status quo.

Jim Kelly, narrator of the novel, occupies a unique position in relation to the other characters and also the status quo. Jim, as narrator, turns his discerning gaze to the characters surrounding him. Everything the readers learn about the events of the plot is first filtered through Jim's perspective, granting him complete command over our understanding, similar to that of Yunior de Las Casas, narrator of *The Brief Wondrous Life of Oscar Wao*, discussed in chapter 5. Thus, Jim's view—like the panoptic gaze preserving the plantation status quo—controls our perceptions. For most of the novel, Jim is a force for keeping things as they are, although he has revolutionary inclinations and intends in the future to stand up to injustice.[10] While he relates well to the other laborers, Jim drives the tractor on the plantation, which sets him apart from them. Nevertheless, Jim is "a good listener and a sensitive and intelligent man" (Griffin 76), to whom both the White Cajun overseer and Black convict laborer open up, giving him even more of an insider's perspective in the style of Nick Carraway of F. Scott Fitzgerald's *The Great Gatsby*. He is well respected by those in the quarters although he has only been there three years and did not grow up on the plantation (Costello 104), positioning him as an outsider on the inside.

While the events are filtered through Jim, he relies on other voices and perspectives to relate certain scenes, which he then weaves together like scraps of cloth into a cohesive whole. Stylistically Gaines's prose is less experimental than a modernist like Faulkner; however, his engagement with multiple voices and perspectives underscores the importance of orality and storytelling for his novels. As a result of these aesthetic choices, Gaines emphasizes the role of porch talk in the regulation of behavior formally through having multiple community voices collated by the narrator. The narrative style is comparable to that employed in *The Autobiography of Miss Jane Pittman*, aligning the novel with both oral culture and a communal voice. In this way, the "viewpoints accumulate but their effect is the gradual revelation of a coherent perspective" (Wideman 82), perhaps due to Gaines bestowing on Jim "the power to tell a tale which incorporates the voices of that community" (Wideman 78). While Jim is the central narrator, a number of other characters describe events to Jim, which he then relays to the readers. For instance, Marcus's death is described through two layers of removal: Sun Brown tells Jim, and Jim tells the readers.[11] As a result of his ability to reconstruct word-for-word dialogue that he was not present to overhear, Jim is more of a convention the reader must accept than a realistic character (Wideman 78).[12] Nevertheless, through his unique positioning on the plantation and the open nature of his character, Jim is able to reconstruct the story of two entwined and boundary-crossing relationships for the readers, while simultaneously influencing our perceptions of them.

In order to introduce the complicated portrayal of gender and sexuality in the novel, I first consider Jim's gaze as fixed on the central characters and what his descriptions of them reveal. In direct opposition to *The Autobiography of Miss Jane Pittman* and *Catherine Carmier*, in *Of Love and Dust* Jim's gaze is turned more precisely on male as opposed to female characters, and he spends more time detailing physical descriptions of the men. Jim never gives a physical description of Pauline—a significant absence that may reveal his feelings for her to be deeper than he lets on. Partway through the novel, Jim reveals that he too likes Pauline (97); he especially appreciates her kindness and "respect for the old people on the plantation" (63). Jim introduces her in the novel with a focus on her slow walk and style of dress: "Pauline wore a pink, flowery dress and a big white straw hat. She was walking slow—she always walked slow with her head high like she's always thinking about something far away" (55). His observant gaze upon her, Jim later notes that Pauline had stayed the same person, aside from her clothes. This description emphasizes her position as "Bonbon's woman," which enables her to move from the fields into the main house and to upgrade her wardrobe (55). Pauline's example emphasizes the limited options for women, as well as intersecting forms of oppression—although neither are explicitly highlighted by Jim. His recognition of Pauline as Bonbon's woman may also explain his failure to describe her body, since, given this fact, spending too much time thinking about her would only lead to trouble. Nevertheless, Pauline's legs are later given attention, as even the "little white salesgirl" does not want to look away from them (142). A direct description of the legs from Jim's perspective is missing—only others' reactions to them are given. The lack of physical description of Pauline is a notable absence on Jim's part and likely speaks to deep unrequited feelings he holds for her, adding layers to the scene in which Bonbon relies on Jim's presence to code his shopping trip to Baton Rouge with Pauline as acceptable.[13]

In contrast, Jim grants Bonbon an entire paragraph of description in which he depicts his face and body in detail:

> Bonbon was about six-four or -five, and I must say he was an impressive-looking man. He was handsome—I think very handsome—but nothing pretty or cute. Marcus, I think, was pretty. Young gals would say that Marcus was "dreamy." Nobody would say Bonbon was dreamy, like nobody would say he was ugly. He was handsome in a rough way. He had a good build—maybe two hundred, two hundred and ten pounds. He had light gray eyes, a long, good-shaped nose, and a dry-shuck-color mustache. His mustache was lighter than his tan face and much lighter than his red neck. (79)

This emphasis on the appearances of the male characters subverts the common trope of sexualizing or overvaluing the bodies of female characters—often of color—as described in chapter 2 through the eroticized focus on the physicality of Creole of Color characters like Catherine Carmier and Mary Agnes Lefebvre. Moreover, the repetition of "I think" reveals his (potentially performative) self-doubt when assessing the attractiveness of the other men. He grounds his own view in young girls' claims that Marcus is "dreamy," adding distance between himself and the assessment of another man's good looks. Jim's description also indicates differences in the geographic associations of the men ("pretty" Marcus is of the city, while "rough" Bonbon is of the country), as well as maturity (Marcus is "cute," while Bonbon is "handsome"). Although he is Black, Marcus considers himself to be above Bonbon in the social hierarchy, viewing him as "not even a solid white man, but a bayou, catfish-eating Cajun" (57). Bonbon is a layered and sympathetic character even though he takes advantage of the exploitative entitlements of his class.[14] He is confined by the expectations of the plantation system. He cannot openly love Pauline or avoid killing Marcus in the end, since allowing Marcus to escape with Louise would set a target on his back. Due to the interactions between various competing hierarchies, every character in the novel is confined in some way. Even Marshall Hebert, who exists at the top of each hierarchy, is restricted by the rules, as well as his indebtedness to Bonbon.

Jim's gaze lingers more openly on Marcus as well, describing him at length: "a pretty handsome fellow and he knew it. He was about six feet tall, slim, but well-built; he had medium brown skin and a pile of curly black hair. He had light brown eyes, a kind of straight nose, thin lips and a well-shaped mustache. Marcus had a lot of Indian blood in him, and he probably had a lot of white blood in him, too" (57). While not technically a Creole of Color, Marcus's physical description puts him in conversation with Catherine Carmier and Mary Agnes Lefebvre discussed in chapter 2—attractive, somewhat tragic characters of mixed lineage. Unlike Catherine and Mary Agnes, Marcus does not escape the fate of the "tragic mulatto" trope. He is eventually killed by Bonbon, as dictated by the rules and orchestrated by Marshall Hebert, for attempting to leave the confining structure of the plantation with Louise and her daughter, Tite. I'll refer to this attempt as his love rebellion, building on Michael Bibler's assertion that the couple's acts of rebellion are "primarily sexual" to emphasize the equally threatening emotional component (40). Love rebellion in place of sexual rebellion further emphasizes the fact that Marcus is not concerned with challenging the hierarchies of gender and sexuality but solely the racial constrictions on his own love relationship. Nevertheless, these longer descriptions are fitting, since both Bonbon and Marcus are more developed characters than either Pauline or Louise, feeding into the complex positioning and representation of women in the text.

Taking this one step further, this focus on the physicality of the male characters, particularly when juxtaposed with the emphasis on women's bodies in Gaines's other novels, leaves space for a more complicated view of Jim's sexuality. Bibler argues that the openly homosexual relationship between

John and Freddie, who are described by Jim as "punks" (Gaines 33), is "a kind of narrative preventative that tries to stop us from reading Jim's increasing affection and sympathy for Marcus as homoerotic" (41).[15] The directness of John and Freddie's affection for each other leads readers to simplify or willfully ignore the complications of Jim's sexuality. After opening a beer for an ailing Marcus, Jim suggests, "Why don't you take a bath . . . You'll feel better" (44). Marcus replies, "You a freak or something?" (44), which Jim takes (and Marcus intends) as an insult. Jim's concern provokes a homophobic eruption from Marcus, who also refers to John and Freddie as "freaks" who can "kiss [his] ass" (32). This tension does not distract too much from the fact that Jim cares for a beaten down Marcus in this scene, cooking him dinner and offering uplifting words, yet ultimately the fear of homosexuality prevents the friendship from developing more fully.

While Gaines portrays the love between Marcus and Louise as immature and unrealistic throughout the novel (Costello 110), the friendship between Marcus and Jim—whether read as purely platonic or homoerotic—is more developed in comparison. The friendship has a positive effect on both men, for instance, eventually pushing Jim to act, leaving the plantation and rejecting Marshall's recommendation letter. Similarly, although Marcus is too stubborn for anyone's influence to do much good, Jim is a positive force in his life, providing him with clothes, food, beer, and a listening ear. Jim succeeds, however briefly, in getting Marcus to wear clothes appropriate for plantation labor and encourages him to factor in others beyond himself. If Marcus had listened more fully this would have given his actions greater subversive potential. A relationship between Black men would have been more acceptable to the plantation culture on the Hebert plantation than that between Marcus and Louise because it does not directly disrupt the hierarchies (Bibler 44). While not overtly subversive in itself, this partnership could have had revolutionary possibility as a result of the combination of Marcus's strong defiance of plantation structures and Jim's relationships and knowledge of the community and its history. Just as the mutability and *métissage*, represented by the biracial, sexually fluid Charles Bon, could have been a potential way out of the cyclical repetitions of colonial crimes for the Sutpen family, described in chapter 1, the balance present in a relationship between Jim and Marcus may have had the capacity to challenge the restrictive plantation culture. Nonetheless, this prospective pairing never develops beyond a fragile friendship in part due to the two's derogatory view of homosexual relations, resulting from the rigid views of gender roles and sexuality common to the plantation system. Love here—whether platonic or homoerotic—has unexplored revolutionary potential.

Further, although dismissed by Jim and Marcus as freaks and punks, the relationship between Freddie and John may just be "the most radical example of the possibility for social change in the novel" (Bibler 41), given their mutuality and the lack of any visible power differentials between them (Bibler 42). Freddie and John are openly gay men, who seem to always find something to giggle about even in the brutal Louisiana heat. Gaines's portrayal of these characters is complex. At the same time that Freddie and John giggle like "perfumed gals going to the dance" (33) or shout "more than any two women" at church (25) (Jim's narration positions giggling and shouting as gendered behaviors), their corn-pulling prowess puts Marcus's skills to shame (Bibler 42). Freddie and John do not care about the watchful eyes of the community. They are overt about their relationship, which positions them alongside Bonbon and Pauline, as a pair more or less sanctioned by the community. The couple may be seen as an exception to the claim that racialized, gendered, and queer bodies are often policed more ardently, since in this case the horizontal relations between Black men do not directly disturb the hierarchies in place on the Hebert plantation.[16] While their relationship may not explicitly disrupt the social order, it contains "the potential for 'changing the rules' of the plantation by proposing an alternative model of egalitarian social relations that defies both racism and sexism" (Bibler 44), which a partnership between Marcus and Jim would have also achieved. Moreover, if Marcus's rebellion had incorporated a sense of the bigger picture in terms of plantation hierarchies and relations in this way, it may have accomplished change on a broader scale. While progressive when it comes to issues of racial oppression, Marcus holds conservative views of both sexuality and gender relations, and this limits the overall effectiveness of his rebellion. Marcus confronts racial hierarchies, but he ignores the others, which, along with his self-interest and alienation from the community, holds his love rebellion back from becoming the full-scale intersectional revolution needed on the Hebert plantation that would disrupt multiple forms of oppression.[17]

In addition to his views on sexuality, Marcus has a traditional approach to gender relations. He buys into the hierarchies that position men above women on the Hebert plantation—perhaps his central means of power—while simultaneously challenging those that value white skin above black. Plantation ideologies stipulating that women should be subservient to men are complicated by a multiplicity of hierarchal relations spanning race, gender, sexuality, ethnicity, and class. Thus, for instance, while Louise Bonbon's Whiteness places her in a position of comparative privilege on the Hebert plantation, her ethnicity, class, and gender add complexity to this positioning. Gender roles prescribe that Louise should be submissive to Marcus, which here conflicts with the characters' racial categorizations. Further, Marcus holds himself above White Cajuns like Louise in terms of class status and ethnicity. The easiest way out of the confining, contradictory webs of social positioning is to cut away the threads and meet each other as individuals, which Marcus and Louise appear able to do eventually. If Marcus had been able to extrapolate from his acceptance of Louise to a tolerance of difference more broadly, then his rebellion could have resulted in more substantial change for the community. However, the rigid plantation structure and unspoken rules that accompany it normalize restriction as the standard, as opposed to freedom, regulating the behavior of individuals on each rung of the social ladder to uphold adherence to the status quo.

For example, although positioned on one of the higher rungs, Sidney Bonbon, the Cajun overseer, described by Jim as "a simple and a brutal man," followed the unwritten rules of the plantation and accepted restriction as the norm (67). This constraining system allowed him some power that he wouldn't have otherwise had, as Maria Hebert-Leiter has observed. Bonbon played his part, "taking" every Black woman who caught his eye in the fields as his position permitted and perpetuating the system of degradation and "monstrous intimacies," or "a set of known and unknown performances and inhabited horrors, desires and positions produced, reproduced, circulated and transmitted, that are breathed in like air and often unacknowledged to be monstrous" (Sharpe 3). Such abuse is so engrained in the system and central to its preservation that it is no long identifiable as monstrous. This type of behavior reinforced the hierarchical system in place and thus was not only accepted but encouraged by the White planter class. The assessing gaze of the White community was omnipresent to evaluate how well he acted on this "privilege" resulting from his Whiteness, exemplifying the mechanisms of policing, such as surveillance and porch talk, at work. Bonbon's violent behavior then zeroed in on Pauline Guerin, and she became the sole object of his abuse before he slowly fell in love with her. In this way, although the novel positions her as reciprocating Bonbon's feelings, "Pauline is essentially sparing other women in the field from sexual exploitation" (J. Morrison, "Politics of the Plate"). Further, the shift from exploitative sex to emotional attachment on Bonbon's end went against the restrictive rules, making him even more subject to the regulatory gaze of the plantation.

When Bonbon began to recognize Pauline's humanity, the relationship fell out of line with the expected behavior of an overseer. The system relies on everyone doing their parts to uphold the dehumanizing plantation hierarchies designed to keep individuals separate. Gaines describes their relationship as "love" in the novel—stating, "After so many years, Pauline did fall in love with Bonbon" (66)—and indeed critics have rightly pointed out that he portrays this pairing as "one more real than the love that exists between husband and wife" (i.e., Bonbon and Louise) (Hebert-Leiter 103). However, it is important to keep in mind that this is a relationship founded on rape, adding complexity to the novel's portrayal of romantic love.[18] Their relationship is depicted in terms of sounds. The ears of the community stand in for the eyes, since the bedroom is one of the few spaces off limits to their observant gazes: "now the shuck mattress was quiet. There wasn't any need for all that noise, because now Bonbon and Pauline's love was much softer—more tender" (66). Can a connection grounded in sexual violence transform into a quiet, tender love? Or is this another instance of Gaines asking us to suspend our disbelief, as with Jim's uncanny ability to replicate conversations he was not present to overhear? Can a relationship with such exploitative origins have revolutionary potential?[19]

While more consensual than their counterparts', the love depicted between Marcus and Louise is similarly complicated. Their affair began with each lover attempting to use the other for revenge on Bonbon, and as a possible way out of the bonds of marriage for Louise, before transforming first into vigorous sexual encounters and later into deep emotional attachments.[20] The soundscape of their relationship mirrors that of Bonbon and Pauline's, progressing from noise to quiet: "There wasn't any noise tonight. No dresser behind the door, no armoire falling. No chairs slamming against the wall; no running, no jumping, no slapping. The room was quiet as the gallery, quiet as the yard, quiet as the whole plantation" (203). The shift from sound to stillness underscores the change in their relationship at the same time that it emphasizes the building tensions on the plantation in the days leading up to their escape attempt. In spite of this change, Gaines continually portrays the love between Louise and Marcus to be immature, describing them as playing "like two children who didn't have a thing in the world to hide" (183). Louise "worshipped" Marcus (Gaines 205)—a verb emphasized by its repetition twice within two pages—and his love for her is based off of how strongly she loves him, not any qualities innate to her (Gaines 260). Although their bond develops beyond the physical, illustrated by their shifting soundscape, this relationship is never idealized or presented unproblematically as a model for future interracial interactions. The seeds for future resistance are more subtly located on a lower level.

The complicated portrayal of romantic love extends to the problematic, often contradictory treatment of women in the novel. The story is primarily told from Jim's masculine perspective—affecting how women are depicted— yet some events are also shown from the viewpoints of female characters, such as Jim's friend Margaret.[21] Although through the novel's structure the female characters are not entirely voiceless, everything from their perspectives is first filtered through Jim. All of the scenes between Marcus and Louise that take place at the Bonbon home are witnessed by Margaret, who later describes their interactions to Jim, who conveys them to us. This structure connects the novel to a communal voice. Porch talk and gossip play an important role in the surveillance of the community, as mentioned above, and this is emphasized through the form of the novel itself with its inclusion of multiple perspectives. Nevertheless, Jim's is the only voice the reader receives unmediated. His power over the narrative, and subordinate voices such as Margaret's, should not be overlooked.

In addition to narrator Jim's control over the other voices of the text, character Jim also has complex interactions with women—from the Bayonne girl that he pays for sex and the unrequited feelings he harbors for Pauline, to reciprocal respect he shares with Margaret and his pining for his departed lover, Billie Jean. The novel echoes this complexity with layered female characters who exert power in their own ways, like Margaret, Pauline, and Julie Rand, existing alongside the overt misogyny of the majority of the male characters in the text. Women are "taken" at whim by those who feel entitled to exploit their bodies, objectified as possessions, and beaten for attempting to escape, such as when Louise's father threatens to "beat hell out her" (163) if she attempts to run away again. However, Gaines's representations of characters and relationships are never two dimensional. The misogyny in the novel is not without consequence and is in part what prevents Marcus's rebellion from reaching fruition.

Indeed, a good deal of the text's misogyny emanates from Marcus, who, after killing a man over the man's girlfriend, cavalierly states, "'Any man's a fool to die over a woman,' he said. 'They got too many of 'em'" (78).[22] Marcus's misogyny is best represented by the scene in which he grabs and kisses a woman who was begging him not to hurt her in the fight: "That's the best thing for 'em when they carrying on like that at a fight" (109–10). Marcus both assumes she would want his lips on hers and presumes to know what is best for her. To top it off, he characterizes her concerns for her children during a violent altercation as "carrying on." In addition to this sexual assault, Marcus physically attacks Pauline. He hits her multiple times, knocks her down, and calls her a "white man bitch" (98) and a "bloody whore" (99) after she rejects him.[23] Once again, the eyes of the community prove omnipresent: they "had heard about him" (99) by the time he gets to the bar, and the tension he creates leads to an all-out brawl. While Pauline has the agency to refuse Marcus's advances, she pays a price for subverting the gender hierarchy, and the violence directed toward her spirals out to impact the rest of the community. Just as Marcus only loves Louise as a result of her feelings for him, he only wanted Pauline as a possession whose presence would have a positive affect him on him: "He thought how he would be a completely different person with a lovely body like that to come home to. Then he realized that that body was for a white man, and he got mad again" (117). Here, he does not consider Pauline as a person, only as a body that would be a physical comfort to him after a long day in the fields, illustrating the tension between the misogynistic representation of women in the text and layered representations of sexual and romantic relationships.

Marcus and Louise's rebellion would not structurally alter the plantation system, as Michael Bibler observes, but only lead Black men to rise in the social hierarchies above White women and, thus, equal to or even above White men (40). This would threaten the power of White men by asserting an equality that they do not want to admit. However, the positioning of Louise and the other women would remain the same (Bibler 40). Through Marcus's reliance on traditional gender roles and relations, his love rebellion ends up resembling the confining relations already in place. Marcus's misogyny holds back any potential for an intersectional revolution that would challenge the multiple, interconnected hierarchies of plantation cultures. Even though Marcus's love for Louise causes him to shirk the ethnic hierarchies that in his mind position her beneath him, he is still firmly committed to those of gender, illustrating the ways in which the "intrinsically subversive character of the romantic love complex was for a long while held in check by the association of love with marriage and motherhood" (Giddens 46). While love—particularly the passionate, border-crossing love depicted here—can be revolutionary in character, that subversive quality is limited by the hierarchical constraints upheld. If Marcus's boundary-defying love had developed further and had spread not only to Jim but to the others on the plantation whom he disdains, the disruptive potential could have been amplified.

In the same way that Marcus feels entitled to Pauline's affection and views her as a potential possession, his relationship with Louise quickly falls into traditional patterns. Although it was Louise's bold, active gaze that jumpstarted the affair (unbeknownst to Marcus), she quickly takes a deferential position in relation to Marcus's maleness, displaying her body for him and providing meals for him in Jim's place. Suzanne Jones argues that "Gaines bases the possibility of the unconventional interracial love affair on the conventionality of the gender roles they assume" (156). This limited disruption of hierarchies is central to the project of the novel itself. Introduced as "Bonbon's little yellow-head wife" (49), Louise is defined throughout by her relationships with men. Louise is described at length midway through the novel with a focus on her small, childlike stature and pale coloring: "Louise was about twenty-five, but she was the size of the average twelve- or thirteen-year-old girl... Her hair was yellow (the same color with that hay in August) and her face was more cream-color than it was white. Her sad gray eyes were the only thing about her that made you feel Louise wasn't a child. They had seen too much sorrow, they had seen it much too long" (119). As a result of this description, coupled with her behavior, Louise is infantilized throughout the novel, particularly compared with the maturity and self-possession of Pauline.[24] Her immaturity and Whiteness are highlighted in this passage: her submission to Marcus as a woman in a plantation society brushes up against the privileges granted by her Whiteness. That Whiteness—conveyed by her hay-colored hair, cream-colored skin, and sad gray eyes—comes off as grotesque here.[25] In her white dress, she is compared to a ghost, and in truth, trapped in that house, she is not dead but neither is she fully alive (120).

Below Marcus in consideration of gender hierarchies but above him concerning those of race, Louise with her Cajun identity occupies a complex position in relation to the various overlapping hierarchies and forms of domination highlighted in the novel. However, Louise's grotesque Whiteness, and its connection to the monstrous intimacies and subjections of the plantation, holds particular weight in this society. As Louise is well aware, her Whiteness is a form of power: it can be used as a weapon causing the death of Black men—no questions asked. According to her servant, Margaret, Louise originally intends to cry rape, using the marks on her body to have Marcus lynched and Bonbon taken away (165). This intention puts Louise's plan in conversation with the myth of the Black rapist. As a White woman raised in a plantation culture, Louise knows she holds a certain power for her role in raising heirs and maintaining White lines of descent—safeguarding Whiteness as economic, social, and political privilege. Louise is aware that the protection of her sexuality, and by extension Whiteness itself, could easily be used as a pretext for the lynching of Black men, which, like plantation hierarchies, continued far beyond Emancipation. Between the end of Reconstruction and the Great Depression, at least 2,462 Black Americans were lynched in the United States (Tolnay and Beck 272). The myth of the Black rapist obscured the institutionalization of the sexual exploitation of Black women by White men, which entitled men like Bonbon to rape whichever sharecroppers they wanted even after the demise of the slave system.

Although Louise knows allegations of rape do not need to be accompanied by proof, she isn't sure she has "anything worthwhile" for a rapist and wants to have a mark as evidence. Louise, in her immaturity and ignorance, believes rape to only be about desire and physical attraction, as opposed to power; however, rape was, of course, institutionalized by White men as a weapon of control in the plantation system. Her desire for a visual mark (proof) may result from her living her life beneath the regulatory gaze of the plantation community: "You had white women who had just said it and had had the n*** lynched; you had some who had dreamed it and had had a n*** lynched; others had done it themselves and had had a n*** lynched; but Louise needed the mark" (165). The repetitive structure of this sentence emphasizes the frequency with which these events occur. Crying rape is depicted here as a twisted entitlement of White womanhood in a plantation culture, speaking to the panic around interracial sexuality and the defense of Whiteness as power, privilege, and protected capital. It doesn't matter whether the White women had said it, dreamed it, or done it themselves—all circumstances in which the allegations are fabricated—the result is the same: the accused Black man is lynched.

The sympathy garnered for Louise due to her brutal family situation, which was so bad that "physical hurt didn't matter any more" for her (165), is complicated by her intention to cry rape and then further by her falling in love with Marcus instead. Nevertheless, her false allegations would have not only led to Marcus's death but also resulted in violent repercussions against those in the quarters. The rules of the plantation culture stipulate that a man like Bonbon can sleep with a woman like Pauline without her consent. Further, according to the same rules, White womanhood is of such value that even false allegations of sexual contact lead to certain death, as the community is well aware. Gaines notes in unpublished commentary on the novel that by the time "Marcus comes along, she has been sitting on the gallery three years, trying to entice, with her eyes, any of the men on the plantation. None of the men have been willing to risk death in order to sleep in her bed" (Gaines Papers 4.11, 195/164).[26] The rules may be unwritten, but they are widely understood and tacitly accepted.

Louise's calculated looking and its role in her plan are worth exploring in more detail. I want to shift the focus from the regulatory potential contained within the gaze to looking as an erotic act. While other forms of sexual activity proved nearly impossible to effectively regulate, looking takes this even further. For instance, how would one enforce laws against looking at individuals of a certain race, gender, or class? Looking is central to the start of Louise and Marcus's affair. Her empowered coopting of the male gaze is responsible for everything that follows. Reciprocal looking here is both an erotic act and a way to signal emotions and intentions, as we saw through Tee Bob's look of love in chapter 2. It is precarious for Marcus, a Black man, to overtly look at the White wife of his overseer; however, it is just as dangerous for Louise, a married White woman, to be seen visibly gazing at Black men. That does not stop her. For as long as Jim has been on the plantation, Louise has been looking at Black men: "She just sat there on that gallery and looked at you when you went by, like she wished you would come in there, like she was waiting for you to try" (50). The readers later discover that looking is only the first stage of Louise's plan to achieve freedom from her husband through seduction. She uses her bold looking to entice a man with the intention of getting a mark on her body, crying rape, and having the man lynched by Bonbon and herself freed as a result. This scenario overtly illustrates George Yancy's claim that "white *gazing* is a violent process" (243, italics in the original). Louise plans to use her White womanhood to trigger racialized violence, which she believes will lead to her freedom. The hierarchies of race and gender are deeply entwined in this example. Louise is in a position of comparative privilege, due to her race, and subservience, as a result of her gender, which she challenges through her appropriation of the male gaze. This is another instance in which contradictory hierarchies complicate a moment of potential resistance.

Louise begins looking at Marcus, the only man on the plantation brazen enough to pursue her, and eventually he notices and begins looking back. Jim marks the day and the hour—Monday, twelve o'clock—when the looking becomes reciprocal (109), and the two "would watch each other like that until they couldn't see each other any more for the dust" (124).[27] While the Whiteness of Louise's gaze may be branded dehumanizing and regressive, objectifying the Black body as "that which is to be feared and yet desired, sought out in forbidden white sexual adventures and fantasies" (Yancy xxx), the maleness of her gaze is simultaneously a subversive force. At the start of their interactions, Louise controls the erotic looking, traditionally associated with a male gaze. Although *Of Love and Dust* is not a film, applying Laura Mulvey's theories of cinema and pleasurable looking to the text gives us a sense of the traditionally gendered associations that often accompany this act. For instance, Mulvey states, "There are circumstances in which looking itself is a source of pleasure, just as, in the reverse formation, there is a pleasure in being looked at" (835). Typically, the pleasure of looking is reserved for men, and the pleasure in being looked at for women: "In a world ordered by sexual imbalance, pleasure in looking has been split between active/male and passive/female. The determining male gaze projects its phantasy on to the female form which is styled accordingly" (837). This pattern is much more complex in *Of Love and Dust*. Louise's active looking functions as the catalyst for the entire affair, placing Louise in the traditional position of the man in this scenario. If Louise is masculinized through the position of control granted to her as the looker, Marcus is unknowingly feminized in a shift that is simultaneously progressive, through its inversion of gender norms, as well as regressive, emasculating the Black man in line with the intended consequence of the broader practice of lynching (Louise's original end goal). While Mulvey notes that typically men "cannot bear the burden of sexual objectification" (838), Louise does not care. For years, she subjected the men of the plantation to her gaze. Louise's objectification of the Black men on the plantation is certainly a privilege of her Whiteness and dangerously in sync with the mentality of lynch culture; nonetheless, it also has the effect of inverting the typical gendered associations with looking.

Louise's role as the instigator here is complicated by the fact that Marcus was unaware of her intentions: "The funny thing about all this, Marcus didn't know Louise had been looking at him for a week already. If he had, I doubt if he would have wanted Louise. Because, you see, he wanted her only for revenge. He wanted to get to her, not her getting to him" (116). As a result of his misogynistic views of women, outlined above, Marcus would not have been interested in the affair had he known Louise was initially in the position of power—or indeed that Louise intended to use him for the same purpose he intended to use her: revenge on Bonbon. Given his investment in traditional gender hierarchies, Marcus presumably is more comfortable when the looking becomes reciprocal and even more so after Louise passes the male gaze along to him, openly displaying her body for him: "He was looking at Louise laying there on the cot. But Louise pretended he wasn't anywhere around. Laying there with half of her belly out and with that skirt pulled halfway up her thighs, and still pretending he wasn't anywhere around" (153). In this scene Marcus is raking leaves in the yard, while stealing glances at Louise's static body, bringing their interactions more in line with the active/male and passive/female dynamic, where it remains for the rest of the novel. The repetitive references to Louise looking first at men generally and later at Marcus specifically highlights the subversive start to their relationship before it recedes into a sea of traditional gender relations, in addition to emphasizing the impact of conflicting, interacting hierarchies on moments of potential resistance.

During the scene in which Marcus and Louise get together for the first time, Margaret is depicted as "watching both of them" (151) before they escape her vigilant eyes and make it to the bedroom upstairs. In this scene the subversive nature of this erotic, interracial looking brushes up against the use of surveillance in the novel as a mode of social control, connecting the panoptic gaze of the plantation to looking as an erotic act. The goal of sexual policing is control over the erotic, and by extension the romantic and familial, exemplified by the consideration of these gazes in tandem. Through regulating sexuality, those invested in maintaining the status quo on the plantation can dampen the revolutionary power of love and familial bonds. As a result, the stakes for controlling private behavior through the public gaze of the community are very high because the continuation of the plantation system itself lies in the balance. Thus, Marcus's love rebellion not only jeopardizes his own life and well-being but also that of the entire community.

As Gaines states in his commentary, "if Marcus is caught, he and perhaps half the people on the plantation will pay in blood for that relationship" (Gaines Papers 4.11, 202/172). Jim speaks for the collective community when he tells Marcus: "We don't want any trouble on this plantation, hear?" (122). In addition to his ignorance of other forms of oppression that do not directly impact his position, Marcus's alienation from the community also contributes to his failure. One of the most unforgivable aspects of his character is his knowledge and subsequent dismissal of his actions' effects. Jim tells Marcus early on that if he is caught, Bonbon and his brothers would burn him alive along with half the people in the quarters, yet he proceeds with the affair anyway (122). While Marcus's love rebellion may be read as such for its challenge to plantation social structures, his disregard for other lives complicates his depiction as a hero and Gaines's usage of positive archetypes in addition to stereotypes. Gaines's repetition of the community's concerns throughout the novel, as voiced by Jim, Margaret, and house servant Bishop, emphasize this self-involved aspect of Marcus's character. Once more, his lack of love for others in his community limits what he is able to achieve with his gaze fixed solely on Louise.

Similar to the Tee Bob episode in *The Autobiography of Miss Jane Pittman*, the whole community attempts to police this couple: Marshall and the Cajuns to preserve the status quo and their relatively privileged position and the Black community because their collective memory "equates this form of individual risk-taking with death" (Beavers 79). Further, because a White woman is involved, the weight of this risk for the community is much heavier than in Gaines's other novels. Bishop voices the fear of the community: "That boy touch Bonbon them brothers go'n ride," leaving violence and destruction in their wake (222). The community, and in particular the older members, remember past lynchings—"'Member the time they lynched Coon boy" (263)—and know enough to be frightened for their lives, even if Marcus and Louise do not. In this way, "it is the memory of violence rather than actual force that enforces passivity and thus upholds the status quo" (Beavers 71). Scenes of past violence that have been imprinted on the community's collective memory have the consequence of keeping the same structures in place.[28] This demonstrates the powerful effects of this racialized violence, not only on the immediate present, but for generations to come. The Black community attempts to keep Marcus and Louise apart, as opposed to Bonbon and Pauline or Freddie and John, because they know a threat to the plantation hierarchies endangers their lives. Further, the patterns portrayed in Gaines's work indicate that the closer the interracial couple is on the race/class/color spectrum, the more likely they are to survive in the novels. The same goes for if the lighter skinned partner is male: the pairing upsets the racial but not gender hierarchies. Relationships like Marcus and Louise's that subvert multiple hierarchies pose a more substantial threat to the plantation system and as a result have greater revolutionary potential. This may explain the difference in outcomes for the two relationships depicted in this novel. Bonbon and Pauline escape the plantation together, while Marcus is killed and Louise is sent to Jackson, "the insane asylum" (278).[29]

A number of scholars agree that Marcus's rebellion, leaving the plantation with Louise Bonbon, had the potential for a more concrete impact. Herman Beavers argues that Marcus "possesses the potential, were it to become collectivized, to topple the plantation system and render social ritual incomprehensible" (79). Similarly, according to Maria Hebert-Leiter, both of the "interracial couples represent the possibility of love and acceptance regardless of racial notions of superiority and inferiority constructed by those in power" (104). Through disregarding his own prejudices against Cajuns, in addition to the racial hierarchies, Marcus's love rebellion had the potential to disrupt the status quo, yet failing to acknowledge his adherence to other societal restrictions, such as hierarchies of gender and sexuality, limits his impact and chances of success. Toward the end of the novel, however, Jim shifts from viewing Marcus and Louise as unforgivably selfish to brave: "They were starting something that others would hear about, and understand, and would follow" (270). While disrupting the paternalism and patriarchy of the plantation is a brave endeavor, I agree with Jim on both counts and, thus, regret all the more Marcus's self-interest and alienation from the community, which lead to his failure.

In ignoring the forms of oppression that do not directly impact his life, Marcus only looks out for himself. He admits as much to Jim: "You, you want care for everybody. Me, I don't care for nobody but me. I been like that too long now to go round changing" (225). Gaines humanizes Marcus in the final sections of the novel, providing the readers with the backstory behind this mentality: the cycles of violence and exploitation Marcus encounters first through his job parking cars and later through his experience in prison cause this mindset.[30] As a result, Marcus promises himself that he would look out for himself alone in the future (253), which he delivers on up until the end of the novel. He could have run away from Louise and Bonbon—observer Sun Brown claims he had all the time in the world to do so (275)—but he remained behind to fight and is cut down by a scythe, echoing Thomas Sutpen's demise in *Absalom, Absalom!* (another character with a grand design). Nevertheless, Marcus's self-interest has the effect of alienating him from the community and limiting the impact of his actions. This would be of no consequence to him, however, since he is not concerned with the well-being of others.

Had he been able to see beyond himself more effectively, Marcus would have recognized the asset before his eyes: Jim. As noted above, Jim's knowledge of the community and its history, only having been there for three years, and his relationships could have aided Marcus by providing him with an understanding of the weight of his actions. Marcus's stubborn disregard for others and their advice leads to his tunnel vision, where his only concern is escape for himself and Louise. While Marcus appears to be a "figure of resistance," according to Herman Beavers, and Jim solely a witness, there is a necessary symbiosis between Marcus and Jim: "Marcus needs Jim to tell his story, Jim tells his story because of Marcus's impact on his life" (Beavers 72). However, had this symbiotic relationship begun earlier or developed more fully into a balanced partnership, Marcus's rebellion might have succeeded. Marcus needs Jim to connect him with the community and its history, and Jim needs Marcus as a catalyst to act on the impulses he has buried for years. Jim has intended to fight the rule that Black men can only have their beers in the side room of the store, for instance, telling himself, "One of these days I'm going to stop this" (43). In part as a result of Marcus's impact, Jim leaves the Hebert plantation behind, rejecting Marshall's recommendation letter, symbolic of his system of influence and control, leaving the readers to wonder what will be next for him. Will he deliver on his positioning as a figure of hope (Bibler 40)?

Aside from his tenuous friendship with Jim, Marcus does not attempt to connect with the others in the Black community. He shows a disrespect for those in the quarters and their way of life, considering them to be "slaves," presumably due to the plantation hierarchies that remain in place from the earlier period. When Jim encourages him to make an effort, he retorts: "Be a contented old slave, huh?" (225). Through forging connections with the community, and perhaps developing an interest in lives beyond his own, Marcus could have learned from the collective memory of the quarters in a way that would have helped him to better anticipate the actions of both Bonbon and

Marshall. While the collective memories of violence are what hold the rest of the community back from action, Marcus's lack of the appropriate level of fear had the potential to balance this effect, which might have led to more concrete change for the community.

Although neither Marcus's rebellion nor Jim's narration result in large-scale alterations to the plantation structure (Beavers 82), they both demonstrate the potential for future change. By refusing the White paternalistic patriarch's letter of recommendation, Jim chooses to break out of the system and go it alone, branding him a figure of hope. Jim's recognition in the end that they—Marcus, Bonbon, Pauline, and Louise—are all tools for rich Whites positions him to act accordingly in the future (269). Bonbon's sincere observation that everything is decided by those on top of the hierarchies impacts Jim's reading of the events that follow and even allows him to see beyond Marcus's selfishness to its accompanying bravery. Bonbon states, "Me and you—what we is? We little people, Geam. They make us do what they want us to do, and they don't tell us nothing" (258). The awareness that the poor White Cajuns and Black community alike have no agency or control over their situations opens Jim's eyes to reality and potentially will lead to future action. Through the character of Jim, individuals can recognize paternalism for what it is and envision ways in which plantation workers oppressed by the system can forge new alliances across the boundaries of race and class (Costello 118). The moments during which the hierarchies are thwarted in favor of relating on an individual level hold the potential for future disruption. The relationships between Marcus and Louise and between Bonbon and Pauline are the obvious examples of this, but so is the interracial understanding between Jim and Bonbon before it is crushed by Bonbon's obligatory killing of Marcus (Hebert-Leiter 107). The potential to shirk the rules that dictate interracial interactions and disregard the intersecting hierarchies of race, gender, sexuality, ethnicity, and class leave space for a more effective revolution against a crumbling plantation system.

Along the same lines of viewing others as individuals as opposed to members of a socially defined race, class, or gender group, utilizing the gaze for ends other than regulating private interactions contains a small seed of rebellion: an alternative to the blind replication of destructive relations. Reclaiming the simple act of looking from the nefarious purposes to which it is attached under the panoptic plantation system is a small step in the direction of dismantling the system in its entirety, alongside shirking the entrenched rules and loving who you want to love. If Marcus and Louise, Bonbon and Pauline, Catherine and Jackson, and perhaps also Tee Bob and Mary Agnes (if we suspend disbelief for a moment and imagine she reciprocated his feelings, which we can never know for sure) can love each other, then small seeds take hold in the earth and soon multiply. As Giddens states, the "possibility of intimacy means the promise of democracy" (188). Love is not only revolutionary but can also be transmittable. Defying the rules and recognizing the full humanity of others in spite of difference has the potential to spread. Just as Marcus's rebellion causes Jim to finally act, moments of subversion can result in others until cracks in the foundation grow large enough to destabilize the entire system. The actions of individuals, in this case Marcus and Louise, have larger social ramifications. To give Jim the last word, "they were starting something that others would hear about, and understand, and would follow," as Jim does on a small scale through removing himself from the toxic plantation environment.

Chapter 4

"FOR FEAR OF A SCANDAL"

Sexual Control, Racism, and the Public Nature of Private Relations in Marie Chauvet's Twentieth-Century Haiti

The mechanisms employed to police sexuality explored in chapter 2, such as the surveying gaze and gossip of the community, directly connect the spaces previously examined to the twentieth-century Caribbean—particularly under the dictatorships of François Duvalier in Haiti and Rafael Leónidas Trujillo Molina in the Dominican Republic. The individualized examples portrayed in novels by Marie Chauvet and Edwidge Danticat in Haiti and Julia Alvarez, Junot Díaz, and Nelly Rosario in the DR elucidate the structural similarities between Caribbean dictatorships and US democracies: the shared legacies of racial and sexual policing across the diverse topographies of Mississippi, Louisiana, Haiti, and the Dominican Republic. For instance, Ernest Gaines's representations of the Panopticon-like structure of surveillance utilized by postbellum plantations in rural Louisiana are mirrored clearly through Marie Chauvet's careful, even cloaked, depiction of a small Haitian town under a terrifying authoritarian regime, in which multiple levels of society work together to police one another's behavior. The remaining two chapters will illustrate the deep connections between the US and the Caribbean as spatially and culturally diverse twinned inheritors of colonial control over racialized sexuality—an inheritance that remains in the bones of both regions' twentieth-century societies.

Marie Chauvet's novella *Love*, the first story of the triptych *Love, Anger, Madness* (1968), illustrates the reciprocal relationship between the public and private spheres of Haitian society, which connects back to the island of Hispaniola's colonial history and the inheritance of European pan-Caribbean laws, such as the 1685 Code Noir. Although much criticism on the novella has centered on Chauvet's purposeful collapse of the post-US occupation era (1934–1957) and François Duvalier's regime (1957–1971), I explore the ways that these two tumultuous periods recall the colonial era and reveal the resulting effects on race and gender relations, sexuality, and individual subjectivities.[1] As a result of the veiled setting, Chauvet was not able to overtly portray Duvalier's regime, and, thus, I incorporate contemporary Haitian American writer Edwidge Danticat's depictions of sexual violence under Duvalier in order to deepen this discussion. Further, my readings in this chapter push back on the concept of Haitian exceptionalism through connecting the problems found in the post-occupation and Duvalier periods explicitly back to the legacies of colonialism and external intrusions, in addition to the similarities between twentieth-century Haiti's policing cultures and those of Mississippi and Louisiana, explored in the previous chapters. These temporal and spatial overlaps challenge the view, held by journalists like David Brooks, that the "Haitian people and their 'progress-resistant culture'" are to blame for natural disasters, such as the earthquake in 2010 (Daut 606).[2] Such views only serve to act as "a shield that masks the negative contribution of the Western powers to the Haitian situation" (Trouillot 7), as well as the points of connection shared by nations of the circum-Caribbean, such as a colonial inheritance of surveillance and policing.[3] Further, as *Love* reveals, the influence of France, and later the United States, is responsible for many of the social, political, and economic issues plaguing Haiti into the twentieth century.

This chapter examines the novella's broader critique of the narrator Claire Clamont's Haitian community—including 1) the policing of interpersonal interactions, 2) the social stratification, sexual violence, and racism that result, and 3) the reliance on sexual and racial stereotypes. The collective fear of scandal in this community connects to the fear of destabilizing the status quo, jeopardizing the privileged position of the *Mulâtres-Aristocrates*, a distinct and primarily biracial class comparable to the Creoles of Color in Louisiana, explored in chapter 2: the analogous racial structures form another link between the US and Caribbean communities explored here. Through a scandal, the private is made public, and the collective is responsible for policing the individual.[4] I then turn more specifically to the individual through Claire's personal experiences, connecting together intimate and larger-scale histories, since in a distorted way private and public seem to reflect each other. As shown through Claire's repressed and consequently skewed sexuality, the regulation of the individual by the community through the fear of scandal helps to maintain colonial hierarchies and ideologies at the personal and the collective levels—similar to the plantation policing depicted in the work of William Faulkner and Ernest Gaines. Only through dismantling these structures can Claire's community hope to alter the cycles of hatred and violence that continue to impact their society in the twentieth century.

Marie Chauvet's *Love* is set in 1939—a period of transition four years after the almost twenty-year US occupation of Haiti, during the reign of Sténio Vincent. Vincent instituted vengeful policies against the *Mulâtres-Aristocrates*, a class that never fully accepted him as their rightful leader (Munro, "Avenging History" 34). The novella was written, however, in 1967 during another period of upheaval, the regime of authoritarian dictator François "Papa Doc" Duvalier (Lee-Keller 1293), and also evokes this era, denouncing Duvalier's regime in addition to Vincent's. The story is told through undated journal entries written by Claire Clamont, a dark-skinned member of the elite *Mulâtres-Aristocrates* who has raised her sisters, Annette and Félicia, and attempts to retain her family's position in the years after the American occupation, alongside others of her class, such as the Audiers, the Camuses, the Duclans, and the Soubirans. Claire's narrative flashes between the events of the past and the present and includes her own personal thoughts, musings, and fantasies, such as the desire to murder her sister Félicia and take her place as wife to White Frenchman Jean Luze and mother to Jean-Claude. Eventually Jean Luze joins a group of persecuted poets, including Joël Marti, and a few members of the peasant class to lead an uprising against the dictator figure, Commandant Calédu, and his cronies.[5] Claire, in an uncharacteristic moment of action, stabs Calédu in the novel's closing scene, an instant that synthesizes her inner and outer worlds. Claire's chaotic moment of personal rebellion simultaneously functions as an essential political act.[6] The structure of the novella, coupled with Claire's first-person narrative voice, allows Chauvet to bring the individual experiences of the Clamont family into focus against the backdrop of palimpsestic historical periods—with references to Duvalier's regime written over the post-occupation moment.

Since the novella doubles as Claire's diary, the intimate aesthetics mirror the text's wider project of using the personal to critique the political. Through Claire, Chauvet criticizes Haitian society more broadly, as a result of her treatment as a dark-skinned member of the *Mulâtres-Aristocrates*, her own racism toward members of the Black lower class, and her distorted relationship to sexuality. Stylistically the text grows more fragmented and frenzied toward the end, revealing her increasingly agitated mental state. In this way, Claire's reliability is called into question as a result of her own progressively fragmented subjectivity, depicted through her skewed relationship to her sexuality, her family, and her community. However, Claire's viewpoint is the sole lens through which the events of the story are narrated. Thus, while readers are always conscious of the filtered quality of the story, which is inseparable from Claire's subjectivity, the fragmented nature of the narrative does not so much cast doubt on its veracity as transform it into

Claire's personal story and subjective experience of the events. The particular and internalized nature of this fictionalized version of a nonfictional mode of writing raises the question of whether accounts of history can ever be anything other than the personal, blurring the border between history and fiction through the form of the narrative.

It is striking that Claire is responsible for the death of the dictator, given that she is a member of the privileged yet presently persecuted *Mulâtres-Aristocrates* and does not appear on the surface to be politically engaged. Claire watches the uprising led by Jean Luze and Joël Marti from her window before she participates in it by stabbing Calédu—arguably during one of her less lucid moments that increase in frequency as the novella continues (155). In a direct way, this public figure infiltrates her personal space. When running for his life, Calédu makes his way toward Claire's house and appears on her balcony. Claire wonders if he is aware that it is her house and balcony to which he runs. Her own conflicted relationship to Calédu comes to a head here: his intensions are uncertain, but her action is not. She takes a dagger, previously coded with phallic imagery—she notes earlier, "I've been spending too much time stroking the dagger Jean Luze gave me" (149)—and significantly housed in her blouse, and she stabs Calédu in the back three times.[7] Although Claire is not portrayed as particularly clearheaded when she stabs him, I argue that we should still view this as a moment of rebellious action, in addition to the climax of her personal inner conflicts. It is an act with personal and political weight, demonstrating the interplay of these factors throughout the novella.

Overall, Claire's journal focuses more overtly on her sexuality and contradictory feelings for the commandant, masking her growing political consciousness. Nevertheless, Claire's act of violence carries important revolutionary weight and is not entirely out of character, as a close reading of her journal reveals. Kaiama L. Glover asserts that Claire's sole political act "has only to do with keeping her brother-in-law—whom she is determined to seduce—from leaving Haiti" (19), which is surely a factor; however, I argue that Claire's motivations and the depth of her political sentiments are more ambiguous.[8] While Claire's journal reveals her obsession with sexuality, it also exposes her growing revolutionary impulses, although she is often not bold enough to act on them. Since childhood, she hated her father, owner of a coffee plantation, for whipping the farmers' sons for no reason, and throughout she is internally resistant to the narrow-minded gossip of women like friend of the family and fellow *Mulâtress-Aristocrate*, Mme Audier, while externally appearing in agreement. Claire does not fully acknowledge these impulses herself, preferring Jean Luze to see her hatred of Calédu as "ma haine amoureuse, ma révote amoureuse" (30), or "a lover's loathing, a lover's outrage" (17), as opposed to a more politically engaged sentiment (although to an extent the love or hatred of a dictator figure is also political). Nonetheless, there are shades of recognition, such as when she decides to befriend Jane Bavière again, a woman shunned by the community as a result of her bearing a child out of wedlock: "J'ai déjà suffisamment applaudi des deux mains aux sornettes de nos bon bourgeois. Je m'élève contre" (52), or "I believe I have offered sufficient applause for our proper bourgeois nonsense. I am rising against it now" (33). To understand the act in these terms is to challenge the ways in which women's roles in slave resistance and later revolutionary activities "have thus been obscured by over-emphasis on [their] sexual functions and the highly biased interpretations of these functions" (Bush 147). While in Claire's case her revolutionary act is connected to her sexuality, that fact does not detract from its communal value—the private and public significance of her act meld together in this moment.

Claire's moment of rebellious action and its public significance connect back to the broader history of Haiti. Originally a Spanish colony, the land was ceded to France in 1697 and became the French colony of Saint-Domingue (Dubois 18). In the late 1700s, Saint-Domingue was one of the most profitable pieces of land in the world—thanks to thriving sugar plantations—but also the most deadly: over the course of the colony's history, as many as one million enslaved people were brought to the island to replenish those lost "at a murderous rate" due to harsh conditions (Dubois 4). These conditions led to the slave revolts that began in 1791 and to the abolition of slavery in 1794 (Dubois 5). Between 1794 and 1801, Saint-Domingue was nominally a French colony, led by Touissant Louverture, until the country's declaration of independence in 1804 (Dubois 5). As a result of this history, Haiti has been seen as "the symbolic heart of the colonized, pan-African world," as well as "a symbol of anticolonial revolt" and "the 'first black republic' in the New World" (Munro, "Can't Stand up for Falling down" 3). Although Haiti earns its place as a symbol of hope, freedom, and anticolonial rebellion, as elsewhere, Haiti was not able to fully shake off the bondage of colonial rule through the revolution, due to outside interference.[9] Colonial hierarchies and mentalities continued to structure Haitian society in the twentieth century, as Marie Chauvet's *Love* exemplifies, positioning it alongside Faulkner's Mississippi and Gaines's Louisiana as spaces that retain the imprints of their colonial histories. The novella depicts the experiences of the elite *Mulâtres-Aristocrates* after the ruling Black class usurped the power they historically held since the Haitian Revolution; however, the revolution and the potential it embodies lingers in the background until it is finally brought to the fore through the interracial and interclass uprising in the final pages.

I use the term "biracial" to refer to the combination of the racial groups recognized as Black and White in Haiti, and I follow Hellen Lee-Keller in her use of the term "*Mulâtres-Aristocrates*" to describe Claire's class. The tenuousness of putting these terms together in the attempt to describe this identity category—representative of race, class, color, and other complexities—reflects the societal instability that leaves space for the threat of scandal. This class, the *Mulâtres-Aristocrates*, rose to prominence almost immediately after Haiti abolished slavery and made White land ownership illegal. At this time, "mulatto offspring of former white landowners began to reclaim their land," which along with the Code Rural,[10] supplanted the White master class with a privileged, light-skinned biracial class (Matthews 253), demonstrating the social, economic, and political power that remained attached to Whiteness in the post-slavery period.[11] In her explication, Lee-Keller recognizes the complexities of the term *mulâtre* but chooses to follow Chauvet's language in the novella. Incorporating the term *aristocrate* helps to emphasize the entwinement of race and class in terms of Claire's social position, which comes closer to recognizing the intersectional nature of identity. As Nicole Aljoe has observed, the terms *mulâtre* and *aristocrate* are not typically associated with each other and are even thought of as oppositional in some societies. If identity categorizations and hierarchies were secure, then the fear of the public exposure of the private may be less dominant in Claire's community. Although problematically recalling what Werner Sollers has termed "the calculus of color," or "racial terminologies and taxonomies" reflective of colonial categorizations (29), *Mulâtres-Aristocrates* also embodies the uncertainty of identity categorizations, while similarly descriptive terms, such as "biracial elite," flatten this tension.[12] Further, using the French terminology, the language of Chauvet's original text, also acknowledges the fact that there is no English counterpart to this term or US equivalent of this racial and class group, leaving space for localized specificities.

While it is primarily concerned with the local, Chauvet's novella is also cognizant of hemispheric connections: more overt political links exist alongside the reciprocal reflections of colonial continuities in each society. External forces influenced twentieth-century Haiti—both in a direct way during the 1915–1934 US occupation and less explicitly through the financial and military interference of the United States in the post-occupation period and François Duvalier's rise to power, which began in the 1950s.[13] Haiti's often unstable political situation—only four Haitian heads of state have served a full term without an internal coup, suicide, assassination, or execution ("Haiti: The List")—was justification for one of the most overt forms of neocolonialism in Haiti since the revolution. The United States military occupation was colonialism by another name, due to the economic dispossession,[14] brutally enforced labor system,[15] violence,[16] and sexual violence employed as tools of control.[17] All of these aspects are central to Chauvet's portrayal of Haiti, and of course, reminiscent of postbellum US southern societies, as discussed in previous chapters, but with space left for local particularities. Further, Duvalier, whose reign was referred to by Millery Polyné as "one of the most notorious authoritarian governments in the hemisphere" (179), relied on methods similar to the exploitation and abuse during US occupation.[18]

François Duvalier's cruelty was legendary, and his violence has been described as limitless (Polyné 203), as is seen in Chauvet's novella, where everyone from beggars to the former aristocracy is vulnerable. While Calédu himself—whose name in Creole means "one who hits or beats hard"—is not a direct depiction of Duvalier, critics have recognized him as symbolic of Papa Doc: both are cruel, megalomaniacal dictators with color and class issues (Dayan, "Reading Women in the Caribbean" 234; Scharfman 231; Walcott-Hackshaw 49). Thus, although Chauvet veils her critique through the 1939 post-occupation setting, US intervention and the Duvalier regime's oppressive policies are evoked and condemned in the novel, as well as the sexism, racism, and social stratification that had been a fixture of Haitian society since the colonial era (Danticat, "Introduction" xi).[19] The entwined settings of Marie Chauvet's *Love* elucidate the similarities—such as racism, physical violence, sexual violence, and surveillance—both the US occupation and Duvalier's dictatorship share with the colonial period, conflating historical eras in order to symbolically underscore the continuity of colonial structures. Further, these similarities are also spatially shared with Mississippi and Louisiana in the same period, as the previous chapters reveal, emphasizing links across geography and political regimes—from democracy to dictatorship.

More specifically, *Love* is a scathing critique of Haiti's unstable political and social structures, as well as the "contradictions in relation to patriarchy and racial elitism originating in French colonialism and worsened by intervention from the United States" (Lee-Keller 1294). The importance placed on color distinctions originated during the colonial era (Nicholls 247) and should be traced to the colonizing nations of France and Spain and not seen as an inherently Haitian predicament. The 1685 Code Noir instituted by France in Haiti and other French colonies institutionalized this emphasis on color distinctions and racial hierarchies and aided in the reduction of "humans to proprietary objects" (Dayan, *Haiti, History, and the Gods* 213).[20]

As discussed in chapter 2, this set of laws attempted to regulate the interactions between the different racial and class groups in part through surveillance—the residual effects of which are portrayed in the novels of Ernest Gaines. *Love* depicts the ways in which colonial structures of control, such as the Code Noir, align with later iterations of external influence, such as twentieth-century US intervention, in their attachment to the status quo and interconnected hierarchies of race, color, and class. In addition to the thin veil between the public and private, *Love* exposes the skewed relationship to gender and sexuality, which manifests in the policing of sexuality inherited from the Code Noir, as well as the sexual violence and racism instituted through outside intrusion.

Sexuality in twentieth-century Haiti can be seen as a particular articulation of the neocolonial relationship. The rampant sexual abuse common to the US occupation and Duvalier regime and the drive to control women and sexuality during both periods connect temporally back to the sexual control of the enslaved population in the French American colonies institutionalized by the Code Noir (and, of course, spatially to the plantation system in the US South). While the Code Noir was not always upheld, it was an attempt to regulate the social conditions of slavery, specifically detailing the status of the enslaved, the interactions between enslavers and the enslaved, and the punishments applied if either party should not act according to the code. For example, the 1685 Code Noir states:

> Les hommes libres qui auront un ou plusieurs enfans de leur concubinage avec leurs Esclaves, ensemble les Maîtres qui l'auront souffert, seront chacun condamnez à une amende de deux mille livres de sucre; & s'ils sont les Maîtres de l'Esclave de laquelle ils auront eu lesdits enfans, voulons qu'outre l'amende, ils seront privez de l'Esclave & des enfans, & qu'elle & eux soient confisquez au profit de l'Hôpital, sans jamais pouvoir être affranchis. N'entendons toutefois le present articles avoit lieu, lorsque l'homme n'étoit point marié *à* une autre personne durant son concubinage avec son Esclave, épousera dans les formes observées par l'Eglise sadite Esclave, qui sera affranchie par ce moyen, & les enfans rendus libres & légitimes (*Le code noir ou Edit du roy* 5, transcription mine).

In other words, if free men have one or several children with enslaved women, they are to be fined two thousand pounds of sugar—together with the women's enslavers—and if the men have children with their own enslaved persons, the women and their children are confiscated for the profit of the

LE CODE NOIR
OU
EDIT DU ROY,
SERVANT DE REGLEMENT

POUR le Gouvernement & l'Adminiſtration de Juſtice & la Police des Iſles Françoiſes de l'Amerique, & pour la Diſcipline & le Commerce des Negres & Eſclaves dans ledit Pays.

Donné à Verſailles au mois de Mars 1685.

AVEC

L'EDIT du mois d'Aouſt 1685. portant établiſſement d'un Conſeil Souverain & de quatre Sieges Royaux dans la Coſte de l'Iſle de S. Domingue.

A PARIS, AU PALAIS,

Chez CLAUDE GIRARD, dans la Grand'Salle, vis-à-vis la Grand'Chambre : Au Nom de JESUS.

M. DCC. XXXV.

Figure 4.1: Title page from the 1685 *Le code noir ou Edit du roy*. Courtesy of the John Carter Brown Library at Brown University.

LE CODE NOIR.

jonction, que nous voulons être tenus & réputez, tenons & réputons pour vrais concubinages.

IX. Les hommes libres qui auront un ou plusieurs enfans de leur concubinage avec leurs Esclaves, ensemble les Maîtres qui l'auront souffert, seront chacun condamnez à une amende de deux mille livres de sucre ; & s'ils sont les Maîtres de l'Esclave de laquelle ils auront eu lesdits enfans, voulons qu'outre l'amende, ils seront privez de l'Esclave & des enfans, & qu'elle & eux soient confisquez au profit de l'Hôpital, sans jamais pouvoir être affranchis. N'entendons toutefois le present article avoir lieu, lorsque l'homme n'étoit point marié à une autre personne durant son concubinage avec son Esclave, épousera dans les formes observées par l'Eglise sadite Esclave, qui sera affranchie par ce moyen, & les enfans rendus libres & légitimes.

X. Lesdites solemnitez prescrites par l'Ordonnance de Blois articles 40. 41. 42. & par la Déclaration du mois de Novembre 1639. pour les mariages, seront observées tant à l'égard des personnes libres que des esclaves, sans neanmoins que le consentement du pere & de la mere de l'esclave y soit nécessaire, mais celui du Maître seulement.

XI. Défendons aux Curez de proceder aux mariages des esclaves, s'ils ne font apparoir du consentement de leurs Maître. Défendons aussi aux Maîtres d'user d'aucunes contraintes sur leurs esclaves pour les marier contre leur gré.

XII. Les enfans qui naîtront de mariage entre esclaves, seront esclaves & appartiendront aux Maîtres des femmes esclaves, & non à ceux de leur marié, si le mari & la femme ont des Maîtres differens.

XIII. Voulons que si le mari esclave a épousé une femme libre, les enfans tant mâles que filles suivent la condition de leur mere, soient libres comme elle, nonobstant la servitude de leur pere ; & que si le pere est libre & la mere esclave, les enfans seront esclaves pareillement.

XIV. Les Maîtres seront tenus de faire mettre en Terre Sainte dans les Cimetieres destinez à cet effet, leurs esclaves baptisez : & à l'égard de ceux qui mourront sans avoir reçu le baptême, ils seront enterrez la nuit dans quelque champ voisin du lieu où ils seront décedez.

XV. Défendons aux esclaves de porter aucunes armes offensives, ny de gros bâtons, à peine du foüet, & de confiscation des armes au profit de celui qui les en trouvera saisis ; à l'exception seulement de ceux qui seront envoyez à la chasse par leur Maître, & qui seront porteurs de leurs billets, ou marques connues.

XVI. Défendons pareillement aux esclaves appartenant à differens Maîtres, de s'atrouper, soit le jour ou la nuit, sous prétexte de nôces ou autrement, soit chez un de leurs Maîtres ou ailleurs, & encore moins dans les grands chemins ou lieux écartez, à peine de punition corporelle, qui ne pourra être moindre que du foüet & de la fleur de lys, &

Figure 4.2: Fifth page from the 1685 *Le code noir ou Edit du roy.* Courtesy of the John Carter Brown Library at Brown University.

hospital, remaining perpetually enslaved. However, if a man was not married to the enslaved woman but marries her in the forms observed by the church, she and her offspring will be freed and made legitimate (translation mine). Although not always enforced, the Code Noir attempted to control sexuality between enslaver and enslaved by attaching a fine to any sexual relations with enslaved persons that resulted in children with the threat of the loss of those family members, who doubled as property.

I argue that the policing of sexuality and interracial sex seen in Marie Chauvet's novella originates with the Code Noir, which was instated to work toward similar ends: regulating the sexuality of others. While not always enforced, the Code Noir was a colonial policy that relied on surveillance and the policing of sexuality in order to instate the overlapping hierarchies of race, color, gender, and class by regulating the interactions of individuals, thereby making control of that sexuality an official or national project.[21] Ideologies of race, gender, and class within the French empire have been constructed and reconstructed continually over the centuries; however, this emphasis on surveillance and the regulation of sexuality and behavior passed from the French colonial period of the Code Noir to later decades in distinct but still recognizable forms. The transmission of the surveillance central to the Code Noir to later periods shows the degree to which this ideology was embedded in Haitian society during the colonial era and the far-reaching network of its effects. The Code Noir's emphasis on surveillance and the policing of the interactions between enslavers and the enslaved may be seen as the historical precursor to the observation and regulation of others' behavior depicted in the multilayered setting of *Love*, as well as a point of connection to broader hemispheric regimes, such as Jim Crow in the US South, as demonstrated in the works of Faulkner and Gaines.

Indeed, the policing of sexuality in the novella—such as spying on the every move of others from one's window, gossip, and preoccupation with other people's business—is reminiscent of similar policing through the Code Noir. Commandant Calédu seeks to regulate interpersonal relationships, which requires constant surveillance. Claire wonders: "Est-ce partout pareil? Existe-t-il dans le monde des petites villes comme celle-ci, à moitié engluée dans d'ancestrales habitudes et où les gens épient les uns les autres? Ma ville! Mon pays!" (11–12), or "Is it like that everywhere? Are there towns in the world like this one, half mired in ancestral habits, people spying on each other? My town! My land!" (3–4). Edwidge Danticat notes that Claire's unnamed town of X could "stand in for many Haitian towns," which implies that this surveillance is endemic to small Haitian communities ("Introduction" xi). In these spaces, individuals are expected to watch one another's behavior, and anything outside of the society's standards is spread widely throughout the community until it reaches those in power. Thus, individual interactions are policed collectively, and as we saw in previous chapters, looking is central to this regulation. For instance, the novella's narrator Claire, a dark-skinned member of the typically light-skinned *Mulâtres-Aristocrates*, cannot visit the ostracized Dora Soubiran without the rest of her community knowing it. The streets of Claire's town are empty, but everyone sees and knows everything: "The whole town watches, posted behind windows, curtains, shutters. The other is there, s/he is watching me, but never to share anything. S/he is there, threatening to denounce me without me knowing" (Scharfman 234). Calédu and those in power rely on the complicity of the community for this system of observation to function: the fear of condemnation, ostracization, and violence, in addition to the politics of respectability, all work together to ensure that everyone plays their parts and the status quo is maintained.

The policing of sexuality and gender relations found in the novella can be productively put in conversation with the politics of respectability—first conceptualized in a US context by Evelyn Brooks Higginbotham in her study of early twentieth-century Black Baptist women—another hemispheric point of connection.[22] The politics of respectability equate "public behavior with individual self-respect and with the advancement of African Americans as a group" and striving "to win the black lower class's psychological allegiance to temperance, industriousness, thrift, refined manners, and Victorian sexual mores" (Higginbotham 14).[23] Respectability politics attempt to regulate the public behavior of individuals for the advancement of the collective and rely on a panoptic understanding of social relations in which public behaviors are visibly observed—similar to the forms of regulation seen in the novella. These politics also involve a gendered dimension and "emerged specifically to combat notions about Black women's hypersexuality and (hetero)sexual deviance—a charge which left them vulnerable to rape" (B. Cooper 106), which is in line with the policing of female sexuality imposed by Claire's community. Further, the problematic class dynamics of respectability politics—emphasizing "differences of social status within the working class itself" (Higginbotham 94)—are in part mirrored by those of the *Mulâtres-Aristocrates* in Chauvet's novel. Given the three-tiered racial construction of Haitian society, the *Mulâtres-Aristocrates* may be seen as using the politics of respectability not only to distinguish themselves from stereotypes, but also the Black lower class entirely. In this way, a comparison to the politics of respectability shows the interrelation of race, gender, and class in the public's regulation of private interactions in Claire's community.

Surveillance plays a key role in this public regulation of private behavior. The inhabitants of the town do not know exactly when eyes are on them. There is always the potential that they are being watched closely, and they must regulate their behavior accordingly. This portrayal calls to mind Michel Foucault's description of Jeremy Bentham's Panopticon, an "architectural apparatus [that] should be a machine for creating and sustaining a power relation independent of the person who exercises it," in which power must be visible yet unverifiable (201). As in the Panopticon—or postbellum Louisiana plantations, as depicted in Ernest Gaines's novels—the inhabitants of Claire's town are potentially monitored at all times, since it is not possible for them to know when and where. Along with the others in her community, Claire is caught up in this system of surveillance. She spies on the interactions of others throughout the novella, and at the same time, she is always aware of others' eyes on her and acts accordingly. Claire constantly regulates her own behavior as a result of her "*crainte du scandale*" (41), or "fear of scandal" (25)—the fear that her private desires and behaviors will be made public. This tension between the personal and the collective is central to the novella from the perspective of the characters and their fears. It is also integral to Chauvet's broader understanding of this history, demonstrated by her fusion of the two in Claire's final act of violence that closes the story and the different levels on which it operates.

Given her longing for intimacy and a child—she envies the ostracized Jane Bavière and at one point expresses her wish to switch places with Violette, a sex worker whom she describes as young, beautiful, and free—Claire may have made different sexual choices if not for the prying, damning eyes of her community (38). Along with racism toward Blacks, she has internalized her community's rules concerning sexual conduct and appropriate pairing and admits: "Par crainte du scandale, j'ai refoulé en moi un océan d'amour" (41), or "For fear of scandal, I have repressed an ocean of love within me" (25). This phrase, "fear of a scandal," is repeated elsewhere in the novel, highlighting its centrality not only for Claire but also for the community on which she reports to the reader. Claire notes that it was "par crainte du scandale" (83) that her sister Félicia agreed to reconcile with her other sister, Annette (56), and that if vivacious Madame Audier, a fellow *Mulâtress-Aristocrate*, settled solely for her husband, "seule la crainte du scandale a pu l'arrêter" (84), or "it was only for fear of scandal" (57). The collective fear of a scandal in Claire's community connects to the fear of the loss of colonial order among its former beneficiaries—the *Mulâtres-Aristocrates*. The private, public, and national are inextricably linked, as revealed by the rampant anxiety about keeping the private out of the public. In this way, the fear of a scandal functions as a successor to the policing properties of the Code Noir and connects to the respectability politics in US society during the same period. In other words, colonial values are dispersed among the community at large, which then tries to impose them in the private sphere in order to control the behavior of individuals, as seen overtly in the example of the Code Noir. As part of the *Mulâtre-Aristocrate* community, Claire adheres to the principles regulating sexuality purely for decorum's sake. This results in her abstinence and, to an extent, in her alienation, her obsession with sexuality, and her at times irrational behavior. Claire demonstrates the detrimental effects of the community's regulation of behavior on a more individual level, which when multiplied exposes the far-reaching impact on a collective scale, illuminating this broader history.

Sexuality, an intimate feature of human existence, is reckoned with publicly and policed so severely in Claire's town that even sexless encounters are sexualized by the community. The quasi-paternal bond shared between Tonton Mathurin, a Black man, and Agnès Grandupré, a young *Mulâtress-Aristocrate*, is sexualized both by Agnès's parents and by their neighbors. Claire's parents state that Claire is not to play with Agnès anymore because "c'est une vicieuse qui va en cachette chez le père Mathurin malgré la défense de ses parents" (128), or "she's a nasty little girl who goes to old Mathurin's house behind her parents' back" (89). Licentiousness is seen as transmittable by Claire's parents, who assert that Mathurin lives in sin and "le péché est contagieux" (128), or "sin is contagious" (89). As a result, they also sexualize Claire's encounters with Agnès: "Qui? Combien de fois l'as-tu vue? Que t'a-t-elle raconté? *Qu'avez-vous fait ensemble?*" (129, emphasis added), or "Who? How many times have you seen her? What did she tell you? *What have you done together?*" (90, emphasis added). This form of sexual policing of the community by its own members is sanctioned in the novella: it is committed not only by laypeople, but also by clergy members. For instance, Father Paul interrogates Claire as to why she visits the home of Jane Bavière, another ostracized former friend. Claire shirks decorum through resuming her friendship with Jane, positioning it as resistance to the accepted social forms of her community. Father Paul tells Claire: "Je n'irai pas sans vous dire que cette fréquentation inquiète votre sœur et que c'est elle qui m'a prévenu. J'espère qu'il n'existe rien de coupable dans vos rapports avec Jane Bavière" (185–6), or "I don't need to tell you these visits worry your sister and that she's the one who alerted me. I hope there is nothing untoward in your relations with Jane Bavière" (132). He later states, "La vie vous a refusé certaines joies, mon enfant, tâchez de ne pas les prendre dans le péché" (186), or "Life has denied you certain pleasures, my child; try not to seek them in sin" (132).

Although Father Paul insinuates otherwise, the friendship between Claire and Jane, like that between Old Mathurin and Agnès, does not have a sexual component. Nonetheless, in addition to interracial interactions, same-sex relations are also heavily policed by the community—the collective regulating the personal to uphold the hierarchical relations in place.

In the same way that consensual interracial sexual relationships challenge colonial hierarchies—for example both Roth Edmonds's and Hubert Beauchamp's couplings in Faulkner's *Go Down, Moses* and Marcus Payne and Louise Bonbon's in Gaines's *Of Love and Dust*—"queer egalitarianism," which includes both homosexual and homosocial relationships, "marks the limits of the plantation myth by presenting an image of interpersonal relations not distorted by any kind of power differential" (Bibler 4). Therefore, both consensual sexual relationships and platonic friendships have the potential to uproot social structures, such as the friendship between Claire and Jane, who has been excised from the *Mulâtres-Aristocrates*, crossing lines of class. Consensual same-sex relationships, like this friendship, are more of a threat to the colonial order, due their dismantling of hierarchical associations and modeling of another mode of interaction, than exploitative relations that reinforce such hierarchies, like Calédu's violent cross-racial rape of Dora. At the same time, however, homosexual relationships between individuals on the same hierarchal rung, such as between Freddie and John in *Of Love and Dust*, are less of a challenge than a pairing that reverses hierarchies like that between Marcus and Louise—although they still model alternative ways of interacting. Nevertheless, the policing of sexuality and other nonsexual relationships in the community—particularly of interracial or same-sex pairings as in the cases of Old Mathurin and Agnès, and Claire and Jane—is an attempt by the community to maintain colonial hierarchies and the status quo through dampening the revolutionary potential of love: romantic, platonic, and familial.[24] Sexuality is policed in the attempt to bring love, friendship, and family formations under national control across circum-Caribbean societies. This impulse originated with the Code Noir in Claire's community yet continues unchecked in the post-/neocolonial present of the novella.

In addition to the regulation of individual relations and behaviors, I want to focus more directly on another aspect of sexual control before bringing race and class dynamics more fully into this discussion: the centrality of sexual violence to both the occupation and Duvalier periods. Although depictions of this abuse are present in Chauvet's novella, I briefly highlight the ways in which Edwidge Danticat, a writer continuing Chauvet's politically engaged legacy, has been able to illustrate more overtly the predatorial violence rampant under Duvalier that disproportionately affected women and girls.[25] Literature shines a light on the ways in which rape has historically been used as an instrument of state-instituted violence in Haiti. Rape is "a crime of violence and intimidation with intrinsic connections to sexual aggressiveness and political and economic power" (McKay 248). It is not only a sexual crime but involves exerting power—both in terms of physical power and emotional control—over another human being.[26] This violent act was essential to both colonialism and slavery as a tool to regulate the behavior of women, humiliate both women and the men who were unable to protect them, and produce more children or more laborers.[27] Rape has also been used as "a frequent accompaniment to military conquests . . . a favored means of ensuring the defeat and pacification of entire nations" (Mama 51).[28] Accordingly, through their strategic use of rape as a weapon of control, both the US Marines during the occupation and Duvalier's *tonton macoutes* place themselves within this long history of groups using rape as a means to both traumatize and subdue.[29]

During the occupation, the sexual abuse of Haitian women by US Marines was the norm and created "an atmosphere in which rape would go unrecognized, unnamed, and, of course, unpunished" (Renda 163).[30] The lingering effects of this atmosphere are clearly depicted in the novella, where the representatives of the Haitian government, who succeeded the US Marines, avenge their own past color discrimination through the torture-rape of women of the *Mulâtres-Aristocrates*, such as Dora Soubiran, Claire's childhood friend who is ostracized after her violent rape at the hands of Commandant Calédu. Chauvet depicts rape and sexual abuse as tactics of terror through her veiled portrayal of Duvalier's regime. For Marie Chauvet, "in Duvalier's Haiti light-skinned women became the bodies upon which political power was confirmed" (Dayan, *Haiti, History, and the Gods* 122).[31] Although they are not directly referred to as *tonton macoutes* in the novella due to the setting, the brutality of Calédu's gang of beggars is echoed in the violence of the former. The firepower and skills of both the Haitian army and the *tonton macoutes* were turned against Haitian citizens. Duvalier's "paramilitary force, the *tonton makouts*, did not discriminate or brutalize Haitians based on color or class"—everyone was a potential victim (Polyné 203).

Recalling the ubiquitous violence of the Duvalier regime, Commandant Calédu's persecution affects members of both the Black and biracial groups, such as the members of the Black lower class in his jail and the poets he harasses. Calédu's violence also takes the form of retribution toward the *Mulâtres-Aristocrates*, specifically women reminiscent of those who scorned him before the occupation. When recalling her torture at the hands of Calédu and his men, Claire's friend Dora Soubiran recalls that "à chaque coup, il criant: Aristos, bande d'aristos, mulâtres-aristos, je vous estropierai tous, aristos, aristos" (191), or "with each blow he would yell: 'snobs, you bunch of snobs, mulatto snobs, I'll make cripples of all of you, you snobs'" (136), exposing Calédu's persecutions to be racially and sexually motivated, echoing the obsession with the compounded hierarchies of race and sexuality policed since the Code Noir. This example directly recalls Calédu's real-world counterpart and the "Duvalierist preference for the sexual 'conquest' of females associated with the political opposition, from torture-rape to acquaintance-rape and marriage, infused the politicization of gender with violence" (Trouillot 167). Ranked lower on hierarchies of gender, women and girls are left particularly vulnerable to this form of sexual violence that doubles as political persecution. Once more, sexuality is seen to express neocolonial relations.[32]

Although the sexual aspect of Dora's torture is never openly discussed, the novella implies that Calédu "avenges his own past colour discrimination by raping lighter-skinned, middle-class women" (Munro, "Hatred Chérie" 166), allegedly in reaction to his mistreatment as a member of the Black lower class by the *Mulâtres-Aristocrates*. This dynamic reveals the vicious cycle of racism, violence, and sexual violence that Haiti inherited from its French, Spanish, and later US colonial histories.[33] The cyclical nature of this violence is exemplified through the next story in the triptych, *Anger*, in which the rape victim, Rose, is given an interiority and makes this connection herself, reflecting on "se venge sur moi d'avoir toute sa vie été repoussé par les femmes qu'il désirait" (334–35), or "the man avenging himself through me for having been rejected by the women he desired" (251). The violence of Calédu and his men, as well as the nameless commandant in *Anger*, continues the succession of racism and persecution in Haitian society and is reminiscent of Claire's musings: "Nous nous exerçons à nous entr'égorger depuis l'Indépendance. Les griffes du peuple se sont mises à pousser et se sont acérées. La haine entre nous est née" (17), or "We have been practicing at cutting each other's throats since Independence. The claws of our people have been growing and getting sharper. Hatred has hatched among us, and torturers have crawled out of the nest" (8). Since the pronouns used by Claire do not reference a specific racial group, I read her observation as indicting the Haitian people more generally. The cycles of violence and racial hatred were imposed on the island by the colonizers, and—along with the control of sexuality and the overlapping hierarchies of class, gender, race, and color—are other residual effects that Haiti is left with after independence. Claire's recognition of this speaks to her growing political consciousness and building resistance to her society's status quo.

While Chauvet's veiled literary depictions demonstrate that women were particularly impacted by the racialized and gendered policies, as well as the sexual violence central to François Duvalier's dictatorship, writing in the 1960s, her critique was necessarily cloaked in a post-occupation setting. However, Haitian American author Edwidge Danticat, writing in the 1990s, was able to condemn Duvalier's regime more openly through her portrayal of the violence and sexual abuse accompanying it. I believe exploring this violence more overtly as recounted through literature adds an important layer to the discussion. While present, sexual violence is not directly depicted in Chauvet's novella but is implied through Dora's description of her beating and Claire's portrayal of her "walking with legs spread apart" (135) ["marchait les jambes ouvertes" (190)]. The form of the text, Claire's increasingly convoluted diary entries, necessitates distance from this experience. Danticat, however, builds upon Chauvet's inclusion of the racialized and sexualized violence of Duvalier and his henchmen, the *tonton macoutes*, in a way that elucidates their broader goals of destabilizing family relations, producing psychological trauma, and depriving women of power over their lives and bodies. Under Duvalier's leadership, the *tonton macoutes* capitalized on the fact that rape and sexual violence are enmeshed with networks of power and control, as we will see again with Rafael Trujillo and his henchmen in chapter 5.[34]

For example, in Danticat's short story "Children of the Sea," the violence committed by the *macoutes* is deviously conceived to have a wide-range of negative effects on individuals, families, and communities. This story is written in an epistolary form with a Haitian teenaged girl and the teenaged boy she loves, who presently resides on a raft bound for Miami, writing letters for each other. The emotional impact of the story is heightened by the form, since readers know these letters can never be sent. The girl describes a method of torture imposed by the *macoutes*:

> **if they come into a house and there is a son and mother there, they hold a gun to their heads. they make the son sleep with his mother. if it is a daughter and father, they do the same thing. some nights papa sleeps at his brother's, uncle pressoir's house. uncle pressoir sleeps at our house, just in case they come. that way papa will never be forced to lie down in bed with me ... we know a girl who had a child by her father that way. (12)**

The lack of capitalization and the bold font differentiate the girl's letters from the boy's. Although the story notes that she has not yet had access to the same level of education that he has, it is most striking to see her "I" uncapitalized—perhaps suggesting a still developing sense of herself and her identity. Despite her young age and nascent sense of self, she and her family are exposed to ineffable violence that is designed to produce the maximum psychological, emotional, and sexual trauma. Forcing incestuous rape on a family unit not only has a traumatic impact on the individuals involved but is also destructive to relationships. The family member committing the violence has no choice in the matter and is forced into the position of sexual abuser. His actions, however, still pervert the bonds of familial love through the brutality he involuntarily commits. This imposed incest is echoed by the story the boy tells of Célianne, a young pregnant woman aboard the raft. Soldiers holding a gun to her brother's head force him to be intimate with his mother. He refuses, but eventually "Lionel did as his mother told him, crying as the soldiers laughed at him, pressing the gun barrels farther and farther into his neck . . . Afterwards, the soldiers tied up Lionel and their mother, then they each took turns raping Célianne. When they were done, they arrested Lionel, accusing him of moral crimes" (23–24). Taken together, these examples illustrate a pattern of unspeakable (but nevertheless written about) violence coldly calculated to have a long-lasting impact both on individual psyches and the bonds between families.

Further, rape is a particularly gendered type of violence that is intended to leave the recipient scarred emotionally, physically, and psychologically. The ultimate goal of rape is to divest women of their power (Jean-Charles, "Beneath the Layers of Violence" 247). Edwidge Danticat illustrates this in her novel *Breath, Eyes, Memory* (1994), the coming-of-age story of a Haitian American girl born as the result of sexual violence during the Duvalier era. Sophie pieces together the story of her violent origins and works through her complicated relationship to her family, sexuality, and Haiti itself. Sophie does not know her father, and it is foreshadowed early on in the novel that she does not resemble her mother. Readers discover that Sophie is the product of Martine's sexual assault: "A man grabbed me from the side of the road, pulled me into a cane field, and put you in my body . . . I did not know this man. I never saw his face. He had it covered when he did this to me. But now when I look at your face I think it is true what they say. A child out of wedlock always looks like its father" (59). Sophie later reveals her understanding that her father "might have been a Macoute" (137). As with the forced incest described above, this sexual violence has the effect of skewing family relations, in addition to the traumatic impact on the individuals. Martine has difficulty looking at her daughter's face without recalling her experience of violence. Martine promulgates this violent history through the virginity testing to which she subjects her daughter, as all the women in her family before her have likewise undergone, connecting to intergenerational experiences of violence.[35] Danticat was able to name the *tonton macoutes* and describe their actions in an overt way that would have been impossible for Chauvet and her necessarily cloaked setting. Through her more direct aesthetic approach and the candidness enabled by the later time in which she was writing, Danticat was able to provide more straightforward representations of the malicious violence of the *macoutes*. Moreover, her portrayal of the intergenerational impact of this violence connects to the cyclical nature of hatred and violence in Marie Chauvet's twentieth-century Haiti.

Further, the surveillance inherited from the Code Noir exposes the centrality of the communal fear of a scandal and intergenerational sexual violence, but also the interrelation between racial categorization and the cycles of violence. While I am interested in Chauvet's portrayal of the relationships between characters depicted in the novella as Black, *Mulâtre-Aristocrate*, and White, I analyze this aspect of the text while keeping in mind the social construction of race and acknowledging the complicated history of race in Haiti. Due to the more fluid conception of race in the Caribbean that resulted from the succession of dominant European cultures in that space, including the Mediterranean cultures of France and Spain, a biracial race in Haiti "represents historically a class of racialized identity that is neither black nor white but distinct" (R. Saldívar 104–5). Haiti's racial system is closer to that found in Louisiana before the Louisiana Purchase: a three-tiered system with an elite, light-skinned biracial class functioning as a separate racial group, further evidence of structural similarities linking the circum-Caribbean.[36]

Marlene Daut encourages scholars writing about Haiti not to essentialize groups recognized as "black" and "mulatto," since they were not monolithic and the use of these terms reflects the desire to classify "in the colonialist logic of 'racial' determinacy itself" (21), in effect reproducing "the same colonialist framework" (19). A Haitian saying helps to illustrate this point: "A rich black man is a mulatto, a poor mulatto is black" (Wucker 34). The social groups broadly depicted in the novella as a light-skinned upper class or a dark-skinned lower class were more fluid than is often recognized. For example, Claire's categorization as a *Mulâtress-Aristocrate* is a socially constructed racial and class position determined relationally, and in her case, this positioning diverges from her skin color, illuminating the complications of such classifications.[37] Her skin color (Black) conflicts with her racial group and class (*Mulâtress-Aristocrate*), which accounts in large part for her alienation and fragmented identity.

Not only racial formations but also their accompanying prejudices differ between cultures and societies, and the racism portrayed by Chauvet in *Love* is specifically that of a distinct light-skinned upper-class racial group toward a darker-skinned lower-class group. The racism depicted in the novella differs from the racism traditionally seen in certain regions of the United States, where race adheres to the strict binary division "built on the polar categories of 'black' and 'white,' with American Indians and Asian immigrants occupying a place outside of that central duality" (Hodes, "The Mercurial Nature and Abiding Power of Race" 88).[38] The antipathy of the *Mulâtres-Aristocrates* toward the Black individuals would be characterized as colorism in a binary system; however, given that this group functions as a distinct race in Haiti, here it is racism.

Chauvet's novella depicts hostility between the formerly elite *Mulâtres-Aristocrates* and the primarily dark-skinned military group represented by Commandant Calédu. However, these groupings should be seen more accurately as a complex combination of race, class, color, profession, and other societal factors, following a more intersectional understanding of social identities and overlapping forms of oppression. Early in Haiti's history, Jean-Jacques Dessalines "decreed that all Haitians would 'henceforth only be known generically as blacks'" (Dubois 43), regardless of color or heritage. This decree attempted to make Blackness "unmarked, normative, and dominant"; erase the idea of skin color; and "deny that divisions based on outward appearance can any longer exist in Haiti" (Daut 128). Nevertheless, divisions within Haitian society remained, and "Haiti's independence was built on racial, cultural, and gendered separation" (Garrigus, "Race, Gender and Virtue" 89). Some scholars, such as David Nicholls, have interpreted many of the conflicts in Haitian history as resulting from a divide between "a mulatto, city-based, commercial elite, and a black, rural and military elite," a separation that developed from the caste distinctions of the colonial era (Nicholls 8). Others, however, such as Daut, argue that it was not always clear who would have been classified as "mulatto" and who as "black" (21), understanding the divisions to be based less on essentialist racial groups. Class and race have historically been entwined in Haitian society.[39] Moreover, understandings of race and class in Haiti are fluid—constructed and reconstructed over time. However, while conceptions of race changed from the colonial era into the post-/neocolonial period, certain patterns and relationships remained.[40]

Indeed, the racism between the Black and light-skinned biracial groups is interwoven with classism in the novella, as in general both the White and biracial races compose the upper class in Haiti, while the Black race remains impoverished.[41] Throughout most of Haitian history, the *Mulâtres-Aristocrates* have been able to "concentrate a great deal of the country's wealth and a disproportionate share of the country's political power," but in *Love* this position is endangered by the rise of a movement based on Black power (Bell par. 4).[42] Thus, in the novel, the *Mulâtres-Aristocrates* have aligned themselves with White society and harbor racist feelings toward the Black characters. For example, the Clamont family is pleased by Félicia's decision to marry Jean Luze, a White Frenchman, but balks at Annette's engagement to Paul Trudor, a Black Haitian. As a result of the racial stratification in this community and the status of Paul's nouveau riche family, this reaction encompasses both racism and classism, which are intimately related in Haitian society and at times indistinguishable.

The Europeans are portrayed as returning the affection of the *Mulâtres-Aristocrates* in the novella, and according to Mme Camuse, another family friend of the Clamonts, this circle of fondness stemmed from the colonial period: "Les Européens nous adorent. Il paraît que du temps de la Colonie, les Français délaissaient leurs femmes pour les belles mulâtresses" (114), or "The Europeans adore us. I've heard that back in colonial times, Frenchmen deserted their wives for the beautiful mulatto girls" (79). Mme Camuse's statement about the White colonizers' preference for "mulatto girls" should not be dismissed as mere arrogance but is supported by Patricia Mohammed's scholarship examining the position of the biracial woman as desired in Jamaica and the broader Caribbean. Through her reading of various historical documents and texts, such as Michael Scott's *Tom Cringle's Log* (1833) and the diary of Lady Nugent (written between 1801 and 1805 and published in 1966), Mohammed confirms "the elevated position" biracial women attained compared with Black women in some Caribbean slave societies (30). Mohammed asserts that "the conditions of the past ... may have influenced ideas and constructions of desire" in these spaces, which she traces back to the colonial period (24).

Moreover, according to Martha Hodes, White people generally treated both biracial women and men better than Black people in the British Caribbean, since "it was in their interest as a numerical minority to keep colored [or biracial] people on their side" (Hodes, "Mercurial Nature and Abiding Power of Race" 96). Therefore, while they were not ultimately considered equals by the White population, "a well-to-do, educated, and mostly light-skinned faction among the colored classes [such as the *Mulâtres-Aristocrates* in Haiti and Creoles of color in Louisiana] allied itself with whites and was permitted entry into white society" (Hodes, "Mercurial Nature and Abiding Power of Race" 96). The elevation of Whiteness in this way retained its associations with power, prestige, and protected capital. Hodes's research supports the fact that upper-class biracial men, along with the "desired" biracial women, were treated with a certain amount of respect by the White race, which was absent from their interactions with those who present as racially Black. If we extrapolate from the British to formerly French Caribbean spaces like Haiti, then this may account for Mme Camuse's musings about the colonial period. By treating biracial individuals as allies, White people prevented the Black lower class and biracial upper class from banding together against the White upper class, as occurred during the Haitian Revolution. Although the *Mulâtres-Aristocrates* and the White former colonizers are depicted engaging in romantic and business relationships together in the novella, the *Mulâtres-Aristocrates* are resistant to allow families historically positioned as Black into their circle.

As a dark-skinned member of the *Mulâtres-Aristocrates*, Claire has a unique perspective in relation to the racism and classism of her society: she both exhibits biases against the Black characters and internalizes the racism to which she is exposed. While racism and classism are intertwined in Haitian society, I will focus more specifically on racism and its overt depiction in Claire's narration. Epithets, such as "ces nègres imbéciles" (31), or "these black imbeciles" (18) and "cette affreuse petite négresse" (48), or "that awful little negress" (30), are used without a second thought by Claire and the other women of her class. Félicia's reaction to her sister Annette's engagement illustrates the ingrained nature of racism in this society:

>   --Un nègre! Un nègre dans notre famille. Et l'un des derniers! Tu t'en rends compte?
>   --Mon Dieu! a fait Jean Luze en lui mettant avec indulgence la main sur les cheveux, il n'y a pas de quoi faire un drame.
>   --Ce n'est pas tellement la couleur de sa peau que je lui reproche, mais sa vulgarité, et surtout, d'être le fils de son père . . . a-t-elle bégayé, un peu honteuse d'elle-même. (104)

or

>   "A black man! A black man in our family. And one of the lowest sort! Can you believe this?"
>   "My God!" Jean Luze said, stroking her hair indulgently, "there is no need to get worked up about this."
>   "It's not so much the color of his skin that I mind, but his vulgarity and especially his father," she stammered, a little ashamed of herself. (71)

In this example, Félicia is clearly dismayed at the thought of allowing a Black man into her family, but her racism is mitigated by her White husband who insists that it is of little consequence, resulting in her feeling vaguely ashamed. While Félicia claims that her reaction relates to class after detecting her husband's disapproval of her attitude, her more tempered response does little to mask the fact that it was Paul's Blackness and not his nouveau riche status that precipitated her initial reaction. Jean Luze's reply to his wife's overt racism reflects the antipathy between the Black and biracial races in the novella. The heightened hostility between the Black and biracial races may remain from the inferiority complex imposed by colonialism, which caused colonized peoples to simultaneously reject and unconsciously internalize what they had been told about their own moral, intellectual, and physical failings (Munro, "Hatred Chérie" 163). Claire exemplifies the belief that "even if [the colonized] manifest an outward contempt for the oppressor, they nurture at the same time an impregnable core of antipathy toward themselves and 'their people'" (Munro, "Hatred Chérie" 163). This self-hatred and antipathy toward shared ancestry is observable in the relations between the biracial and Black racial groups in the novella and differentiates the racism found in *Love* from other forms, such as that of the former plantocracy against the Black and biracial populations in the US South, as depicted in the works of Faulkner and Gaines.

The racism portrayed in the novella remains from the colonial era and endures in the post-/neocolonial period in which the *Mulâtres-Aristocrates* took over, leaving the same hierarchical system in place. The racism of Félicia and her sisters is positioned as something that they inherited from their parents, along with their house and servants. At one point Félicia notes "que [elle] n'avai[t] jamais vu de noirs à la table de [s]es parents" (169), or "that [she] had never seen blacks at [her] parents' table" (119), to which Dr. Audier responds that the same was true for the Camuses, the Duclans, the Soubirans, and all the members of their class. Another example of this form of racism and its consequences is seen in Claire's memories of her father, Henri Clamont, and his interactions with the peasants who worked on his coffee plantation and who both feared and respected him. Henri's relationship to his coffee workers is more complex than the relationship between a White enslaver and the enslaved: he has ties both to the White enslaver class and the enslaved community. However, as on slave plantations or in the occupation-era corvée, forced labor for public works projects, the peasants in the novella work hard but are still unable to earn enough food to ease the hunger of their families, such as in the case of Louisor. In contrast, Henri and the other coffee plantation owners enjoy a life of luxury and opulence beyond the basics.⁴³

Henri Clamont's opinion that the Black laboring class lacks discipline elucidates this comparison between himself and a White enslaver: "C'est une race indisciplinée que la nôtre, et notre sang d'anciens esclaves réclame le fouet, comme disait feu mon père . . . Dites-moi, croirez-vous, si vous ne me connaissiez pas de longue date, que j'ai du sang noir dans le veines? Cela signifie que mon sang noir à moi est en voie de régression et que j'ai hérité certaines qualités qui vont lui faire défaut à elle, si je ne la corrige pas" (129–30), or "Ours is a race lacking discipline and our old slave blood requires the lash, as my late father used to say . . . Tell me, if you hadn't known me for so long, would you have believed that I have black blood in my veins? This means that my own black blood has been reabsorbed and that I inherited certain traits that will blemish [Claire] unless I correct her" (90). Henri subscribes to the White supremacist mentality lingering from the colonial to the neocolonial period and believes that Blacks, including his ancestors, inherently want for willpower, which justifies the former enslavers' use of the lash. At the same time, he recognizes that his disdain for the dark-skinned working class encompasses a self-hatred, since, in his mind, a mixture of "black and white blood" flows through his own veins—although of course all blood is red.

Nevertheless, Henri exploits his connection to the culture of the formerly enslaved Haitians to his advantage. He performs "*points vaudous*" (146) or "voodoo spells" and appears to serve his grandmother's loas—Vodou gods or deities in Haitian Kreyòl—in order to make the workers on his coffee plantation afraid to steal from him (103).⁴⁴ This manipulative use of Vodou also recalls François Duvalier's exploitation of *noirisme*, his distortion of concepts like negritude and pan-Africanism in order to win the support of peasant and Vodou communities and rise to power (Chancy, *From Sugar to Revolution* 66).⁴⁵ Duvalier used *noirisme*, or "the psychological game [he] played with colour" as a tool for widespread control (Chancy, *From Sugar to Revolution* 118), which is mirrored by Henri's interactions with the workers. Danticat explains that Duvalier was not interested in celebrating African culture, or he would have done so alongside other cultures, but *noirisme* served his intensions of "divide and conquer" (*From Sugar to Revolution* 119). Duvalier abused this cultural affirmation of Blackness to exacerbate the divisions between Haitians and centralize his authority. In a similar way, Henri uses the blood he believes he inherited from White enslavers to validate his intimidation of his workers, drawing on both his connections to the former enslaver and enslaved communities to achieve the same purpose: the preservation of colonial hierarchies.

In Henri's opinion, as a light-skinned *Mulâtre-Aristocrate*, his "black blood" has been "reabsorbed," and consequently his daughter, a dark-skinned *Mulâtress-Aristocrate*, must work harder to remain unblemished by her inherited "black blood." Henri watches Claire closely and punishes her for such things as the ink blots in her notebook: she would kneel "à quelques pas de [s]on père, les bras croisés et la tête droite" (123), or "with arms crossed, chin up, next to [her] father" until he told her to get up, but the torment would last longer if she cried (85).[46] When repeating her lessons, Henri would pinch his daughter's ear "à la moindre erreur à la faire saigner" (122), or "hard enough to draw blood for the smallest error" (84). This behavior reveals the "extent to which [Henri] has internalized racial self-hatred [that] is shown in the abuse he inflicts on his own daughter; he literally wants to beat the blackness out of her to try to correct this regression" (Walcott-Hackshaw 47). Henri's self-hatred resulting from his White supremacist beliefs extends to his daughter, who despite her name, Claire (which ironically means "clear" or "light" in French), symbolizes the return of the repressed: the Blackness of his ancestors. While both this biracial racism and White racism are about blood—the White fear of "miscegenation" stems from a fear of the contaminating qualities of "black blood" originating in the colonial era—the difference is that Henri's racism turns him against the blood he considers to be running through his own veins.

In addition to ideas about the corrupting features of blood, colonialism institutionalized the belief that black skin is inferior to white or light skin, as "the division of human society in this way [by skin color] is inextricable from the need of colonialist powers to justify the imperial enterprise" (Ashcroft, Griffiths, and Tiffin 198). Despite her propensity for using phrases such as "these black imbeciles," Claire recognizes the connection between the current state of her nation and the overvaluation of light skin resulting from the ideologies left in place from the French colonial era, such as Whiteness as economic, political, and social capital. She states in the beginning of the novel: "Par quel miracle ce pauvre peuple a-t-il pu pendant si longtemps rester bon, inoffensif, hospitalier et gai malgré sa misère, malgré les injustices et les préjugés sociaux, malgré nos multiples guerres civiles? Nous nous exerçons à nous entr'égorger depuis l'Indépendance . . . C'est un héritage colonial auquel nous nous cramponnons, comme au français" (17), or "By what miracle has this poor nation managed to stay so good, so welcoming, so joyful for so long, despite its poverty, despite injustice, prejudice, and our many civil wars? We have been practicing at cutting each other's throats since Independence ... It's a colonial legacy to which we cling, just as we cling to the French" (7–8).⁴⁷ As Claire herself observes, the racist hierarchical structures which continue to govern Haitian society—pitting racial and class groups against each other and developing feelings of inferiority and hatred against one's own blood—were not only inherited from the colonial oppressors but have remained in place since independence, due in part to outside influence.

Racial prejudice is positioned as "*démodés*" (27) or "out of fashion" (15) in the Clamont household. Although these biases are censured by Jean Luze—who is both an outsider and a White Frenchman—they nevertheless endure, as is shown by Félicia's reaction to Annette and Paul's engagement. From the outset, Claire introduces readers to Calédu as "un nègre féroce" (17), or "a ferocious black man" (8), which demonstrates her racism through the language she chooses; "ferocious" carries with it animalistic connotations, at the same time that it accurately depicts Calédu's cruelty. Sympathy for the formerly subjugated Black lower class is obscured by the fact that the individuals who are in control in the novella are portrayed as violent criminals, such as Commandant Calédu, or corrupt social climbers, such as Paul Trudor and his family.⁴⁸ Jean Luze argues that Calédu's situation would be sympathetic to an outsider had he not abused the power he holds over his community: "Je regrette les crimes du commandant ... parce qu'autrement, il me deviendrait sympathique. De toute manière, il s'est fait le représentant de la haine et de la violence et aucun honnête homme ne peut se permettre de l'absoudre" (169), or "Too bad the commandant is a criminal ... because otherwise I might sympathize with him. In any case, he has made himself the representative of hatred and violence and no honest man could agree to absolve him" (120). As Jean Luze demonstrates, the compassion felt toward darker-skinned members of the community—symbolized by Calédu, the novel's central Black figure—while not entirely erased, is tempered by the violence and corruption of the individuals presently in power, as well as their prejudices against the *Mulâtres-Aristocrates*. Thus, Chauvet plays with stereotypes in a complicated way: the correlation of Blackness with criminality is one of the foundations of racism, yet the charge of immoral behavior is nevertheless warranted in the specific case of Calédu and his corrupt upstarts.⁴⁹

The fixation on the intersection of race and sexuality, seen in the policing inherited from the Code Noir, Calédu's sexual violence toward *Mulâtresses-Aristocrates*, and the multifaceted racisms of the community, manifests in a fourth way in Marie Chauvet's depiction of Haiti: the use of stereotypes to marginalize and control women and those lower on the racial hierarchies.

The use of this rhetorical device within the text serves to critique the predominance of stereotypes in Claire's society and the prejudices that produce them. Racial and sexual stereotypes—both acknowledged and subverted by the novella—may also be traced back to Haiti's colonial past and are another attempt to control or confine the sexuality of others. Sexual stereotypes, such as White women as cold or repressed and Black men as virulent, are evoked in revealing ways. The novella seems to affirm these stereotypes at the same time that it subverts them. For example, as has been mentioned before, sympathy for the Black class presently in power, symbolized by Calédu, is assuaged by his portrayal as a violent rapist who targets biracial women, aligning him cross-culturally with the myth of the Black rapist prevalent in the United States during the same period.[50] Further, Annette portrays her Black husband, Paul, in a predominantly sexual manner. When asked by Félicia if Paul is a good husband, Annette replies that he is a good lover: "C'est un nègre et il sait prendre une femme. Il est si fougueux qu'il n'aurait qu'à effleurer ta main pour te désirer" (182), or "He's a black man and he knows how to take a woman. He is so passionate that all he would have to do is brush against your hand to desire you" (129). Annette depicts Paul not only as a primarily sexual being but, in accordance with the stereotypes, as unable to control his own desires and arousal. Along the same lines, Félicia, whose skin is lighter than Claire's, is described by the latter as "trop blanche, trop blonde, trop tiède et mesurée" (21), or "too white, too blond, too lukewarm, too orderly," as if the fact that she is too lukewarm directly results from her Whiteness (11).

At the same time that the text seemingly affirms these racial and sexual stereotypes, it also undoes them through the portrayals of Annette and Claire. As the lighter of the two, Annette is depicted as passionate and promiscuous, while Claire, darker than both of her sisters, hides her passion to the extent that she is sexually repressed. Although the characterization of light-skinned Annette subverts the figure of the "promiscuous Black woman," at the same time, it affirms another stereotype with Haitian origins, the "tropical temptress," or biracial woman who "corrupted white men with highly developed sexual skills" (Garrigus, "Race, Gender and Virtue" 77)—evidence of the complicated ways in which Chauvet plays with both racial and sexual stereotypes in the novel. The "tropical temptress" stereotype traces back to the eighteenth century when "almost all Frenchmen who came to make fortunes in [the French colony of] Saint-Domingue took women of color as concubines" with colonial elites growing "alarmed at the power these brown and black women had over white men" (Garrigus, "Race, Gender and Virtue" 77). During this period Whites stressed the ways in which *ménagères*, or free women of color who worked as housekeepers on plantations, manipulated their French employers, leading to the specifically Haitian stereotype of the "manipulative *ménagère*," the precursor to the "tropical temptress" (Garrigus, *Before Haiti* 57). Emily Clark describes a *ménagère* as "a free woman of color who had managed a white bachelor's household and frequently became his life partner" (59), a detail which does not correlate with Annette's position in the family or the reality of Claire's family situation but more so with her fantasy of replacing Félicia in the lives of Jean Luze and Jean-Claude. Further, Claire's position as the caretaker of the household also connects her with the "manipulative *ménagère*" figure through the control she wields in the home and her attempts to influence the sexual liaisons that occur in that space. For instance, she refers to herself as "directing" (6) ["je les manœuvre" (15)] the interactions between Annette and Jean Luze and notes the pride she takes in being "an impeccable housekeeper" (58) ["une maîtresse de maison impeccable" (85)].[51] While Claire can be read as a version of the "manipulative *ménagère*," Annette represents the "tropical temptress," who attempts to use her sexuality to manipulate a Frenchman into sleeping with her. As Annette ultimately fails to seduce Jean Luze away from his wife and marries a Black man, upon second glance, her character challenges the stereotype of the "tropical temptress" at the same time that it acknowledges it.

Additionally, Claire may seem to occupy the role of another stereotyped figure, the "tragic mulatto," common to literature published in the US and France.[52] The "tragic mulatto" was a popular and typically "white invention and literary vehicle," which allowed White readers to sympathize with heroines closer to themselves in appearance, while at the same time the tragic outcome supported the belief that the mixture of races is a curse (Sollors 225). Although there is much tragedy in Claire's life, in part resulting from the discrepancy between her skin color and social position, she challenges the "tragic mulatto" stereotype. She does this through the depth of her character (the "tragic mulatto" in literature usually lacked individuality and psychological depth and was "quickly and recognizably sketched and given only a few memorable traits"), her darker skin (the stereotype tended to be nearly White in appearance), and the action she takes at the end of the novella (Sollors 228). Thus, like Gaines's heroines, Catherine Carmier and Mary Agnes Lefebvre across the gulf in Louisiana, Claire acts against the typical use of the "tragic mulatto" as a determinist concept (Sollors 228). As opposed to passively watching the tragedy of her story unfold, Claire takes control over her fate through her final action that concludes the novella: her stabbing of Calédu. Therefore, in addition to her use of the "promiscuous black woman" and "sexually repressed white woman," Chauvet plays with other stereotypic figures, such as the "tropical temptress," "*ménagère*," and "tragic mulatto" through her characterizations of Claire and Annette.[53] Chauvet's novella uses these literary vehicles to both evoke and critique the cultural work of stereotypes, but ultimately they emphasize the characters' existence as distinct and multifaceted individuals.

The text may seem contradictory in the way that it both affirms sexual stereotypes, such as the "asexual White woman," the "promiscuous Black woman," and the "virulent Black man," through its portrayal of Félicia and Paul and undermines them through the depiction of Claire and Annette. However, it is important to note that these stereotypes are confirmed not by characters' behavior but by their descriptions of others. For example, through the ways in which they act, Claire and Annette unknowingly undermine the stereotypes, while through their words and own racist views of Paul and Félicia, the two women support them. Through the stereotypic descriptions given by Claire and Annette, Chauvet depicts her characters as prejudiced, as opposed to representing the stereotypes themselves as realistic. Claire's narration seemingly promotes but ultimately subverts stereotypic associations developed to reify colonial hierarchies.[54] Claire and Annette verbally affirm the stereotypes, while at the same time undoing them through their own behavior, which positions the stereotypes along with the characters' racism and the hierarchies themselves as an inheritance from the colonial period. The all-encompassing aspect of this inheritance becomes even more visible when considering not only the characters' views of each other but also of themselves, for example Claire's internalization of her society's racism and the fragmentation of her subjectivity that results.

In addition to *Love*'s critique of racism, sexism, hatred, and violence on the broader scale of the community—shown by Claire's society's self-policing, race and class stratification, sexual violence, and use of racial and sexual stereotypes—Chauvet's novella also depicts the efforts to control sexuality and behavior at the level of the individual, as depicted through the portrayal of Claire's past and present. As previously described, the aesthetics focus on the individual to reflect the collective. Claire internalizes the racism of her father toward his own Black ancestry and, as a result, interrogates her position in the family. After overhearing her father discuss his desire to "correct" the traits she supposedly inherited along with her dark skin, Claire begins to question her race: "Je fixai avec étonnement mes bras foncés posés sur les draps. Étais-je bien leur fille? Non, ce n'était pas possible. Comment pourrais-je être la fille de ces deux blancs?" (130), or "I stared with astonishment at my dark arms resting on the sheets. Was I really their daughter? No, it did not seem possible. How could I be the daughter of two whites?"

(90). Young Claire's labeling of her *Mulâtre-Aristocrate* parents as "whites" is noteworthy, underscoring the group's positioning as closer to White on the class and color spectrums. Claire's racism toward herself and its effect on her subjectivity, relationships with others, and sexuality show the negative effects of hierarchical mentalities and their impact on an individual scale.

In spite of her light-skinned parents and position as a member of the *Mulâtres-Aristocrates*, Claire has dark skin and has been identified as Black by others since her childhood, illustrating the conflict between her class, race, and color. Claire is referred to as Black by a young servant who tells her, "Noire, tu es noire comme moi . . . et je te prendrai pour femme lorsque je serai grand" (130), or "Black, you're black like me . . . and when I am bigger I will marry you" (91); Alcius who says to her father, "c'est une bien belle négresse que vous avez là" (132), or "that's one beautiful black girl you got there" (92); and young Félicia who innocently asks, "Pourquoi Claire est noire, maman?" (140), or "Why is Claire black, Mama?" (98). In response to the latter exchange between Félicia and her parents, Claire states: "Et je me mis à haïr l'aïeule dont le sang noir s'était sournoisement glissé dans mes veines après tant de générations" (140), or "And I began to loathe the forebear whose black blood had slyly flowed into my veins after so many generations" (98). Although her class positions her alongside the other members of her family as a *Mulâtress-Aristocrate*, due to the dark hue of her skin, Claire follows her father's example and turns the racism of her class inward against herself, which both Dr. Audier and Claire herself refer to as her "complexes" (126). Dr. Audier states in conversation with Jean Luze: "que pendant longtemps Claire a souffert de n'être pas à l'égale de ses sœurs, blanche et rose comme un lis" (115), or "for a long time Claire had a complex about not being her sisters' equal, about not being as white and pink as a lily" (79–80).

Claire pulls away from suitors, such as Frantz Camuse, literally and figuratively as a result of "le contraste de nos mains réunies" (141), or "the contrast between [their] joined hands" (99). Later a French officer refers to Claire as "une déesse noire" (150), or "a black goddess," (105) and "la plus jolie noire qu'il eût jamais vue" (150), or "the prettiest black girl he had ever seen" (106), highlighting not only her beauty but also her dark skin. Although part of her appeal to the French officer appears to be her dark hue, both Frantz and the officer are attracted to Claire. She, however, ignores their attentions, believing their flattery and interest to be only owing to her social position; in this way she polices herself, avoiding relationships that cross the lines of color. In her own words: "pendant trop longtemps je m'étais appliquée à tromper les autres sur mon compte et, sous mon masque distant, je continuais à brûler en silence comme une torche" (22), or "I was too practiced in the art of deception, and behind my mask of detachment, I burned in silence like a torch" (11). The eligible bachelors in Claire's town are initially drawn to her and attempt to pursue her, while she gives no indication of her reciprocal interest. Her aloof manner is responsible for her unmarried status, as opposed to the color of her skin.

Claire doubts herself in social situations, as is shown in the previous examples, in part due to her internalization of the racist views of her class. As a consequence of the conflict between her color and racial/class group, as well as the political chaos and violence experienced by her nation, Claire becomes alienated from herself and others, resulting in the fragmentation of her subjectivity, which Hellen Lee-Keller has gone so far as to label her "madness" (1297).[55] While I am unconvinced of Claire's identity as a "madwoman," as opposed to her propensity to commit irrational acts or behave eccentrically, I agree with Lee-Keller that Claire experiences alienation and a fragmented subjectivity due to the contradictions between her race, color, and social position and the racism she internalizes.[56] Chauvet's portrayal of the alienation and fragmentation Claire undergoes due to her treatment as a dark-skinned member of the *Mulâtres-Aristocrates* critiques Haiti's racism, continued adherence to social hierarchies, and the psychological violence inflicted by both racism and social stratification on an individual scale.

Along with her skewed relationship to others and society due to her inferiority complex and resulting alienation, Claire's connection to her sexuality is distorted. A mature, virginal woman, Claire represses her sexual desires, which causes her to have an elevated interest in sexuality and motherhood to the extent that she becomes obsessed with her brother-in-law Jean Luze and fantasizes about murdering Félicia in order to replace her in his bed.[57] This fixation on sex is shown through the way it constantly intrudes on her thoughts and her clandestine devouring of romance novels and pornographic postcards (10). Kathleen Renk argues that "sexual deviance in women defined insanity" in the nineteenth century, which may explain critics' inclination to position Claire as a madwoman as a result of this underlying mentality that considers both women and the colonies themselves as prone to madness (Renk 89).[58] While Claire's behavior can be deemed strange, in my opinion, we should not leap to positioning her as insane, as opposed to just lonely and sexually repressed (10).[59]

In addition to her heightened interest in sex and motherhood, Claire's fragmented/alienated subjectivity and her resulting skewed relationship to her sexuality is revealed through both her sexual fascination with and repugnance toward Commandant Calédu, whom she murders in the final pages of the novel.[60] Although Claire hates Calédu, whose own inferiority complex manifests in his sexual abuse of women of the *Mulâtres-Aristocrates*, he appears often in her sexual fantasies: "Et j'ai fermé les yeux pour attirer contre moi un grand corps musclé, noir et nu que je n'ai pas voulu reconnaître" (97), or "I closed my eyes and drew him to me, a naked, big, and black athletic body I did not want to recognize" (66) and "Ce n'est plus lui que je vois mais un autre. Qui? Je n'ose pas comprendre" (101), or "I am no longer seeing him [Jean Luze] but another. Who is it? I don't dare comprehend" (69). Claire is explicit that she hates Calédu and loves Jean Luze, yet the same passionate foundation of visceral emotional response underlies her reactions to both, and at a certain point, hate and attraction may be seen to intersect in Claire's subconscious, exemplified by her dreams.[61] When Claire spies Calédu's "ronde solitaire" (107), or "solitary patrol" (74) beneath her window, she describes it as revealing "ou la haine ou l'amour" (107), or "either love or hate" (74). She does not want to acknowledge the complexity of emotions that could involve a combination of the two.

As a result of her contradictory feelings for Calédu, scholars such as Elizabeth Walcott-Hackshaw and Colin Dayan have convincingly connected Claire (and Rose, the protagonist of *Anger*) to Erzulie, a literary allusion adding another layer to the novella, particularly for Haitian readers. Erzulie is an ambivalent loa who has darker skin (like Claire), often embodies oppositional characteristics, and has been described alternatively as the goddess of love, "Black Venus," "Virgin Mary," or "Mater Dolorosa" (Dayan, "Reading Women in the Caribbean" 239).[62] Erzulie takes forms ranging from "good" Erzulie-Freda to "evil" Erzulie-gé-rouge and from beautiful, young Maitress Erzulie to old Grand Erzulie, dramatizing the separation of women into objects of desire or abhorrence (Dayan, "Reading Women in the Caribbean" 240). In Vodou this dichotomy is dismantled, as is seen through the erotics of Erzulie-Freda, who "takes on the garb of femininity—and even speaks excellent French—in order to discard it" (Dayan, "Reading Women in the Caribbean" 240). Erzulie endorses extremes and subverts binary categorization in the same way that Claire does, for example through Claire's dark skin color and social position as a *Mulâtress-Artistocrate* and her attraction to both White Frenchman Jean Luze and Black military commander Calédu (Dayan, "Reading Women in the Caribbean" 240–1). Claire, as an Erzulie figure, destabilizes a range of other dichotomies, for example through her corrupt yet virginal sexuality, as well as her alternation between passive voyeurism and moments of action. The collapse of conventional binaries is in line with the novella's complicated character portrayals and rejection of easy categorizations. The breakdown of binaries also reflects the complexities of increasing globalization in the post-/neocolonial period in which notions of core versus periphery, First World versus Third World, White versus Black, men versus women, and other similar binaries become more complex, but the mindsets that produce them do not disappear completely.

Further, this combination of opposites structures the final scene of the novel, illustrating the melding of the private with the public and the individual with the collective. Although Claire fantasizes about killing her sister and replacing her in the family unit, she acknowledges that she would never have the courage and considers killing herself instead. These violent, personal impulses, however, culminate in her most overt political act—the stabbing of dictator Calédu. Her compulsion toward more intimate forms of violence against her sister and herself morphs into a critical act of defiance. The personal and political continue to fuse together for Claire: after stabbing Calédu, whom she refuses to recognize in her sexual fantasies, and gently pushing away the other object of her affection, Jean Luze, Claire returns to her bed, her most intimate space. From here, she looks out her window and sees the political revolution she helped to incite. The novella ends with the words "Les portes des maisons sont ouvertes et la ville entière, debout" (219), or "The doors of the houses are open and the entire town has risen" (156). The front doors of the homes, which literally separate the private and public spheres, have been opened, and the individuals merge together collectively, irrespective of social status, to comprise one force. Regardless of the ultimate outcome of this revolution, to which the readers are not privy, it has short-term positive effects for the town: the cessation of the state-sponsored sexual and physical violence of Calédu and the deemphasis of the colonial hierarchies of race, color, class, and gender. The revolution has brought individuals from all levels of society—including White Frenchman Jean Luze, shunned *Mulâtress-Aristocrate* Jane Bavière, rough-hewn intellectual Joël Marti, and "one-armed beggar" Pierrilus (143)—together to rise as one, to borrow from Claire's final characterization.

Therefore, while Claire has strong sexual desires and never acts on them, her journal also hints at her revolutionary impulses, which perhaps she gives way to in the end (again, Claire's motivations are ambiguous, and readers are not granted much clarity through her increasingly frenzied journal). Nevertheless, throughout most of the novella, her "complexes," or sense of her inferiority, in addition to her fear of a scandal, cause her to strictly police her own behavior and in particular her sexuality. Claire chooses to remain repressed and unattached rather than to risk exposing her private desires publicly. Turning her classism and racism toward herself, Claire does not believe she is the equal of her suitors. This depiction of Claire's internalized racism correlates with the novella's broader portrayal of the community's policing, racial stratification, and acceptance of stereotypes. In Chauvet's *Love*, the personal mirrors the collective, underscoring the need for the community to dismantle the tools of colonialism on all levels—for example, through destabilizing reductive hierarchies and disavowing racism and classism, which we see partially and perchance temporarily achieved in the closing scene. Through its interrogation of flat categorizations and the violence that racism perpetuates on individual subjectivities, *Love* critiques the adherence to outmoded ideologies and the effects of international interventions in both the post-US occupation period and the years of the Duvalier dynasty. The novella depicts the persistence of the hierarchies of race, color, class, gender, and sexuality and the complicated ways in which they intersect, but through the ending, the novella leaves space for potential resistance—echoes of Marcus's failed rebellion in *Of Love and Dust* and Charles Bon's possible recuperation by later generations in *Absalom, Absalom! Love*'s closing scene suggests that the recognition of these problems is not enough—revolutionary action and coalitions crossing lines of race, class, color, and gender are needed to break free from the cyclical repetitions of colonial violence and hatred.

Chapter 5

"WE ARE TRAWLING IN SILENCES HERE"

Race, Sexuality, and Unnarratable Histories in Literary Depictions of Dominican Dictatorship

Extending the analyses of the previous chapters, I explore the control over sexuality, structures of policing, and destructive treatment of women in literary depictions of Rafael Leónidas Trujillo Molina's regime, but also link to other nodes in Dominican history—from the US occupation to late twentieth-century diasporic migration, specifically to the US. These connections underscore the shared inheritance of racialized sexual policing, relating the colonial period to the twentieth century across the diverse spaces of the US South, Haiti, and the Dominican Republic. The effects of blind adherence to outmoded colonial hierarchies of race, gender, class, and sexuality shared by these regions persist after the abolition of slavery, after the demise of the plantation system, after the rise of the US as a global power and supposed propagator of democracy abroad, and after the dictatorships of Duvalier and Trujillo in the Caribbean. Thus, the worlds of twentieth-century US democracy with its associated prosperity and Caribbean dictatorships with their presumed poverty and political instability are perhaps not as far apart as those in power would want to showcase.[1]

In the late twentieth century and early twenty-first, the Trujillo dictatorship became an important case study for diasporic novelists situated in the United States. Although the historical context of the events is Hispanophone and the three hyphenated American authors explored here are writing primarily in English, they are invested in the history of the Dominican Republic and their inherited relation to this space.[2] In this way, the positions of the writers themselves illustrate the interconnected histories of the US and Caribbean. The connections between the spaces depicted in the novels, such as violence, racism, and sexual abuse, underscore the shared histories of slavery and colonialism linking Hispaniola to the United States. More specifically, the novels by Junot Díaz, Julia Alvarez, and Nelly Rosario demonstrate how the plantation systems of policing and sexual control examined previously are refracted through the structures of power and privilege generated under dictatorship.

The narrator of Junot Díaz's *The Brief Wondrous Life of Oscar Wao* (2007), Yunior de Las Casas, has complete control over the material presented in the novel, similar to Jim Kelly in Gaines's *Of Love and Dust*, described in chapter 3. He is the only character who speaks directly to readers, and all of the information we have access to first comes through him. In an interview with Katherine Miranda, Díaz states that as a result of this, you can draw a direct line from Dominican dictator Rafael Leónidas Trujillo Molina, in power from 1930 to 1961, to Yunior in Dominican society: "What's ironic is that Trujillo is this horror in the book, but readers don't even recognize that the person telling them the story is Trujillo with a different mask" (36).[3] By positioning the narrator, Yunior, whose colloquial voice, despite his other failings, succeeds in drawing the reader in, as "Trujillo with a different mask," Díaz signals his intensions to use narrative techniques to convey something important about the particular histories with which the novel engages.

Alongside Díaz's novel, I position Julia Alvarez's *In the Time of the Butterflies* (1995) and Nelly Rosario's *Song of the Water Saints* (2002) as historically based fiction that documents the unknowable, yet simultaneously narratable, nature of histories. These writers approach history through literature, using devices such as a dictatorial narrator in the attempt to represent the specifics of a certain time and place.[4] Díaz, Alvarez, and Rosario use the history of the Dominican Republic in the twentieth century—a personal, embodied, traumatic history—and by extension the US in the same period to both position readers as witnesses to the racism, violence, and sexual exploitation of this brutal era and to comment on the nature of History more broadly.[5] I use the term *capital-h-History* to refer to official written accounts of the past, and *history* or *histories* to refer to the events and occurrences of the past, the totality of which can never be fully captured by written texts. While accounts of History are always subjective and incomplete, written records nevertheless validate the experiences of others. Each novel approaches the unspeakable violence of history in a different manner, yet all transmit something unsayable in the past to future generations.

While the past is ultimately unknowable, writers attempt to narrate histories of unspeakable pain: the project of these novels is to attempt to communicate the incomprehensible—what cannot be narrated—through gaps, silences, and palimpsests. Trauma is defined as an event "whose violent singularity overwhelms the psyche's capacity to assimilate or represent it" (Stringer 67). Nevertheless, the unrepresentability of a traumatic experience does not negate the healing potential in speaking, writing, and sharing stories. Narratives of trauma allow the healing subjects to "reconstruct themselves as empowered survivors" and also to connect with others in their communities, replacing their isolation with networks of support (Morgan and Youssef 210). In terms of representing trauma, Dominick LaCapra notes the paradox that "one disorientingly feels what one cannot represent; one numbingly represents what one cannot feel" (42). This paradox reflects what I intend to denote through the idea that traumatic histories are simultaneously narratable and unnarratable. Audrey Small has written about this tension in relation to narratives of the 1994 Rwandan genocide, referring to genocide as "ultimately unthinkable, unspeakable, and certainly unrepresentable," yet in this instance it was still spoken and written about shortly after the event (Small 2).[6] Following Paula Morgan and Valerie Youssef's belief that narrative can function as a palliative and that "major therapeutic intervention resides in the ability to speak one's pain in the face of traumatic events which stun individuals and peoples into silence" (222), I argue that writing or sharing one's experience with a community can help one come to terms with a traumatic experience or, in the case of the novels explored here, broader traumatic histories. In this literature, gaps, blankness, absent-presences, fragmentation, and other experimental techniques can represent the repressed or the unsayable, which has the effect of both expanding understanding of this history, as well as perchance healing the damage it has wrought.

Writing about these histories enables Alvarez, Díaz, and Rosario to both confront and spread awareness about the past—advancing the circum-Caribbean tradition of using literature to represent History, explored throughout this book. From the early twentieth century, William Faulkner employed experimental techniques and forms to critique his culture, society, and historical moment through the substitutions, reversals, and patterns found in his portrayals of intersectional relationships. The structure of the novels simulate the experience of uncovering the resonances of history, blurring the boundary between literature and history. Similarly, the novels by the hemispheric American writers explored in this chapter can be seen as historical recovery projects, as demonstrated through statements by the authors, as well as their chosen narrational strategies in the novels themselves. I argue that History (capital-h-History that centers large-scale events and figures) is incomplete, and histories are ultimately unknowable and untellable. These writers attempt to recount the unrepresentable through the gaps and silences in their fictional accounts, as well as through the use of multiple voices, perspectives, and experiences to illustrate the negative impacts of dictatorship on communities, demonstrating that even though these histories are unnarratable, they nevertheless open themselves up to attempts at representation.

Further, dictatorships are intimately entwined with fictions: they are narrative overlays that are in a sense imposed through seductive storytelling and, at the same time, policed through the use and/or threat of force. Part of the curative potential of these narrative fictions based on Trujillo's regime is that he is contained safely within them. Trujillo cannot reach you from within the novel, posing no direct threat to readers. The novels are fictional reconstructions of his reign and, as a result, create space between the reader and the historical figure, which is heightened by the passage of time, as well as the distancing of place for readers in English-speaking countries like the United States. In this way, these novels can be seen as resisting and reversing the dictator's official narrative, allowing a multiplicity of other voices, experiences, and stories to rise to the surface.

Although using different approaches, Julia Alvarez, Junot Díaz, and Nelly Rosario all wrote historically grounded works of fiction predominately in English in the 1990s and 2000s looking back at the struggles experienced by the Dominican Republic during earlier periods.[7] In terms of the degrees of fiction, Alvarez fictionalizes the experiences of real-world figures, whereas Díaz and Rosario invent the multigenerational histories of two families living before, during, and after Trujillo's reign. Julia Alvarez's *In the Time of the Butterflies* is a fictionalized historical account of the experiences of the Mirabal sisters—Patria, Minerva, and María Teresa—before their untimely deaths, as ordered by dictator Rafael Trujillo in 1960.[8] Both Junot Díaz's *The Brief Wondrous Life of Oscar Wao* and Nelly Rosario's *Song of the Water Saints* span multiple generations of fictional Dominican families to show the widespread effects of the violence of US occupation and neocolonialism, dictatorship, and the diasporic experience, positioning the lives of Dominicans in a hemispheric frame.

Diaspora, often an effect of dictatorship, shapes the novels explored here. To varying extents, they center on both the lives of characters in the Dominican Republic and later generations living in the United States, connecting these spaces as inheritors of racial and sexual policing—the effects of which remain written into each country's infrastructures from democracy to dictatorship. Thus, while they cover a good deal of historical ground, a consideration of these texts together demonstrates the lingering effects of colonial control over sexuality and the intersecting hierarchies of race, color, class, gender, and sexuality not only in the 1930s and 1940s, the focus of the previous chapters, but running throughout the twentieth century and across the hemisphere. In this chapter I build from depictions of democracy and dictatorship in the previous chapters to examine what happens to sexuality under Rafael Trujillo's dictatorship, as illustrated by literature, reading into and between the blank spaces.[9]

For writers representing Trujillo's dictatorship, literature is the only means to make sense of the unreality of these lived realities—perhaps because of the distance it affords. As LaCapra argues, "narratives in fiction may also involve truth claims on a structural or general level by providing insight into phenomena such as slavery or the Holocaust, by offering a reading of a process or period, or by giving at least a plausible 'feel' for experience and emotion which may be difficult to arrive at through restricted documentary methods" (13). Thus, through the nature of the genre, fiction enables writers to engage with traumatic histories in a less restrictive way, incorporating emotions that brim beyond the borders of facts. More specifically, Julia Alvarez writes in the postscript to *In the Time of the Butterflies* that the Trujillo epoch "can only finally be understood by fiction, only finally be redeemed by imagination" (324).[10] For Alvarez, fiction is the only way to provide readers with a sense of life under Trujillo.[11] An aside from the narrator of *The Brief Wondrous Life of Oscar Wao* positions Díaz's understanding of the affordances of fiction similarly: "who can keep track of what's true and what's false in a country as baká as ours" (139).[12] Díaz pushes Alvarez's claim a step further, positioning not only fiction but fantasy specifically as best equipped to recount Trujillo's reign, which he demonstrates through writing in a magical realist mode.[13]

Part of the projects of both novels seems to be spreading awareness of this history among Anglophone readers in the hemisphere more broadly. Alvarez verbalizes this intension directly: she acknowledges that Dominicans may be separated by language from her created world and hopes the book "deepens North Americans' understanding of the nightmare you [Dominicans] endured and the heavy losses you suffered" (324). Directly addressing a US-based audience and centering the present through the investigations of a Dominican American woman, Alvarez might also hold space for the recognition of the enduring colonial ties likewise existing in twentieth-century US society. While some previous historical grounding is helpful, Alvarez provides a solid amount of background information, as demonstrated by the substantial research collected in her papers at the Harry Ransom Center—from clippings of both the Mirabals and Trujillos to Trujillo's *The Basic Policies of a Regime* and the "Anti-Trujillo Pastoral Letter of Dominican Bishops" from January 25, 1960. Similarly, through the inclusion of heavy footnotes, colloquial language, and fictionalized experiences under the dictatorship, Díaz's novel brings readers unfamiliar with Dominican history up to speed, revealing this shared purpose: to educate English-speaking readers in the wider hemisphere about the traumatic history of a fellow American nation, while at the same time leaving space to represent the unknowable nature of history and unspeakable experiences of violence.[14]

In contrast to the historically situated work of Díaz and Alverez, readers of Nelly Rosario's *Song of the Water Saints* are dropped into the US invasion of the Dominican Republic in 1916 with little context. While the novel spans the twentieth century, the events centered by capital-h-History remain in the background and the individual experiences of multiple women emerge in the fore. Similar to the multigenerational structure of *The Brief Wondrous Life of Oscar Wao*, Rosario's novel covers four generations of women and, in this way, is able to consider the Trujillo dictatorship within the broader context of the twentieth century. *Song of the Water Saints* centers the experiences of the women in Graciela's family against a backdrop of occupation, dictatorship, and diaspora—emphasizing colonial continuities extending from the DR to the US. Of the three writers examined here, Rosario confronts the traumatic histories and experiences of her characters most directly through her straightforward style and more candid depictions of violence and sexual abuse. This difference in emphasis illuminates the fact that multiple approaches are necessary to capture the lasting impact of state-sponsored violence on a nation.

In this chapter, I use literature as a means of analyzing the effects of dictatorship on sexuality, gender relations, family formations, and love through exploring each author's approach to capturing these difficult histories. The fragmented, polyvocal novels discussed in this chapter make space for silences, blankness, and repression—confronting the gaps and obfuscation created by the authoritarian narratives imposed from above. I use the term *absent-presence* to denote the felt significance of a substantive gap, where something tangible is perceived in and beyond the blankness. In this way, the writings of Alvarez, Díaz, and Rosario act as correctives and perhaps even palliatives to capital-h-History. Experimental techniques are a means of encapsulating a more inclusive history, containing those aspects often left out of dictatorial narratives and official History, such as institutionalized racism, state-sponsored violence, and sexual exploitation, and thus functioning as resistance to authoritarian accounts.

The novels analyzed in this chapter provide a window into the experiences of Dominicans across the twentieth century in a way that straight historical accounts could not accomplish. As Lynn Chun Ink writes, "History is a tale authorized by those in power, and for this reason, it is always suspect" (799). Each novel relies on experimental formal techniques as an attempt to relate events and experiences as reliably as possible. The novels of Alvarez, Díaz, and Rosario, for instance, incorporate an assortment of voices and experiences—although in Díaz's novel the various voices are mediated by a single narrator.[15] Multiple perspectives and approaches are necessary for a realistic portrayal of any historical event. This chapter follows postcolonial theorists, such as J. Jorge de Alva and Robert J. C. Young, in viewing history not as a linear progression but as "a multiplicity of often conflicting and frequently parallel narratives" (de Alva 245), which are distinct from each other, "products of particular situations and contexts" (Young 10). Ania Loomba positions this strain of postcolonial thought as in line with the post-structuralist understanding that "meaning is always contextual, always shifting" (79). For this literature, it is not that meaning does not exist, but that it is highly contingent on time and place and can only be captured in part from multiple angles. And, of course, the meaning held by the past is always filtered through the lens of the present. In the style of those preceding it, this chapter includes a blend of facts and fictions. I consider historical accounts—for instance, the work of Myriam Chancy, Lauren Derby, Edward Paulino, Milagros Ricourt, and Michele Wucker—alongside an exploration of the textuality of these novels or their engagement with difficult histories through perspective, lacuna, and palimpsests, among other literary techniques. Through centering the work done by these novels in particular, I emphasize that multiple stories, angles, and approaches are needed to unearth the contextual truths buried in History, as well as in our histories.

More specifically, this chapter examines the ways in which the control over sexuality is more overt and expansive under dictatorship, exceeding beyond the rigid confines of circum-Caribbean plantation structures examined in earlier chapters and spanning every level of society. Just as the postbellum US plantation was compared to Foucault's Panopticon, as depicted in the work of Ernest Gaines, Dominican society under Trujillo was under constant surveillance. The stakes for this policing were high for Trujillo, since he drew his power from this unrestricted control, as well as the fear it generated. Comparable to the reach of Haitian dictator François Duvalier, explored in chapter 4, the influence of Rafael Trujillo infamously infiltrated all corners of private lives and experiences through his manipulation of the tensions between race, nationality, and ethnicity, as well as his predatorial sexual control over his subjects. Trujillo maintained his absolute authority through the persistent power granted to colonial ideologies, such as hierarchical relations and the value bestowed on Whiteness. Indeed, society under dictatorship illustrates the culmination of the structures of policing and power, as well as command over the sexuality of others, explored in the previous chapters: this seems a fitting place to conclude the book. Before analyzing the novels' representations of dictatorship in more detail, I first want to situate the literature more fully in terms of the distinct colonial histories and racial formations in Haiti and the Dominican Republic.

While slavery and colonialism took different forms in Haiti and the Dominican Republic, these experiences were common to both nations. Haiti, originally a Spanish colony, was ceded to France in 1697 and became the French colony of Saint-Domingue (Dubois 18) with Santo Domingo, or the present-day Dominican Republic, remaining a Spanish colony until it was occupied by Haiti from 1822 to 1844 (Ricourt 10). Additionally, the two nations have gone through comparable experiences of US occupations and brutal dictatorships with the accompanying impacts on social relationships, sexuality, and family formations. I follow Ian Haney López's definition of race grounded in the intersection of race and law in US society: "the historically contingent social systems of meaning that attach to elements of morphology and ancestry" (*White by Law* 10). This definition is supported by the divergent constructions of race on the two halves of Hispaniola. An intersectional lens reveals that sexuality is entwined with race, gender, class, and other identity categories. As this book is particularly interested in the interrelation of race and sexuality, I consider the differing constructions of race in Haiti and the Dominican Republic and the role specifically played by race in the twentieth-century experiences of the DR, before launching into a discussion of the effects of dictatorship on sexuality as related to race, gender, and class.

The systems of slavery differed in Santo Domingo and Saint-Domingue due to the prevalence of cattle raising in the Spanish part and the predominance of the sugar, indigo, and coffee plantation economies in the French portion, which relied on more intensive slave labor (Ricourt 12).[16] Moreover, the free people of color population, referred to as *castas* in Spanish America (Morelli 143), tended to be larger in the Spanish and Portuguese colonies by 1800 "for the simple reason that slaves were freed at higher rates in Latin America than in the rest of the hemisphere" (Morelli 144). As a result of these factors, the social order in Santo Domingo was less hierarchical, leading to "maximal racial mixture and minimal class differentiation" (Derby, *The Dictator's Seduction* 188). However, the success of Saint-Domingue's sugar production convinced the elites of Santo Domingo that "stronger institutions of control" were needed, leading to reforms by the Spanish Crown in the eighteenth century, such as the first Spanish Black Code (1768) that endeavored to regulate the behavior of enslaved and free Blacks (Paulino 19).[17] The third Spanish Code (1784), known as Código Negro Carolino, reorganized the socioeconomic system (Obregón 6–7) and involved six spheres of racial categorization, which could lead to a generational shift from the classification of "negro" to that of "white" (Chancy, *From Sugar to Revolution* 15). The French Code Noir, on the other hand, listed nine categories of mixed-race offspring and placed more emphasis on the ability to differentiate between them (Chancy, *From Sugar to Revolution* 15).[18] Therefore, the predominant mixed-race population blurred racial lines in Santo Domingo, where "color divisions are still important but moveable" (Wucker 32), while in Saint-Domingue, the main lines separating the Black and biracial elite groups were more entrenched, depending on class as much as color (Wucker 34). In this way, the origins of a bifurcated racial categorization on Hispaniola may be traced back to the French and Spanish colonial periods and their accompanying sets of slave codes in particular.

Further, the US occupations of both spaces played a role in solidifying the constructions of race, in addition to the racialization of Haitians as blacker than Dominicans.[19] Since even before James Monroe's 1823 message to Congress that would become the Monroe Doctrine (Murphy 4), the US has continually interfered in the affairs of other American nations, invading each country of Hispaniola twice in the twentieth century: Haiti in 1915 and 1994 and the Dominican Republic in 1916 and 1965 (Wucker xii).[20] Early in the century, both nations were occupied during overlapping periods—Haiti 1915–1934 and the DR 1916–1924—and the occupations were accompanied by alliances between opposition groups that defied the border (Chancy 59).[21] While cooperation between oppositional forces resulted in a de-emphasis of differences, at the same time, the US military reified any previous distinctions between Haitians and Dominicans.[22] The all-White military force, composed mostly of soldiers from the US South, was accustom to viewing people of color as inferior and brought this mentality to the occupations of both countries (Paulino 35). Additionally, US diplomats saw Haitians as "African and barbarian" and Dominicans as "light skinned and white" (Ricourt 10–11).[23] Colonial racial ideologies and the varying racialization of Haitians and Dominicans during the occupations were both catalysts for the official Dominican racial discourse against Haitians and Blackness that arose under Trujillo's regime (Ricourt 11).[24]

While from the start *Song of the Water Saints* signals that the events of capital-h-History will be secondary to the personal experiences of the protagonists, the novel simultaneously illustrates the negative impact of US intervention on the island. This approach allows Rosario to expose patterns and connections between events throughout the twentieth century. Readers are encouraged not to focus on the occupying US soldiers in the opening scenes, instructed symbolically by young protagonist Graciela who encourages Silvio to concentrate on her and forget "the goddamned yanqui" (8).[25] Rosario's novel engages with History in this way—through the lens of the personal. While foreigners never take center stage in the novel, outside influence detrimental to the Dominican characters lingers in the background. The "yanqui" photographer is an example of this. His relationship with Graciela and Silvio, paying them meagerly to pose for his erotic photographs, takes on the tone of the sexual exploitation and exoticization of the tropics (10). This exploitative dynamic is underscored by the White European man, significantly named Eli Cavalier (his last name doubling as an adjective), who ironically is in possession of one of the exoticized postcards. After a highly problematic sexual encounter with Graciela, Cavalier infects her with the syphilis that she unknowingly brings back to her community. Years after the encounter, the readers learn that "Eli Cavalier's syphilis ate its way throughout the town" (127). Cavalier's syphilis represents the negative forces infecting the island from the outside and eating away at the community, such as the colonial hierarchies, racism, and violence initially imposed during the colonial and occupation periods and reified under the twentieth-century dictators.[26]

Not responsible for the bifurcated understanding of race on Hispaniola, Rafael Trujillo capitalized on it in order to consolidate his growing power. Trujillo's project of *blanqueamiento*, or "the processes of becoming increasingly acceptable to those classified and self-identified as 'white'" (Chancy, *From Sugar to Revolution* 14), would seem to be the conceptual opposite of *noirisme*,[27] the ideological affirmation of Blackness used by François Duvalier to exacerbate divisions between Haitians. However, both capitalized on racial sentiments to attract supporters and centralize authority.[28] Early in his reign Trujillo acknowledged his Haitian lineage, using it as "a source of pride for political ends" in Haiti (Paulino 49), before stepping back and declaring himself a pure European after his power was secure (Ricourt 33).[29] Announcing aspirations to Whiten the country, Trujillo shifted to a belief that the elimination of Haitians was necessary to maintain a boundary—social, cultural, and political—between the island nations (Ricourt 32).[30] Trujillo preserved colonial ideologies that held fast during the US occupation, such as the relationship between Whiteness, power, and prestige, and the accumulation of Whiteness as protected capital. The economic value held by Whiteness in the Dominican Republic under Trujillo connects cross-culturally to the postbellum US southern settings of Faulkner's and Gaines's novels, as well as post-revolutionary Haitian society represented in Chauvet's work—its maintenance a central motivation for racial and sexual policing across these spaces.

Trujillo was obsessed with Whiteness, which he demonstrated on a personal level through his use of white pancake makeup and habit of having his photographs retouched to make himself look lighter (Derby, *The Dictator's Seduction* 197).[31] On a political level, Trujillo evinced this obsession through his *blanqueamiento* and anti-Haitian campaigns (Chancy, *From Sugar to Revolution* 66) that resulted in the 1937 Haitian massacre along the border between Haiti and the DR during which anywhere between twelve thousand and forty thousand Haitians, Dominicans of Haitian descent, and dark-skinned Dominicans were killed, as ordered by Trujillo (Chancy, "Diasporic Disconnections" 176).[32] Historically, the border had a strong Haitian presence: intermarriage and cross-border trade were the standard (Paulino 57), with multicultural families continuing "the trend of cultural convergence and hybridity" that began in the sixteenth century (Paulino 108). Thus, this massacre was not only a rejection of the cultural hybridity of the border region but also the attempted erasure of "a resilient economic and social collaboration from the country's history books" (Paulino xviii). It was not enough for Trujillo to control relations in the present: he wanted to influence the way the past was remembered as well. The dictator's official narratives, here Trujillo's racist social fictions about Haitians, are taken as truth, resulting in violence, genocide, and a rewriting of the nations' pasts. Through the violence of the massacre and policies of exclusion that followed, the power of the dictator extended to national belonging—revising who could be accepted as Dominican and emphasizing the association of Dominicanness with Whiteness.

In terms of the project of writing back to official narratives, Julia Alvarez's *In the Time of the Butterflies* contains scant reference to the slaughter of tens of thousands of Haitians, even though the events of the novel begin in 1938, the year following the massacre.[33] Through alternating sections from the perspective of each sister, the novel centers the experiences of the Dominican Mirabals in their early lives and years of growing political involvement, which ultimately resulted in the deaths of Minerva, María Teresa, and Patria. The novel, focusing on the revolutionary efforts and subsequent deaths of the Mirabal sisters, is very aware of the vulnerability of Dominican citizens, yet chooses not to focus on the destruction of Haitian lives.[34] The massacre is mentioned once in a list of Trujillo's other offenses: "But others had been suffering great losses. There were the Perozos, not a man left in that family. And Martínez Reyna and his wife murdered in their bed, and thousands of Haitians massacred at the border, making the river, they say, still run red" (53). Although Alvarez perhaps purposely positions this violence as marginal to the text to reflect the peripheral relation the massacre would have had to the lives of Dominicans living away from the border, at the same time, this brief mention reduces the violent deaths of tens of thousands to thousands and positions the genocide of Haitians as almost an afterthought to the murders of individual Dominicans.[35] The gap where a more direct engagement with the massacre should be embodies what gets told and what does not, mirroring the similarly opaque silence surrounding instances of racism, violence, and sexual abuse in more official accounts of this history, as opposed to correcting them.

Conversely, in *The Brief Wondrous Life of Oscar Wao* not only is casual racism toward Haitians littered throughout the novel but Yunior also directly references the massacre in his footnotes, beginning with the tongue-in-cheek listing of "the 1937 genocide against the Haitian and Haitian-Dominican community," as one of Trujillo's "outstanding accomplishments" (3).[36] A more descriptive note, however, refers both to the "historically fluid border with Haiti" and the "horrifying ritual of silence and blood, machete and perejil, darkness and denial, [through which he] inflicted a true border on the countries" (224–25). Yunior speaks insightfully to the powerful consequences the massacre had for national belonging in this note, cutting a border deep within the histories and imaginaries of Dominicans. Although the massacre is relegated to the footnotes, this does not necessarily imply that it is tangential to the broader project of the book. Part of the novel's structural play with form is to include footnotes that in some cases take over entire pages.[37] Further, the death of the novel's central antagonist, "Rafael Leónidas Trujillo Molina, the Dictatingest Dictator who ever Dictated" (80), occurs in a footnote. In this way, the footnotes could represent the return of the repressed—the unsayable pushing to be spoken, the histories that cannot be contained—symbolizing the power dynamics existing between official and less official narratives and histories.

In opposition to the indirect approaches taken by Alvarez and Díaz, the portrayal of Haitians and the 1937 massacre in Rosario's *Song of the Water Saints* is complex and direct. For instance, in terms of complexity, one of the novel's protagonists, Mercedes, voices explicitly anti-Haitian views (until finally seeing the violence of the massacre as "the horror out west" [183] when someone close to her is affected). Rosario bluntly describes the month of October 1937 as opening "with thirty-six hours of carnage in which drunken Dominican soldiers, on orders from Trujillo, took their machetes and built a damn of human bodies in the western Dajabón River" (181). She references facts drawn from historical accounts of the massacre, such as the machetes used "so that the Dominican peasantry could spontaneously participate in the massacre," the killings that "happened within Dominican families with

Haitian, part-Haitian, or dark-skinned relatives," and "pregnant women [who] were raped, then disemboweled like cattle," as a result of the heightened threat they embodied of giving birth to more Haitians on Dominican soil (181).[38] Rosario's novel includes the most historically informed confrontation of this violence of the three Dominican-American texts explored here. Rosario is able to narrate what seems unnarratable for Alvarez and Díaz, a pattern we will see again in each writer's representation of sexual violence. The (un)narratability of difficult events is individualized and not standardized across the novels, resulting in various approaches and degrees of engagement.

Moreover, it is inaccurate to consider racism, colorism, and ethnic discrimination apart from classism, sexism, and heterosexism without acknowledging "the convergence, co-constitution, imbrication, or interwovenness of systems of oppression" (Carastathis 55). In addition to Trujillo's manipulation of national, racial, color, and ethnic tensions, resulting in the Haitian massacre, the related exploitative relationship to sexuality is a feature of his dictatorship that had a brutal impact on individual lives and interpersonal experiences, including gender relations, family structures, and love. Racism, colorism, and classism are entwined with predatorial sexuality under Trujillo through his womanizing and explicit targeting of elite, light-skinned women to elevate his own status.[39] In yet another time and place, sexuality expresses neocolonial relations, linking the Dominican Republic under Trujillo explicitly to Haiti under Duvalier and the plantation cultures of Louisiana and Mississippi.

Trujillo and his followers were widely known for the sexual exploitation of women of all social classes, which Michele Wucker notes was more attributable to "coercion than to charm" (45).[40] Trujillo was associated with traditional (and even hyper-) masculinity, as a result of the high number of women he slept with (particularly those of the elite class) and his "prowess as lover, father, and husband, as well as defender of his extended family" (Derby, *The Dictator's Seduction* 111).[41] The predatory sexuality associated with the dictatorship is captured well by Peruvian novelist Mario Vargas Llosa's *Fiesta Del Chivo* (2000) or *The Feast of the Goat* (2005).[42] The novel includes sections from the perspectives of Trujillo and the men that killed him but also, most revealing for the entwinement of power and sexuality, Urania Cabral, the fictional daughter of a former confidant of the dictator whose virginal body is offered to him in an attempt to regain favor. In addition to constant sexualization, women were not accepted as full and equal participants in social and political life under Trujillo (Derby, *The Dictator's Seduction* 166).[43] Others occupying the lower end of identity-based hierarchies, including queer, nonbinary, or darker-skinned individuals also tend to be disproportionately affected by policies grounded in intolerance; however, women and their experiences are Yunior's focus in *The Brief Wondrous Life of Oscar Wao*.[44] Hypermasculinity, gender-based discrimination, and the sexual exploitation of women were modeled from the top of society—the president—all the way down to the lower social classes.

In his colloquial, blunt, and often crude voice, Yunior reminds readers throughout Díaz's novel of these aspects of Trujillo's dictatorship, highlighting stereotypical notions of Dominican hypermasculinity.[45] Yunior states, "If you think the average Dominican guy's bad, Trujillo was five thousand times worse. Dude had hundreds of spies whose entire job was to scour the provinces for his next piece of ass," noting that hiding your family's women was "tantamount to treason" (217). As described earlier, Díaz intended there to be a direct line running from Trujillo to Yunior, due to the latter's absolute narrative power over the text. However, readers can draw connections between the textual and the real-world dictators, not only through Yunior's complete control over the story but also his hypersexuality (Machado Sáez 543). Elena Machado Sáez positions these "male agents of history," like Trujillo and his former son-in-law/pseudo-son, Porfirio Rubirosa, known for his exploits as a "Dominican Casanova" (Torres-Saillant 101), as the problem of postcolonial regimes deriving their power from violence and the exploitation of women's bodies, such as those of Oscar's mother, Beli Cabral, and Ybon, Oscar's love interest whose boyfriend ultimately kills him (544). As dictatorial narrator, Yunior becomes "the spokesperson for a disturbing model of diasporic masculinity that the novel figures as a by-product of dictatorship" (Machado Sáez 544).[46] While Yunior outwardly disapproves of Trujillo and his methods, critics and the author himself encourage readers to recognize the ways Yunior is complicit in this history of exploitative sexuality and violence, as revealed through his voice, narrative control, and hypersexuality.[47] Díaz utilizes Yunior as a narrative convention that enables him to comment on the negative impact of dictatorship on sexuality more broadly.

Regardless of his complicity, Yunior understands the far-reaching negative influence of Trujillo, portraying the dictator's infamous affairs, exploits, and abuses as having a major impact on the plot of the novel. The novel is in a sense anti-chronological, writing back to Eurocentric conceptualization of History: although the events of protagonist Oscar de Léon's life advance in a linear fashion, the sections focusing on other characters progress backward from Oscar's sister Lola in the 1980s to his mother Belicia in the 1950s and 1960s and his grandfather Abelard in the 1940s. More specifically, in the fifth section ("Poor Abelard 1944–1946"), the novel flashes from a focus on Oscar and Lola growing up in New Jersey in the 1980s and 1990s to the story of their grandfather Abelard and his family living in the DR during Trujillo's dictatorship—demonstrating the colonial continuities connecting these spaces. Trujillo's interest in Jacquelyn, Abelard's beautiful daughter, begins the family's downfall, which, although fictional, aligns with historical accounts of the regime. As a result of his attempts to protect his daughter, and supposedly some disrespectful comments he was overheard making about the president, Abelard's family ends up dead, with the exception of his third daughter, Beli, at the time an infant. Beli, who would become the mother of Oscar and Lola, is later exiled to the United States as a result of her own brush with the regime. She has a relationship with a henchman who happens to be married to Trujillo's sister, illustrating once more that the horrific reach of Trujillo can only be realistically captured through fiction. As a result of this reach, Trujillo as sexual predator was relegated to the realm of rumor—the histories spoken but not written down.

As the novels elucidate, there are many stories from throughout the nation of Trujillo's "abduction of virginal girls during his provincial travels and of beautiful victims spied and romanced during official balls and functions" (Derby, *The Dictator's Seduction* 112). Yunior voices this directly: "The rap about The Girl Trujillo Wanted is a pretty common one on the Island . . . Trujillo took your houses, your properties, put your pops and your moms in jail? Well, it was because he wanted to fuck the beautiful daughter of the house! And your family wouldn't let him!" (244). Minerva Mirabal, the most headstrong and vocal of the four sisters, depicts the circulation of similar rumors in *In the Time of the Butterflies*, stating, "We've heard the stories. Young women drugged, then raped by El Jefe" (95). Both Derby's scholarship and the examples from Díaz's and Alvarez's novels show not only that Trujillo's destructive sexual exploits were widespread but also that these stories circulated throughout the nation, accurately describing his actions and simultaneously contributing to the mythos (and contrived, yet well-founded, fear) surrounding him. Fictionalizing the stories captured about the history of the regime allows both Alvarez and Díaz to emphasize the high stakes for sexuality under dictatorship on an individual level.

In a society where women are continually objectified and parents fear that no daughter is too young to Trujillo's rapacious eye, female beauty is a hazard. Women were systematically dehumanized by an elevated emphasis on their bodies and social statuses, linking back to Old Carothers McCaslin's violation of his own daughter in *Go Down, Moses*, Bonbon's exploitation of Black women on the Hebert plantation in *Of Love and Dust*, and most similarly, Calédu's torture rape of *Mulâtres-Aristocrates* women in *Love*. Beauty as a threat connects the novels of Alvarez and Díaz, as on the day of Trujillo's party, Minerva Mirabal's older sister Patria warns her, "The worse you look, the better for you" (93). Similarly, Yunior describes the physical development of Beli, who according to him "hit the biochemical jackpot" (91), as a power in its own way but also a "newly acquired burden" (93). Beli's aunt and mother-figure, La Inca, having lived through the first round of Trujillo's obsessive pursuit of Beli's sister, desperately inquires, "Why would God give you that burden in this country of all places!" (94). While, according to Yunior, Trujillo had been "on his last erections" during the "Summer of [Beli's] Secondary Sex Characteristics" (91), it was her relationship with his henchmen that "catapulted her and hers into Diaspora" (115). Beli's experience echoes what happened to her sister fourteen years earlier—the resonances of dictatorship's violent effects—in an example that blatantly shows the entwinement of the personal and political under the regime. Trujillo's abuse of women both exemplified and helped solidify his power through the exploitation of those beneath him on the social hierarchies.

Just as the beauty of Abelard's daughter Jacquelyn led to the downfall of the Cabrals in *The Brief Wondrous Life of Oscar Wao*, Alvarez's novel portrays Minerva Mirabal's appearance (along with her underground anti-regime activities) as leading to the deaths of her father, her two sisters, and ultimately herself. In a scene ripped from a combination of historical accounts and Mirabal lore, Minerva attends a dance at "El Jefe's favorite party mansion" after having been requested by name via a handwritten note on the family's invitation (94). Minerva dances with the dictator, debates politics, and rebuffs his advances, allegedly with a slap to his face.[48] Trujillo is portrayed as forceful in this scene, leading to her surprising reaction: "he draws me to him, so close I can feel the hardness at his groin pressing against my dress . . . He yanks me by the wrist, thrusting his pelvis at me in a vulgar way, and I can see my hand in an endless slow motion rise" (100).[49] Through this description, Minerva's actions take on the character of self-defense during sexual assault: she must act to free herself from Trujillo's erect member and thrusting pelvis, echoing both Calédu's abuse in *Love* and his representation in Claire's dreams, as a live statue with an erect "phallus [that] wagged feverishly" (120). Shortly after this scene, Enrique Mirabal is arrested and before long dies. As a result of their underground revolutionary activities, in addition to Minerva's slight, Minerva, Patria, María Teresa, and their husbands are soon jailed as well. In this way, Alvarez reveals that Trujillo's hypersexuality not only impacted individuals but, like the sexual violence of the *tonton macoutes* described in chapter 4, had a destructive impact on family structures and relationships.

According to Lauren Derby, family structures in the Dominican Republic are complicated, at times contradictory, and characterized by "concubinage, serial unions, female-headed households, de facto polygamy, and a rigid set of unattainable gender-role expectations" (*The Dictator's Seduction* 114).[50] For instance, a Dominican man is expected to serve as the father in an official household, or *oikos*, that shares his last name and additionally to maintain a *casa chica* (small house), or secret family unit (Derby, *The Dictator's Seduction* 114). Thus, Derby notes that Dominican family structures often take the form of a "husband-wife-mistress triangle" (*The Dictator's Seduction* 114) with the maintenance of (often serial) co-wives or concubines and the fathering of many children bestowing power and prestige onto the man (Derby, "Haitians, Magic, and Money" 514). This family dynamic is illustrated both through Abelard's relationship with Lydia in Díaz's novel, who briefly believes herself to be pregnant, as well as Enrique Mirabal Fernandez's formation of an alternative family of the *campesino*, or farming class, in In the Time of the Butterflies. The key aspect of this configuration is that the secondary family should not be flaunted openly in the community, in order to keep the family's honor intact (Derby, "Haitians, Magic, and Money" 514). This stipulation may explain the heartbreak experienced by Enrique's wife and daughters upon the discovery of his second family.

Rafael Trujillo's womanizing and numerous affairs negatively impacted Dominican family ideals and were destructive to the accepted structures. The stories of the sexual intrigues of the Trujillo family, not only Rafael but his son Ramfis, pseudo-son Porfirio Rubirosa, and daughter Flor, made the family relatable, "translating the apparently superhuman first family into a vernacular language and mode of expression drawn from daily life" (Derby, *The Dictator's Seduction* 114). Nevertheless, at the same time, the Trujillos and their exploits also eroded more conventional formations through the acceptance of infidelity beyond the *oikos* and *casa chica* systems. During his dictatorship, Trujillo passed laws that were developed to loosen familial bonds, including a law that allowed children to be disinherited and one that enabled divorce (Derby, *The Dictator's Seduction* 133–34). As a result of Trujillo's leadership, some of the most liberal divorce laws in the Americas were passed in the Dominican Republic (134), underscoring the impact he had on family configurations, which expanded outward to affect the broader community.[51] According to the novels, the hypermasculinity and accompanying infidelity, for which Trujillo himself is infamous, appear to be pervasive and tacitly accepted throughout the country, having a lasting impact on Dominican society. Through their portrayals of the intricacies of gender relations and family life—from the infidelity of Enrique and Abelard during the dictatorship to widespread focus on women's bodies in later periods, illustrated by Oscar and Yunior—Alvarez and Díaz demonstrate the ways in which Trujillo's hypermasculinity and the resulting policies negatively affected individuals, families, communities, and the nation at large. Further, the novels portray a connection between Dominican identity, hypermasculinity, and sexual violence that is worth unpacking more directly.

Narrator Yunior is invested in the hypermasculinity that he depicts in the novel and in society's expectations of him as a Dominican man. While Yunior acknowledges the detrimental effects of dictatorial narratives and hypermasculinity and allows readers to fleetingly glimpse his own guilt and vulnerability, at the same time, he engages in these problematic behaviors himself. Retaining complete control over the narrative until the last of the novel's multiple endings, Yunior never fully divorces himself from his dictatorial narrational style, and his misogynistic rhetoric is constant throughout the novel. He goes overboard with references to his own sexual exploits and "player" lifestyle in the fourth section of the novel—for example, "I should have been happy for the Wao. I mean, honestly, who was I to begrudge Oscar a little action? Me, who was fucking with not one, not two, but three fine-ass bitches *at the same time* and that wasn't even counting the side-sluts I scooped at the parties and the clubs" (185, italics in the original). Yunior cares what his readers thinks of him, and he *really* wants readers to know that he is doing well with the ladies, using demeaning terminology such as "side-sluts" and "fine-ass bitches," the descriptor solely emphasizing their appearances, to refer to them.

Yunior's rhetoric has an impact comparable to Trujillo's exploitative sexuality: the dehumanization of women. Yunior buys into this mentality through his emphasis on women's bodies and his sex life (and Oscar's lack thereof).[52] However, at the same time, he recognizes the harmful effects of this mentality both on a broader level through the connection he narrates between Trujillo's rapacity and the downfall of families and communities, as well as on a personal level. Although he never says it directly, it is clear to readers that Yunior is deeply in love with Lola, but he is unable to refrain from cheating on her and eventually loses her for good.[53] Hypermasculinity and the resulting dehumanization of women as bodies skews a society's relationship to love. If love is revolutionary in its resistance to hierarchies and fixation on difference, as discussed in relation to Marcus's love rebellion in *Of Love and Dust*, then this aspect is lost when the humanity of women is ignored. Through his portrayal of Yunior and his relationship to stereotypical

Dominican hypermasculinity, Díaz deconstructs this mentality as a result of both the gap between readers' views of Yunior and his view of himself, as well as the overall negative effects of this behavior on his life.

Yunior's reductive focus on bodies and sex reflects the dehumanization of women institutionalized by Trujillo's regime—an outmoded colonial ideology persisting across the circum-Caribbean, alongside the exaltation of Whiteness. Pushing this further, Yunior's emphasis may also have significance in terms of his relationship to the traumatic histories that he narrates. If "*the breakage of the verse enacts the breakage of the world*," then narratives of trauma necessarily depend on experimental formal techniques to portray the inner turmoil of a subject (Felman and Laub 25, italics in original). I argue that formal techniques, such as Yunior's crass voice and repetitive emphasis on female bodies, are literary devices purposely used to distance readers (and also Yunior himself) from the traumatic stories represented. The impact of this history is not always approached directly but must be inferred through the gaps, silences, and misinformation, as well as the detachment with which Yunior reconstructs the histories of the Cabrals and the de Léons. Although readers only have access to the narrative through Yunior, he keeps us at a distance from his interiority and the truth of his experiences. For instance, Yunior does not reveal his own name and identity until about halfway through the novel. Readers must work to put the pieces of his personal relationship to the story together, such as his feelings for Lola, in spite of this.[54] Further, Yunior's fixation on bodies runs throughout the novel. In a way, bodies and the corporeal may be seen to function as a counterpoint in the text to traumatic histories and the mental anguish they cause. In other words, a focus on the physical may be an attempt to relieve the emotional: the traumatic weight of these histories and Yunior's personal connection to them. Of course, the machismo encouraged in his culture in part explains this emphasis; however, I argue that it goes deeper, revealing an attempt to distract from his mental anguish, sadness, and guilt over the loss of Oscar and ultimately also Lola.

Another aspect of Díaz's project of deconstructing the mind of a misogynist like Yunior is to interrogate the link between this hypermasculinity, pervading the country from the president down, and the sexual violence that accompanies it. The hypermasculine aspects of Díaz's text are intimately linked to its representations of sexual violence. The threat of rape is responsible for the deaths of Jacqueline Cabral and her family, and Minerva Mirabal and her family—alongside other factors in the latter case, such as their activism.[55] The thread runs intergenerationally between the novels, connecting the experiences of the Cabrals in the 1940s to the Mirabals primarily in the 1950s. Beli

Cabral's early life in the DR during the late 1950s and early 1960s echoes that of both the Mirabals and her deceased family. In a similar way, Lola's experiences in the 1970s through 1980s, primarily in the US, are a reverberation of her mother's, in addition to those of the previous generations, which are also layered palimpsestically on top.[56] While resonances of traumatic experiences are said to linger and impact subsequent generations, the ties depicted in these novels involve the added layer of shared experiences of dehumanization and violence—extending from the DR to the US. The hypermasculinity associated with Dominican society has an expansive effect on the experiences of women across the century and throughout the diaspora.

Love across boundaries can be revolutionary, as demonstrated by border-crossing relationships highlighted in previous chapters that challenge the confining hierarchies of the status quo, such as between Charles Bon, Judith, and Henry Sutpen in *Absalom, Absalom!* and Marcus and Louise in *Of Love and Dust*. However, as *The Brief Wondrous Life of Oscar Wao* shows, love can also be destructive—particularly within the confines of restrictive social formations. For instance, pregnant Beli is abandoned by her lover, the husband of Trujillo's sister, and almost loses her life at the hands of the secret police "for having transgressed the rigid island love laws" (J. D. Saldívar, "Conjectures on 'Americanity'" 128). That this pivotal scene occurs in the sugarcane fields is no accident, connecting back to the sexual violence experienced by Martine in Edwidge Danticat's *Breath, Eyes, Memory*.[57] The historic resonances of sugar run backward through the 1937 Haitian massacre all the way to the "farming of bones" during slavery—a phrase used to describe the harvesting of this brutal crop that Danticat takes as the title for her novel about the massacre. Flashing ahead to the concluding sections, Oscar will be beaten and later will meet his end in the cane fields at the hands of similar figures—corrupt policemen.

Rather than sensationalize the violence of Beli's beating, Yunior focuses on the bodily harm that resulted, giving the readers a list of her injuries with about "167 points of damage in total" (147). Once again, sometimes the traumatic weight of violent incidents is best approached indirectly by writers to build its significance through an absent-presence, the perceivable substance of a gap.[58] Moreover, the rhetoric used to describe this violence (i.e., "points of damage") is taken from the role-playing gamer language that permeates the novel, adding to the distancing that occurs and the tension between reality and fantasy. Regarding Beli's beating in the cane fields, Yunior wonders in his characteristic, though here unsettling, cavalier tone, "Was there time for a rape or two? I suspect there was, but we shall never know because it's not something she talked about" (147). I will return to the absent-presence and the unknowable nature of Beli's sexual violence—what is narrated versus what falls into the novel's gaps and blank spaces—but if we take Yunior at his word that it was likely, then this abuse directly connects Beli's experiences to those of her daughter, Lola, in New Jersey, linking the cultures of the US and the DR through the residual impacts of their colonial histories on the bodies of girls and women.

At the age of eight, Lola was attacked by a family acquaintance, which Yunior describes as "common knowledge" throughout the family and the community, as well as neighboring towns. Yunior notes that her long, beautiful hair, "a source of pride," was likely something that attracted the attention of her attacker (25). In this way, the mentality modeled by Trujillo during his reign, men taking what they want regardless of circumstances, can be blamed. Yunior makes a direct connection between the emphasis on women's bodies (here, Lola's long hair), hypermasculinity, and sexual violence. The narrator also implies that Beli's own experience of violence, in addition to her young age (just fourteen) and inability to work through her own trauma, causes her harmful reaction, perpetuating the cycle of abuse discussed in relation to Martine and Sophie in *Breath, Eyes, Memory* in the previous chapter. Through leading readers to draw certain connections, Yunior—and ultimately Díaz himself—demonstrates his dictatorial control over readers' thoughts and reactions.

Lola recalls to Yunior, "When that thing happened to me when I was eight and I finally told her what he had done, she told me to shut my mouth and stop crying, and I did exactly that, I shut my mouth and clenched my legs, and my mind, and within a year I couldn't have told you what that neighbor looked like or even his name" (56–57). This example represents an attempt at narrating the unsayable and also shows the mechanism of repression at work. The weighty impact of the unsaid here spirals out to affect Lola's life and relationships more broadly. Yunior, who attempts to control our understanding of the information we receive in the text, leads us to view the wider ramifications of this unaddressed sexual trauma: Beli's experience precipitates her cold reaction to her daughter's abuse, and Lola's experience shapes her interactions with others later in life. Two examples on the same page illustrate this clearly. After Lola runs away to the boardwalk to be with a boy she thinks she loves and the relationship begins to deteriorate, she states about her boyfriend and his father, "I guess I should count myself lucky that they didn't just decide to bury the hatchet by gangbanging me" (65). When boys approach her at the beach with lines such as, "You a good-looking girl, you should be in a bikini," she responds, "Why, so you can rape me?" (65). These are indications that like her mother, Lola has not been able to process her experience. Lola, Beli, and Jacqueline (in addition to generations of Haitian women, such as Martine and Sophie) experience abuse, harassment, and the encouraged repression that accompanies them. This speaks to the intergenerational impact of sexual violence in hypermasculine societies traversing the hemisphere, which Díaz highlights, although in a subtle, indirect manner.[59] The experiences of sexual violence shared by mother and daughter join the DR with the diasporic community in the US, linking these spaces in a similar way to the intergenerational, transamerican connections drawn by Rosario.

Although she engages less directly with Trujillo's reign, Nelly Rosario also centers the abuses, as well as the successes, experienced by multiple generations of women in her novel. *Song of the Water Saints* focuses primarily on the experiences of Graciela during the US occupation and early twentieth century and Mercedes during Trujillo's regime, as well as a brief focus on Amalfi, Mercedes's daughter who stays behind in the DR, and Leila, Mercedes's granddaughter whom she raises in the United States—once more highlighting the relationship between the DR and the US. Rosario strives to "contrast four generations of women and the distinctive cultural expectations bestowed upon them by their gender," noting that trauma does not happen once but "unfolds between generations; its aftermath is experienced by the survivors" (Ayuso 58). The novel places Trujillo and his regime within the scope of the broader century and hemisphere through its expanded focus and foregrounding of the multigenerational experiences of these women. Tactics relied on during Trujillo's dictatorship, such as violence, discrimination, and sexual exploitation, in reality were part of the Dominican experience carrying through from the occupation at the start of the century into the present period with the treatment of Haitians in the DR (and the US) today, to be explored in the coda. However, just as Junot Díaz plays with narrative form and resonances of power through having Trujillo die in a footnote, Rosario's novel suppresses his name for twenty years during his regime (Ayuso 58) and also depicts his assassination as secondary to Amalfi's birth.[60] The section begins with this sentence, "Mercedes had given breath to Amalfi on the day of the assassination, in 1961, of El Generalisimo Doctor Rafael Leónidas Trujillo Molina" (191), and the succeeding section focuses on Mercedes's experience of birth, not the death with which it is paired. Similarly, the opening sections of the novel are structured in part around men: chapters in Graciela's section bear the names of her lovers, Silvio and Casimiro. Yet, this is increasingly less the case with latter sections named after locations, events, or the female characters at the center. These formal techniques underscore the novel's emphasis on Graciela and her descendants. The women and their experiences are always the focal point, which speaks to the struggles and also strengths of Graciela's family throughout the generations.

Further, if we trace the portrayal of sexuality in the novel, threads manifest, such as the danger of sexual violence toward women. While this concern is common to all three novels, Rosario is the only writer to confront it thoroughly and directly. The US soldiers represent a sexual threat to the women of the DR, as the experiences of Graciela and her mother Mai show: "The yanqui-men's rifles and giant bodies confirmed stories that had already filtered into the city from the eastern mountains . . . women left spread-eagled right before their fathers and husbands" (13). Graciela witnesses a woman, referred to by the soldiers as a "Negro wench," shot down, and after she falls, "some already had their shirts pulled out of their pants," underscoring the sexual nature of this violence (14). After witnessing this encounter, Graciela comes home to find her mother kneeling by a soldier "whose fists entangled her hair and had undone the cloth rollers" (14)—a position encapsulating the threat of sexual violence. The soldiers then clamp Graciela's nose and hold it until it bleeds (15). Readers are aware of the stakes in this scene, due to the rumors and the violence seen by Graciela in the previous pages, which heightens the relief felt when the soldiers leave before forcing themselves on either woman.

Rosario's explicit engagement with multigenerational experiences of sexual violence may be seen as a form of textual resistance to what gets emphasized in official accounts of History. The novel spans from the violence of the occupation, which also likely claimed Graciela's husband Silvio, whose body unbeknownst to her was found "riddled by bullets" (33), to more personal experiences of sexual exploitation. One such example is the encounter Graciela has with Eli Cavalier, possessor of syphilis and consumer of racialized erotica (of which Graciela unknowingly became a part through posing for the postcard in the novel's opening section). As discussed previously, Rosario links tactics of rape directly with the genocide of Haitians at the border in 1937, carrying this thread of sexual violence across the course of the century from occupation to dictatorship to diaspora. Diaspora here illustrates the reciprocal lines of connection between the DR and the US, with the DR directly influencing US culture. In the final section of the novel, Rosario portrays a later iteration of exploitative sexuality associated with the experience of immigration. Mercedes, Andrés, and their granddaughter, Leila, are "part of the largest immigrant group to settle in New York City during the 1980s" (198), and through a focus on Leila's particular experiences, Rosario humanizes and individualizes the impact of those statistics. Leila left her mother, community, and home behind in the DR to be raised by her grandparents in New York City, an urban landscape full of anonymity and unknowns. She demonstrates that rebelling against one's parental figures in New York City comes with higher stakes without the support of a broader community on which Mercedes and Graciela before her both relied. Her experience underscores the continuities of exploitative sexuality spanning the hemisphere, linking the Global North to the Global South through their complicity in the abuse and dehumanization of women.

At the age of fourteen (connecting to Beli's young age during the violent episode in the cane fields), Leila begins flirting and sexually experimenting with Miguel, an older married man who lives in her grandparents' building. Leila gets in over her head once she escapes her grandparents' watchful eyes to meet her neighbor at a club, echoing her mother's brief abandonment of her family and experience with Eli. Leila accompanies Miguel to a motel in the Bronx where the encounter turns violent with Miguel pulling Leila by the shoulders, throwing her, smacking her thighs (232). He calls Leila by his wife's name, he calls her "slut," echoing Yunior's demeaning language, and she whimpers, "Migo, please kiss me at least" (232). Leila doubles during the rough sex, thinking of the loving actions of Mercedes and viewing herself from the outside: "Leila saw them. She witnessed the man on top of the girl, her legs twisted under him, her brand-new breasts crushed. She winced with the digging of his feet into the mattress at each thrust, the horse-buttocks tightening, the shock in her own eyes, then her face extinguished" (233). Leila witnesses what is being done to her body from without. This distancing is mirrored by the language of the passage, referring to herself as "the girl," and is complicated by the recognition that it is at the same time "her legs" twisting, "her brand-new breasts" crushed, "the shock in her *own* eyes" (emphasis added). Whereas Yunior distances himself from mental distress through a focus on the physical, here Leila mentally disassociates herself from the physical. Beyond the violent sex, Miguel tells her that he could kill her with a hanger, "wrap it around your neck, and spill you on this bedspread," or throw her out the window (233), a moment that resonates with the various instances of violence to Dominican women cataloged throughout the book.

Miguel gains her trust back with gentle kisses but is soon rough again, "as Leila floated back to the ceiling and waited by the curtain rods" (234). Doubling, or witnessing actions to your body as if you were apart from it, appears often in circum-Caribbean novels depicting traumatic encounters, such as *Breath, Eyes, Memory*; *Song of the Water Saints*; and Shani Mootoo's *Cereus Blooms at Night* (1996).[61] Doubling is a way to formally represent the mental anguish and bodily pain experienced by the characters in that moment. Although doubling helps distance characters from their realities,

Rosario does not allow readers that space. This depiction of sexual violence is the most direct, unflinching portrayal across these novels: it is not melodramatic but realistic, understated, and difficult to read, adeptly transmitting the trauma of this experience to readers. Leila's brutal sexual encounter is highly individualized, and yet at the same time, put in conversation with the systemic totality of other generations' experiences. While specific to Leila, the abuse contains within it the imbricated layers of her predecessors' experiences across different times and spaces—discernable in the text through her dreams.

Like her great-grandmother's encounter with Eli, Leila's violent sexual experience occurs on a smaller scale than that portrayed during the US occupation or the Haitian genocide. Nevertheless, all of these examples are depicted in tandem with one another. Through describing, and even foregrounding, these more personal experiences alongside the larger-scale events, Rosario gives weight to everyday traumas, in addition to those accompanying the events of capital-h-History. Leila's dreams following her encounter with Miguel connect her to the collective memories of the women in her family and to everyday hardships, but also the pleasure and hopes of those preceding her:

> Her dreams were a collage of confounding images: two copulating lizards . . . cumulonimbus clouds shaped like ships . . . small brown hands paring an apple . . . the map of the world on a face . . . La Virgen de la Altagracia without a face . . . a peppermint stick inside a coffee cup . . . lavender tangled in pubic hair . . . a hatbox . . . mercury-stained skin . . . an uncombed baby under a chair . . . a thorned and bleeding plaster heart. (238)

These images are unknowable to Leila yet speak to a visceral bond beyond understanding that unites her with the women who came before her. While their personalities and experiences are diverse, the women in Leila's family are connected by some intangible and unnamable entity, which is underscored by the ellipses or blank spaces in between the flow of images.

The inexplicable quality of this bond Leila shares with Amalfi, Mercedes, and Graciela connects back to other unknowable aspects of the novels, such as the experiences of sexual violence linking the women depicted in Alvarez's and Díaz's texts. For example, in *In the Time of the Butterflies*, Dedé Mirabal, the fourth and surviving sister, notes that it isn't known if her murdered sisters were violated: "They killed them good and dead. But I do not believe they violated my sisters, no. I checked as best I could. I think it is safe to say they acted like gentlemen murderers in that way" (303). Isabel Zakrzewski Brown observes that the historical accounts differ from the fictional and biographical when it comes to this point (109–10). Historians Piero Gleijeses and Robert Crassweller state that the sisters were violated, and Alvarez and biographers William Galván and Ramón Alberto Ferreras insist that they were not (I. Brown 109–10), illustrating the unknowable nature of history. This unrecoverable knowledge is paralleled by the fictional character of Beli in *The Brief Wondrous Life of Oscar Wao*. Yunior notes that she may have been raped during her beating in the cane fields, but we can never know because she never talked about it (146). Here Yunior does not attempt to narrate Beli's unsayable/unknowable experiences. Through both acknowledging the probability of sexual assault, as well as the impossible nature of that knowledge, he creates space for that which can never be recovered, similar to the space Faulkner holds at times for the missing perspectives of women and people of color—gaps he acknowledges but does not attempt to fill in. This illustrates the different degrees of repressed experiences in the novel: from those that are recoverable through fictional narratives to those that can never be recuperated.

Further, the unknowability of sexual violence in the face of persistent threats connects more broadly in the novels to what gets told and what does not: for instance, the relative silence around the Haitian genocide in Alvarez, the relegation of official History to the background in Rosario, and the use of blankness in Díaz, which I turn to next.[62] For Rosario, these experiences are narratable in a way that they are not for Alvarez and Díaz, in whose novels they are referenced but not fully developed.[63] This is not to privilege one approach over the other. Díaz and Alvarez succeed in conveying much through the absent-presence of sexual violence, the shadowy outlines of abuse potentially experienced. To have approached the topic more directly in these novels, particularly via Díaz's unapologetically crass narrator, may not have the same profound effect. However, Rosario's almost matter-of-fact style is conducive to a candid examination of the violence and sexual abuse disproportionately affecting women in the twentieth-century Dominican Republic. The combination of her simple style and frank approach directly confronts this intergenerational violence in a way that is at once poignant and disturbing, lingering in readers' thoughts after the book is put down. As these incidences are highly individualized, multiple approaches—both direct and indirect—are needed to even come close to capturing the impact of these experiences.

One technique common to the approaches of Rosario, Alvarez, and Díaz, however, is the use of absent-presence, gaps, and blankness to represent the inscrutable nature of the past. Blankness can include a felt absent-presence or simply a gap or silence left by something unsaid or unwritten. Blankness is directly linked to the novels' contextual backgrounds and the silencing writers experience under dictatorship: the blankness in the novels correlates with the blankness in historical accounts. *Song of the Water Saints* does not focus equally on each of its four protagonists. Gaps are present in the accounts of their lives, especially Mercedes's daughter, Amalfi, who remains in the Dominican Republic after Mercedes, her husband, and her granddaughter emigrate to the United States. Further, blankness appears in Alvarez's novel in the form of missing pages from María Teresa's prison diary, which happen to also be the accounts of prison torture, denoted in the novel by the phrase "[pages torn out]" throughout the section (234).[64] Alvarez alludes to the violence: its absence is visceral, but it is ultimately outside of her capacity to narrate. Similarly, Díaz uses the trope of the blank page to represent the silencing and silences in accounts of History. The various manifestations of blankness in Díaz's novel, from blank pages to the surreal figure of the blank-faced man, represent that which cannot be contained within capital-h-History, such as resistant aspects that have been silenced and multiplicities that have been flattened.

Just as Díaz links Yunior to Trujillo, Yunior draws a connection between writers and dictators (97), since both are "narrative makers and narrative controllers. Both the dictator and the novelist create metanarratives and produce meaning" (Harford Vargas "Dictating a Zafa" 8). This connection between writing and dictatorships is brought to the fore in a note describing former Dominican president Joaquín Balaguer. Balaguer is famous for "ordering the death of journalist Orlando Martínez. Later, when he wrote his memoirs, he claimed he knew who had done the foul deed (not him, of course) and left a blank page, a *página blanco*, in the text to be filled in with the truth upon his death. (Can you say *impunity*?) Balaguer died in 2002. The página is still blanca" (Díaz 90, italics in original).[65] Writers have the power to counter authoritarian narratives and expose the dictatorship: they pose a threat and must be kept silent. The blank page in the novel represents the purposeful silencing that accompanies dictatorships. Dictators attempt to control information and perceptions through excising a multiplicity of accounts, leaving only their version of History. This again connects back to Yunior's dictatorial control over the narrative, leading us to view characters and events how he chooses. Thus, the blank spaces hold meaning in their blankness, depicting the gaps that necessarily accompany historical narratives. Harford Vargas notes that the blank pages speak, "functioning as testifying silences" through which "repressed stories can be dictated and chronicled in the archive of fiction" ("Dictating a Zafa" 23).⁶⁶ In this way, Díaz creates meaning through the silences and their broader significations, both for the dictatorship and History in general. However, through the inclusion of gaps in the accounts and references to blank pages, Díaz nods to the fact that neither Trujillo nor Yunior can have complete control over individual stories or official History.

The novel includes numerous repeated references to *páginas en blanco* throughout, leaving space for the aspects of narrative that escape dictatorial control, in addition to secrets safeguarded by the regime.⁶⁷ The blank pages are also accompanied by a surreal creature, the man without a face, who is connected to another fantastic element, the Mongoose that appears in our characters' times of grave need.⁶⁸ Yunior's dream after Oscar's death connects the imagery of the blank page with the blank face.⁶⁹ The two are standing in a ruined bailey full of books with Oscar in a "wrathful mask" (325). Oscar holds up a book, and Yunior notices that "the book's pages are blank" (325). Sometimes Oscar's eyes smile behind the mask, and sometimes, Yunior states, "I look up at him and he has no face and I wake up screaming" (325). Oscar's death clearly haunts Yunior, which accounts for the fact that he is the figure to combine two forms of blankness: the emptiness of redacted or unwritten accounts and the blankness of faces undergoing strong emotions.

Blankness is not only a motif central to the content of *The Brief Wondrous Life of Oscar Wao* but is also a recurring aesthetic technique: the appearance of blank spaces represent missing words on the page. The most pertinent examples of this include the Mongoose's blank words in Oscar's dream, "'- ----- ----- -----,' said the Mongoose" (301); the name of Ybon's other man, known only as the *capitán*, "Me and ------- are getting married" (305); and Yunior's admission that he could have saved his relationship with Lola, if he had tried to say the words "----- ----- -----" (327).⁷⁰ This last example is closely followed by another place where Yunior's narration breaks down, and he cannot say the missing words even to his readers: "Could have been my daughter if I'd been smart, if I'd been -------" (329). The appearance of this blankness on the page highlights Díaz's attempt to engage with this history through his formal techniques. On an aesthetic level, the blanks where words should be hold space for what is missing, what is left out, what cannot be said. Stories are never entirely comprehensible to those who have not lived them: something is always lost in translation. Accounts that include blankness acknowledge, in a more direct way, the ultimately unknowable nature of History—the discontinuous histories, the histories left out of History, the history that appears and disappears at the moment of action.

Additionally, beyond missing words, pages, and faces, Yunior speaks of other forms of lacuna, including missing books and blank stories: Abelard's missing book or "an expose of the supernatural roots of the Trujillo regime!" (245); Oscar's dreams of a blank book (302); the missing second package containing his writing (333); and the missing story of the family's experiences under Trujillo (243). Concerning the final example, Yunior states:

> What's certain is that nothing's certain. We are trawling in silences here. Trujillo and Company didn't leave a paper trail—they didn't share their German contemporaries' lust for documentation. And it's not like fukú itself would leave a memoir or anything . . . A whisper here and there but nothing more . . . Which is to say if you're looking for a full story, I don't have it. Oscar searched for it too, in his last days, and it's not certain whether he found it either. (243)

Yunior emphasizes the uncertainty and incomplete nature of History: nothing is ever definite, and we are left to sift through silences.[71] Nevertheless, narratives like Yunior's work around the gaps left by the repressed, the unsayable, through the range of formal techniques he employs, including polyvocality, palimpsests, and blankness. In this way, the novel's experimental aesthetics represent what is left out and perhaps aid in lightening the traumatic weight of history. The fact that Yunior and Oscar were determined to find the complete story but came up short raises the question, Can there ever be a full story? Does every story contain blank pages? If so, what do we as readers do with this information? How does the blankness, or even more so the absent-presence, in recorded accounts interact with the palimpsestic violence layered beneath the surface of spaces and individual experiences? The answer to this final question lies in the relationship between official accounts and personal stories of trauma.[72] In varying ways, all of the literature considered in this chapter explores the connections between History—with a capital H, signifying the official recorded writings of an event—and more individual stories and experiences.

Yunior states at one point, "There were no papers, no civil rights groups, no opposition parties; there was only Trujillo" (247). Indeed, an exploration of what gets told and what does not in these novels, which represent the unreality of Dominican history, reflects the silencing and disappearances often associated with dictatorships. This includes the absence of accounts of violence in official state records; the lack of data, such as an exact number of the casualties of the Haitian massacre of 1937; the disappearance or assassination of political dissidents, students, and writers; reliance on surveillance; and the stripping away of civil liberties. Often the experiences of women, people of color, and other marginalized groups are not the first to be narrated. Thus, I analyze these novels with an eye to the gaps in the texts and what they might reveal, for instance, about the unnarratability of genocide, sexual violence, and life under Trujillo more broadly. The work of writers both during and after dictatorship plays a key role in combating propaganda and official narratives, accounting for the racism, state-sponsored violence, and sexual exploitation often left out. Through the use of polyvocality, absent-presences, palimpsests, and other techniques, these novels confront the gaps produced by obfuscating, reductive dictatorial narratives and official versions of History by simultaneously holding space for the unknowable and narrating the unsayable. Thus, resistance to the powerful and their accounts is found in these writers' approaches to history. Although history is incomprehensible, fiction and the affordances of form provide a means of capturing, at least in part, the stories and experiences of those who came before us, challenging authoritarian narratives of control.

* * *

To conclude, I turn briefly to the passing down of stories between generations and the significance this holds in terms of the relationship between the past and the present across multiple novels, before engaging with the present more directly in the coda. The transmission of stories from one generation to the next is vital, even in the face of gaps, absent-presences, and unnarratable trauma. How stories are exchanged and the traces that remain impact future generations. As Resmaa Menakem describes, "Our very bodies house the unhealed dissonance and trauma of our ancestors" (10).[73] The concept of the transgenerational phantom, as discussed by Nicolas Abraham, Maria Torok, and later Nicholas Rand, may be of use here in consideration of the transmission of trauma from parents to children, spanning the novels examined throughout this book. According to the concept of the transgenerational phantom, some people "unwittingly inherit the secret psychic substance of their ancestors' lives" (Abraham and Torok 166), where the dead do not actually return but "their lives' unfinished business is unconsciously handed down to their descendants" (Abraham and Torok 167). Abraham asserts that unfinished business is transferred to later generations in the form of the phantom through the survival of the traces of memory (168).[74] The transmission of the phantom or traumatic traces occurs overtly in a number of hemispheric American novels—particularly those with an intergenerational focus, such as *Song of the Water Saints* and *The Brief Wondrous Life of Oscar Wao*, in addition to *Breath, Eyes, Memory* and *Absalom, Absalom!*, discussed in previous chapters. Inherited traumas are experienced in a different way in part because traumatic experiences are not preserved whole cloth and passed down to posterity. The transgenerational phantom is made up only of the traces of traumatic memories and may progressively fade after transmission to succeeding generations until it disappears completely (Abraham and Torok 176).

The inheritance of intergenerational trauma takes many forms in these novels, ranging from spoken accounts of the past to the more public records of plantation ledgers. In Leila's case, intergenerational memories are passed down to her through her dreams, although she lacks the knowledge to fully grasp the meaning of the images.[75] This passing from one hand to another of the pieces of a traumatic story can have a material component beyond the traces of memory.[76] In this case physical artifacts take the place of the nebulous psychic substance of our ancestors' memories, such as the letter written to Judith by Charles Bon in *Absalom, Absalom!*, the McCaslin plantation ledgers in *Go Down, Moses*, the tape recordings of Miss Jane's voice in *The Autobiography of Miss Jane Pittman*, and Clare Clamont's diary in *Love*. These tangible objects add another layer: through their existence in the physical world, they can be used to widen the audience of transmitted stories, in a similar way to that accomplished through the books written by Alvarez, Díaz, and Rosario and their circulation in the world. As explored by Gayl Jones's novel *Corregidora* (1975), there is a murky line between preserving and learning from histories and re-traumatizing later generations, and perhaps literature and its fictive elements are more solidly on the former side of that line.[77] As fiction, there is a necessary distance from lived experiences that enables writers to attempt to crystalize something unsayable in the past that is continually transmitted. As demonstrated by Alvarez's stated intension of "deepen[ing] North Americans' understanding of the nightmare" endured by Dominicans under Trujillo (324), the publication of these works ensures the continued circulation of these histories. Even if, like memory traces, stories are not inherited whole cloth and pieces are fictionalized or lost in translation, they still play a vital role in preserving this history, capturing the contextual truths of the past for future generations.

As Rita Felski notes, "We cannot ever know the past as it really was, that history is always, at least in part, the history of the present" (577). Although complete knowledge is not possible, it is the attempt that matters, as in the passage between hands of a material account of the past, regardless of the comprehension of the content: "History is not entirely knowable but it must be related so that it can become known, so that it can be proved that it 'did truly happen'" (Ink 799). In this way, written accounts of history, like the traces of memories passed down between the generations, are always necessarily incomplete. Nevertheless, it is important to tell the stories and bear witness to what has gone before. Further, no historical events can be captured in their entirety through a singular perspective. This calls to mind John Berger's quote used as the epigraph to Arundhati Roy's *The God of Small Things* (1997): "Never again will a single story be told as though it's only one."[78] Multiple stylistic approaches to and viewpoints of these histories are needed in the hope of capturing even a shadow of reality. Thus, in addition to the physical representation of blankness on the page, signifying an absent-presence, the focus on various stories in the novels speaks to the incomplete nature of both official History and more individual histories. The sharing of multiple stories, perspectives, and accounts, as illustrated through the structure of the novels by Díaz, Rosario, and Alvarez, is the closest we can come to an accurate understanding of this history. The aesthetics of all three writers explored in this chapter connect to their conceptions of history, returning full circle to the question of why literature is the necessary mode to represent the unreality of reality.

Coda

LOOKING BACK IN RESISTANCE, LOOKING TO THE PRESENT

In its examination of twentieth-century literature from the hemispheric American South, *Policing Intimacy* reveals certain patterns in the relationships between sexuality and other interconnected identity-based hierarchies, grounded in historical and local specificities but also as related to broader social forces.[1] These patterns persist into our current moment, linking the colonial period to the present day across the diverse terrain of the US South, Haiti, and the Dominican Republic. This literature exposes the continuing coloniality connecting depictions of US democracy to Caribbean dictatorships in the twentieth century through the shared inheritance of racialized sexual policing across these spaces. The novels by William Faulkner, Ernest Gaines, Marie Chauvet, Edwidge Danticat, Julia Alvarez, Junot Díaz, and Nelly Rosario reveal the widespread abusive relations that result from the continued adherence to colonial ideologies in the twentieth century; however, resistance to this policing is also a point of commonality, which can open up for alternative ways of interacting. I choose to end with a final emphasis on the thread of resistance running through the work of the writers explored in this book in the hope of making space for change in the present, before considering twenty-first-century sites where racialized and sexualized policing happens. How does literature reacting to these contemporary iterations of colonial violence engage in resistance, and how might this resistance relate to previous articulations?

Compared with Ernest Gaines, a former sharecropper, or Marie Chauvet, a target of Duvalier's regime, the politics of William Faulkner's fictional reconstructions from the early twentieth century are less explicit. Faulkner's subject position distances him from the epicenter of violence, allowing him to write more ambiguously about the issues of sexual exploitation, racism, and physical violence. However, chapter 1 demonstrates how resistance in Faulkner's novels works on different levels to expose the destruction wrought by the racist social fictions particular to his time and place. For instance, Faulkner directly writes back to the myth of the Black rapist and the predominance of lynch culture in his novels by putting characters of uncertain racial backgrounds who do not commit rape or White men who do in dialogue with the figure of the Black rapist. Further, resistance to racial hierarchies is grounded not only in the form of Faulkner's novels but also in the content, including the characters he depicts and their actions. More specifically, he leaves space for less destructive patterns of relations in the form of consensual interracial relationships, such as those between Hubert Beauchamp and his unnamed cook, and Roth Edmonds and his unnamed distant relative, and more fluid forms of identity, as exemplified by Charles Bon. The potential acceptance of these relations and individuals suggests a different way of interacting that is less constrained by hierarchies and prejudices.

Resistance to plantation hierarchies and the status quo is central to Ernest Gaines's depictions of his characters and their interactions and relationships. As is shown through the example of *Loving v. Virginia* described in chapter 3's opening, boundary-defying love has the power to subvert dehumanizing hierarchical mentalities. The moments during which characters relate on the level of their common humanity by putting aside the hierarchies of race, ethnicity, gender, class, and sexuality contain the greatest potential for structural alterations to the plantation system. Similar to Faulkner's subversion of the myth of the Black rapist, Gaines also invokes racial and sexual stereotypes, such as the "tragic mulatto," while simultaneously challenging their dominance through his characters' incongruous outcomes and limited agency. For instance, Catherine Carmier has the agency to stay with her father or to leave with her lover, and Mary Agnes has the agency to refuse Tee Bob's advances—even if she cannot fully deter his pursuit. Further, in her lack of interest in men and relationships and passion for her career, Mary Agnes is also able to resist ideologies of gender and the confining roles that result. While there is a subversive aspect of Tee Bob's pursuit of Mary Agnes and his refusal to let the rules dictate who he can love, this is tempered by his imposition of his wishes on Mary Agnes, regardless of her desires. Nevertheless, I read the friendship between Jules and Jane as a more authentic example of resistance to the colonial hierarchies of the plantation system. Their respect for and enjoyment of each other's company challenges their Louisiana community's violent plantation history.

The structure and form of *Of Love and Dust* likewise expose Gaines's interest in resistance to the status quo. For example, Jim as narrator relies on the voices of others from all levels of the community to build a polyvocal story in contrast to official historical narratives. Jim's focus on the physicality of the male characters subverts the overemphasis on the bodies of female characters—often of color—employed by tropes such as the "tragic mulatto." Finally, in his positive portrayal of the same-sex relationship between Freddie and John, Jim leaves space for future relationships not grounded in power differentials (Bibler 44), such as his own potentially subversive partnership with Marcus, which never attains its full promise. The relationship between Marcus and Louise is radical for its challenge to racial hierarchies and has the potential to be more broadly subversive, as demonstrated through the complex example of Louise's usurpation of the male gaze. However, the pairing ultimately would not structurally alter the plantation beyond placing Black men above White women (Bibler 40). Marcus falls short of his status as a revolutionary figure: his misogynist and heterosexist mentality holds him back from achieving the full-scale intersectional rebellion needed on the plantation. The novel, nevertheless, includes the seeds of future revolution. For instance, Jim recognizes that Marcus, Bonbon, Pauline, and Louise are all tools for rich White men to manipulate. This realization will influence Jim's future actions, as we see in the novel's final scenes with his decision to leave the confining plantation system behind and his outright rejection of Marshall's letter of recommendation, symbolic of his power and influence.

Moreover, the fact that Marie Chauvet wrote *Love, Anger, Madness*, which is highly critical of notorious dictator François Duvalier, during his reign exemplifies her resistance to the regime. By conflating historical eras, she symbolically underscores continuity of colonial structures. Through her descriptions of her characters' relationships and categorizations of one another, she both invokes and subverts racial and sexual stereotypes—ultimately affirming her characters as unique and multifaceted individuals. She breaks down reductive binaries and assumptions through her complex character portrayals and rejections of easy classifications. And finally, through focusing on Claire's negative treatment as a darker-skinned *Mulâtresse-Aristocrate*—including her racism toward herself, as well as her skewed relationship to others and her sexuality—Chauvet criticizes the status quo on the communal but also individual level. Further, writing almost a generation after the demise of the Duvalier dynasty, Edwidge Danticat is able to verbalize her denunciation of the powerful more directly, emphasizing their tactics of violence and sexual exploitation. She names the *tonton macoutes* and Duvalier himself openly in her depiction of the physical, psychological, and emotional trauma their actions produce in a way that Chauvet was unable to do.

While in part existing more subtly within Chauvet's writerly techniques, resistance also operates on other levels within her novella from the nation's history of revolution that led to the first free Black republic in the New

World to the characters' actions in the present. Claire's stabbing of Calédu is the most obvious example, alongside the collective defiance of hierarchies and violence symbolized by the town rising as one in the closing scene. A careful reading reveals that this final action can be seen as the culmination of Claire's growing revolutionary impulses. She had been internally resistant to the status quo since childhood, as revealed by her earlier choices, such as the decision to renew her friendships with Jane and Dora—ostracized members of her community. The seeds of revolution are located in Claire's recognition of the negative effects of Haiti's inheritance from colonialism and more recent outside intervention.

Similarly, in chapter 5, the actions of the characters embody resistance to those in control, such as the revolutionary activities of the Mirabals in Julia Alvarez's *In the Time of the Butterflies*, Oscar's decision to return to the DR despite the *capitán*'s threats in Junot Díaz's *The Brief Wondrous Life of Oscar Wao*, and Mercedes's successful maintenance of a business under dictatorship in Nelly Rosario's *Song of the Water Saints*. Through Yunior's narration, Díaz questions the hypermasculinity that has become an accepted aspect of Dominican society. He resists the status quo by directly connecting the overemphasis on women's bodies, analyzed in other chapters through the trope of the "tragic mulatto," to sexual violence, speaking to the intergenerational effects of such violence in hypermasculine societies. Rosario confronts the exploitation spanning women's experiences in the DR and the US throughout the twentieth century thoroughly and overtly, while both Díaz and Alvarez include more indirect denunciations.

On another level, resistance to the powerful and their narratives is found in the writers' approaches to this history—for instance, in the foregrounding of multiple perspectives, the telling of an unnarratable story, or the sharing of a traumatic experience. The expressed intentions behind these works are to educate Anglophone readers in the broader Americas about Dominican history, while also leaving space to represent ultimately unknowable histories and unspeakable experiences of violence and sexual abuse. Through the use of experimental techniques, these writers are able to build more inclusive histories with an eye to institutionalized racism, state-sponsored violence, and sexual exploitation. The blankness employed by all three writers leaves space for what is missing—the unrecoverable aspects of histories and experiences. Additionally, Faulkner's reversals and fragmentation of time, Gaines's polyvocality and play with stereotypes, Chauvet's symbolism and substitutions, and Danticat's direct engagement with rape and violence are all techniques employed to get at a fuller account of the past, beyond the eye of the historian.

In this way, the writers explored in this book work to combat the influences of official histories and authoritarian narratives through both the form and content of their novels and attempt to elucidate the enduring legacy of colonialisms in theses spaces and its lasting impact on sexuality and interpersonal relations. Looking back and learning from the resistance of the past may help us to build momentum toward the full-scale intersectional revolution required for our future. Patterns of resistance found running throughout the novels include relating to others as individuals in spite of destructive hierarchies, challenging racist and sexist social fictions, as well as the potential acceptance of racial, national, gender, sexual, and other forms of fluidity. If these values are to be respected more broadly—especially by those topping the social hierarchies—new ways of interacting should take the place of the vestigial cycles of destruction and hatred set in motion by multifaceted colonialisms in the hemispheric south.

Indeed, the negative ramifications of colonial relationships across these spaces are still present with us today, woven into current legal, economic, and political infrastructures of US and Caribbean societies. This leads me to inquire explicitly: What are twenty-first-century sites of policing, violence, and dehumanization that reflect this history? Some of the most overt examples include mass incarceration in the US, the immigration industrial complex, and the mistreatment of Haitians and Dominicans of Haitian descent living in the DR. More specifically, in the US, the control over gendered and racialized bodies enabled by the prison industrial complex should be seen as the logical continuation of legal policies like the Code Noir in Louisiana and the Black Code in Mississippi. Michelle Alexander convincingly argues that mass incarceration in the US emerged as "a stunningly comprehensive and well-disguised system of racialized social control that functions in a manner strikingly similar to Jim Crow" (4). Alexander contends that despite the fact that many people would deny it, the US criminal justice system can be viewed as a tool of racial control (183) and that African Americans are kept as a racialized undercaste through "the system of mass incarceration, a wide variety of laws, institutions, and practices—ranging from racial profiling to biased sentencing policies, political disenfranchisement, and legalized employment discrimination" (184).[2] In this way, the rhetoric may have changed—"felon" taking the place of the "N-word" as one Black minister in Mississippi asserts (Alexander 164)—but the effects of the social control initiated by systems of laws, such as the Code Noir and the Black Code, are still deeply embedded in our legal and judicial systems.

Changes in laws and policies, not an increase in crime, are responsible for the US prison population rising from 350,000 to 2.3 million in less than thirty years (Alexander 93).³ A parallel may be drawn here to how the phenomenon of mugging functioned in Great Britain in the 1970s. Great Britain adopted the concept of mugging from the US in 1972 (S. Hall et al. 6)—a new conceptualization of an old crime, violent street robberies—as well as the fear and "panic about race, crime, riot, and lawlessness" surrounding it (28). The crime predated the term, yet "the label helped to break up and recategorize the general field of crime—the ideological frame which it laid across the field of social vision," as we entered "the realm of the relation of facts to the ideological constructions of 'reality'" (S. Hall et al. 29). These examples demonstrate more specifically how fixation on crime and the rhetoric of law and order came to supplant previous systems of racialized control. In this way, "everyone knows—but does not say—that the enemy in the War on Drugs can be identified by race" (Alexander 103). The masking of this shared knowledge has led to a system extraordinarily difficult to uncover and dismantle. I argue that literature, however, provides a means for unmasking and spreading awareness of these structures of racialized policing.

Moreover, under the umbrella of the US prison industrial complex is the issue of privatized prisons and the related immigration industrial complex, both of which can be seen as the extension of the policing enabled by early slave codes. As a result of the extreme rise in the prison population due to mass incarceration, courts passed legislation that allowed prisons to be privatized (Price and Morris 4). The privatization of prisons complicates issues of accountability in terms of the power held over prisoners as a result of the "greater institutional distance between citizens and those producing and delivering services on their behalf" (Price and Morris 3).⁴ Yijia Jing states that private prisons are "punishment centered and benefit from high growth in inmate populations, longer terms, higher recidivism, and less rehabilitative spending" (64), and Michelle Alexander asserts that "prisons are big business and have become deeply entrenched in America's economic and political system" (230).⁵ Thus, with decreased accountability and increased financial gain to be had, privatized prisons can be seen specifically as the inheritance of earlier state-mandated systems of control established by slave codes and legal systems, which ensured that those with the power reaped the economic benefits of others' labor.

Relatedly, immigration detention centers in what Tom Wong refers to as "Western immigrant-receiving democracies" are a cog in the wheel of the immigration industrial complex and share similarities with the US prison system (3).⁶ Both the prison population and number of immigrants have risen inordinately, with data from the World Bank showing a nearly 200 percent increase in the number of international migrants in the last half-century (Wong 1). Unlike the issue of mass incarceration, those detained because of their immigration status have not typically been found guilty of any crimes, and a broad population—including torture survivors, victims of human trafficking (groups afforded protections under international human rights laws), legal permanent residents, and US citizens—is brought under the control of US immigration detention facilities (Wong 120). In general, "detention is a technique of government through which individuals and mobile populations become managed as illegal, undesirable or threatening" (A. Hall 7), illuminating an overt line of connection between immigration detention and earlier transnational systems for the management of racialized, gendered, and marginalized bodies. In detention centers, the bodies of the detainees—their health and overall physical state—are invested by politics and become the sites of battles for control (A. Hall 11). Thus, the bodies of detainees accrue meaning beyond their physicality for the political system at hand, reflecting the control over bodies perpetrated by the plantation system throughout the circum-Caribbean, as well as that required by the twentieth-century dictatorships of Rafael Trujillo and François Duvalier.

Corrections Corporation of America (CCA) became the first US federal agency to contract out the detention of immigrants to private prisons in 1984 (Taylor-Grover et al. 188), blurring the border between state-sponsored control of individuals, seen clearly in the example of the dictatorships, and corporate control. Privatization created a similar problem for immigration detention centers as that seen in the example of prisons (Taylor-Grover et al. 188). In addition to issues of cost, human rights violations—including allegations of subpar medical treatment, overpopulation, maltreatment or death, and lack of accessible legal resources (Taylor-Grover et al. 193–94)—are a major concern. Immigration detention centers have become notorious as the places most likely to see human rights violations occur within liberal democracies (Fiske 7) with frequent accusations of abuse—both physical and sexual (Fiske 6).[7] As of September 2019, "more than 52,000 immigrants [have been] confined in jails, prisons, tents and other forms of detention—most of them for profit" with thousands alleging physical and sexual abuse within those facilities (Kassie). Further, as of June 2019, 24 immigrants had died in the custody of US Immigration and Customs Enforcement during Donald Trump's presidency with at least 4 others dying shortly after their release (Rappleye and Seville). This figure does not include the deaths of immigrants in the custody of other federal agencies, including 5 children (Rappleye and Seville). Additionally, around 5,500 immigrant children have been separated from their parents by the Trump administration (Aguilera).[8] These sites are present-day examples of the ways in which the societal structures of the US, among other Global North countries, retain the hierarchical shape of previous systems, granting those at the top absolute power over the racialized and gendered bodies of individuals beneath them on the social ladders, resulting in flagrant, widespread dehumanization.[9]

If the echoes of previous systems of control from slavery to Jim Crow were not clear enough, making distinctions between people as a result of immigration status is "a haphazard or even deliberate exercise in racial and ethnic discrimination" (Wong 24), forming the basis for the racialization of immigration control with "illegal" becoming "synonymous with broad and often ill-defined racial and ethnic categorizations, such as Hispanic and Latino in the U.S. context or African and Asian (which subsumes those from the Middle East, South Asians, and East Asians) in the European context" (Wong 113). Similar to the minister's assertion that "felon" is "the new N-word" (Alexander 164), the language used to talk about immigration becomes racially coded, emphasizing the role of the US immigration industrial complex in the enduring state-sponsored systems of control that remain in place to regulate the bodies of people of color within its borders.

Not surprisingly, Haitians are one of the populations that the US targets through the immigration industrial complex. According to Carl Lindskoog, the criminalization of immigrants arose with the influx of Haitian immigrants four decades ago during François Duvalier's regime with "racist and xenophobic opposition at the state and local level" that contributed to a reversal of national immigration policy in 1981. The US did not want to alienate Duvalier, an anti-communist ally in the region, and when local officials protested the arrival of Haitian immigrants, the government classified them as "economic migrants," as opposed to "refugees," which made them ineligible for asylum (Lindskoog). Further, in November 2017, the Trump administration announced that it would not renew the Temporary Protected Status granted to sixty thousand Haitians with provisional legal residency, giving them eighteen months to leave; some have been in the country for more than seven years (Rubin). Thus, before turning to the fraught relationship between Haitians and Dominicans in our present period, it is important to acknowledge the appalling treatment Haitians received and continue to receive at the hands of the US government throughout the twentieth century and into the twenty-first.

The present-day relationship between Haiti and the Dominican Republic is another example of the ways in which governments, corporate powers, and dominant classes extend their control over marginalized bodies into the twenty-first century. Those topping the Dominican and Haitian social hierarchies have frequently colluded and continue to collude in the exploitation of Haitian migrants and the movement of this workforce across the border (Fumagalli 21). However, in 2013 a Dominican court ruling instituted policies preventing Haitian migration, as well as stripping 200,000 Dominicans of Haitian descent and their descendants of Dominican citizenship (Alarcon). The law is part of *la apatrida*, or "civil genocide," declaring Dominicans of Haitian descent born up until the 1930s as "'in transit'—only passing through—even if they had spent their entire lives in the Dominican Republic" (Ariza).[10] The Dominican legislature passed the Naturalization Law, or Law 169-14, supposedly to help Dominicans reclaim their citizenship, but unfortunately, to do so, they would need to provide records of their births or their parents' births in the DR—births that were deliberately denied this registration (Alarcon). Law 169-14 did little to mitigate the damage of the original ruling. The Dominican government is ignoring the fact that this ruling was found to violate the United Nations' Universal Declaration of Human Rights and is using it to exert power over the 750,000 Haitians living and working in the Dominican Republic (Ariza).

While Dominican President Danilo Medina claimed in 2015 that mass deportations would not occur and issued a moratorium through June 2015 (Ariza), between August 2015 and May 2016, more than 40,000 people (including several hundred children unaccompanied by adults) were deported to Haiti according to the International Organization for Migration (IOM) and Haitian civil society organizations (Amnesty International). Additionally, 68,000 people returned to Haiti, in many cases due to threats or the fear of persecution and violence in the DR (Amnesty International). Maria Cristina Fumagalli states that mutual respect and collaboration would be essential for the creation of a "less dysfunctional Hispaniola," as well as "a much needed social change that can counteract across-the-border structural violence only by putting people's social and economic rights, human dignity and environmental integrity and sustainability before profit and market forces" (312). New priorities running counter to colonial and neocolonial ideologies are necessary in order to break free from the ceaseless cycles of hatred, exploitation, and violence. This work is essential to stop the damage produced not only by the treatment of Haitians and Dominicans of Haitian descent in Dominican society but also by the US criminal justice and immigration systems into the twenty-first century.

I conclude with an invitation for future scholarship emanating from the intersection between literature and racial and sexual policing: How is twenty-first-century literature responding to and engaging with the exigencies and crises in our current moment?[11] What bodies of literature, both existing and developing, analyze these sites—for instance, the prison and the detention center? And importantly, how does this literature identify resistance, in relation to previous articulations of literary resistance, such as the examples explored at the start of this coda? To date and to my knowledge, there is a burgeoning collection of nonfiction texts responding to these spaces and experiences, including John Edgar Wideman's memoir detailing his brother's incarceration, *Brothers and Keepers* (1984); Edwidge Danticat's memoir involving her uncle's confinement in Krome Detention Center in *Brother, I'm Dying* (2007); and multidisciplinary artist Tings Chak's *Undocumented: The Architecture of Migrant Detention* (2014), which explores Canada's immigration detention system through interviews, comics, and architectural sketches.[12] *The Book of Rosy* (2020), coauthored by Rosayra Pablo Cruz, a Guatemalan asylum seeker, and Julie Schwietert Collazo, founder of Immigrant Families Together, tells the story of Rosy and her family's journey north to the border, forced separation, and devasting experience of detention. Published in the spring of 2020, this example demonstrates the developing nature of this genre. In terms of fiction, Mississippian Jesmyn Ward's *Sing, Unburied, Sing* (2017) centers on a family's road trip to Parchman Prison with stories from inside and outside this space interwoven together, while Rachel Kushner's *The Mars Room* (2018) centers on the experiences of women in a fictional correctional facility in California. Additionally, a few recent novels engage with these experiences in a more speculative way, including US novelist Ben Winters's *Underground Airlines* (2016), which takes place in a contemporary alternative-history US where slavery remained legal in Alabama, Louisiana, Mississippi, and an integrated Carolina; Egyptian Canadian writer Omar El Akkad's *American War* (2017), set in a US devastated by climate change during a second civil war in the 2070s; and Pakistan-born novelist Mohsin Hamid's *Exit West* (2017) about a young couple escaping their war-torn city through a system of magical doors connecting various points across the globe.[13] As this body of literature continues to expand, I invite scholars to explore connections to the previous systems of policing captured by their literary antecedents, as well as to forms of resistance to the status quo, overt and subtle, found in both the aesthetic choices and content.

NOTES

INTRODUCTION

1. I follow Régine Michelle Jean-Charles in referring to the author as Marie Chauvet, as opposed to Marie Vieux-Chauvet, since that is the name she chose for herself during her writing career ("Naming, Claiming, and Framing" 73).

2. I refer to the era following the colonial period as "post-/neocolonial" to imply through the juxtaposition of "post" and "neo" that the postcolonial period becomes neocolonial as a result of the lingering effects of the colonial system.

3. In times of turmoil, those at the top of the hierarchies with the most to lose—frequently straight, White, cisgender men—have a pronounced investment in retaining the status quo, while those beneath them in the social structure fervently police sexuality to retain their comparatively elevated positions. For instance, lower-class Whites violently enforced Jim Crow—a feat accomplished in part by appealing to the "racism and vulnerability of lower-class Whites, a group of people who are understandably eager to ensure that they never find themselves at the bottom of the American hierarchy" (Alexander 22). Gaines's *Of Love and Dust* examined in chapter 3 effectively explores the roles played by the upper-class White planter class and the lower-class White Cajuns in relation to the upholding of hierarchies.

4. The capitalization at the start of some quotations has been altered for readability.

5. This book builds on previous scholarship on intimacy, including the work of Michael Bibler, Sheryll Cashin, Francis Smith Foster, Anthony Giddens, Randall Kennedy, Rachel Moran, Christina Sharpe, and Ann Laura Stoler.

6. The conceptualization of the circum-Caribbean recognizes culture as "dynamic, nomadic, flowing" (Lowe, *Calypso Magnolia* xi) in a way that accounts for the reciprocal effects of the South and the Caribbean on each other, as well as the transnational expanse of the plantation economy (Lowe, *Calypso Magnolia* 1).

7. *Policing Intimacy* intends to contribute to the version of American Studies labeled "post-nationalist," which is defined by the authors of *Post-Nationalist American Studies* as a method that is "less insular and parochial and more internationalist and comparative" (Rowe 2).

8. American exceptionalism involves the dual beliefs that the US has something unique to offer the world (Lagon 44), as well as that the US is an exception to the rules, "exempting

itself from the norms it promotes, from multilateral agreements and bodies, and from scrutiny" (Lagon 45). Southern exceptionalism is the belief in a "cultural and historiographical construct," validating the "regional distinctiveness [that] moves the South outside the major historical currents in US history" (Edwards 533). Haitian exceptionalism is the belief that Haitian people are resistant to progress and that the devastation Haiti experiences, such as the 2010 earthquake, results from the nation's poverty and culture (Daut 607). Such a view does not acknowledge the culpability of Western powers in terms of Haiti's social, political, and economic issues (Trouillot 7), or the poverty and natural disasters occurring within the borders of the US.

9. The term *the color line* is generally used to refer to racial structures in the United States; however, W. E. B. Du Bois applied the term more broadly in *The Souls of Black Folk*, stating, "The problem of the twentieth century is the problem of the color-line,—the relation of the darker to the lighter races of men in Asia and Africa, in America and the islands of the sea" (9). The concept maps onto different spaces, shifting according to the cultural context in which it is located.

10. Immanuel Wallerstein describes "the extended Caribbean" as "stretching from northeast Brazil to Maryland" (167).

11. A significant amount of existing scholarship calls into question the all too neatly demarcated temporal and geographical boundaries that form when applying postcolonial concepts to the US South. To characterize the South merely as the periphery to the core of the North would be simplistic, given that the South technically exists within the boundaries of a First World nation and is a bivalent space that is "simultaneously center and margin, colonizer and colonized, global north and global south, essentialist and hybrid" (J. Smith, "Hot Bodies and 'Barbaric Tropics'" 105). I build on the work of scholars considering the US South in all of its postcolonial complexity, including Hosam Aboul-Ela, Sara Gerend, Édouard Glissant, Taylor Hagood, George Handley, John T. Matthews, and Jon Smith, as well as the anthologies *Look Away! The US South in New World Studies* and *Global Faulkner*.

12. I draw on the work of Anna Brickhouse, Myriam Chancy, Marlene Daut, Kirsten Silva Gruesz, Carlos Hiraldo, Caroline Field Levander, Robert S. Levine, John Wharton Lowe, Gretchen Murphy, Lucía M. Suárez, and Michele Wucker, among others.

13. In order to retain specificities of historical experiences of colonialism, conflicts, and resulting cultures, I work within the nation-state frame; however, at the same time, I value a consideration of multiple divergent spaces within the same conversation to take the pressures off of the limiting and reductive confines of the nation-state model. Ideas of America, Latin America, and the Western Hemisphere were not found but invented (Levander and Levine 4), and therefore, I consider nation as another socially constructed phenomenon, alongside race and other identity markers.

14. Public discussions of this topic date back to the multiracial movement, which began in the late 1970s, grew in the 1980s, and was organized around the need to bring changes to the methods of recording racial information on the US Census in the 1990s (Daniel et al. 6). Critical mixed race studies, however, solidified as a distinct academic field around 2004 (Daniel et al. 8).

15. Kimberlé Crenshaw is credited with coining the term *intersectionality* in her articles from 1989 and 1991 that explore "the various ways in which race and gender intersect in

shaping structural, political, and representational aspects of violence against women of color" ("Mapping the Margins" 1244). Crenshaw focuses specifically on the intersection between race and gender to emphasize "the need to account for multiple grounds of identity when considering how the social world is constructed" (1245). It is not accurate to consider racism as separate from sexism, as in reality aspects of identity are constantly present and overlapping—not neatly compartmentalized.

16. Although I follow Judith Butler in recognizing gender as "an identity instituted through a *stylized repetition of acts*" through time that "constitute the illusion of an abiding gendered self" without any deeper essence (519), in the majority of the texts considered here, gender is mapped onto a binary system with characters interpellated as either men or women. When I use the term "class," I refer to the comparative socioeconomic standing of an individual and whether or not he/she/they hold an upper-, middle-, or lower-class position in relation to others in the society.

17. Anna Brickhouse notes that the bulk of work in hemispheric American studies is written from within the United States, typically in English, and that the field has a "responsibility to consider and make self-conscious the geopolitics of knowledge delimiting the work that we do" ("Hemispheric Jamestown" 33).

18. In recognition of my own particular situatedness as a scholar, I leave space for local differences in my consideration of literature developed in specific places and also historical moments. Susan Gilman impresses on her reader the need for a "reading practice attuned to such a multidimensional, multidirectional comparability that can effect a union of temporality with its spatial complement, but not necessarily as equal partners" (331). Thus, throughout this project, I continually situate my exploration of the literary examples in a discussion of the context of the work in terms of both time and space.

19. A range of fields, including multilingual American studies, legal studies, postcolonial theory, global feminisms, critical mixed race studies, and hemispheric American literature, all have a stake in this conversation and could add meaningfully to its extension from different angles.

20. As identity has been proven to be fluid (even for literary characters), I do not mean to imply that I present the authentic or true version of Bon. I propose another way of seeing his character that tries to be conscious of Quentin and Shreve as narrators and the baggage they bring to their task of storytelling.

21. According to Valérie Loichot, *métissage*, "unlike *miscegenation*, not only defines race, but can also describe cultural, social, and gender blurring" (117). This term is thus more fluid and open.

22. In my work with Chauvet's fiction, I follow Hellen Lee-Keller's use of the term *Mulâtres-Aristocrates*. While *mulâtre* is a weighted, and even offensive, historical term, Lee-Keller adheres to Chauvet's language and incorporates *aristocrate* to emphasize the entwinement of race and class in Haitian society.

23. Additionally, the free people of color in the Spanish American colonies such as Santo Domingo, or today's Dominican Republic, were referred to as "*castas*," which were a more fluid population, since "familiar prestige and social status, beyond color, could determine a person's position in the colonial hierarchy" (Morelli 146). While the more fluid constructions of race found throughout the Caribbean and Latin America may appear less rigid

than, and by extension superior to, the binary system found in regions of the United States, Carlos Hiraldo leads by example in refraining from positioning one racial system as preferable to another, problematizing "the popular notion that race relations are more benevolently constructed within mulatto Latin American societies than within more hierarchical US structure" through exploring literary examples that undermine this framing (7).

24. Had the Bons not decided to pass in Louisiana, they may have lost their elite position, since "persons of mixed ancestry were 'redefined' as part of the black or 'slave' race during the 1830s" (Ladd xv) when the policy of segregation displaced that of assimilation following the Louisiana Purchase in 1803 (Ladd xiv).

25. Southern Mississippi, specifically the formerly French territory of Natchez, became part of British West Florida in the 1760s (Libby 18). In British regions, "the status of a mixed-blood child followed that of the mother, from the very beginning of the eighteenth century" (Ladd 21). This dualistic understanding of race in the colonial era was reified as a strict Black/White binary, resulting in the official adoption of the one-drop statute in Mississippi in 1917, which positioned every individual with any claim to African ancestry as Black (Sweet 318). The one-drop rule was in the air much earlier than its adoption as state law (beginning with Tennessee in 1910) (Sweet 318). For instance, the one-drop rule appeared in court cases in the US around 1850, lasting for about a century (Sweet 316). The adoption of the one-drop rule directly illustrates the ways in which the construction of race was shaped by law, as well as the vestigial effects of colonial policies in the post-/ neocolonial period.

26. I discuss the ways in which the various narrators' contradictory portrayals of Bon align with their divergent colonial mindsets in "Postcolonial Palimpsests: Entwined Colonialisms and the Conflicted Representation of Charles Bon in William Faulkner's *Absalom, Absalom!*"

27. Faulkner, as well as Quentin and his siblings, was born during the Radical era, and Richard Godden notes that "neither Faulkner nor the Compson children would have escaped apprenticeship to its pathologies" (*Fictions of Labor* 24).

28. In his portrayal of Bon as an extravagant European, Jason Compson may be aware of the phrase's potential as a euphemism for *biracial*, as a result of the racial flexibility connected with the French and Spanish colonies, or he may not have taken it this far, seeing in Bon only a foreignness that positions him outside Compson's acknowledged boundaries of the US South.

29. Interestingly, on a symbolic level, Bon's actions are also mediated by law in Quentin and Shreve's version of the events. The lawyer hired by Eulalia Bon manipulates Bon's behavior by sending him to the University of Mississippi to befriend Henry and ultimately seduce Judith—"*daughter? daughter? daughter?*" (Faulkner 241). For Bon's mother and the lawyer, incestuous sex and marriage across the color line matter less than family ties and inheritance in terms of the revenge plot.

30. According to Haney López, viewing race in a binary system also "forecloses an examination of the ways in which Asians and Blacks have been racialized against each other, rather than simply each in contrast to Whites, and impedes as well the conceptualization of Asians as members of diverse communities with particular histories" (*White by Law* 117). This is another obvious drawback to simplistic, binaristic understandings of race.

31. I adhere to Juana María Rodríguez's use of the term queer not as simply an umbrella term for sexual identities but as "a challenge to constructions of heteronormativity" that "creates an opportunity to call into question the systems of categorization that have served to define sexuality" (24). Rodríguez argues that queerness involves the critical practice of rejecting explication (24) and, in this way, is a term reflecting both fluidity and resistance to cultural norms and boundaries.

32. As Crenshaw notes, the interconnection of race, sexuality, and gender may have originated during colonial periods but remains a part of society today: "Much of the problem results from the way certain gender expectations for women intersect with certain sexualized notions of race, notions that are deeply entrenched in American culture. Sexualized images of African Americans go all the way back to Europeans' first engagement with Africans" ("Mapping the Margins" 1270–71).

33. This term is an abbreviation for Lesbian, Gay, Bisexual, Transgender, Queer, Intersex, and Asexual. The plus clarifies that this is an umbrella term meant to stand in for other related communities.

34. Terms such as colonial, postcolonial, and neocolonial are not only inadequate as a result of their inability to cleanly differentiate temporal periods, but also for their failure to account for the multiplicity of relations (McClintock, "The Angel of Progress" 86). Nevertheless, neocolonialism occurs when a region appears independent on the surface, while its economic and political systems are controlled from the outside. This power structure is evident in the way the Black population remains constrained and exploited by the former plantocracy after Emancipation. If the South existed in a colonial relation to the North during Reconstruction, this relationship may be seen as neocolonial in the post-Reconstruction era after the exodus of Northern troops.

35. As Martha Hodes notes, in the US South, the Ku Klux Klan was ultimately responsible for offering White southerners a "a new language of sexualized politics" (172–73).

36. For instance, in the US, naturalization laws determined who was allowed citizenship, segregation laws regulated where people could live and work, and antimiscegenation laws controlled sexual relationships (Haney López, *White by Law* 85). Together these laws "altered the physical appearances of this country's people, attached racial identities to certain types of features and ancestry, and established material conditions of belonging and exclusion that code as race" (Haney López, *White by Law* 85).

37. Both also enjoy wide readerships abroad and are particularly popular in France. Faulkner's popularity in France began in the 1930s: the first French translation was of *Sanctuary* in 1933 (Pitavy 85) with nine translations between 1946 and 1951 (Pitavy 88). The Legion of Honor was awarded to him in 1951 (Pitavy 88). A number of Ernest Gaines's works have also been translated into French, and he was made a Chevalier of the French Order of Arts and Letters in 2000 ("The Author"). *The Autobiography of Miss Jane Pittman* is a required text for high school national exams in France ("The Author").

38. As opposed to coming directly from the regime, the "pressure to stop distribution of the text came from the author's family" (Spear 14). After 1968, Chauvet's work circulated primarily in rare copies and photocopies with contracts for new editions and translations turned down by the family: "rumors circulated of family intrigues and political dramas that led to the persistent censorship of the trilogy, despite the fall of the dictatorship in 1986," resulting in contradictory myths (Spear 14).

39. Chauvet is a fearless writer who, like Faulkner and Gaines before her, uses her art to critique her current social and political moment, for instance, through what Colin Dayan describes as her "scathing analysis of Duvalier's dictatorship—more particularly, of women's place in a society crippled by color conflicts and social injustice" (*Haiti, History, and the Gods* 119).

40. Although she writes primarily in English, Danticat seems more interested in educating a Haitian and Haitian diasporic readership than a US-based one. She stated in reference to her motivations for *The Farming of Bones* (1998), written about the 1937 massacre of Haitians in the border region shared with the Dominican Republic, that "the massacre is not as well-known here as it is in Haiti . . . I wasn't thinking so much I wanted to popularize it with a larger audience as with younger people, like my brothers, who didn't know about it at all. It's a part of our history, as Haitians, but it's also a part of the history of the world. Writing about it is an act of remembrance" (Charters).

41. This information was conveyed to me by Gaines's biographer John Wharton Lowe at the 2018 Society for the Study of Southern Literature Conference in Austin, Texas.

42. All sources from the Gaines Papers are from the 115 collection. The citations list the box and folder numbers. I included the original page numbers from the documents whenever possible. This research was completed before the archives were reorganized. The citations refer to the former system; however, both systems are included under the images in chapter 2.

43. In contrast, given the complex publication history of *Love, Anger, Madness*—Marie Chauvet blocked the distribution, due to threats of retribution by Duvalier's regime, and prohibited further printings (Glover 14)—it is unsurprising that her papers have not been collected outside her family's archives (Jean-Charles, "Naming, Claiming, and Framing" 56). Of the contemporary writers included in this project, only Julia Alverez's papers have been collected thus far, and they are located at the Harry Ransom Center in Austin, Texas. Like Faulkner's, her work does not dramatically change from draft to draft, although the sheer amount of research incorporated into her historically based fiction is worth noting. Her extensive files include clippings of the Mirabals and the Trujillos, in addition to primary source documents, such as a published message that Trujillo addressed to his countrymen, "On the Tenth Anniversary of assuming the Political Direction of the Dominican People," and excerpts from *The Pocket Guide to Ciudad Trujillo* written by Erwin Walter Palm and published by Ciudad Trujillo in 1951.

44. For a more involved discussion of the relationship between historical works and fiction or art, see Hayden White's *Metahistory: The Historical Imagination in Nineteenth-Century Europe*. White notes that it is sometimes said that "the difference between 'history' and 'fiction' resides in the fact that the historian 'finds' his stories, whereas the fiction writer 'invents' his. This conception of the historian's task, however, obscures the extent to which 'invention' also plays a part in the historian's operations" (6). For more on historiographic metafiction, which "works to situate itself within historical discourse without surrendering its autonomy as fiction" (4), see Linda Hutcheon's "Historiographic Metafiction Parody and the Intertextuality of History."

45. Sadiya Hartman observes that some perspectives are left out of the archive entirely, such as autobiographical narratives by enslaved women who survived the Middle Passage ("Venus in Two Acts" 3–4). In her own work, Hartman narrates "counter-histories of

slavery" and represents "the lives of the nameless and the forgotten, to reckon with loss, and to respect the limits of what cannot be known" ("Venus in Two Acts" 4).

46. Hartman refers to the method guiding her writing as "critical fabulation" through which she rearranges aspects and reworks the sequence of events in different stories from contested perspectives to "jeopardize the status of the event, to displace the received or authorized account, and to imagine what might have happened or might have been said or might have been done" ("Venus in Two Acts" 11). In this way, she elucidates "the contested character of history, narrative, event, and fact, to topple the hierarchy of discourse, and to engulf authorized speech in the clash of voices" ("Venus in Two Acts" 12). As Nicole Aljoe has clarified, this does not mean inventing things whole cloth but "turning up the volume and refocusing on what had only seemed to recede into silence in comparison to what was going on in the foreground" (33).

CHAPTER 1
"WE WILL HAVE TO WAIT": RACIAL HIERARCHIES, PLANTATION INTIMACY, AND SEXUAL POLICING IN WILLIAM FAULKNER'S MISSISSIPPI

1. Although the Black Code focused on regulating the behavior of Black, White, and biracial people, Mississippi was home to people of other racial backgrounds, such as Indigenous populations like the Chickasaws, who appear in *Go Down, Moses* and *Absalom, Absalom!*

2. Michelle Alexander argues that segregation laws were calculated to deliberately separate lower-class Whites from African Americans through encouraging the former "to retain a sense of superiority over blacks, making it far less likely that they would sustain interracial political alliances aimed at toppling the white elite" (34). Thus, those with the power in society, upper-class White men, devised the system to retain their privileged positions.

3. The sharecropping system replaced slavery, and while the formerly enslaved were nominally free and compensated for their labor with a share of the crop, the system did not allow them to escape the grip of poverty or White control (Mandle 13). Since laborers had to remain on a plantation until the end of the crop year to receive any payment for their work, the sharecropping system allowed limited mobility, as well as inadequate opportunity for advancement and landownership (Mandle 22). Debt peonage, violence, and corruption, embedded within this system, restricted the rights of the formerly enslaved in the neocolonial period, further collapsing the distance between the pre- and post-Emancipation eras (Mandle 23).

4. Shades of slavery are also seen in the convict lease system in place after the Civil War. Convicts were leased out by southern states to work on railroads, in mines, or on large plantations, and employers did not have much capital invested in convict laborers or incentive to treat them well, as opposed to during the time of slavery (PBS). According to Douglas Blackmon, under the convict lease system, "the questions of who controlled the fates of black prisoners, which few black men and women among armies of defendants had committed true crimes, and who was receiving the financial benefits of their re-enslavement would almost always never be answered" (54).

5. The Black Code of 1865 in Mississippi was another attempt by White southerners to restrict the liberties of freed Black Americans, deny them justice, and restrain the social

effects of the Emancipation Proclamation as much as possible (T. Davis, *Games of Property* 31). Even though Mississippi ratified the Fourteenth and Fifteenth Amendments to the US Constitution in 1870, the oppressive conditions that the Black Code (most of which was repealed in 1870 after the damage was done) helped to keep in place continued and primed the country for the Jim Crow laws that followed the Mississippi Constitution of 1890 (T. Davis, *Games of Property* 33).

6. The Jim Crow laws were a segregationist strategy that produced racial stratification. The era was defined by "the legal construct of separate-but-equal segregated government services" (Blackmon 86).

7. For a discussion of the shadow family William C. Falkner potentially formed in his own backyard, see Joel Williamson's *William Faulkner and Southern History*.

8. These ties typically remained unacknowledged, however, and alternative domestic relations were purported. For instance, Clytie works as a house slave in *Absalom, Absalom!*, and Sutpen cannot say "my son" to Charles Bon (see figure 1.1).

9. These rules were invented to prevent sex across the color line (and also inbreeding), in order to uphold colonial hierarchies and ideologies. However, plantation culture granted White men complete authority over African Americans, women, and children.

10. Following in the footsteps of *Absalom, Absalom!*'s Henry Sutpen, Isaac McCaslin ultimately cannot accept the interracial as opposed to the incestual aspects of the relationship in "Delta Autumn." Isaac's thoughts confirm this: "*Maybe in a thousand or two thousand years in America ... But not now! Not now!*" (344).

11. In 1870, an era of political change in Mississippi following the Civil War, the ban was lifted, along with the punishments associated with marriage across the color line (Wallenstein 82). Like Reconstruction itself, this reprieve was short lived, and renewed regulation was enacted in 1880, according to which a person defined as White could no longer marry someone who had at least one-fourth African ancestry (Wallenstein 93).

12. This official state ban was written into the 1890 Constitution and continued into the twentieth century, later expanding to include individuals from other racial backgrounds, such as Chinese Americans (Mississippi Department of Archives and History 2).

13. Nevertheless, these restrictions remained on the books and in the constitutions of many states, with Louisiana and Mississippi waiting until 1972 to repeal their antimiscegenation laws, South Carolina not doing so until 1998, and Alabama holding out until 2000 (Kennedy 279).

14. Jesmyn Ward, a contemporary Mississippian writer, engages with similar themes to those explored by Faulkner—however, from the perspective of Black and biracial protagonists. In her novels, such as *Salvage the Bones* (2011) and *Sing, Unburied, Sing* (2017), women's perspectives are more developed. Thus, her work may be seen as filling in gaps left by Faulkner's.

15. The White fear of "miscegenation" or amalgamation can be traced back to a fear of the contaminating qualities of "black blood" that originated in the colonial era. Although all blood is red, White racists believed in biological differences between the races, which may explain the fixation on differences in blood.

16. In addition to his feminized style, and worldly ways, Bon is depicted as having spent his youth in pursuit of pleasure and indulgence, spending a large portion of his mother's money "on his whores and his champagne" (241).

17. As discussed in the introduction, Charles Bon's racial categorization shifts depending on his location: he is potentially a member of the *Mulâtres-Aristocrates* in Haiti, the Creoles of Color in New Orleans, and the Black race in Mississippi.

18. And perhaps this trace also exists on his father's side. Scholars such as James Snead have understood Sutpen, who merges with the "wild" enslaved men he meets in the ring and his biracial son through "the characteristic 'not smiling,'" to be "the source of a certain censored blackness in the narrative" (132–33). Similarly, Richard Godden argues that Sutpen's "mastery (white), embodied in Sutpen's Hundred ('*Be Light*' [p. 4]), derives from the labor of the slave and is experienced as doing so by a master who almost made himself black to get his Hundred built" (*Fictions of Labor* 54). In laboring with his enslaved men, Sutpen blackens himself; however, he reaffirms his mastery through fighting the enslaved men in the ring, as slavery "rests on a continuous repression of revolution" (*Fictions of Labor* 56).

19. I follow scholarship on Marie Chauvet's novella through my use of *Mulâtres-Aristocrates*, a term I will explicate more directly in chapter 4.

20. The lack of an English equivalent of the French *métissage* and the Spanish *mestizaje* is "explained by the extreme binary classification of people of the imagined 'black' and 'white' races in the United States while the French and Spanish legal systems included articles on various intermediate categories" (Loichot 124).

21. Loichot notes that Joe Christmas of *Light in August* embodies *métissage* and is the most threatening of Faulkner's mixed-race characters because his Blackness is speculative (125). However, as far as each of the narrators before Quentin's final retelling of the story is concerned, Eulalia Bon is a White Creole, making Bon's racial origins as uncertain as Christmas's. I agree with Loichot that Christmas is a social *métis* who embodies the neither-nor stretch in between social categories, yet while Bon lives as a refined upper-class White Creole in New Orleans, even down to his participation in what scholars have described as the *plaçage* system, in reality he too is a social *métis* as a rich (possibly) biracial man who offers an example "of difference becoming sameness" (127).

22. The Caribbean has been stereotypically associated with fluidity, license, and licentiousness from the interracial sex rampant during the colonial period, which brought into being an elaborate and precise color scale for determining social rank, to the modern-day portrayal of the Caribbean as America's tourist playground (Mohammed 25). As Benítez-Rojo states: "The Caribbean is the natural and indispensable realm of marine currents, of waves, of folds and double folds, of fluidity and sinuosity" (11).

23. His status as a law student at the university, his *plaçage* relationship with his Black "wife," and his engagement to the White planter's daughter Judith are experiences that would have been closed off to Bon in the antebellum South due to his race and lineage. While the *plaçage* system, formal relationships between White men and women of color in New Orleans, has been unmasked by Emily Clark as a concept developed in the twentieth century through a "circular feedback phenomenon" (149), Faulkner bought into the trope in his description of Bon's "marriage."

24. Given the association of race with economics and class in the antebellum South (and also in Haiti during Bon's time except with light skin supplanting white), Bon may also be seen as a type of economic *métis*. Through his lineage, Bon is literally an amalgamation

of the Black laboring body and the body of the White master at leisure. The linkage of race with economics remained central in the South through Faulkner's time, given that the "regime of accumulation," which depended on the abuse of Black labor, resisted transformation until the 1930s (Godden, "Faulkner at West Point"), underscoring Bon's economic status as *métis* in both Quentin and Shreve's turn-of-the-century period and the time of Faulkner's writing.

25. Not only was the myth of the Black rapist used as a political weapon to keep African Americans disenfranchised and disparage interracial sexuality, but it was also employed by White racists as justification for the practice of lynching. During the period after the Civil War, the lynching of Black men by White men was no longer the destruction of their own property but a type of compensation or catharsis through which they channeled the rage that accompanied the economic loss they endured through Emancipation (Wiegman 84). Alongside the rape of Black women and the creation of the myth of the Black rapist, lynching was an important tool used by southern Whites to maintain plantation hierarchies in the neocolonial period and particularly in the Radical era.

26. I discuss Faulkner's racially ambiguous bootleggers more fully in "Racial Ambiguity, Bootlegging, and the Subversion of Plantation Hierarchies in Faulkner's South."

27. Theresa Towner states that Christmas "murders and is murdered because of the American color line, yet who never knows where he stands in relation to it" (21). The last words of Percy Grimm to Christmas after he has killed and castrated him—"Now you'll let white women alone, even in Hell"—serve to connect Christmas more solidly to the myth of the Black rapist than anything in his life (464).

28. The myth of the Black rapist also had the consequence of dissuading White people from supporting the cause of Black equality. Angela Davis writes: "Not only was opposition to individual lynchings stifled—for who would dare to defend a rapist?—white support for the cause of Black equality in general began to wane" (187). Further, the depiction of Black men as rapists "reinforces racism's open invitation to white men to avail themselves sexually of Black women's bodies" (Angela Davis 182).

29. Additionally, the destruction of family units directly results from the murder and specifically the castration of Black males, as these acts can literally be seen as attempts to thwart Black male lineage in the post-slavery period, as observed by Elizabeth Hopwood.

30. Faulkner also wrote against lynching in a number of his public letters. For example, in "Press Dispatch Written in Rome, Italy, for the United Press, on the Emmett Till Case" published in the *New York Herald Tribune* on September 9, 1955, Faulkner states that "if we in America have reached that point in our desperate culture when we must murder children, no matter for what reason or what color, we don't deserve to survive, and probably won't" (*Essays, Speeches & Public Letters* 223).

31. I find Isaac's choice of pronouns in this statement interesting. His use of "we" places himself and Roth's mistress in the same position in relation to interracial sex, although the issue is much more real and immediate for her than it ever was for Isaac. This would seem to reduce or demean the immediacy of the woman's predicament, as well as the possibility that her situation could be resolved were Roth Edmonds to form a family unit with her and her son.

32. Although they were rendered unenforceable by the Supreme Court in the *Loving v. Virginia* case (1967), Mississippi did not repeal its antimiscegenation laws until 1972 (Kennedy 279).

33. I credit John Matthews with this complication of Lucas's resistance.

34. Joel Williamson describes how southern women remained "pedestalized" after Emancipation (386). While he claims that interracial sex diminished, he writes: "Prostitution was another way in which white men might spare their wives the 'indignity' of a lusty sex life" (386).

35. Her voice is notably absent from the excerpted passages written in her husband's hand described on pages 254 and 255. Indeed, as Jay Watson observes, *Go Down, Moses* contains no evidence that Mrs. McCaslin received a genealogical entry in the ledgers.

36. Women attorneys were not allowed to practice in federal court until 1879 (B. Burns 108). Interestingly, Black litigants "participated in over 600 civil cases in eight Southern appellate courts between 1865 and 1920" (Milewski 723), often hiring White lawyers for civil trials and sometimes Black lawyers for criminal trials (Milewski 732). Even though Black lawyers existed in the fifty years following the Civil War, they made up only 2 percent of lawyers in the US South (Milewski 732), which I argue likewise exemplifies the silencing of particular voices.

37. In a letter to Hal Smith describing his decision to have Quentin Compson narrate *Absalom, Absalom!* (then titled "Dark House"), Faulkner writes: "I use his bitterness which he has projected on the South in the form of hatred of it and its people to get more out of the story itself than a historical novel would be. To keep the hoop skirts and plug hats out, you might say" (Blotner 327).

38. This may speak to the fact that the baby is more of a plot device than a fully formed character; however, Temple's baby joins the other unnamed female characters described above.

39. Doreen Fowler argues that Nancy's act of infanticide, as well as Sethe's in Morrison's *Beloved*, needs "to be read in the context of a patriarchal culture that seeks to make women abject. Pressed by this culture, Nancy and Sethe are driven to a last desperate alternative. Both women choose death for the child over life in a life-destructive patriarchal culture" (143). I agree with this argument but also note that it is important not to collapse the actions of Nancy and Sethe, given the temporal difference between the two (Sethe acts during the antebellum period and Nancy in the 1930s). Moreover, as Fowler notes, the threat that the schoolteacher in *Beloved* poses to Sethe and her children is much more concrete than the danger Pete represents in *Requiem* (143–44).

40. Temple references her split identity at other points in the book as well. She states, "So already you've got two different people begging for the same clemency; if everybody concerned keeps on splitting up into two people, you wont even know who to pardon, will you?" (123) and, in reference to asking the judge to save Nancy, "whether you want to save her or not, will consider saving her or not; which if either of us, Temple Drake or Mrs Gowan Stevens either, had any sense, would have demanded first of you" (101).

41. Nancy's physical and sexual abuse at the hands of a White man exposes the bodily trauma essential to the colonial system, which granted White men license over female and Black bodies. Temple recounts how the White man "knocked [Nancy] across the pavement

into the gutter and then ran after her, stomping and kicking at her face or anyway her voice which was still saying 'Where's my two dollars, white man?'" (96).

42. In Temple's words: "I met the man, how doesn't matter, and I fell what I called in love with him and what it was or what I called it doesn't matter either because all that matters is that I wrote the letters—" (116). Red was hired by Popeye to rape Temple for Popeye's viewing pleasure, and Temple became attached to Red. It is unclear to the reader whether or not we are meant to read this as an instance of Stockholm syndrome or something like it.

43. I argue that Temple's level of consent here is ambiguous. If she was attached to Red as a result of something like Stockholm syndrome, then her desire to leave with Pete could be attributed to a similar reaction.

44. While, as Doreen Fowler notes, the threat to the baby is questionable, Gavin Stevens at least appears to believe the child would have been at risk, stating "that the adults, the fathers, the old in and capable of sin, must be ready and willing—nay, eager—to suffer at any time, that the little children shall come unto Him unanguished, unterrified, undefiled" (129). I read this statement by Gavin as implying that the suffering of Nancy and Temple through the child's murder is warranted to protect the children from anguish, terror, and defilement, which they may have received at the hands of Pete or Gowan.

45. Orlando Patterson describes "natal alienation" as "the loss of ties of birth in both ascending and descending generations," as well as the "loss of native status, of deracination" (7). Natal alienation, or the destruction of Black kinship ties, was a horrible effect of slavery that has remained "throughout the twentieth century with the separation of families and the denial of familial bonds" (T. Davis, *Games of Property* 234).

46. Doreen Fowler connects Faulkner's *Requiem for a Nun* and Morrison's *Beloved* through the authors' refusal to "recoil" (139) from infanticide and the shared plot device wherein "a mother or mother-surrogate kills an infant" out of love as opposed to hate (139–40). Morrison's Pulitzer Prize–winning novel was inspired by the story of Margaret Garner, an enslaved woman who made it into the newspapers for killing her child.

47. However, there is also a sense in which Nancy's actions recall the trope, common in earlier US southern and Caribbean literature, of the good slave who sacrifices herself—often for her White family. One of the first instances of this trope is found in "Friendly Advice to the Gentlemen-Planters of the East and West Indies" (1684), reprinted in *Caribbeana: An Anthology of English Literature of the West Indies, 1657–1777* (edited by Thomas W. Krise). The trope of the good slave recurs in abolitionist literature throughout the eighteenth and nineteenth centuries and is perhaps most overt in Maria Edgeworth's "Grateful Negro," published in 1804. I thank Nicole Aljoe for suggesting this connection.

48. For more on the intersection of race and class in the mid-twentieth-century South, see Brannon Costello's *Plantation Airs: Racial Paternalism and the Transformations of Class in Southern Fiction, 1945–1971*.

49. Glissant notes that this incest would not be uncharacteristic for Sutpen (see figure 1.1), as he notes that for some time General Compson had believed that Bon's child, brought to the plantation by the child's biracial mother, was actually the son of Clytie (Sutpen's daughter with an enslaved women) and Sutpen—a situation that would directly mirror that of Old Carothers, Eunice, and Tomasina (136).

50. Other examples not covered in this chapter include the fellowship created by Judith, Clytie, and Rosa when the men are away fighting in the Civil War in *Absalom, Absalom!* and Dilsey's preservation of the Gibson family in the face of societal upheaval in *The Sound and the Fury* (1929).

CHAPTER 2
"THERE IS NO IN-BETWEEN": COMMUNITY, SEXUALITY, AND THE SHIFTING CONSTRUCTION OF RACE IN ERNEST GAINES'S LOUISIANA

1. Although often conceived as such in popular culture, the US South is not a monolith. Jessica Adams emphasizes the South "as a heterogeneous region that blurs not only into other parts of the United States but into the larger plantation region of the Americas" (17). Alecia Long adds that New Orleans, Tampa, Miami, and El Paso are often viewed as in but not of the South, as a result of the diversity and complexity of these cities; however, not including them creates a false sense of southern homogeneity (5).

2. The Haitian Revolution had a significant impact on Louisiana. It led to the Louisiana Purchase, contributed to national slavery debates, and caused slavery to become more entrenched in New Orleans (Aslakson 13). The first wave of immigration due to the Haitian Revolution was caused by the burning of Cap Français in 1793, followed by a wave in 1798 after the defeat of British forces, and another in 1803–04 following the victory of Jean Jacques Dessalines's forces (Aslakson 21).

3. Since many enslaved people in Saint-Domingue were brought directly from Africa to replace those lost at a murderous rate to the brutal labor of the sugar plantations, these immigration waves fostered connections between Louisiana and not only the West Indies but also Africa. In addition, enslaved people were brought straight to Louisiana from Africa between 1719 and 1731, which aided in the development of what Gwendolyn Midlo Hall terms the "Afro-creole slave culture of New Orleans" based on "a separate language community with its own folkloric, musical, religious, and historical traditions" (59). The mélange of different languages, cultures, and customs in this early period, resulting from the slave trade and other forms of immigration from Europe and the West Indies, helped establish the region's racial fluidity and multiculturalism.

4. It was easier for the formerly enslaved in Latin America and the French West Indies to assimilate into free society than it was in Anglo-American colonies, and due to the proximity and cultural influence of that region, this was true to a certain extent in the territory that would become Louisiana (Aslakson 5). The French and Spanish colonial governments allowed free people of color more rights and privileges than were found in other states, and this difference survived the Louisiana Purchase (Aslakson 5).

5. The legal differences between the English, French, and Spanish colonies had far-reaching effects on the lives of those spanning all levels of society. For instance, slavery in the English colonies, which lacked a comprehensive set of slave laws, was known to be harsher than in the Spanish and to a lesser extent the French colonies (Aslakson 5). At the same time, however, the threat of being sold "down river" to Louisiana was a terrifying prospect for enslaved people in the upper South. This seems to support the opposite claim but may also speak to shifts in the system as Louisiana reached statehood or to the

"murderous work of sugar" (Sublette 170), which a refugee from Saint-Domingue, Antoine Morin, helped Louisiana planter Etienne Boré first granulate in 1794 (Baptist 51). H. Sophie Burton adeptly summarizes the debate over the nature and severity of Louisiana's slave system in the foreword to *The Forgotten People: Cane River's Creoles of Color*. Scholars, such as Gwendolyn Midlo Hall, state that the French slave regime was harsher than the Spanish, and others like Gilbert S. Din argue that Louisiana's regime was consistent with other Spanish colonies, due to Iberian slave laws (xv). Thomas N. Ingersoll asserts that "the shift in regimes from French to Spanish to American had little appreciable impact on the colony's social order, which remained consistently one of brutally enforced white planter control over a black majority" (xv).

6. While other racial groups, such as Indigenous peoples, inhabited Louisiana, the codes were established to police the interactions between Black, White, and biracial populations.

7. The Carmiers, however, are distinct from their Creole of Color ancestors. As Thadious Davis observes, "They are rural, uneducated tenant farmers and sharecroppers, who, by their refusal to recognize that for a century before Raoul Carmier's time Creoles of color no longer had any official sanction, persist in empty, self-isolating forms" ("Headlands and Quarters" 7–8).

8. Nelson is Catherine's son by a dark-skinned man who was driven off by Raoul before he could marry her. We can read this example as evidence of Raoul's racism and also his fear of losing his daughter to another man.

9. Sterling Brown, a professor of African American literature and folklore, was the first scholar to call attention to the stereotype of the "tragic mulatto" in his writings from the 1930s through the 1960s (Sollors 223). While scholars typically note that the trope of the "tragic mulatto" originated with Lydia Maria Child's short stories, "The Quadroons" published in 1842 and "Slavery's Pleasant Homes" in 1843, a cross-cultural lens directs us toward Victor Séjour's "The Mulatto" (1837). Although published before Child's work and in a different language and country—French and France—the tale is also in conversation with the stereotype in interesting ways.

10. Raoul exists in a liminal position as neither White nor Black, alienating himself from both communities: "He hates one as much as he does the other" (Gaines, *Catherine Carmier* 114). As a result, Aubert rightly asserts that Raoul is "the truly tragic mulatto, but individualized to the point of universality, and abrogative of literary stereotype" (70).

11. These types of marriages were also popular due to Louisiana inheritance laws, according to Maria Hebert-Leiter. Hebert-Leiter explains that forced heirship was written into the Digest of 1808: this meant that all inherited, not just the first son, and the family land was divided. Therefore, Cajuns, for instance, married first cousins in order to keep land within the family.

12. The stakes for the interracial pairings could not be higher in *Of Love and Dust*: the safety of the entire Black community is on the line.

13. Scholars have long depicted the antebellum system of *plaçage* as based on "formal and sometimes even contractual arrangements between white men and women of color [or placées] in New Orleans," which resembled marriage but without the legal sanction of the state (Long 7). Emily Clark convincingly argues against the existence of the system, positioning the *plaçage* complex as a "circular feedback phenomenon that fed the invention

and proliferation of activities in New Orleans designed to satisfy the market for encounters with quadroons aroused by the earliest accounts" (149). She provides evidence of the connection between the first uses of the term and the culture and customs of Haitian refugees living in New Orleans, such as the ménagère system (156), the tradition of balls in Saint-Domingue (155), and the use of the word *plaçage* to refer to relationships between men and women of the same racial ancestry (159–60). Clark asserts that it is not possible to find "good evidence for the use of the term *plaçage* by antebellum New Orleanians" (148) and instead that it is "a term commentators began applying in the twentieth century to liaisons between white men and free women of color in antebellum New Orleans" (66). She goes as far as to position the concept as almost as fanciful as the trope of the "tragic mulatto" (149).

14. Jane's narrative exists within the frame of a young Black history teacher who has interviewed and recorded her words. The readers do not have direct access to Miss Jane or to the other voices she catalogues in the text. Jane is nevertheless "a believable narrator with an authentic voice" (Gaudet 23). Jane's voice is so convincing that many believe she is an actual person: for example, Hugh Carey, a former New York governor, included her on a list of historical Black women (Gaudet 24).

15. Michel Foucault builds on Jeremy Bentham's figure of the Panopticon: a circular structure surrounding a central tower "pierced with wide windows that open onto the inner side of the ring; the peripheric building is divided into cells, each of which extends the whole width of the building; they have two windows, one on the inside, corresponding to the windows of the tower; the other, on the outside, allows the light to cross the cell from one end to the other," making highly visible the inhabitants of each cell to the occupants of the tower (200). Those in the cells know they could be watched at any time but are unable to verify when the tower is occupied. Thus, it does not matter who occupies the tower, or even if anyone does, since the structure itself and this accompanying uncertainty cause the feeling of uninterrupted surveillance.

16. The day Tee Bob saw Mary Agnes for the first time (170), as well as the day he saw her face for the first time (172), are important moments recorded by the community, which also speaks to the important role played by looking—and appearances—in the formation of their friendship.

17. Mary Agnes has no control over the situation. Although she is not interested in Tee Bob, she can't prevent him from pursuing her: "'I can't help it if he want ride through the quarters side me,' she said. 'I can't make him leave his own gate'" (178).

18. Matthew Teutsch and Katharine Henry astutely point to a moment from Tee Bob's past to illustrate his ignorance of the rules, which his family never effectively explain to him: "After his father Robert sends Timmy [Tee Bob's biracial half-brother] away for beating the white overseer Tom Joe, Miss Jane says that Tee Bob understood Timmy was different but he could not comprehend why Timmy had to leave the plantation" (518).

19. These multiple voices are especially pronounced in the description of Mary Agnes and Tee Bob's last confrontation. We do not get a direct account of the action but only what Clamp Brown sees and hears. He relies on other members of the community, Jane, Ida and Joe Simon, to care for Mary Agnes and alert the Samson household.

20. This motivation to present as a higher class is made clear in the text. Jimmy's father and his brothers owned a place "no more than a small farm but they called it a plantation—just so people would think they was in the upper class" (176).

21. In the earlier drafts, Jimmy leads a lynch mob calling for Mary Agnes's death. After hearing Tee Bob's mother read his suicide note out loud, the mob disperses except for Jimmy, who is about to lynch Mary Agnes by himself before a glance at Robert turns him around (Gaines Papers 6.18, 248).

22. Teutsch and Henry argue that the letter opener "symbolizes a relic of the Samsons' robust political and economic power," illustrating how the logic behind the plantation rules "is internally inconsistent and unstable such that the Samson house is dismantled from the inside out" (522). I agree with this observation. The fact that Tee Bob moves from the quarters to the interior of the plantation home to take his own life also supports the claim.

23. Further, Tee Bob kills himself in the library, surrounded by "too many books on slavery in that room" (206) and "pictures of the old people" (195) that shake as Robert attempts to break down the door, symbolizing the suffocating weight of History that in part leads to Tee Bob's suicide.

24. Gaines seems to anticipate Bhabha's phrasing here. A similar instance of this language appears in Faulkner's *Go Down, Moses* (1942): the arms of Tomey's Terrell (a biracial enslaved man who is both the son and grandson of Old Carothers McCaslin) were "supposed to be black but were not quite white," similar to Terrell's Sunday shirt that was "supposed to be white but wasn't quite either" (28).

25. We can connect Tee Bob's use of the term *looking* here back to the depictions of him casting his White, male gaze on Mary Agnes, discussed previously. However, here, how you look at someone also stands in for how you treat someone.

26. This view of Tee Bob is complicated by the fact that suicide itself is often considered to be a sin.

27. The system of slavery was founded on the abuse of nonwhite bodies and subjectivities—abuse that was considered acceptable since nonwhite bodies were thought to be less than human and therefore to not suffer in the same way as White bodies. Thus, racism in postplantation/neocolonial societies, such as the United States, is not just found in "isolated instances of conscious bigoted decisionmaking or prejudiced practice, but [is] larger, systemic, structural, and cultural, as deeply psychological and socially ingrained" (Matsuda et al. 5).

28. This passage continues: "Everything was for teaching. But she wanted to stay pure. She wanted to be pure all her life. When Tee Bob raped her, it was just like killing her. Life—nothing mattered. Definitely no more teaching" (Gaines Papers 6.18, 242–43). Tee Bob may have lost his life at the end of the episode, but Mary Agnes lost her life's meaning, which is also substantial.

CHAPTER 3
"THEY WERE STARTING SOMETHING": RACE, GENDER, AND FAILED REVOLUTION IN ERNEST GAINES'S *OF LOVE AND DUST*

1. Gaines references this process in an interview with John Wharton Lowe. He notes in particular that there were several drafts of *Of Love and Dust* that he saved ("An Interview with Ernest Gaines" 328).

2. Further, one of the most discussed Hollywood films in 1967 was *Guess Who's Coming to Dinner*, which positively portrayed an interracial couple (Kennedy 104). This example demonstrates the broader representation of interracial relationships in US culture at that time.

3. These interracial connections went beyond the sexual in this community as well: Richard Loving's White father worked for a Black man for twenty-three years, and Richard himself co-owned a drag-racing car with two Black friends (Kennedy 273).

4. In this way Richard was "dangerous both to the creamy class that evaded its Negroness and to whites that dated or copulated interracially and surreptitiously" (Cashin 106). By trying to make his relationship legal, Richard brought attention to the interracial mingling in Central Point, which, given the laws against interracial relationships, would have been better left out of the spotlight at that time.

5. Valerie Babb sees this as characteristic of Gaines's "vision of protest and change" overall (75). According to Babb, "his characters do not effect large social and racial transfigurations; they simply attempt to make sense of their personal world against the larger backdrop of society's forces. The most important battle they wage is that for their individual dignity; without this, no true social change will be possible or effective" (75). She views Gaines as interested in social change but through the lens of the individual.

6. In a draft of his speech entitled "Another Frontier," Gaines notes that although the novel was written about people on a Louisiana plantation in 1948, he does not feel society has changed much since then: "Men and women no longer work the fields as they did then, but the same old prejudices still survive" (Gaines Papers 4.7, 7). Writing from the 1960s about the 1940s, Gaines recognized the entrenched effects of the plantation system on this community.

7. Marcus further illustrates this type of irrational passionate love through refusing to leave Louise and Tite behind to save himself in the moments before he is killed. Ordinarily, his sole obligation is to himself, but in this example, he shirks that responsibility as a result of his feelings for Louise.

8. The year 1948 was an important one for Gaines himself. It was the year he left Louisiana to live with family in California, which according to Lowe was "a move that he credits as a kind of salvation" ("Transcendence in the House of the Dead" 143).

9. Although he is a combination of multiple races and ethnicities, Marcus is taken to be Black in the novel. Since race is a social construction determined relationally in communities, I consider him in those terms in this chapter.

10. Diane Chiriani Russo discusses Marcus's accusation of Jim as "whitemouth" (6) as a metaphor for the narrative voice, which on the surface is "often dominated by the standardized language associated with white control" (95).

11. It is necessary for Sun Brown to narrate the scene of Marcus's death. If Jim were present, he may have interfered in the fight between Marcus and Bonbon, as opposed to neutrally observing.

12. Just as interesting as what Jim relates that he could not have had access to is what he leaves undepicted. As the stories of the lovers are told from without, no one is in the room to describe the acts themselves—a reticence Suzanne Jones believes to be "embedded in the novel's structure" (156). Indeed, the lovemaking is expressed based on shifting sounds

overheard by Pauline's neighbors, which is later mirrored by Margaret listening to Marcus and Louise. While possibly just a convention of the time and genre, this absence of direct depictions of the interracial sex emphasizes its importance in the novel.

13. Given the time period, it would be unacceptable for Bonbon and Pauline to travel alone to Baton Rouge together, which necessitates Jim's presence. Securing a room for the interracial couple causes Jim to feel like a pimp, which forces him "to take a long hard look at how he is implicated in maintaining the status quo for black people when he facilitates the southern racial customs that discriminate against them" (Jones 154). These interactions, in addition to his friendship with Marcus, lead him toward the action he takes at the end of the novel.

14. Maria Herbert-Leiter astutely observes that Gaines's portrayals of Cajuns are often as sympathetic as his depictions of Black characters (98).

15. When asked to rake Marshall's lawn, Marcus is concerned Marshall might be "one of them fat old punks" and confirms that he will labor physically but that he "ain't messing with no punk—I don't care who he is" (186). After learning about the sexual exploitation that Marcus witnessed in jail committed by a prisoner named Horse Trader, this fixation, while not excused, can be understood a bit better.

16. Although silence surrounds the pervasiveness of homosexual relationships during the early history of the United States, Frances Smith Foster argues there is evidence that, like other antebellum groups, "African American communities recognized enduring, personal relationships that were not heterosexual" (38).

17. Diane Russo Chiriani effectively summarizes scholars' characterizations of Marcus, such as Thadious Davis's depiction of him as a blues subject or urban badman, Sherley Anne Williams's consideration of him as a hero in an untraditional, non-Western sense, Marcia Gaudet's positioning of him as a type of folk hero, and H. Nigel Thomas's portrayal of him as the "Bad N*** of folklore" (101–2). I agree that the text positions Marcus as rebel and unconventional hero, but I am also interested in the ways in which he complicates these roles.

18. In a draft of "Another Frontier," Gaines describes the four central characters in *Of Love and Dust* as finding "ways to love each other" even with everything against them: "Nothing permanent—no. That could not be possible under the condition in which they lived. But until society caught up with them, they did love. Loved as well, as truly, as they had ever done in the past, or as they would ever do in the future. But they were the first, they were breaking a [new] ground, and they had to be destroyed" (Gaines Papers 4.7, 7). Gaines believes the characters were capable of love for each other under these circumstances, in spite of the problematic origins of the two relationships.

19. Eventually perhaps, yet this type of relationship between a White man and Black woman is a less explicit threat to the hierarchies in place given a plantation culture's institutionalization of this pattern of abuse.

20. As discussed in chapter 2, Gaines likes to employ and ultimately undermine common stereotypes, such as the figure of the "tragic mulatto." He places his characters in this novel in conversation with the "notion popular in the 1960s that black men have sex with white women as revenge for past racial wrongs," yet complicates this connection through Louise's own revenge motivation (Jones 155) and their subsequent emotional bond.

21. Although she is referred to as Aunt Margaret throughout the text, she does not appear to be anyone's aunt, linking her name with the use of the term *aunt* to show respect to older enslaved women during the antebellum period. As a result, I choose to refer to her as Margaret in this chapter.

22. This echoes Roth Edmonds's comment in Faulkner's *Go Down, Moses*, when he is overheard saying, "does and fawns—I believe he said women and children—are two things this world aint ever lacked" (331), and also asking Isaac McCaslin if he hasn't discovered that "women and children are one thing there's never any scarcity of?" (323).

23. As Gaines states in unpublished commentary on the novel: "Marcus is not just a rejected suitor; he is a Black man who has been rejected by a Black woman in favor of a white man" (Gaines Papers 4.11, 190/159). This does not excuse but may explain his explosive reaction to Pauline.

24. As Keith Byerman raised at the 2016 National Endowment for the Humanities Summer Institute, "Ernest J. Gaines and the Southern Experience," this description of Louise would seem to put Marcus in conversation with pedophilia, adding further complications to the portrayal of sexuality in the novel. I agree with Byerman that this aspect adds complexity; however, I consider the intended effects of Louise's infantilization to be the emphasis on her difficult childhood and resulting mental and emotional arrested development, as well as the immaturity she shares in common with Marcus.

25. Louise's grotesque Whiteness is further exemplified by the episode in which she and Tite appear in blackface, positioning her as a White minstrel figure exploiting and appropriating Blackness in service of her escape. Louise puts soot on herself and her daughter in the hope that they will be able to pass as Black and escape Louisiana with Marcus. One of the strangest aspects of this scene is Margaret's assertion that it works: "you couldn't tell Louise wasn't colored" (243). This illustrates the complicated entwinement of race, gender, class, and ethnicity in the novel.

26. Pages from this incomplete commentary are located in the archives at the Ernest J. Gaines Center. There are no notes mentioning another author, which led head archivist Cheylon Woods to conclude that Gaines himself wrote the document. It includes two sets of page numbers: one type-written and the other written by hand.

27. Gaines stated in an interview with John O'Brien that "dust is the opposite of love" and that "the dust is death" (Lowe, *Conversations with Gaines* 35). Thus, we can read into the fact that dust keeps the couple from seeing each other in this scene—just as death will ultimately separate them at the end of the novel.

28. As John Wideman puts it, "Black people had feared Marcus because they recognized in him a threat to stable order; they preferred enduring a known evil to challenging the established order and opening the door to chaos" (78). Memories of past violence are responsible for this preference for the "stable order."

29. This is the same asylum that Benjy Compson is sent to at the end of *The Sound and the Fury*.

30. After Marcus's mother passes away and his dad leaves him, he gets a job in a parking lot where a man named Big Red would take his earnings. Eventually young Marcus hits Big Red over the head with a bottle and is sent to jail, where he is also exploited. A series of men in jail force Marcus to give them cigarettes until one day Marcus refuses to submit,

thinking, "If I had to go through life like that, life wasn't worth it" (252–53). He is beaten each time he refuses. When he gets out of jail, he commits to the mentality of only looking out for himself.

CHAPTER 4
"FOR FEAR OF A SCANDAL": SEXUAL CONTROL, RACISM, AND THE PUBLIC NATURE OF PRIVATE RELATIONS IN MARIE CHAUVET'S TWENTIETH-CENTURY HAITI

1. The day after François Duvalier's death on April 21, 1971, his son Jean-Claude was made president for life (Dubois 350). His reign lasted fourteen years, and thus in total, the Duvalier family was in charge of the country from 1957 to 1986 (Dubois 350).

2. Marlene Daut notes that the article by David Brooks subscribing to such beliefs, "The Underlying Tragedy," was published in the *New York Times* twelve days after the earthquake (606).

3. Daut effectively argues against Haitian exceptionalism in *Tropics of Haiti*, stating, "We can find the new narratives we seek" (611).

4. According to Colin Dayan, the publication of the trilogy itself created a scandal. Chauvet had "occupied a privileged position as a beautiful, light-skinned member of the Port-au-Prince bourgeoisie" but that the "publication of this scathing analysis of Duvalier's dictatorship—more particularly, of women's place in a society crippled by color conflicts and social injustice—caused a scandal" (*Haiti, History, and the Gods* 119). While the publication history of *Love, Anger, Madness*, such as the threats of reprisal from the regime and family pressure to stop distribution that led Chauvet to retract the book (Bell, "Permanent Exile"; Spear 14), is truly fascinating, I agree with Régine Michelle Jean-Charles that it is extraneous to literary analyses of the text ("Naming, Claiming, and Framing" 54). Jean-Charles astutely observes that the myths and rumors reduce Chauvet to "a tragic figure whose work was stifled, unappreciated, and forgotten" ("Naming, Claiming, and Framing" 55).

5. Not only his name, Joël Marti, but also his status as a revolutionary-minded poet calls to mind Cuban literary, cultural, and political figure José Martí (1853–1895).

6. An added complication, at one point Calédu alludes to knowing about Claire's past. In a flashback, we learn that during Claire's tenure as head of the Clamont's coffee plantation, she set the price for the coffee too low one year to "ruin the peasants and get [her] revenge on them" (112). The farmers paid with their lives for Claire's scheme: twenty planters murdered them with machetes in order to remove the unnaturally low coffee prices from the market. Practically, Claire's motivation here may also be to silence Calédu from spreading the word about her guilt.

7. In the original text, Claire states, "Je caresse trop souvent le poignard que m'a offert Jean Luze" (209). The French quotations come from the 2005 version published by Édition Zellige, and the English quotations come from the 2010 Modern Library Paperback Edition. Since Jean Luze gave her this knife, we could even read it as not only symbolically phallic but as representing Jean Luze's phallus specifically.

8. While I agree with Glover that Claire's radical act is "committed in the absence of any clear or coherent political conviction" (20), I do not believe this entirely excuses the act's revolutionary weight.

9. During this period, Haiti's former colonizer, France, refused to recognize the new nation's independence, with England and the United States following suit, politically isolating Haiti (Dubois 5). Thus, not only the legacies of slavery and colonialism on the island but also "the continuing threat of French invasion in the two decades after independence" (Daut 22) had a damaging impact on the nascent nation. In addition to France's continued political, social, and economic influence on Haiti, British, German, and American gunships were known to "brazenly intervene in Haitian affairs" (Dubois 166). In 1825 President Jean-Pierre Boyer accepted an indemnity to compensate France for loss of property suffered by the French planters through the Haitian Revolution in exchange for a recognition of independence (Dubois 99).

10. According to Eric Williams, in addition to reinstituting slavery, the Code Rural "revived and stimulated the colour distinctions by which the mulatto regarded himself as the superior of the black man" (334, qtd. in Matthews 253).

11. Chauvet's writing also "exposes how the revolution, proclaimed in the name of the people, did not change the broad outlines of the social system. Mulattoes and blacks merely took over the top ranks of society" (Dayan, *Haiti, History, and the Gods* 89).

12. I thank Nicole Aljoe for her observations about this terminology.

13. With an eye to hemispheric connections, US southerners played the role of colonizers of the Haitian population during the US occupation (Danticat, "Introduction" x)—another direct link between the spaces explored in this book. The occupation has been described as President Woodrow Wilson (himself a southerner) "carrying on a reign of terror, browbeating, and cruelty, at the hands of southern white naval officers and marines" (Danticat, "Introduction" x). Some historians, such as Laurent Dubois, argue that there was a purposeful policy of dispatching marines from the US South to Haiti "with the assumption that they would be particularly effective at controlling a black population" (Dubois 226).

14. When the US Marines arrived on Haiti, they removed $500,000 worth of gold (the equivalent of $11 million today) belonging to the Haitian government to New York (Dubois 204). The United States took control of Haiti's national bank through this raid and the processes leading up to it, such as the purchase of a majority share from the French by two US banks in 1909 (Dubois 205). Moreover, a number of US companies gained government contracts for agricultural and infrastructure projects in Haiti, such as banana plantations and railroads (Dubois 207). This threatened the autonomy of rural residents by supplanting their local way of life—growing coffee, harvesting wood for export, and cultivating livestock—with "monoculture plantation production for export" (Dubois 208).

15. The Code Rural instituted by President Boyer in 1826, which Eric Williams states "was the restoration of slavery, minus the whip" and "made of Haiti two nations," had remained on the books but had not been enforced since Boyer's presidency (334). Article 54 of the 1864 Code Rural gave the government the power to conscript men to labor on public works projects, which the US Marines took advantage of, forcing rural residents to work as road-building crews as early as 1916 at the start of the occupation (Dubois 239). Although the corvée was described as humane on paper, in reality workers were forced to labor under armed guard, tightly roped together, not given enough to eat, and "frequently shot" (Dubois 239–43). We can see parallels here to the neocolonial convict lease system instituted in the southern United States after Emancipation—another hemispheric connection.

16. Mary Renda notes that violence in Haiti had been "couched as discipline" (55), but also that the fiction "of paternalism unraveled in the 'excesses' of violence that attended the corvée" (139). The abuses of the corvée and the overall violent, exploitative atmosphere exacerbated the conflict between the US Marines and Haitian citizens and resulted in the revolt of the Cacos under Charlemagne Péraulte, who had himself escaped from forced labor in Le Cap (Dubois 248). According to Nicholls, "the clumsy actions of the Americans, who insisted on treating all Haitians of whatever colour as 'n***s,' contributed to this growing solidarity," as the Americans inadvertently succeeded where Dessalines had failed—uniting Haitians of different hues under the label "black" for a short period (142).

17. The occupation was an instance of neocolonialism: "as soon as the marines landed in Haiti, Wilson's administration shut down the press, took charge of Haiti's banks and customs, and instituted a system of compulsory labor for poor Haitians," and by the end of the occupation, more than fifteen thousand Haitians loss their lives (Danticat, "Introduction" x).

18. Duvalier was not above seeking paternalistic aid from the US (Polyné 179). After his victory in the 1956 presidential election, he publicized his hope for Haiti to "become the 'spoiled child of the United States, with the help of American capital'" (Dubois 334). As if in answer to his prayers, direct financial aid began to flow from the United States, and by 1961, $13.5 million was given to Haiti, making up about half of the Haitian budget (Dubois 335). Additionally, the US provided military aid and training to Duvalier's regime (Dubois 335), linking US democracy directly to the Haitian dictatorship.

19. Scharfman notes that Calédu represents Duvalier's regime as "one that imprisons mulatto women from the bourgeoisie in order to torture them, whipping their genitalia, while screaming furiously..." (231). Walcott-Hackshaw also positions Calédu as "Chauvet's representative of the Duvalier regime" (49).

20. In addition to reducing people to property, the code also helped in the effort of "the central state to gain greater control over the slaveholding colonies" (Miller 28). While the code was intended to provide marginal rights to enslaved people, "owners were barely punished for violating slaves' meager entitlements, while actual atrocities were prescribed by the Code against slaves who attempted escape or committed other offenses" (Miller 28), making it instead a "guarantee of tyranny" (Dayan, *Haiti, History, and the Gods* 207).

21. As Sander Gilman notes, the laws place "great emphasis on the control of the slave as sexual object, both in terms of permitted and forbidden sexual contacts as well as by requiring documentation as to the legal status of the offspring of slaves" (231), demonstrating the attempt to regulate sexuality through law.

22. Higginbotham notes that with the dominance of crude stereotypes and "scientific" racism in the form of social Darwinism, Black Americans' assertions of respectability were subversive (188) and were "used to expose race relations as socially constructed rather than derived by evolutionary law or divine judgment" (192).

23. While the politics of respectability worked to reify hierarchies of class, Brittney C. Cooper complicates the discussion, arguing that "respectability discourse also constituted one of the earliest theorizations of gender within newly emancipated Black communities" (19) and is "a complicated, contingent, and (rightfully) contested mode of articulating Black gender identity vis-à-vis the social resuscitation of Black women's sexual morality" (22). Viewing these politics within an intersectional framework reveals that problematic class relations existed alongside early articulations of gender in Black communities.

24. This regulation of sexuality, particularly of what the community would deem nonnormative sexuality, also connects to the situation of Charles Bon in *Absalom, Absalom!* whose relations were heavily policed due to their interracial and same-sex components. In both Faulkner's novel and *Love*, heteronormative relationships are at times monitored less closely. For example, Jean Luze and Fèlicia—who are of different racial but not class groups—conceived Jean-Claude before they were married, a "scandal" of which the town was not aware.

25. The explicit violence Haitian women in particular experienced at the hands of Duvalier's *tonton macoutes* connects directly to the regime of Rafael Trujillo (1930–1961), the focus of the next chapter, and the anti-Haitianism it espoused. Haitians in general were affected by the hatred Trujillo fostered; however, pregnant Haitian women were excessively targeted due to their potential to produce more Haitians on Dominican soil, revealing the similarly gendered policies of Trujillo's regime (Ricourt 42). Both dictators sought to control women's bodies and to gain control through women's bodies. Trujillo's obsession with Whiteness and notoriety for his exploitation of Dominican women of every class, including elite light-skinned women, in addition to the violence he encouraged toward Haitian women, is best considered alongside the reliance on tactics of sexual violence under François Duvalier's rule and the historical exploitation of women on both sides of the island.

26. The use of rape as a tool for control spanned the Americas. For example, Angela Davis notes that slavery in the United States relied as much on institutionalized sexual violence as it did on the whip and the lash (175). Therefore, sexual violence and the rape of women were not only endemic to the Middle Passage but also constitutive of the plantation system (Morgan and Youssef 172).

27. Marie-Chantal Kalisa argues that "gendered violence is a corollary to imperialism and colonialism" (185). For example, the violent occupation of a land by a foreign imperial power is often characterized as the possession of a woman's body in colonial texts. As a result, the body of the colonized woman has come to represent both a national emblem and land itself (Kalisa 25)—land that has been "violated by external assailants" (Kalisa 164). Sexual violation of colonized women is central to the colonial system, both at the metaphoric level representing the occupation of land and, more concretely, as a direct and pervasive consequence of colonialism.

28. The use of rape as a tactic of terror was widespread during the 1994 Rwandan genocide to the extent that it was established as a crime of genocide by the United Nations' International Criminal Court for Rwanda following the events (Kalisa 4). Moreover, this is not only a strategy common to postcolonial nations or guerilla warfare; during the Vietnam War, US soldiers were instructed to use rape as a tactic of terror, which they were told was justifiable because they were fighting against an "inferior race" (Angela Davis 177).

29. The *tonton macoutes* take their name from a fairy tale creature, "a bogeyman, a scarecrow with human flesh . . . [who] always had scraps of naughty children, whom he dismembered to eat as snacks" in his knapsack (Danticat, *Breath, Eyes, Memory* 137); however, they expressed a ubiquitous, corporeal threat, ever-present throughout communities during the reign of François Duvalier. Backed by the omnipotent dictator and recruited primarily from the urban poor—like Calédu's army of beggars (Dayan, "Reading Women in the Caribbean" 234)—the members of Duvalier's army are secure in their power and

brazen in their use of rape as a tactic of terror in line with the nightmarish creature with which they are associated.

30. In alignment with racialized understandings of sexual abuse in the US, marines, such as Captain Craig, were of the belief that Haitian women were "of easy virtue" (Dubois 235) and incapable of denying a sexual advance, echoing the detrimental stereotype of Black women as hypersexual used to alleviate White guilt for the systematic rape of Black women in hemispheric plantation societies.

31. Myriam Chancy extends this, noting that the use of rape "as an instrument of state-instituted violence"—used under Duvalier—greatly increased from the late 1980s to late 1990s, and that women have always been used as "political pawns between male-dominated political factions" with the violence against them only increasing after the Duvaliers' departure (*Framing Silence* 44).

32. Perhaps as a result of this knowledge, as well as their lack of a son, the Clamonts decided to raise Claire as if she were a boy with the understanding that she would take over the family business, complicating her society's seemingly traditional understanding of gender roles.

33. As Scharfman notes, "Calédu's obsessive-compulsive behavior fuses race, class, and gender in one single horrific gesture of punishment" (231), and in this way, Calédu's actions are not only realistic for the time and place but simultaneously work on a symbolic level.

34. Lucia Suárez notes that rape as a political weapon also threatened the reputation of the victim and her family, as often victims would not report crimes to preserve their standing in the community (62). Further, the police or military officers to whom they would report were frequently "authorized" as rapists themselves (Suárez 62). The rape of women, often in front of family members, has been used as "a political tactic of terror by several repressive regimes," including the reign of the Duvaliers and the brutal de facto regimes (Suárez 64).

35. It is significant that this violence occurs in the sugarcane fields. Like the Massacre River, the space of the cane fields is a palimpsest of postcolonial violence. The brutal nature of sugar as a crop and the harsh conditions surrounding its farming in Saint-Domingue led to the enslaved population dying "at a murderous rate" (Dubois 4). As will be explored in chapter 5, the violence of the Haitian massacre also took place around and within the cane fields in the border region, and similarly key moments of violence in Junot Díaz's novel occur in the cane fields, linking the experiences of the two parts of the island through the symbolic resonances of cane.

36. This supports the idea that race is not only a social construction but also "a practical device for policy implementation" (Constant x), dependent on the racial configuration of a certain society.

37. According to Michele Wucker, "a small elite with light skin counts for no more than a tenth of the population; the vast majority of Haitians occupy the darkest end of the color spectrum" (33–34), and today "Haiti's main (if moveable) dividing line separates blacks and mulattoes in a distinction that depends on class as much as color" (34). Wucker speaks to the fact that the lines of race and class are movable in Haitian society and result from both class and color distinctions.

38. While the *Mulâtres-Aristocrates* exist as a separate racial group in Haiti—distinct from both White elites and a Black lower class—this was not the case in most regions of the United States where according to the one-drop rule, "all persons of African ancestry were lumped together as Negro both socially and legally" (Mohammed 36–37), as we saw in the case of Charles Bon and his trace of African ancestry in the introduction.

39. Before the 1770s–1780s, old colonial biracial families who usually owned property and enslaved people were classified as "White," but after this time they were considered "nonwhite," causing a dramatic growth in the free population of color (Garrigus, *Before Haiti* 144). Therefore, it was not until the 1770s–1780s that race joined social class as a defining feature of local relationships and the separation of the biracial upper class from the White upper class became significant (Garrigus, *Before Haiti* 53).

40. One example of this is the tension between the need to join together as Haitians to combat foreign interference—symbolized in the novella by the US Marines and later by Mr. Long's American export company—or to dominate each other in the nation's political and economic spheres.

41. This fact opened the way for François Duvalier to use *noiriste* ideology to acquire the backing of the Black middle class in Port-au-Prince and win the presidency (Nicholls 209). In his campaign addresses, Duvalier praised the army and the "dignity of peasant life," and promised to raise the wages of the lower classes—pledges that did not reflect the policies of his regime (Nicholls 210–11).

42. This corresponds historically with the rise of the *noiriste* movement during the 1930s in Haiti, which "emphasized Haiti's African past" (Nicholls 167). Nevertheless, Madison Smartt Bell notes that although Chauvet sets the story in 1939, this power reversal "resembles nothing so much as the Duvalier regime" (par. 5).

43. The price paid for coffee is so low that the peasants working at the Clamont's Lion Mountain do not make enough money to feed their children. The peasants have the illusion of mobility and the freedom to leave for a different coffee plantation, but the wages are fixed by the management throughout the region, preventing the peasants from improving their lot (93).

44. Henri does not seem to respect or believe in Vodou, but he uses what he refers to as "voodoo spells" to keep his workers afraid of him. Claire acknowledges as much and wonders if he is "a good enough actor to play at voodoo to keep his naïve farmers in check" (103). I use the term Vodou to refer to the folk religion of Haiti, since according to Leslie Desmangles, it is more phonetically correct and "corresponds to the nomenclature used by the Haitians themselves for their religion" (xi–xii).

45. The Negritude movement was a political and aesthetic movement born in Paris, which freed members of the African diaspora from isolation and "contributed to the emergence of African literature between the 1930s and the 1960s" (Constant and Mabana 5). Pan-Africanism, a term that arose in the 1950s, is "an educational, political, and cultural movement which had a lasting impact on the liberation of people of African descent, in the continent of Africa and the Diaspora" (Malisa and Nhengeze 28). Pan-Africanism promotes an understanding of Africa as the ancestral home for Black people, as well as the aspiration to work for Africa's liberation (Malisa and Nhengeze 29).

46. This stance also has sexual connotations and is reminiscent of the threat of sexual violence embodied through the position in which Graciela finds her mother at the hands of occupying US soldiers in *Song of the Water Saints*, discussed in chapter 5.

47. This line is echoed in *Madness,* the final story of the triptych, in which René, a persecuted poet, states: "I wrote verse in French about Christophe, Dessalines, Toussaint and Pétion. I am clinging to the colonial legacy like a louse" (322).

48. In addition to Calédu and those in power with him, the other Black characters in the novella's present period are relegated to the background, such as the poor peasants who have been armed by Calédu. Along with the coffee plantation workers, who also remain in the background, Tonton Mathurin is another Black character who exists in Claire's reconstruction of the past, but he is dismissed by Claire's parents as a licentious old man and instigator, who denounces Henri Clamont as a "phony" (101).

49. Khalil Gibran Muhammad traces the "ideological currency of black criminality" back to the 1890s, specifically in the US (3). The publication of the 1890 census was the first time that prison statistics were used to portray Black people as "a distinct and dangerous criminal population" (Muhammad 3) in a way that ignored the "race-conscious laws, discriminatory punishments, and new forms of everyday racial surveillance" institutionalized by that time (Muhammad 4).

50. Although Dora's torture is not explicitly described by Claire as rape, scholars such as Martin Munro have used that term to characterize Calédu's actions. Madison Smartt Bell argues that Dora was clearly beaten and gang-raped at Calédu's headquarters: "the rape is unmistakable, and for a long time afterward Dora 'hobbles along with legs spread apart like a maimed animal'" (Bell par. 7).

51. Another complication of Claire's alignment with the *ménagère* stereotype is that she is not the sole housekeeper. The family employs a Black woman named Augustine who actually completes the majority of the household labor, although her efforts are largely hidden from the readers of Claire's journal. An example of Augustine's invisible labor is seen when Félicia is giving birth, and Dr. Audier asks Claire to boil some water (59). Augustine brings a pot of boiling water to Claire who then brings it to Dr. Audier.

52. The "tropical temptress" and "*ménagère*" stereotypes have Saint-Dominguan/Haitian origins. The trope of the "tragic mulatta" is thought to have originated with Lydia Maria Child's short stories in the US, yet I argue that the use of the trope is more widespread. Victor Séjour's "The Mulatto" (1837), written in French and published in France before Child's work, takes place in Saint-Domingue/Haiti and is also in direct conversation with the stereotype.

53. Claire is also linked to the mammy stereotype—more prevalent in the United States, while the *ménagère* figure was more widespread in Haiti—whom Christian describes as "black in color, fat, nurturing, religious, kind, above all strong, and . . . enduring" (2). Claire is seen to nurture and care for her family. She serves as a surrogate mother to Félicia's baby (and in her mind, wife to Jean Luze) while her sister is ill, and appears religious to those who have not read her journal. Readers know, however, that Claire resents her role as parent to her sisters and would like to kill Félicia to earn a more permanent place in the life of Jean Luze and his son. In this way, Claire subverts the flat characterizations usually

found of the mammy stereotype, who was "so loyal to her white family that she was often willing to risk her life to defend them" (Pilgrim par. 10). Through her actions, such as the risk she takes in murdering Calédu—a threat not only to her family but also her class and community more broadly—Claire would seem to comply with the mammy figure, yet through her thoughts and the hatred they reveal toward that same family, she simultaneously undermines the stereotype.

54. This work done by Claire's narrative links her purposefully with Erzulie, the Haitian loa who often embodies oppositional characteristics, such as good and evil or young and old, only to destabilize easy categorizations (Dayan, "Reading Women in the Caribbean" 239).

55. Using Frantz Fanon's analysis in the *Wretched of the Earth*, Lee-Keller argues that the fragmentation of the individual subject, as well as the subject's alienation from herself and others, is a destructive and enduring effect of colonialism: "The colonial system implicitly denied the humanity of the colonized peoples during colonization, the colonized learned to separate what they knew about themselves ('we are human') from what they had to dissimulate to their colonizers ('we are less than human')" (1296). I agree that Claire's identity has been fragmented in this way, but I am not as comfortable positioning her as a "madwoman" given the weight of this language.

56. Similarly, Evelyn O'Callaghan argues that "the figure of the schizophrenic madwoman in the work of Caribbean women writers works as a 'social metaphor' to explain the 'damaged West Indian psyche . . . fragmented as a result of colonial/postcolonial conflict'" (Renk 89). I prefer to characterize her acts as irrational, as opposed to labeling Claire mad, in part to avoid the pathologization that would accompany such a positioning.

57. Colin Dayan connects Claire to one of the most frightening ghosts of Haitian folklore: the djablesse, a female ghost who lives in the woods for years before entering heaven as punishment for having died a virgin, which may help explain Claire's obsession with her virgin status ("Reading Women in the Caribbean" 235).

58. The colonies and the Caribbean in particular were thought to be "loci of madness" with English visitors becoming "maddened by the tropics, supposedly through association with the climate and the cultural practices visitors observed" (Renk 89). Thus, madness was considered a feature of the Caribbean landscape—a trope running back to the colonial era. It was believed that White Europeans would go mad if they spent too much time in the Caribbean and that creoles were "tropicalized" by their environment and were "emotionally high-strung, lazy, and sexually excessive" (Rhys 33, note 1). Marie-Chantal Kalisa notes that Caribbean "madness" is rooted in historical violence (120).

59. Claire's desire for a baby has led her to purchase a doll that she secretly cares for (and successfully fights the urge to breast feed), which is surely eccentric, but I argue is evidence of her lonely, repressed lifestyle and alienation, not her "madness" (34)

60. Scholars such as Walcott-Hackshaw and Scharfman trace Claire's obsessions with Jean Luze and Calédu back to her relationship with her father: "The complex, violent, and ambiguous relationship that Claire has with her father translates into perverse desire for her brother-in-law, Jean Luze, a white Frenchman, and for the local commandant, Calédu, another terrorizing patriarchal figure" (Walcott-Hackshaw 49). Both scholars cite Claire's dreams as evidence of this connection.

61. In one dream a naked Claire in the midst of a crowded arena throws herself at the feet of a statue of Calédu that has come to life with an erect "phallus [that] wagged feverishly" (120), or in the original French "le phallus s'agita, fiévreusement" (170). The crowd incites Calédu to murder Claire, which here can be seen as standing in for rape given Calédu's state of arousal, and he beheads her (120–1). In the next paragraph, Claire describes another dream from her childhood in which her father was "transformed into a roaring two-legged creature with a lion's mane" (121) or "metamorphose en un animal bipède à crinière de lion" (171), who whips her as she attempts to exit his cage. The juxtaposition of these two dreams supports the connection between her suppressed attraction to Calédu and her complex relationship with her abusive father, as well as the overlap between sexuality and violence in Claire's subconscious, which may account for her unwanted attraction to the commandant.

62. If further evidence of this connection is needed, Erzulie is often associated with Catholicism's Saint Claire (Dayan, "Reading Women in the Caribbean" 234).

CHAPTER 5
"WE ARE TRAWLING IN SILENCES HERE": RACE, SEXUALITY, AND UNNARRATABLE HISTORIES IN LITERARY DEPICTIONS OF DOMINICAN DICTATORSHIP

1. For more on the dictatorship novel as a subgenre of Latina/o literature, see Jennifer Harford Vargas's *Forms of Dictatorship*, which explores "what these novels and their formal literary devices can tell us about the haunting afterlives of dictatorship and about dictatorial power relations that Latina/os grapple with in the United States" (4–5). She speaks to this "hemispheric binary" associating Latin America with dictatorship and the US with democracy, which "veils and disavows the United States' constitutive and imperialist role in fomenting and colluding with authoritarian regimes in Latin America" (13).

2. Although many style systems, such as *The Chicago Manual of Style*, have moved away from including a hyphen within terms such as Haitian American and Dominican American, "hyphenated American" refers to bicultural and/or transnational American identities.

3. The regime of Rafael Trujillo was one of the longest and most repressive in the history of Latin America, in part due to his reliance on forms of everyday terror, including random abductions, surveillance, and systematic forms of ridicule (Derby, *The Dictator's Seduction* 2). His methods of control were widespread and included elements ranging from violence and torture to "popular forms such as gossip, gift exchange, fictive kinship, and witchcraft" (Derby, *The Dictator's Seduction* 7). Trujillo was known from the beginning as a caudillo, or military man, who "openly preyed on the country's most beautiful young women" and was barred entry into elite circles due to his reputation as a thief, forger, and blackmailer (Wucker 45). Parallels to the rise of François Duvalier may be seen in these class dynamics.

4. For a discussion of the relationship between history and fiction from the perspective of narrative theory, see Hayden White's "The Burden of History," "The Politics of Historical Interpretation," and *Metahistory: The Historical Imagination in Nineteenth-Century Europe*, as well as Linda Hutcheon's "Historiographic Metafiction Parody and the Intertextuality of History."

5. These diasporic writers focus less on the perspective of the dictator figure, differing from the approaches of boom generation authors, such as Alejo Carpentier, Augusto Roa

Basto, Gabriel García Márquez, and Mario Vargas Llosa, and their successors, including Roberto Bolaño and Cristina Peri Rossi (Harford Vargas, *Forms of Dictatorship* 9). Jennifer Harford Vargas describes dictatorship novels by boom writers, such as Carpentier's *El recurso de método* (*Reasons of the State* 1974), Roa Basto's *Yo el supremo* (*I the Supreme* 1975), García Márquez's *El otoño del patriarca* (*The Autumn of the Patriarch* 1975), and Vargas Llosa's *La fiesta del chivo* (*The Feast of the Goat* 2000), as fictional worlds "organized around an anonymous dictator" with "an inequitable distribution of power and voice similar to the hierarchy of power that exists under dictatorship" (*Forms of Dictatorship* 40). Harford Vargas contrasts these novels to Díaz's, which "displaces the dictator from the center of the historical narrative and redistributes attention to the subjects at the *bottom* of the hierarchy" (*Forms of Dictatorship* 40, emphasis in the original).

6. For more information about the relationship between trauma and literature, see Nicolas Abraham and Maria Torok's *The Shell and the Kernel: Renewals of Psychoanalysis*, Cathy Caruth's *Unclaimed Experience: Trauma, Narrative, and History*, Greg Forter's *Gender, Race, and Mourning in American Modernism*, E. Ann Kaplan's *Trauma Culture: The Politics of Terror and Loss in Media and Literature*, Dominick LaCapra's *Writing History, Writing Trauma*, Elaine Scarry's *The Body in Pain: The Making and Unmaking of the World*, Susan Sontag's *Regarding the Pain of Others*, and Dorothy Stringer's *Not Even Past: Race, Historical Trauma, and Subjectivity in Faulkner, Larsen, and Van Vechten*.

7. Each of these writers publishes primarily in English, although Spanish words and phrases appear in the texts. Therefore, this is the language of the quotations in this chapter.

8. The fourth Mirabal, known in the novel as Dedé, does not get involved with revolutionary activities and survives her sisters.

9. While the extremes of Trujillo's reign correspond with exoticized conceptions of despotism, it is important to leave space for the particularities of the regime to avoid reproducing "a long European tradition of projecting the most extreme forms of political despotism and otherness onto non-Western societies and imagining beyond the edges of the European universe oddly passive or irrational peoples who mysteriously accept intolerable regimes" (Turits, *Foundations of Despotism* 4). This also applies to the dictatorships of François Duvalier and his son, Jean-Claude.

10. Echoing this sentiment, scholar Lauren Derby states, "The terror was so appalling that it has been described more readily in literature than in history" (*The Dictator's Seduction* 3).

11. Much has been written on the relationship between *In the Time of the Butterflies*, capital-h-History, and collective memory. Trenton Hickman describes Alvarez's novel as "a haunted fiction that she argues isn't history but is truer than it—aims to raise a monument to the Mirabals that will endure the march of diachronic time, difference in language, and distances in physical space" (116). Similarly, according to Steve Criniti, Alvarez not only positions North American collective memory of Dominican history and the involvement of the US as inadequate, but she also actively reconstitutes that memory, advocating for those who are often excluded from the process (45). He views Alvarez as "subtly embedding a disruptive memory into North American collective memory with the hope of ultimately altering that memory's shape and constitution" (54). Maya Socolovsky expands on this idea, arguing that Alvarez's works of historical fiction "extend the American historical

imaginary, and allow Dominican events to write themselves into U.S. history, thereby blurring the U.S.'s own historical boundaries" (6). Alvarez's novel disrupts the set boundaries of the United States, opening up for a more hemispheric conceptualization of the region. While Lynn Chun Ink acknowledges that the novel "remains a significant intervention in American imperial history because of its attempt to recover local Dominican history and to foreground women's roles in this history," she argues that the "problematic rendering of Dominican collectivity ultimately echoes imperial history and the power relations it produces" (798). Ink critiques the ways in which the novel also reifies the region's broader power dynamics, for example, through Alvarez's choice to write in English, the privileging of US culture over Dominican, and the measuring of Dominican women according to US standards (798). Although in an imperfect and at times problematic way, Alvarez's novel spread awareness of this history to an expanded readership and opened the door for the writers coming after her to build on and respond to her account. Writing after Alvarez, both Díaz and Rosario include a more expansive focus on Dominican history and the place of the dictatorship within it.

12. Díaz defines *baká* in an interview as something that changes its shape nonstop (Miranda 39).

13. Tim Lanzendörfer notes that Díaz's novel recognizes that it is problematic to offer "supernatural explanations for historical events, but it insists that history must be interpreted through narrative and suggests that it is best interpreted through fantasy" (129).

14. Sean O'Brien argues that Yunior's "almost challenging tone" with readers and assumptions that we are ignorant of Dominican history "indicate that his implied audience is not primarily other Dominicans (who presumably study more than two seconds of Dominican history), but rather English-speaking outsiders" (84).

15. Charlotte Rich speaks well to the impact of the polyvocality of Alvarez's novel: "The various voices within Alvarez's novel challenge such a representation of reality, and in their decentering, centrifugal emphasis, they serve to both humanize the mythic Mirabal sisters and to speak subversively in response to the official discourses of Trujillo's regime" (179). In this way, Alvarez's use of multiple voices is a direct response to official perspectives voiced by the regime. Elena Machado Sáez argues that Díaz's novel only appears to have a polyvocal structure, since Yunior is really the sole narrator (528). I agree that everything the readers have access to comes by way of Yunior. However, the readers are still presented with multiple mediated voices, such as Lola's first-person account and Beli's third-person story based on Yunior's interviews with her and other research.

16. One French chronicler, Médéric Louis Elie Moreau de Saint-Méry, concluded in 1797 that "masters and slaves in the Spanish colony lived in relative harmony as compared with the brutal system in the island's French colony" (Ricourt 12).

17. The Spanish Black Codes were modeled after the French Code Noir, as well as the thirteenth-century Spanish *Siete Partidas*, "colonial compendiums of laws from 1567 and 1680, ordinances on slaves from Hispaniola dating as far back as 1528, Roman law, and slave laws from other colonies" (Obregón 4).

18. As discussed in earlier chapters, the 1685 French Code Noir and later 1724 Louisiana Code Noir attempted to standardize the treatment of the enslaved in the French colonies, defining racial groups as White, enslaved, and free Black (typically biracial) and regulating sexuality as an essential aspect of these categories.

19. A group of experts commissioned by the United Nations in 2007 reached the conclusion that the DR has a "'profound' and 'entrenched' problem of racism and discrimination against Haitians, Dominicans of Haitian descent, and blacks in general" (Ricourt 37). The present-day ramifications of colonial policies in the hemispheric Americas will be confronted more directly in the coda.

20. As occurred previous to the US occupation of Haiti, outlined in chapter 4, the military occupation of the DR was preceded by an overtaking of the economic system: an American firm took over the Dominican foreign debt in 1892, and the US assumed control of the customshouse in 1905, preserving control until 1941 (Derby, *The Dictator's Seduction* 17). The US was the "real third-party witness on the ground" through this control over both Haitian and Dominican customs (Paulino 77).

21. The porous border between the nations became a "symbol of and stage for a racist anti-insurgency program to pacify the region" (Paulino 38) with forgotten stories of the binational resistance to US forces that prevented them from controlling or closing the border (Paulino 40).

22. Lauren Derby notes more specifically that Dominican conceptions of *raza* (nation or people) "came to be mapped along several contradictory axes, including kinship, ritual, and association with money," as opposed to skin color or genealogy ("Haitians, Magic, and Money" 490). Further, "Haitianism" would seem to be similarly socially constructed: "A Dominican could become Haitianized if he lived in Haiti long enough that his speech, bodily movements, and way of life were affected" ("Haitians, Magic, and Money" 521).

23. Paulino argues this difference is evident in the withdrawal of US troops from the DR in 1924—ten years earlier than the evacuation from Haiti—verifying the United States' view of a divide between the primarily White Dominicans and the Black (read: ignorant, savage) Haitians (Paulino 9). Further, according to April Mayes, anti-Black racism in the DR "emerged as a reaction against Haitians *and* Afro-Antilleans," who immigrated to work in the sugar region (emphasis in original 7) with "the political significance of race chang[ing] as a result of Afro-Antillean immigration and the country's integration into the US sphere of influence" (6). For more on the role of Afro-Antillean immigration in the development of Dominican anti-Blackness, see Mayes's *Mulatto Republic: Class, Race, and Dominican National Identity*. She explores anti-Haitianism as a "tool of labor management and control" (8) in San Pedro de Macorís, the center of the eastern sugar-growing region (7).

24. Edward Paulino asserts that the "violence Hispaniola experienced under the US occupation laid the foundation for 1937 massacre," due to the United States' complicity in training Trujillo in the national guard and in anti-insurgency campaigns that led to the torture of Haitians and Dominicans, particularly in the border region (55).

25. Graciela "couldn't care less that Theodore Roosevelt's 'soft voice and big stick' on Latin America had dipped the yanqui the furthest south he had ever been from New York City" and refers sardonically to the debauchery of "the Marines stationed on her side of the island, who were there to 'order and pacify'" (8).

26. At one point in Alvarez's *In the Time of the Butterflies*, Patria Mirabal falls asleep and dreams that the "Yanquis" are back and are burning houses again (52), and later Mamá states that the Yanquis "killed anyone who stood in their way" (57). Junot Díaz directly states in a footnote that the story of the violence experienced by the Cabral family during

Trujillo's dictatorship really begins "when the Spaniards 'discovered' the New World—or when the U.S. invaded Santo Domingo in 1916" (211). Díaz draws a direct line of connection between the impact of Trujillo's regime and the occupation and colonial period. Díaz refers to the curse impacting Oscar's family as "*Fukú americanus* . . . the Curse and the Doom of the New World" (1). This connects to the concept of *fucú* in Dominican history—associated with Columbus's imperial efforts. Twice Columbus's attempts to "discover" new regions of the Caribbean were stopped by tempests: Columbus was said to have "cursed the island in retribution," bringing his *fucú* or his wrath to the region (Derby, *The Dictator's Seduction* 67). In his explanation of *fukú americanus*, the narrator Yunior does not refer to Columbus by name but only as the Admiral (O'Brien 80).

27. Myriam Chancy and Edwidge Danticat discuss the harm caused by Duvalier's *noirisme* or "the psychological game Duvalier played with colour in order to control as many people as he could throughout the country" (Chancy, *From Sugar to Revolution* 11).

28. Trujillo's rise challenged "traditional elite notions of race and class" (Paulino 49) in a comparable way to how Duvalier's would across the border. Lauren Derby draws a connection between Trujillo's and Duvalier's forms of populism: Duvalier "drew upon the most marginal of social constituencies—urban shantydwellers—those who lacked any kind of organized occupational identity whatever," while Trujillo imposed order "on the undisciplined masses through the schools and the military" (*The Dictator's Seduction* 23).

29. Trujillo announced publicly that, like his maternal grandmother, Diyette Chevalier, he was not solely Dominican but also Haitian (Paulino 54), before dropping this sentiment when it no longer served him. Examining the first seven years and nine months of the dictatorship, Dominican scholar Bernardo Vega was unable to find any anti-Haitian racist and/or political materials in Dominican magazines, newspapers, or books (Paulino 54). Unlike other ethnic genocides in the twentieth century, "no prior state policy, local tension, international conflict, official ideology, or escalating attacks had signaled the possibility of such state-directed carnage" (Turits, "A World Destroyed" 620). The regime's anti-Haitianism resulted from rather than produced the state-sponsored violence.

30. Trujillo's racism revealed itself: he continued his "Dominicanization" campaign at the border, banned immigrants of color, encouraged White immigration, and embraced Nazi and Spanish Falange ideologies (Ricourt 33).

31. Lauren Derby uses Trujillo's high voice (223), penchant for face makeup, affinity for spectacle and elaborate costumes, vanity, and whispered love affairs with men to position his masculinity as ambivalent (186). This is interesting juxtaposed against his reliance on conventional conceptions of masculinity through his seduction and exploitation of women, complicating traditional hierarchies of gender.

32. At first machetes were used in order to give the appearance of an internal conflict among the working classes (Suárez 40). The massacre went on for more than a week and eventually the weapon of choice shifted from the machete to the more efficient rifle (Wucker 50). Despite US Military Intelligence Division reports to the contrary, Dominican civilians, in addition to soldiers, participated in the murders (Turits, "A World Destroyed" 619), while others endangered their own lives to protect Haitians—a fact not frequently focused on in discussions of the massacre (Paulino 66). The dictator scapegoated Haitians as responsible for the violence when his desire for complete control over the border and

his obsession with Whiteness were truly to blame (Wucker 51). Trujillo capitalized on the racialization of Haitians not only as blacker than Dominicans but also as a subspecies associated with forms of bodily pollution, such as disease and contagion (Chancy, "Diasporic Disconnections" 176).

33. For an extended discussion, see "'A Border that Exists Beyond Maps': Contextualizing State-Sponsored Violence in Contemporary Haitian American and Dominican American Literature," in which I use representations of the 1937 Haitian Massacre as a test case essential for distinguishing the approaches and positionings of Alvarez, Díaz, Rosario, and Danticat.

34. Myriam Chancy directly states that none of Alvarez's novels can "find room to voice the genocidal impulse of the Trujillo regime" and that she does not reference Trujillo's anti-Haitian campaigns (*From Sugar to Revolution* 77). Through the failure of *In the Time of the Butterflies* to address these aspects of Dominican history, Chancy goes as far as to say that the novel bears false witness consistent with collective amnesia, which she describes as both an unconscious and violent omission (*From Sugar to Revolution* 79). I agree that it is likely unintentional on Alvarez's part and may result from the historic silence surrounding the horrific event.

35. Julia Alvarez, however, has publicly voiced opposition to the present-day treatment of Haitians in the Dominican Republic. Along with Edwidge Danticat, Junot Díaz, and journalist Mark Kurlansky, she published a letter to the editor in the *New York Times* in response to the Dominican high court Ruling 0168-13, which revoked citizenship from Dominicans of undocumented parents retroactive to 1929.

36. Additionally, Abelard's father allowed Trujillo's army to borrow his horses when "the army had started murdering all the Haitians" and didn't say anything when they were never returned (231).

37. Jennifer Harford Vargas argues that the novel "mobilizes underground storytelling modes—specifically hearsay, footnotes, and silences—to represent and contest formally the dissemination and repression of information under and after dictatorship" ("Dictating a Zafa" 11). Thus, the footnotes and the structure of the novel work to challenge the totalitarian power of the dictator.

38. While there is no direct evidence of sexual violence toward Haitian women during the genocide, some scholars such as Milagros Ricourt believe this type of violation did occur, since the anti-Haitian policies that followed were highly gendered. According to Richard Lee Turits, "women and children were reportedly less successful than men in escaping and hence composed the majority of those murdered" (Turits, "A World Destroyed" 615). Violence against Haitians during Trujillo's regime specifically targeted women, due to their capacity to produce more Haitians within the borders of the Dominican Republic (42).

39. Trujillo's defiance of the Dominican aristocracy took the form of stealing their daughters in an attempt to elevate his standing (Derby, *The Dictator's Seduction* 115); however, his exploitation of women surpassed class lines, including women from "families of modest means in small towns or from those of important Dominican officials" (Turits, *Foundations of Despotism* 6). This behavior earned Trujillo the moniker of "the goat" (Derby, *The Dictator's Seduction* 1).

40. While Trujillo's son, Ramfis Trujillo, and son-in-law for a brief period, Porfirio Rubirosa, were known for their womanizing as part of the Hollywood jet set (Derby, *The Dictator's Seduction* 182), this predilection for numerous liaisons also crossed gender lines when it came to Trujillo's family. Trujillo's daughter Flor de Oro would anger her father by indulging in erotic escapades reserved for the men in the family (Derby, *The Dictator's Seduction* 175). Similar to Trujillo's ambivalent masculinity, his daughter's emulation of this rapacious sexuality served to complicate the regime's relation to traditional conceptions of gender roles and sexuality.

41. Trujillo's embodiment of the womanizing *tiguere* type—a Dominican underdog who grows in power, esteem, and status through his "impeccable attire, implacable charm, irresistible sexuality, and a touch of violence" (Derby, *The Dictator's Seduction* 114)—brought him respect among the marginalized lower classes (Derby, *The Dictator's Seduction* 175).

42. Mario Vargas Llosa's novel is not a focus here due to its more straightforward narrative techniques and realist style; however, its addition would productively extend the discussion in this chapter—particularly around sexuality, violence, and power.

43. Although women were frequently denounced—a common method of control employed by the regime—they were penalized less often than men and not held to the same moral standards (Derby, *The Dictator's Seduction* 166). A law in 1940 extended rights to Dominican women and simultaneously declared men the heads of the households, "legislat[ing] patriarchal authority and gender hierarchies" (Turits, *Foundations of Despotism* 220). While the regime encouraged men to be responsible for the women they had sexual relationships with and the children that resulted, this solidified their control over the private sphere at the same time and also resulted in the formation of multiple households (Turits, *Foundations of Despotism* 221).

44. Yunior does not depict any openly queer, transgender, or nonbinary characters. When Oscar is teased for being different, his heterosexuality is questioned by his harassers, possibly leading him to stand in for other nonnormative or marginalized individuals. Oscar receives the nickname Oscar Wao when his Doctor Who costume causes him, according to Yunior, to look like "that fat homo Oscar Wilde" (180). Although indirectly present through Yunior's language, for instance his use of racial epithets and asides, such as referring to tans as "Mulatto Pigment Degradation Disorder" (213), race is also not a central focus of the novel. We do, however, see Beli attract negative treatment as a result of her dark skin, revealing the colorism deeply embedded in Dominican society.

45. Yunior emphasizes this aspect of Trujillo's legacy from the start, noting that Trujillo is known for changing the names of all the landmarks to his name, building monopolies and one of the largest armies in the Western hemisphere, stripping allies and friends of positions and property for no reason, and "for fucking every hot girl in sight, even the wives of his subordinates, thousands upon thousands upon thousands of women" (2).

46. Machado Sáez argues that Díaz's novel beguiles readers into "becoming complicit with the heteronormative rationale used to police male diasporic identity" (523). She reads Yunior, the embodiment of the Dominican diaspora, as silencing Oscar's queer otherness, represented by his virginity and sentimentality (524). Through his ending of the novel, Yunior projects onto Oscar "a transformation into full-fledged heterosexuality," while also hinting at a suppressed homosocial romance, unrenderable as part of the history of the

Dominican diaspora (524): a connection back to the relationship between Henry and Bon in *Absalom, Absalom!* or between Marcus and Jim in *Of Love and Dust*. According to Machado Sáez, Yunior, who is Dominican-born, enforces the code of nationalist belonging through which Oscar can become a diasporic subject. This reading is made particularly convincing by the fact that Yunior has complete control over the narrative, including the portrayal of characters and their development.

47. This complicity may be seen to extend to Díaz himself. In May 2018, authors Zinzi Clemmons, Carmen Maria Machado, Monica Byrne, and Alisa Valdes came forward to accuse Junot Díaz of inappropriate actions ranging from sexual misconduct to verbal abuse. This suggests that like his protagonist Yunior, Díaz himself is not free from the detrimental effects of the hypermasculinity that he often deconstructs through his writing. In "The Silence: The Legacy of Childhood Trauma," Díaz reveals his own experience of sexual violence at the age of eight, perhaps speaking to the cyclical nature of exploitation. Díaz writes, "Eventually what used to hold back the truth doesn't work anymore. You run out of escapes, you run out of exits, you run out of gambits, you run out of luck. Eventually the past finds you."

48. Trenton Hickman notes that although the slap was discussed in the press, many scholars agree that it probably did not happen (107). Nevertheless, the fictional slap had an effect on ten-year-old Julia Alvarez after reading about it in *Time Magazine*.

49. Minerva had witnessed Trujillo's sexual aggression before, although from afar, during his pursuit of an older girl at her high school, Lina Lovatón. Trujillo's wife discovered that Lina had gotten pregnant and attacked her with a knife (Alvarez 23). Like Díaz's Beli, Lina was sent out of the country. According to Lauren Derby, Lina Lovatón "provided erotic imagery for the body politic" through her participation in the Carnival of 1937 (*The Dictator's Seduction* 113)—the same year of the massacre of Haitians on the border.

50. Raymond Smith links the dual marriage system of the West Indies to kinship structures under slavery. Building on Smith's work, Derby describes the dual marriage system as a result of the "colonial European practice of simultaneous marriage to a status equal and of concubinage with status inferiors, in which the mistress performed all wifely duties" except for presiding at table (Derby, "Haitians, Magic, and Money" 514).

51. The government also increased legislation requiring men to support the children resulting from all sexual relationships: this had the effect of collapsing the distinction between legitimate and illegitimate children (Turits, *Foundations of Despotism* 221). Further, the regime altered adultery laws to make them gender neutral, excusing either a husband or a wife for murders resulting from exposed adultery (Turits, *Foundations of Despotism* 222).

52. Yunior was born in the Dominican Republic and lived the early years of his life there—unlike Oscar, who was born in the United States. He presents himself to readers as a gatekeeper for understandings of Dominicanness in the novel (Machado Sáez 530) with his hypermasculinity mirroring that of Trujillo (Machado Sáez 544). When Oscar's Dominicanness and masculinity are measured according to Yunior's standards, the former is found to be lacking.

53. In between descriptions of his sexual exploits, Yunior betrays his feelings for Lola. He describes her body in detail, along the lines of the hypermasculinity that he exudes throughout the text, but at the same time, seems impressed by her accomplishments as "the

president of her sorority, the head of S.A.L.S.A. and co-chair of Take Back the Night" (168). He notes that he would have to be a better version of himself with Lola: "of all the chicks I'd run up on ever, Lola was the one I'd never gotten a handle on. So why did it feel like she was the one who knew me best?" (198).

54. Although I do not argue that Yunior is traumatized necessarily by Oscar's death, he is certainly haunted. This narrative fragmentation, however, relates to that experienced by traumatized subjects who can "tell it only in bits and pieces. The event has annulled in them the possibility of recounting the totality. In essence, the event is such that beyond it there remains only a speech in pieces, splinters and fragments of speech" (Nichanian, *Loss: The Politics of Mourning* 112).

55. Along with their husbands, three of the Mirabal sisters, Patria Mercedes, Minerva, and María Teresa, joined an underground movement against Trujillo in the late 1950s (Rich 165), making them targets of the dictatorship.

56. Monica Ayuso also positions Rosario's novel alongside Danticat's story "Nineteen Thirty-Seven," discussed in chapter 3, as "works about the transmission of traumatic memory primarily from mothers to daughters" (52).

57. As described in the previous chapter, Martine was raped by a *tonton macoute* in the cane fields, a traumatic experience that produced her daughter Sophie. Martine continues the cycle of violence through conducting invasive virginity tests on her daughter.

58. Harford Vargas uses similar terminology to discuss Trujillo himself as "an overwhelmingly absent presence, a kind of backstage character who is continually invoked and described but whose appearance onstage is extremely brief in relation to his overall manifestation in the narrative" (*Forms of Dictatorship* 41).

59. Yunior's interest in intergenerational violence is evident from the first page. He starts off the narration with the concept of *fukú*, which is itself intergenerational with the *fukú* incurred by Trujillo lasting "down to the seventh generation and beyond" (3).

60. Harford Vargas notes the novel's power reversal in depicting Trujillo as a minor and flat character whose depiction is mediated by others—Yunior and by extension Díaz ("Dictating a Zafa"11).

61. In Danticat's novel, Sophie doubles during the virginity testing to which her mother subjects her. Shani Mootoo's *Cereus Blooms at Night* takes place on the fictional Anglophone island of Lantanacamara, likely modeled after Trinidad, and is also interested in the intergenerational impact of sexual violence and colonial hierarchies.

62. A connection may also be made here to the many unknown factors regarding Sophie's violent conception in *Breath, Eyes, Memory*: for instance, Martine tells her, "I did not know this man. I never saw his face. He had it covered when he did this to me" (59). There is a blankness in Martine's memory where her rapist's face would be, and Sophie can never know the identity of her father.

63. It is outside of the purview of this chapter to speculate on why this is, but the early publication date of Alverez's novel and Díaz's own experience of abuse, revealed in his *New Yorker* article, might be factors.

64. Scholars have a range of views concerning Alvarez's device of Mate's diary. Isabel Zakrzewski Brown and Steve Criniti believe that the fictionalized journal entries overemphasize the character's innocence in line with stereotypical conceptions of the characters.

Charlotte Rich notes that the diary form "convincingly dramatizes her growing political consciousness" (170) and that her entries in the prison reveal the most about her consciousness with the ripped-out pages as "the omitted center" of her prison narrative (171). Lynn Chun Ink agrees that the diary lends "insight into life in the SIM prison, but it is a peculiarly G-rated version of prison life that sheds little light on the horrors the Mirabals endured," particularly due to the "significant and literal gaps in the account" and the "generally idealized" conditions (796). She concedes that the missing pages speak to the unknowable nature of history, but also contribute to the Mirabals's positioning as legend as opposed to flesh and blood (796).

65. Sean O'Brien notes an important erasure that occurs previous to this example on the novel's opening page: Yunior refers to Christopher Columbus as "the Admiral" and never provides his name (80). This may be seen as part of a zafa, or counterspell, since Columbus was the figure who supposedly created the New World curse. In this sense, it is fitting for him to go unnamed.

66. Harford Vargas expands on this concept in *Forms of Dictatorship*, describing how the postmemory generation, including Yunior, Oscar, Lola, and Díaz himself, "inherit[s] these gaps and silences, which, in turn, condition how they understand and speak about the past" (57).

67. For instance, Yunior refers to Beli's time with her abusive foster family as something neither she nor La Inca spoke about, "their very own página en blanco" (78). Yunior references the "páginas en blanco" left by Beli's and others' refusal to discuss the regime (119), as well as his own "silences" and "páginas en blanco," surrounding the phenomenon of the Mongoose (149).

68. Importantly the mongoose-like creature is defined in opposition. It is described as "a creature that would have been an amiable mongoose if not for its golden lion eyes and the absolute black of its pelt" (149). Although it is referred to as the Mongoose, Yunior explains that's not what it was. The Mongoose is a walking contradiction—an entity embodying a combination of opposites.

69. The "Man Without a Face" (321) is first seen by Beli preceding the beating in the cane fields that almost breaks her: "when she looked up she saw that there was one more cop sitting in the car, and when he turned toward her she saw that he *didn't have a face*. All the strength fell right out of her" (141). Similarly, Oscar believes he saw a man that "had no face" before he is also beaten in the cane fields (298): his own moment of violence layered palimpsestically on top of his mother's and the historic weight of cane on the island. In addition to these linked incidents, the figure often haunts the dreams of characters in the intense periods of anticipation preceding a difficult event, such as Socorro's dreams before Abelard is taken by the Secret Police (236–37) and Oscar's before he returns to Ybon and the DR, knowing the violence he is likely to trigger. The Man Without a Face is not a singular figure or fairy tale villain but is a more complex feature.

70. The missing name of the *capitán* is particularly interesting, since it might represent information unknown or redacted, but also could signify his ability to stand in for many others in his position of power.

71. This connects to the blankness in Edwidge Danticat's "Nineteen Thirty-Seven." The daughter of a survivor of the genocide is not allowed to speak the name of the Dominican Republic but refers to it as "the Spanish-speaking country" (33).

72. Moreover, characters' faces turn blank during moments of elevated emotion, whether anger or fear, at different points in the story. The face of Beli's adoptive "father" had "turned blank at the moment he picked up the skillet" to pour hot oil on his adopted daughter's back (261), and Ybón's face "was a blur" before telling Oscar that she is marrying the *capitán* (304). In these examples, "blank-faced-ness" is a condition tied to emotions or negative acts, as opposed to a singular character.

73. In *My Grandmother's Hands: Racialized Trauma and the Pathway to Mending Our Hearts and Bodies*, Menakem describes how trauma responses can become internalized and passed down over generations within groups and states that racialized trauma lives in the bodies of both White and Black Americans (9). He refers to the transmission of intergenerational trauma as a *soul wound*, which can occur through abusive family dynamics; abusive systems, structures, institutions, and cultural norms; and through our DNA expression (10).

74. Greg Forter conceptualizes the transgenerational phantom in different terms and argues that each of us inherits family trauma "from some mythically primal 'fatherhead'"—a term Forter takes from Bon's musing that "all boy flesh that walked and breathed stemming from that one ambiguous eluded dark fatherhead and so brothered perennial and ubiquitous everywhere under the sun" (Forter 129; Faulkner 240). According to Forter, this shows not only how one comes to "'naturalize' the social injuries of the world one inhabits but how one might come to see human history as a ceaseless repetition of a traumatization that resides at the origin of time" (Forter 129).

75. In a comparable way, the past is incomprehensible in Faulkner's *Absalom, Absalom!*, as discussed in chapter 1, even with multiple narrators attempting to reconstruct it. However, it is the effort at recollection, the telling itself, that matters, as Judith Sutpen observes to General Compson's wife: "And so maybe if you go to someone, the stranger the better, and give them something—a scrap of paper . . . at least it would be something just because it would have happened, be remembered even if only from passing from one hand to another, one mind to another . . ." (101). As Judith describes, the process of telling, or acting as a witness to an aspect of the past's existence, affects both the speaker and the hearer, regardless of how much the hearer understands or even pays attention. The same applies to other interactions between the narrators and their listeners in the novel: Miss Rosa or Mr. Compson speaking to Quentin, and later Quentin speaking to Shreve, as well as Shreve speaking back to Quentin in the "happy marriage of speaking and hearing" that exists between the two (Faulkner 253).

76. Scholars such as Bill Brown, Bruno Latour, Jane Bennett, Karen Barad, Nick J. Fox, Pam Alldred, Rosi Braidotti, and others in the field of new materialism explore the agency of material or things.

77. *Corregidora* centers on blues singer Ursa Corregidora, whose family history includes incestual intergenerational sexual exploitation at the hands of "Old man Corregidora, the Portuguese slave breeder and whore monger" (8–9). While the official records of Brazilian slavery were destroyed, Ursa's family attempts to keep evidence of their experiences alive through "*making generations*" and the oral transmission of trauma (emphasis in the original 22).

78. Arundhati Roy's *The God of Small Things* is a multigenerational story of a family in Kerala, India, that is invested in exploring the relationship between large-scale and small-scale historical events.

CODA: LOOKING BACK IN RESISTANCE, LOOKING TO THE PRESENT

1. Although race is socially constructed differently in each space through the legal systems—according to a binary model, three-tiered structure, and even more fluid constructions—all of the novels explored here focus primarily on the interactions among racial groups positioned as Black, White, and biracial. Future scholarship would do well to bring representations of other socially constructed racial groups into the conversation. Similarly, the experiences of transgender, nonbinary, and gender nonconforming individuals are primarily absent from the novels examined here. A more expansive exploration of novels that encompass a wider range of gender identities and subject positions in general would add another essential layer to this discussion.

2. Ruth Wilson Gilmore provides an alternative perspective: she positions the view that prisons are majority Black as a widely accepted and harmful misconception (Kushner, "Is Prison Necessary?"). The Black population is the most impacted, but 33 percent of those in prison are Black, 23 percent are Latinx, and 30 percent are White, according to the Bureau of Justice Statistics (Kushner, "Is Prison Necessary?"). However, Gilmore acknowledges that prison is a human rights catastrophe, like slavery, and the suffering of Black people is a central aspect of mass incarceration (Kushner, "Is Prison Necessary?"). She sees the connection between mass incarceration and Jim Crow as prompting concern about a population that may otherwise be ignored (Kushner, "Is Prison Necessary?").

3. More overtly, "violent crime is *not* responsible for mass incarceration" (Alexander 101, emphasis in the original). Violent crime rates have been shown to fluctuate over the years, not directly correlating to incarceration rates, which have continued to climb in the past three decades (Alexander 101).

4. While the privatization of prisons was an attempt to alleviate fiscal stress, it is not clear if states actually save money as a result (Eugene and Morris 4). What is clear is that the desire to exploit inmate labor is a significant factor behind the impetus for privatization (Price and Morris 6).

5. Ruth Wilson Gilmore states that private prisons are not driving mass incarceration: "They are parasite on it. Which doesn't make them good. Which doesn't make them not culpable for the things of which they are culpable. They are parasites" (as qtd. in Kushner, "Is Prison Necessary?"). According to Gilmore, the purpose of prisons is to separate people from society, which costs money (Kushner, "Is Prison Necessary?").

6. The immigration industrial complex includes "multilateral deportation regimes, public-private partnerships between states and publicly traded prison firms, increasingly dense networks of immigration detention sites and asylum processing centers, external border controls, [and] interior immigration enforcement," which together form the international systems of immigration (Wong 2).

7. As of October 2017, 65 percent of detainees held by the Department of Homeland Security are held in privately run detention centers (Gomez). Deplorable conditions are

sometimes found: people do not know the length of time for which they will be detained; rules and punishments can be arbitrary (Fiske 6). Tom Wong adds discrimination, racism, shackling, the use of tasers, and regular coercion to perform sexual favors for early release experienced by female detainees (including minors) to this list of harms (121).

8. Further, approximately one thousand children have been separated from their parents since the Trump administration declared the practice over in June 2018 (Aguilera).

9. During the editing of this manuscript, the connections between the policing of sexuality and family structures and immigration detention became even more blatant through allegations that immigrant women were subjected to unwanted gynecological procedures, such as hysterectomies, in a privately run facility in Georgia (Dickerson).

10. The law prevents this segment of Dominican society from owning property, voting, securing employment in the private sector, and sending children to school beyond fourth grade (Ariza).

11. The climate crisis, which will disproportionately affect people of color living in the Global South, is another direction in which this work could develop. As Christopher Todd Beer succinctly states, "Having contributed a fraction of the historical GHG [greenhouse gas] emissions, the Global South is currently experiencing the greatest harm," according to the Intergovernmental Panel on Climate Change (85).

12. In recent years, there has been an increase in nonfiction works dealing with the experiences of undocumented Americans, such as Pulitzer Prize–winning journalist Jose Antonio Vargas's memoir *Dear America: Notes of an Undocumented Citizen* (2018), José N. Ángel's *Illegal: Reflections of an Undocumented Immigrant* (2014), and Jenny Rodriguez's *Undocumented: The True Stories of Illegal Immigrants and Their Children* (2014).

13. Thank you to my fellow members of the Society for the Study of Southern Literature for pointing me in the direction of these texts.

WORKS CITED

Abdur-Rahman, Aliyyah I. "'The Strangest Freaks of Despotism': Queer Sexuality in Antebellum African American Slave Narratives." *African American Review* 40 no. 2 (2006): 223–37.

Aboul-Ela, Hosam M. *Other South: Faulkner, Coloniality, and the Mariategui Tradition*. Pittsburgh: University of Pittsburgh Press, 2007.

Abraham, Nicolas, and Maria Torok. *The Shell and the Kernel: Renewals of Psychoanalysis*. Edited and translated by Nicholas Rand. Chicago: University of Chicago Press, 1994.

Abrahams, Yvette. "Images of Sara Bartman: Sexuality, Race, and Gender in Early-Nineteenth-Century Britain." In *Nation, Empire, Colony: Historicizing Gender and Race*, edited by Ruth Roach Piernon and Nupur Chaudhuri, 220–36. Bloomington: Indiana University Press, 1998.

Adams, Jessica. *Wounds of Returning: Race, Memory, and Property on the Postslavery Plantation*. Chapel Hill: University of North Carolina Press, 2007.

Aguilera, Jasmine. "Here's What to Know About the Status of Family Separation at the US Border, Which Isn't Nearly Over." *Time*, 1 February 2020, https://time.com/5678313/trumpadministration-family-separation-lawsuits/.

Alarcon, Javiera. "It's Really Happening: The Dominican Republic Is Deporting Its Haitian Residents." *Foreign Policy in Focus*, 4 April 2016, https://fpif.org/really-happening-dominican-republic-deporting-haitian-residents/.

Alexander, Michelle. *The New Jim Crow: Mass Incarceration in the Age of Colorblindness*. New York: New Press, 2011.

Aljoe, Nicole. *Creole Testimonies: Slave Narratives from the British West Indies, 1709–1838*. New York: Palgrave Macmillan, 2012.

Alvarez, Julia. *In the Time of the Butterflies*. New York: Hudson, 1995.

Amnesty International. "Haiti/Dominican Republic: Reckless Deportations Leaving Thousands in Limbo." 15 June 2016. https://www.amnesty.org/en/latest/news/2016/06/haiti-dominican-republic-reckless-deportations-leaving-thousands-in-limbo/.

Ángel, José N. *Illegal: Reflections of an Undocumented Immigrant*. Champaign: University of Illinois Press, 2014.

Ariza, Mario. "*La Apatrida*: Dominicans of Haitian Descent are Deported and Forgotten." *Miami New Times*, 21 February 2017, https://www.miaminewtimes.com/news/la-apatrida-dominicans-of-haitian-descent-are-deported-and-forgotten-9153733.

Ashcroft, Bill, Gareth Griffiths, and Helen Tiffin. *Post-Colonial Studies: The Key Concepts*. London: Routledge, 2000.
Aslakson, Kenneth R. *Making Race in the Courtroom*. New York: New York University Press, 2014.
Aubert, Alvin. "Ernest J. Gaines's Truly Tragic Mulatto." *Callaloo* 3 (May 1978): 68–75.
"The Author." Ernest J. Gaines Center, 7 July 2018, https://ernestgaines.louisiana.edu/author.
Ayuso, Mónica G. "'How Lucky for You That Your Tongue Can Taste the "r" in "Parsley"': Trauma Theory and the Literature of Hispaniola." *Afro-Hispanic Review* 30 no. 1 (2011): 47–62.
Babb, Valerie Melissa. *Ernest Gaines*. Twayne's United States Authors Series 584. Boston: Twayne, 1991.
Baptist, Edward E. *The Half Has Never Been Told: Slavery and the Making of American Capitalism*. New York: Basic Books, 2014.
Beavers, Herman. "Tilling the Soul to Find Ourselves: Conversion, Labor, and [Re]membering in Gaines's *Of Love and Dust* and *In My Father's House*." In *Wrestling Angels into Song: The Fictions of Ernest J. Gaines and James Alan McPherson*. Philadelphia: University of Pennsylvania Press, 2015.
Beckert, Sven, and Seth Rockman, eds. *Slavery's Capitalism: A New History of American Economic Development*. Philadelphia: University of Pennsylvania Press, 2016.
Beer, Christopher Todd. "Climate Justice, the Global South, and Policy Preferences of Kenyan Environmental NGOs." *The Global South* 8 no. 2 (2014): 84–100.
Bell, Madison Smartt. "Permanent Exile: On Marie Vieux-Chauvet." *The Nation*. 14 January 2001. https://www.thenation.com/article/permanent-exile-marie-vieux-chauvet/.
Benítez-Rojo, Antonio. *The Repeating Island: The Caribbean and the Postmodern Perspective*. Durham, NC: Duke University Press, 1997.
Bhabha, Homi. *The Location of Culture*. London: Routledge, 1994.
Bibler, Michael P. *Cotton's Queer Relations: Same-Sex Intimacy and the Literature of the Southern Plantation, 1936–1968*. Charlottesville: University of Virginia Press, 2009.
"Black Code of Mississippi 1865 (Document Text)." *Milestone Documents in African American History*. Hackensack, NJ: Salem Press, 2017.
Blackmon, Douglas A. *Slavery by Another Name: The Re-Enslavement of Black Americans from the Civil War to World War II*. New York: First Anchor Books, 2009.
Blotner, Joseph L. *Faulkner: A Biography*. New York: Vintage International, 1991.
Bond, Julian. *Southern Exposure: A Journal of Politics & Culture* 29. Institute for Southern Studies, 2000.
Brasseaux, Carl A. "Creoles of Color in Louisiana's Bayou Country, 1766–1877." In *Creoles of Color of the Gulf South*, edited by James H. Dormon, 67–86. Knoxville: University Press of Tennessee, 1996.
Brasseaux, Carl A., Keith P. Fontenot, and Claude F. Oubre. *Creole of Color in the Bayou Country*. Jackson: University Press of Mississippi, 1994.
Brickhouse, Anna. *Transamerican Literary Relations and the Nineteenth-century Public Sphere*. Cambridge: Cambridge University Press, 2004.
Brooks, David. "The Underlying Tragedy." *New York Times*, 15 January 2010, www.nytimes.com/2010/01/15/opinion/15/brooks.html?_r=0.

Brown, Isabel Zakrzewski. "Historiographic Metafiction in *In the Time of the Butterflies.*" *South Atlantic Review* 64 no. 2 (Spring 1999): 98–112.

Brown, Kimberly Juanita. *The Repeating Body: Slavery's Visual Resonance in the Contemporary*. Durham, NC: Duke University Press, 2015.

Burns, Brian. *Gilded Age Richmond: Gaiety, Greed, & Lost Cause Mania*. Charleston, SC: History Press, 2017.

Burns, Francis P. "The Black Code: A Brief History of the Origin, Statutory Regulation and Judicial Sanction of Slavery in Louisiana." In *An Uncommon Experience Law and Judicial Institutions in Louisiana 1803-2003*, edited by Judith Kelleher Schafer and Warren H. Billings, 305–11. The Louisiana Purchase Bicentennial Series in Louisiana History, vol. XIII. Lafayette: Center for Louisiana Studies at University of Southwestern Louisiana, 1997..

Burton, H. Sophie. "Foreword to the Revised Edition." *The Forgotten People: Cane River's Creoles of Color*, 2nd ed. by Gary B. Mills, xi–xvi. Baton Rouge: Louisiana State University Press, 2013.

Bush, Barbara. "Defiance or Submission? The Role of the Slave Woman in Slave Resistance in the British Caribbean." In *We Specialize in the Wholly Impossible: A Reader in Black Women's History*, edited by Darlene Clark Hine, Wilma King, and Linda Reed, 147–70. New York: New York University Press, 1995.

Butler, Judith. "Performative Acts and Gender Constitution: An Essay in Phenomenology and Feminist Theory." *Theatre Journal* 40 no. 4 (December 1988): 519–31.

Byerman, Keith. "Bloodlines: Creoles of Color and Identity in the Fiction of Ernest Gaines." In *Songs of the New South: Writing Contemporary Louisiana*, edited by Suzanne Disheroon Green and Lisa Adney, 193–201. Westport, CT: Greenwood, 2001.

Camp, Cyrus C. *Labor, Capital and Money; Their Just Relations*. Sydney: Wentworth Press, 2016. First published 1887 by Lerch (Bradford, PA).

Candelario, Ginetta E. B. "Voices from Hispaniola: A Meridians Roundtable with Edwidge Danticat, Loida Maritza Pérez, Myriam J. A. Chancy, and Nelly Rosario." *Meridians: Feminism, Race, Transnationalism* 5 no. 1 (2004): 69–91.

Carastathis, Anna. *Intersectionality: Origins, Contestations, Horizons*. Lincoln: University of Nebraska Press, 2016.

Carpentier, Alejo. *El recurso de método*. Havana: Editorial de Arte y Literatura, 1974.

Caruth, Cathy. *Unclaimed Experience: Trauma, Narrative, and History*. Baltimore: Johns Hopkins University Press, 1996.

Cashin, Sheryll. *Loving: Interracial Intimacy in America and the Threat to White Supremacy*. Boston: Beacon Press, 2017.

Chak, Tings. *Undocumented: The Architecture of Migrant Detention*. Westmount, Quebec: Architecture Observer, 2014.

Chancy, Myriam J. A. *Framing Silence: Revolutionary Novels by Haitian Women*. New Brunswick, NJ: Rutgers University Press, 1997.

Chancy, Myriam J. A. *From Sugar to Revolution: Women's Visions of Haiti, Cuba, and the Dominican Republic*. Waterloo, Ontario: Wilfrid Laurier University Press, 2012.

Charters, Mallay. "Edwidge Danticat: A Bitter Legacy Revisited." *Publishers Weekly*, 17 August 1998. https://www.publishersweekly.com/pw/by-topic/authors/interviews/article/30020-pw-edwidge-danticat-a-bitter-legacy-revisited.html.

Child, Lydia Maria. *Slavery's Pleasant Homes & Other Tales*. Roxwell: OK Publishing, 2017.
Christian, Barbara. *Black Feminist Criticism*. New York: Pergamon Press, 1985.
Clark, Emily. *The Strange History of the American Quadroon*. Chapel Hill: University of North Carolina Press, 2013.
Collins, Patricia Hill. *Black Feminist Thought: Knowledge, Consciousness, and the Politics of Empowerment*. London: Routledge, 2008.
Constant, Fred. Foreword to *The Color of Liberty: Histories of Race in France*, edited by Sue Peabody and Tyler Stovall. Durham, NC: Duke University Press, 2003.
Constant, Isabelle, and Kahiudi C. Mabana. *Negritude: Legacy and Present Relevance*. Newcastle upon Tyne: Cambridge Scholars Publishing, 2009.
Cooper, Brittney C. *Beyond Respectability: The Intellectual Thought of Race Women*. Urbana: University of Illinois Press, 2017.
Cooper, Frederick. *Colonialism in Question: Theory, Knowledge, History*. Ewing: University of California Press, 2005.
Costello, Brannon. *Plantation Airs: Racial Paternalism and the Transformations of Class in Southern Fiction, 1945–1971*. Baton Rouge: Louisiana State University Press, 2007.
Crassweller, Robert D. *Trujillo: The Life and Times of a Caribbean Dictator*. New York: Macmillan, 1966.
Crenshaw, Kimberlé. "Demarginalizing the Intersection of Race and Sex: A Black Feminist Critique of Antidiscrimination Doctrine, Feminist Theory and Antiracist Politics." University of Chicago Legal Forum Vol. 1989, Iss. 1. Article 8 (1989): 139–67.
Crenshaw, Kimberlé. "Mapping the Margins: Intersectionality, Identity Politics, and Violence against Women of Color." *Stanford Law Review* 43 no. 6 (July 1991): 1241–99.
Criniti, Steve. "Collecting Butterflies: Julia Alvarez's Revision of North American Collective Memory." *Modern Language Studies* 36 no. 2 (Winter 2007): 42–63.
Cruz, Angie, and Nelly Rosario. "Angie Cruz in Conversation with Nelly Rosario." *Callaloo* 30 no. 3 (Summer 2007): 743–53.
Daniel, G. Reginald, Laura Kina, Wei Ming Dariotis, and Camilla Fojas. "Emerging Paradigms in Critical Mixed Race Studies." *Journal of Critical Mixed Race Studies* 1 no. 1 (2014): 6–65.
Danticat, Edwidge. *Breath, Eyes, Memory*. New York: Soho Press, 1994.
Danticat, Edwidge. *Brother, I'm Dying*. New York: Vintage Contemporaries, 2007.
Danticat, Edwidge. *The Farming of Bones*. New York: Penguin Books, 1998.
Danticat, Edwidge. Introduction to *Love, Anger, Madness*, by Marie Vieux-Chauvet. New York: Modern Library, 2001.
Danticat, Edwidge. *Krik? Krak!* New York: Vintage Contemporaries, 1996.
Daut, Marlene L. *Tropics of Haiti: Race and the Literary History of the Haitian Revolution in the Atlantic World 1789–1865*. Liverpool: Liverpool University Press, 2015.
Davis, Adrienne. "'Don't Let Nobody Bother Yo' Principle': The Sexual Economy of American Slavery." In *Sister Circle: Black Women and Work*, edited by Sharon Harley and the Black Women and Work Collective, 103–27. New Brunswick, NJ: Rutgers University Press, 2002.
Davis, Angela. *Women, Race, and Class*. New York: Vintage, 1983. First published 1981 by Random House (New York).

Davis, Thadious. *Games of Property: Law, Race, Gender, and Faulkner's* Go Down, Moses. Durham, NC: Duke University Press Books, 2003.

Davis, Thadious. "Headlands and Quarters: Louisiana in Catherine Carmier." *Callaloo* 7 (Spring-Summer 1984): 1–13.

Davis, Thadious. *Southscapes: Geographies of Race, Religion, & Literature*. Chapel Hill: University of North Carolina Press, 2011.

Dayan, Colin. *Haiti, History, and the Gods*. Berkley: University of California Press, 1995.

Dayan, Colin. "Reading Women in the Caribbean: Marie Chauvet's *Love, Anger, Madness*." In *Displacements: Women, Tradition, Literatures in French*, edited by Joan DeJean and Nancy K. Miller, 228–53. Baltimore: Johns Hopkins University Press, 1991.

De Galíndez, Jesús. *The Era of Trujillo: Dominican Dictator*. Tucson: University of Arizona Press, 1973.

Delgadillo, Theresa. "The Criticality of Latino/a Fiction in the Twenty-First Century." *American Literary History* 23 no. 3 (Fall 2011): 600–24.

Derby, Lauren. *The Dictator's Seduction: Politics and the Popular Imagination in the Era of Trujillo*. Durham, NC: Duke University Press, 2009.

Derby, Lauren. "Haitians, Magic, and Money: Raza and Society in the Haitian-Dominican Borderlands, 1900 to 1937." *Comparative Studies in Society and History* 36 no. 3 (July 1994): 488–526.

Desmangles, Leslie G. *The Faces of the Gods: Vodou and Roman Catholicism in Haiti*. Chapel Hill: University of North Carolina Press, 1992.

Diamond, Raymond T., and Robert J. Cottrol. "Codifying Caste: Louisiana's Racial Classification Scheme and the Fourteenth Amendment." *An Uncommon Experience: Law and Judicial Institutions in Louisiana 1803–2003*, edited by Judith Kelleher Schafer and Warren H. Billings. The Louisiana Purchase Bicentennial Series in Louisiana History, vol. XIII. Lafayette: Center for Louisiana Studies at University of Southwestern Louisiana, 1997.

Díaz, Junot. *The Brief Wondrous Life of Oscar*. New York: Riverhead, 2007.

Díaz, Junot. "The Silence: The Legacy of Childhood Trauma." *New Yorker*. 16 April 2018. https://www.newyorker.com/magazine/2018/04/16/the-silence-the-legacy-of-childhood-trauma.

Dickerson, Caitlin. "Inquiry Ordered into Claims Immigrants Had Unwanted Gynecology Procedures." *New York Times*, 27 September 2020. https://www.nytimes.com/2020/09/6/us/ICE-hysterectomies-whistleblower-georgia.html.

Diederich, Bernard, and Al Burt. *Papa Doc: Haiti and its Dictator*. Maplewood, NJ: Waterfront Press, 1991.

Domínguez, Virginia R. *White by Definition: Social Classification in Creole Louisiana*. New Brunswick, NJ: Rutgers University Press, 1986.

Dubois, Laurent. *Haiti: The Aftershocks of History*. New York: Metropolitan Books, 2012.

Du Bois, W. E. B. *The Souls of Black Folk*. Mineola: Dover Publishing, 1994. First published 1903 by A. C. McClurg (Chicago).

Edgeworth, Maria. *The Grateful Negro*. Gloucester, England: Dodo Press, 2008. First published 1804.

Edwards, Laura F. "Southern History as US History." *Journal of Southern History* 75 no. 3 (August 2009): 533–64.
El Akkad, Omar. *American War: A Novel.* New York: Knopf, 2017.
Fanon, Frantz. *The Wretched of the Earth.* New York: Grove Press, 1963.
Faulkner, William. *Absalom, Absalom!* New York: Vintage International, 1990. First published 1936.
Faulkner, William. *Essays, Speeches, & Public Letters.* Edited by James B. Meriwether. New York: Modern Library, 2004.
Faulkner, William. *Go Down, Moses.* New York: Vintage International, 1990. First published 1942.
Faulkner, William. *Intruder in the Dust.* New York: Vintage International, 1991. First published 1948.
Faulkner, William. *Light in August.* New York: Vintage International, 1990. First published 1932.
Faulkner, William. *Requiem for a Nun.* New York: Vintage International, 1994. First published 1950.
Faulkner, William. *Sanctuary.* New York: Vintage International, 1985. First published 1931.
Faulkner, William. *The Sound and the Fury.* New York: Vintage International, 1984. First published 1929.
Felman, Shoshana, and Dori Laub. *Testimony: Crises of Witnessing in Literature, Psychoanalysis, and History.* New York: Routledge, 1992.
Felski, Rita. "Context Stinks!" *New Literary History* 42 no. 4 (Autumn 2011): 573–91.
Ferrante, Joan, and Prince Brown Jr. *The Social Construction of Race and Ethnicity in the United States.* Upper Saddle River, NJ: Prentise Hall, 2001.
Ferreras, Ramón Alberto. *Las Mirabal.* Santo Domingo: Media Isla, 1982.
Fiske, Lucy. *Human Rights Refugee Protest and Immigration Detention.* London: Palgrave Macmillan, 2016.
Forter, Greg. *Gender, Race, and Mourning in American Modernism.* Cambridge: Cambridge University Press, 2011.
Foster, Frances Smith. *'Til Death or Distance Do Us Part: Love and Marriage in African America.* Oxford: Oxford University Press, 2010.
Foucault, Michel. *Discipline and Punish: The Birth of the Prison.* Translated by Alan Sheridan. New York: Vintage, 1977.
Fowler, Doreen. "Reading for the 'Other Side': *Beloved* and *Requiem for a Nun*." *Unflinching Gaze: Morrison and Faulkner Re-Envisioned.* Edited by Carol A. Kolmerten, Stephen M. Ross, and Judith Bryant Wittenberg. Jackson: University Press of Mississippi, 1997.
Fredrickson, George M. *The Black Image in the White Mind: The Debate on Afro-American Character and Destiny, 1817–1914.* New York: Harper Torchbooks, 1972.
French, B. F. "Black Code of Louisiana" (1724). In *Historical Collections of Louisiana: Embracing Translations of Many Rare and Valuable Documents Relating to the Natural, Civil, and Political History of that State.* New York: D. Appleton, 1851.
Fumagalli, Maria Cristina. *On the Edge: Writing the Border between Haiti and the Dominican Republic.* Liverpool: Liverpool University Press, 2015.

Gaines, Ernest J. Draft of "Another Frontier." Ernest J. Gaines Papers, N.d. Box 4, Folder 7, Collection 115, Ernest J. Gaines Center, University of Louisiana at Lafayette Libraries, Lafayette, LA. Accessed 5 June 2016.

Gaines, Ernest J. *The Autobiography of Miss Jane Pittman*. New York: Bantam Books, 1996. First published 1972.

Gaines, Ernest J. Draft of *The Autobiography of Miss Jane Pittman*. Ernest J. Gaines Papers, N.d. Box 5, Folder 71, Collection 115, Ernest J. Gaines Center, University of Louisiana at Lafayette Libraries, Lafayette, LA. Accessed 5 June 2016.

Gaines, Ernest J. Draft of *The Autobiography of Miss Jane Pittman*. Ernest J. Gaines Papers, N.d. Box 5, Folder 76, Collection 115, Ernest J. Gaines Center, University of Louisiana at Lafayette Libraries, Lafayette, LA. Accessed 14 June 2016.

Gaines, Ernest J. Draft of *The Autobiography of Miss Jane Pittman*. Ernest J. Gaines Papers, N.d. Box 6, Folder 10, Collection 115, Ernest J. Gaines Center, University of Louisiana at Lafayette Libraries, Lafayette, LA. Accessed 8 June 2016.

Gaines, Ernest J. Draft of *The Autobiography of Miss Jane Pittman*. Ernest J. Gaines Papers, N.d. Box 6, Folder 18, Collection 115, Ernest J. Gaines Center, University of Louisiana at Lafayette Libraries, Lafayette, LA. Accessed 23 June 2016.

Gaines, Ernest J. *Catherine Carmier*. New York: Vintage Books, 1993. First published 1981.

Gaines, Ernest J. "A Conversation with Ernest Gaines." By Ruth Laney. *Conversations with Ernest Gaines*. Edited by John Lowe, 56–71. Jackson: University Press of Mississippi, 1995.

Gaines, Ernest J. "An Interview with Ernest Gaines." By John Lowe. *Conversations with Ernest Gaines*. Edited by John Lowe, 297–328. Jackson: University Press of Mississippi, 1995.

Gaines, Ernest J. *Of Love and Dust*. New York: Vintage Books, 1994. First published 1967.

Gaines, Ernest J. Draft of *Of Love and Dust*. Ernest J. Gaines Papers, N.d. Box 3, Folder 27, Collection 115, Ernest J. Gaines Center, University of Louisiana at Lafayette Libraries, Lafayette, LA. Accessed 23 June 2016.

Gaines, Ernest J. Unpublished Commentary. Ernest J. Gaines Papers, N.d. Box 4, Folder 11, Collection 115, Ernest J. Gaines Center, University of Louisiana at Lafayette Libraries, Lafayette, LA. Accessed 23 June 2016.

Galván, William. *Minerva Mirabal*. Santo Domingo: Universidad Autónoma de Santo Domingo, 1982.

García Márquez, Gabriel. *El otoño del patriarca*. Bogatá: Grupo Editional Norma, 2003.

Garrigus, John D. *Before Haiti: Race and Citizenship in French Saint-Domingue*. New York: Palgrave Macmillan, 2006.

Garrigus, John D. "Race, Gender and Virtue in Haiti's Failed Foundational Fiction: *La Mulâtre comme il y a beaucoup de blanches* (1803)." In *The Color of Liberty: Histories of Race in France*, edited by Tyler Stovall and Sue Peabody, 73–94. Durham, NC: Duke University Press, 2003.

Gaudet, Marcia. "Miss Jane and Personal Experience Narrative: Ernest Gaines' *The Autobiography of Miss Jane Pittman*." *Western Folklore* 51 no. 1 (January 1992): 23–32.

Gerend, Sara. "'My Son, My Son!': Paternalism, Haiti, and Early Twentieth Century American Imperialism in William Faulkner's *Absalom, Absalom!*" *Southern Literary Journal* 42 no. 1 (2009): 17–31.

Giddens, Anthony. *The Transformation of Intimacy: Sexuality, Love, and Eroticism in Modern Societies*. Stanford, CA: Stanford University Press, 1992.

Gillman, Susan. "Afterword: The Time of Hemispheric Studies." In *Hemispheric American Studies*, edited by Caroline Field Levander and Robert S. Levine, 328–36. New Brunswick, NJ: Rutgers University Press, 2008.

Gilman, Sander L. "Black Bodies, White Bodies: Toward an Iconography of Female Sexuality in Late Nineteenth-Century Art, Medicine, Literature." *Critical Inquiry* 12 no. 1 (Autumn, 1985): 204–42.

Gilroy, Paul. *Postcolonial Melancholia*. New York: Columbia University Press, 2006.

Gleijeses, Piero. *The Dominican Crisis: The 1965 Constitutionalist Revolt and American Intervention*. Translated by Lawrence Lipson. Baltimore: Johns Hopkins University Press, 1978.

Glissant, Édouard. *Faulkner, Mississippi*. Translated by Barbara Lewis and Thomas C. Spear. New York: Farrar, Straus and Giroux, 1999.

Glover, Kaiama L. "'Black' Radicalism in Haiti and the Disorderly Feminine: The Case of Marie Vieux Chauvet." *Small Axe* 17 no. 1 (March 2013): 7–21.

Godden, Richard. *Fictions of Labor: William Faulkner and the South's Long Revolution*. Cambridge: Cambridge University Press, 1997.

Godden, Richard. "Re: Faulkner at West Point." Email message to the author. 31 July 2012.

Gomez, Alan. "Trump Plans Massive Increase in Federal Immigration Jails." *USA Today*, 17 October 2017. https://www.usatoday.com/story/news/world/2017/10/17/trump-plans-massive-increase-federal-immigration-jails/771414001/.

Griffin, Joseph. "Ernest J. Gaines's Good News: Sacrifice and Redemption in *Of Love and Dust*." *Modern Language Studies* 18 no. 3 (Summer 1988): 75–85.

Hagood, Taylor. *Faulkner's Imperialism: Space, Place, and the Materiality of Myth*. Baton Rouge: Louisiana State University Press, 2008.

"Haiti: The List." *Haiti Net*. Northeastern University, 2011. Accessed 20 March 2014. http://www.northeastern.edu/haitinet/haiti-facts/.

Hale, Grace Elizabeth. *Making Whiteness: The Culture of Segregation in the South*. New York: Vintage International, 1999.

Hall, Alexandra. *Border Watch: Cultures of Immigration, Detention and Control*. London: Pluto Press, 2012.

Hall, Gwendolyn Midlo. "The Formation of Afro-Creole Culture." In *Creole New Orleans: Race and Americanization*, edited by Arnold R. Hirsch and Joseph Logsdon, 58–90. Baton Rouge: Louisiana State University Press, 1992.

Hall, Jacquelyn Dowd. *Revolt Against Chivalry: Jessie Daniel Ames and the Women's Campaign Against Lynching*. Revised edition. New York: Columbia University Press, 1993.

Hall, Stuart, Chas Critcher, Tony Jefferson, John Clarke, and Brian Roberts. *Policing the Crisis: Mugging, the State, and Law and Order*. London: Macmillan, 1978.

Hamid, Mohsin. *Exit West: A Novel*. New York: Riverhead Books, 2017.

Handley, George B. *Post Slavery Literatures in the Americas: Family Portraits in Black and White*. Charlottesville: University of Virginia Press, 2000

Haney López, Ian F. "The Social Construction of Race" (2000). In *Literary Theory: An Anthology*, edited by Julie Rivkin and Michael Ryan, 964–74. Malden: Blackwell Publishing, 2004.

Haney López, Ian F. *White by Law: The Legal Construction of Race*, 10th Anniversary Edition. New York: New York University Press, 2006.

Harford Vargas, Jennifer. "Dictating a Zafa: The Power of Narrative Form in Junot Díaz's *The Brief Wondrous Life of Oscar Wao*." *MELUS* 39 no. 3 (Fall 2014): 8–30.

Harford Vargas, Jennifer. *Forms of Dictatorship: Power, Narrative, and Authoritarianism in the Latina/o Novel*. Oxford: Oxford University Press, 2018.

Hartman, Saidiya. *Lose Your Mother: A Journey Along the Atlantic Slave Route*. New York: Farrar, Straus and Giroux, 2008.

Hartman, Saidiya. "Seduction and the Ruses of Power." *Callaloo* 19 no. 2 (1996): 537–60.

Hartman, Saidiya. "Venus in Two Acts." *Small Axe* 12 no. 2 (June 2008): 1–14.

Hebert-Leiter, Maria. "A Breed Between: Racial Mediation in the Fiction of Ernest Gaines." *MELUS* 31 no. 2 (2006): 95–117.

Hickman, Trenton. "Hagiographic Commemorafiction in Julia Alvarez's *In the Time of the Butterflies* and *In the Name of Salome*." *MELUS* 31 no. 1 (2006): 99–121.

Higginbotham, Evelyn Brooks. *Righteous Discontent: The Women's Movement in the Black Baptist Church 1880–1920*. Cambridge, MA: Harvard University Press, 1993.

Hiraldo, Carlos. *Segregated Miscegenation: On the Treatment of Racial Hybridity in the US and Latin American Literary Traditions*. New York: Routledge, 2015.

Hirsch, Arnold R., and Joseph Logsdon. *Creole New Orleans: Race and Americanization*. Baton Rouge: Louisiana State University Press, 1992.

Hodes, Martha. "The Mercurial Nature and Abiding Power of Race: A Transnational Family Story." *American Historical Review* 108 no. 1 (February 2003): 84–118.

Hodes, Martha. *White Women, Black Men: Illicit Sex in the Nineteenth-Century South*. New Haven, CT: Yale University Press, 1999.

Holloway, Karla F. C. *Legal Fictions: Constituting Race, Composing Literature*. Durham, NC: Duke University Press, 2014.

hooks, bell. *Yearning Race, Gender, and Cultural Politics*. New York: Routledge, 1990.

Hutcheon, Linda. "Historiographic Metafiction Parody and the Intertextuality of History." In *Intertextuality and Contemporary American Fiction*, edited by P. O'Donnell, and Robert Con Davis, 3–32. Baltimore: Johns Hopkins University Press, 1989.

Ink, Lynn Chun. "Remaking Identity, Unmaking Nation: Historical Recovery and the Reconstruction of Community in *In the Time of the Butterflies* and *The Farming of Bones*." *Callaloo* 27 no. 3 (Summer 2004): 788–807.

Intergovernmental Panel on Climate Change. *Climate Change 2007: Synthesis Report*. Geneva: IPCC, 2007. www.ipcc.ch.

Jacobs, Harriet. *Incidents in the Life of a Slave Girl, Written by Herself*. Edited by Nellie Y. McKay and Frances Smith Foster. New York: W.W. Norton & Co., 2001. First published 1861.

Jean-Charles, Régine Michelle. "Beneath the Layers of Violence: Images of Rape in the Rwandan Genocide." In *Local Violence, Global Media: Feminist Analyses of Gendered Representations*, edited by Lisa Cuklanz, 246–66. New York: Peter Lang, 2009.

Jean-Charles, Régine Michelle. "Naming, Claiming, and Framing Marie Chauvet." *Meridians* 16 no. 1 (2017): 50–76.

Jing, Yijia. "The US Experience in Prison Privatization." In *Prison Privatization: The Many Facets of a Controversial Industry*. Vol. 1, edited by Byron Eugene Price and John Charles Morris, 55–86. Santa Barbara, CA: Praeger, 2012.

Jones, Gayl. *Corregidora*. Boston: Beacon Press, 1987.

Jones, Suzanne. *Race Mixing: Southern Fiction Since the Sixties*. Baltimore: Johns Hopkins University Press, 2004.

Jordan, Winthrop D. *White over Black: American Attitudes Toward the Negro, 1550–1812*. Kingsport, TN: Kingsport Press, 1968.

Kalisa, Chantal. *Violence in Francophone African & Caribbean Women's Literature*. Lincoln: University of Nebraska Press, 2009.

Kaplan, Amy, and Donald E. Pease, eds. *Cultures of United States Imperialism*. Durham, NC: Duke University Press, 1994.

Kaplan, E. Ann. *Trauma Culture: The Politics of Terror and Loss in Media and Literature*. New Brunswick, NJ: Rutgers University Press, 2005.

Kassie, Emily. "Detained: How the US Built the World's Largest Immigrant Detention System." *The Guardian*, 1 February 2020. https://www.theguardian.com/us-news/2019/sep/24/detained-us-largest-immigrant-detention-trump.

Kein, Sybil. *Creole: The History and Legacy of Louisiana's Free People of Color*. Baton Rouge: Louisiana State University Press, 2000.

Kennedy, Randall. *Interracial Intimacies: Sex, Marriage, Identity, and Adoption*. New York: Pantheon Books, 2003.

Klor de Alva, J. Jorge. "The Postcolonization of the (Latin) American Experiences: A Reconsideration of 'Colonialism,' 'Postcolonialism,' and 'Mestizaje.'" In *After Colonialism Imperial Histories and Postcolonial Displacements*, edited by Gyan Prakash. Princeton University Press, 2001.

Krise, Thomas W. ed. *Caribbeana: An Anthology of English Literature of the West Indies, 1657–1777*. Chicago: University of Chicago Press, 1999.

Kurlansky, Mark, Junot Díaz, Edwidge Danticat, and Julia Alvarez. Letter. *New York Times*, 1 November 2013, A30.

Kushner, Rachel. "Is Prison Necessary? Ruth Wilson Gilmore Might Change Your Mind." *New York Times Magazine*, 1 February 2020. https://www.nytimes.com/2019/04/17/magazine/prison-abolition-ruth-wilson-gilmore.html.

Kushner, Rachel. *The Mars Room*. New York: Scribner, 2018.

LaCapra, Dominick. *Writing History, Writing Trauma*. Baltimore: Johns Hopkins University Press, 2000.

Ladd, Barbara. *Nationalism and the Color Line in George W. Cable, Mark Twain, and William Faulkner*. Baton Rouge: Louisiana State University Press, 1996.

Lagon, Mark P. "Reflections on Global Justice and American Exceptionalism." *World Affairs* 180 no. 1 (Spring 2017): 42–63.

Lanzendörfer, Tim. "The Marvelous History of the Dominican Republic in Junot Díaz's *The Brief Wondrous Life of Oscar Wao*." *MELUS* 38 no. 2 (Summer 2013): 127–42.

Le code noir ou Edit du roy. (1724). Paris: De l'Imprimerie royale, 1727. John Carter Brown Library.

Le code noir ou Edit du roy. (1685). Paris: Chez Claude Girard, 1735. John Carter Brown Library. RememberHaiti. http://www.archive.org/stream/lecodenoirouedioofran#page/4/mode/2up.

Lee-Keller, Hellen. "Madness and the Mulâtre-Aristocrate: Haiti, Decolonization, and Women in Marie Chauvet's Amour." *Callaloo* 32 no. 4 (2009): 1293–1311.

Levander, Caroline Field, and Robert S. Levine, eds. *Hemispheric American Studies*. New Brunswick, NJ: Rutgers University Press, 2008.

Libby, David J. *Slavery and Frontier Mississippi, 1720–1835*. Jackson: University Press of Mississippi, 2004.

Lindskoog, Carl. "How the Haitian Refugee Crisis Led to the Indefinite Detention of Immigrants." *Washington Post*, 9 April 2018. https://www.washingtonpost.com/news/made-by-history/wp/2018/04/09/how-the-haitian-refugee-crisis-led-to-the-indefinite-detention-of-immigrants/?utm_term=.379d4dc4694c.

Loichot, Valérie. *Orphan Narratives: The Postplantation Literature of Faulkner, Glissant, Morrison, and Saint-John Pearse*. Charlottesville: University of Virginia Press, 2007.

Long, Alecia P. *The Great Southern Babylon: Sex, Race, and Respectability in New Orleans, 1865–1920*. Baton Rouge: Louisiana State University Press, 2004.

Loomba, Ania. *Colonialism/Postcolonialism*, 3rd ed. London: Routledge, 2015.

Lowe, John. *Calypso Magnolia: The Crosscurrents of Caribbean and Southern Literature*. Chapel Hill: University of North Carolina Press, 2016.

Lowe, John, ed. *Conversations with Ernest Gaines*. Jackson: University Press of Mississippi, 1995.

Lowe, John. "Transcendence in the House of the Dead: The Subversive Gaze of *A Lesson Before Dying*." In *The World is Our Home: Society and Culture in Contemporary Southern Writing*, edited by Jeffrey J. Folks and Nancy Summers Folks, 142–62. Lexington: University Press of Kentucky, 2000.

Machado Sáez, Elena. "Dictating Desire, Dictating Diaspora: Junot Díaz's *The Brief Wondrous Life of Oscar Wao* as Foundational Romance." *Contemporary Literature* 52 no. 3 (Fall 2011): 522–55.

Maillard, Kevin Noble, and Rose Cuison Villazor, eds. *Loving v. Virginia in a Post-Racial World: Rethinking Race, Sex, and Marriage*. Cambridge: Cambridge University Press, 2012.

Malisa, Mark, and Phillippa Nhengeze. "Pan-Africanism: A Quest for Liberation and the Pursuit of a United Africa." *Genealogy* 2 no. 3 (August 2018): 28–43.

Mama, Amina. "Sheroes and Villains: Conceptualizing Colonial and Contemporary Violence Against Women in Africa." In *Feminist Genealogies, Colonial Legacies, Democratic Futures*, edited by M. Jacqui Alexander and Chandra T. Mohanty, 46–62. New York: Routledge, 1997.

Mandle, Jay R. *Not Slave, Not Free: The African American Economic Experience Since the Civil War*. Durham, NC: Duke University Press, 1992.

Martin, Joan. "*Plaçage* and the Louisiana *Gens de Couleur Libre*: How Race and Sex Defined the Lifestyles of Free Women of Color." In *Creole: The History and Legacy of*

Louisiana's Free People of Color, edited by Sybil Kein, 57–70. Baton Rouge: Louisiana State University Press, 2000.

Matsuda, Mari J., Charles R. Lawrence III, Richard Delgado, and Kimberlé Williams Crenshaw. *Words that Wound: Critical Race Theory, Assaultive Speech, and the First Amendment*. Boulder, CO: Westview Press, 1993.

Matthews, John T. "Recalling the West Indies: From Yoknapatawpha to Haiti and Back." *American Literary History* 16 no. 2 (2004): 238–62.

Mayes, April J. *Mulatto Republic: Class, Race, and Dominican National Identity*. Gainesville: University Press of Florida, 2014.

McClintock, Anne. "The Angel of Progress: Pitfalls of the Term 'Post-Colonialism.'" *Social Text* 31/32 (1992): 84–98.

McClintock, Anne. *Imperial Leather: Race, Gender, and Sexuality in the Colonial Contest*. London: Routledge, 1995.

McKay, Nellie Y. "Alice Walker's 'Advancing Luna—and Ida B. Wells': A Struggle Toward Sisterhood." *Rape and Representation*, edited by Lynn A. Higgins and Brenda R. Silver, 248–62. New York: Columbia University Press, 1991.

Menakem, Resmaa. *My Grandmother's Hands: Racialized Trauma and the Pathway to Mending Our Hearts and Bodies*. Las Vegas, NV: Central Recovery Press, 2017.

Milewski, Melissa. "Slave to Litigant: African Americans in Court in the Postwar South, 1865-1920." *Law and American History Review* 30 no. 3 (August 2012): 723–69.

Miller, Christopher L. *The French Atlantic Triangle: Literature and Culture of the Slave Trade*. Durham, NC: Duke University Press, 2008.

Mills, Gary. *The Forgotten People: Cane River's Creoles of Color*. Baton Rouge: Louisiana State University Press, 2013.

Miranda, Katherine. "Junot Díaz, Diaspora, and Redemption: Creating Progressive Imaginaries." *Sargasso, Quisqueya: La República Extended* 2 (2008–09): 23–39.

Mississippi Department of Archives and History. "Miscegenation Law: Mississippi and the Nation." 2015. http://www.mdah.ms.gov/new/wpcontent/uploads/2014/08/MiscegenationLaw.pdf.

Mississippi Legislature. "Mississippi Black Code (1865)." America's Reconstruction: People and Politics After the Civil War. 2003. http://www.digitalhistory.uh.edu/exhibits/reconstruction/section4/section4_blackcodes.html.

Mohammed, Patricia. "'But Most of All Mi Love Me Browning': The Emergence in Eighteenth and Nineteenth-Century Jamaica of the Mulatto Woman as Desired." *Feminist Review* 65 (2000): 22–48.

Mootoo, Shani. *Cereus Blooms at Night*. New York: Grove Press, 1996.

Moran, Rachel. *Interracial Intimacy: The Regulation of Race & Romance*. Chicago: University of Chicago Press, 2001.

Morelli, Federica. "Race, Wars, and Citizenship: Free People of Color in the Spanish American Independence." *Journal of the History of Ideas* 79 no. 1 (January 2018): 143–56.

Morgan, Jennifer. *Laboring Women: Reproduction and Gender in New World Slavery*. Philadelphia: University of Pennsylvania Press, 2004.

Morgan, Paula, and Valerie Youssef. *Writing Rage: Unmasking Violence through Caribbean Discourse*. Kingston, Jamaica: University of the West Indies Press, 2006.

Morrison, Adele. "*Black v. Gay?* Centering LBGT People of Color in Civil-Marriage Debates." In *Loving V. Virginia in a Post-Racial World: Rethinking Race, Sex, and Marriage*, edited by Kevin Noble Maillard and Rose Cuison Villazor. Cambridge: Cambridge University Press, 2012.

Morrison, Jennifer. "The Politics of the Plate: Foodways and Southern Culture in Ernest Gaines's 'Of Love and Dust.'" Folklife in Louisiana. 2016. 2 July 2018.

Morrison, Toni. *Beloved*. New York: Vintage, 2004. First published 1987.

Muhammad, Khalil Gibran. *The Condemnation of Blackness: Race, Crime, and the Making of Modern Urban America*. Cambridge, MA: Harvard University Press, 2011.

Mulvey, Laura. "Visual Pleasure and Narrative Cinema." In *Film Theory and Criticism: Introductory Readings*, edited by Leo Braudy and Marshall Cohen, 833–44. New York: Oxford University Press, 1999.

Munro, Martin. "Avenging History in the Former French Colonies." *Transition* 99 (2008): 18–39.

Munro, Martin. "Can't Stand up for Falling down: Haiti, Its Revolutions, and Twentieth-Century Negritudes." *Research in African Literatures* 35 no. 2 (Summer, 2004): 1–17.

Munro, Martin. "Hatred Chérie: History, Silence and Animosity in Three Haitian Novels." In *Echoes of the Haitian Revolution 1804-2004*, edited by Martin Munro and Elizabeth Walcott-Hackshaw, 163–75. Kingston, Jamaica: University of the West Indies Press, 2008.

Murphy, Gretchen. *Hemispheric Imaginings: The Monroe Doctrine and the Narratives of US Empire*. Durham, NC: Duke University Press, 2005.

Nicholls, David. *From Dessalines to Duvalier: Race, Colour and National Independence in Haiti*. Piscataway, NJ: Rutgers University Press, 1996.

Nugent, Maria. *Lady Nugent's Journal: Jamaica One Hundred Years Ago: Reprinted from Journal Kept by Maria, Lady Nugent, from 1801 to 1815, Issued for Private Circulation in 1839*. Los Angeles: HardPress Publishing, 2018.

Obregón, Liliana. "Black Codes in Latin America," Microsoft Encarta Africana Third Edition. 1998–2000.

O'Brien, Sean P. "Some Assembly Required: Intertextuality, Marginalization, and *The Brief Wondrous Life of Oscar Wao*." *The Journal of the Midwest Modern Language Association* 45 no. 1 (Spring 2012): 75–94.

Oppenheim, Leonard. "The Law of Slaves: A Comparative Study of the Roman and Louisiana Systems." In *An Uncommon Experience: Law and Judicial Institutions in Louisiana 1803-2003*, edited by Judith Kelleher Schafer and Warren H. Billings, 312–30. The Louisiana Purchase Bicentennial Series in Louisiana History, vol. XIII. Lafayette: Center for Louisiana Studies at University of Southwestern Louisiana, 1997.

Pablo Cruz, Rosayra, and Julie Schwietert Collazo. *The Book of Rosy: A Mother's Story of Separation at the Border*. New York: HarperOne, 2020.

Padgett, John B. "The McCaslin Family Legacy." William Faulkner on the Web. Accessed 12 September 2012. http://cypress.mcsr.olemiss.edu/~egjbp/faulkner/gen-mccaslin.html.

Padgett, John B. "Thomas Sutpen's Dynasty." William Faulkner on the Web. Accessed 12 September 2012. http://cypress.mcsr.olemiss.edu/~egjbp/faulkner/gen-sutpen.html.

Palmer, Vernon. "The Origins and Authors of the *Code Noir*." In *An Uncommon Experience: Law and Judicial Institutions in Louisiana 1803-2003*, edited by Judith Kelleher Schafer and Warren H. Billings, 331–59. The Louisiana Purchase Bicentennial Series in Louisiana History, vol. XIII. Lafayette: Center for Louisiana Studies at University of Southwestern Louisiana, 1997.

Patterson, Orlando. *Slavery and Social Death: A Comparative Study*. Cambridge, MA: President and Fellows of Harvard College, 1982.

Patterson, Richard F. "Resurrecting Rafael: Fictional Incarnations of a Dominican Dictator." *Callaloo* 29 no. 1 (Winter 2006): 223–37.

Paulino, Edward. *Dividing Hispaniola: The Dominican Republic's Border Campaign Against Haiti, 1930-1961*. Pittsburgh, PA: University of Pittsburgh Press, 2015.

PBS. "Convict Leasing." *Slavery by Another Name*. http://www.pbs.org/tpt/slavery-by-another-name/themes/convict-leasing/.

Peabody, Sue, and Tyler Stovall, eds. *The Color of Liberty: Histories of Race in France*. Durham, NC: Duke University Press, 2003.

Pilgrim, David. "The Mammy Caricature." Museum of Racist Memorabilia. October 2000. Ferris State University. 11 December 2010. http://www.ferris.edu/jimcrow/mammies/.

Pitavy, François. "The Making of a French Faulkner: A Reflection on Translation." *Faulkner Journal* 24 no. 1 (Fall 2008): 83–97.

Polyné, Millery. *From Douglass to Duvalier: US African Americans, Haiti, and Pan Americanism 1870-1964*. Gainesville: University Press of Florida, 2010.

Prakash, Gyan, ed. *After Colonialism Imperial Histories and Postcolonial Displacements*. Princeton, NJ: Princeton University Press, 2001.

Price, Byron Eugene, and John Charles Morris. *Prison Privatization: The Many Facets of a Controversial Industry*. Vol. 1. Santa Barbara, CA: Praeger, 2012.

Rappleye, Hannah, and Lisa Riordan Seville. "24 Immigrants Have Died in ICE Custody During the Trump Administration." NBC News, 1 February 2020. https://www.nbcnews.com/politics/immigration/24-immigrants-have-died-ice-custody-during-trump-administration-n1015291.

Renda, Mary A. *Taking Haiti: Military Occupation and the Culture of US Imperialism, 1915-1940*. Chapel Hill: University of North Carolina Press, 2001.

Renk, Kathleen J. *Caribbean Shadows & Victorian Ghosts: Women's Writing and Decolonization*. Charlottesville: University Press of Virginia, 1999.

Rhys, Jean. *Wide Sargasso Sea*. New York: W. W. Norton & Company, 1999. First published 1966.

Rich, Charlotte. "Talking Back to El Jefe: Genre, Polyphony, and Dialogic Resistance in Julia Alvarez's *In the Time of Butterflies*." *MELUS* 27 no. 4 (Winter 2002): 165–82.

Ricourt, Milagros. *The Dominican Racial Imaginary: Surveying the Landscape of Race and Nation in Hispaniola*. New Brunswick, NJ: Rutgers University Press, 2016.

Riddell, William Renwick. "Le Code Noir." *Journal of Negro History* 10 no. 3 (July 1925): 321–29.

Rizzo, Tracey, and Steven Gerontakis. *Intimate Empires: Body, Race, and Gender in the Modern World*. Oxford University Press, 2017.

Roa Basto, Augusto. *Yo el supremo*. Bogatá: Siglo Veintiuno Editores, 1988.

Rodriguez, Jenny. *Undocumented: The True Stories of Illegal Immigrants and Their Children.* Morrisville, NC: Lulu.com, 2014.

Rodríguez, Juana María. *Queer Latinidad: Identity Practices, Discursive Spaces.* New York: New York University Press, 2003.

Rosario, Nelly. "Seeing Double: Creative Writing as Translation." *Callaloo* 35 no. 4 (Fall 2012): 1001–5.

Rosario, Nelly. *Song of the Water Saints.* New York: Vintage Contemporaries, 2002.

Rowe, John Carlos, ed. *Post-Nationalist American Studies.* Berkeley: University of California Press, 2000.

Roy, Arundhati. *The God of Small Things.* New York: Random House, 1997.

Rubin, Jennifer. "Abject Cruelty: Deporting 60,000 Haitians." *Washington Post*, 21 November 2017. https://www.washingtonpost.com/blogs/right-turn/wp/2017/11/21/abject-cruelty-deporting-60000-haitians/?utm_term=.aabd61f9133c.

Russo, Diane Chiriani. "'Whitemouth': A Bakhtinian Reading of Narrative Voice in Ernest J. Gaines's Transitional Novel *Of Love and Dust*." *Studies in the Literary Imagination* 49. (Spring 2016): 93–111.

Saldívar, José David. "Conjectures on 'Americanity' and Junot Díaz's 'Fukú Americanus' in *The Brief Wondrous Life of Oscar Wao*." In "The Global South and World Dis/Order." Special issue, *The Global South* 5 no. 1 (Spring 2011): 120–36.

Saldívar, Ramón. "Looking for a Master Plan: Faulkner, Paredes, and the Colonial and Postcolonial Subject." In *The Cambridge Companion to William Faulkner*, edited by Philip M. Weinstein, 96–122. Cambridge: Cambridge University Press, 1995.

Scarry, Elaine. *The Body in Pain: The Making and Unmaking of the World.* Oxford: Oxford University Press, 1985.

Scharfman, Ronnie. "Theorizing Terror: The Discourse of Violence in Marie Chauvet's *Amour Colère Folie*." In *Postcolonial Subjects: Francophone Women Writers*, edited by Mary Jean Green, 229–45. Minneapolis: University of Minnesota Press, 1996.

Sciuto, Jenna Grace. "'A Border that Exists Beyond Maps': Contextualizing State-Sponsored Violence in Contemporary Haitian American and Dominican American Literature." In "Contextualizing the Anglophone Novel," edited by Shun Y. Kiang. Special issue, *The Global South* (forthcoming, 2021).

Sciuto, Jenna Grace. "'For Fear of a Scandal': Sexual Policing and the Preservation of Colonial Relations in William Faulkner and Marie Vieux-Chauvet." In *Faulkner and the Black Literatures of the Americas*, edited by Jay Watson and James G. Thomas, Jr., 183–93. Jackson: University Press of Mississippi, 2016.

Sciuto, Jenna Grace. "Postcolonial Palimpsests: Entwined Colonialisms and the Conflicted Representation of Charles Bon in William Faulkner's *Absalom, Absalom!*" *Ariel: A Review of International English Literature.* 47 no. 4 (Oct. 2016): 1–23.

Sciuto, Jenna Grace. "Racial Ambiguity, Bootlegging, and the Subversion of Plantation Hierarchies in Faulkner's South." In *Southern Comforts: Drinking and the US South*, edited by Conor Picken and Matthew Dischinger, 193–206. Baton Rouge: Louisiana State University Press, 2020.

Scott, Michael. *Tom Cringle's Log.* Ithaca, NY: McBooks Press, 1998. First published in 1833.

Sedgwick, Eve Kosofsky. *Between Men: English Literature and Male Homosocial Desire*. New York: Columbia University Press, 1985.

Sedgwick, Eve Kosofsky. *Epistemology of the Closet*. Berkeley: University of California Press, 2008.

Seiden, Melvin. "Faulkner's Ambiguous Negro." *Massachusetts Review* 4 no. 4 (1963): 675–90.

Séjour, Victor. "The Mulatto." Translated by Philip Barnard. In *The Norton Anthology of African American Literature*, 2nd Edition, edited by Henry Louis Gates, Jr. and Nellie Y. McKay, 353–65. New York: Norton, 2004. Originally published as "Le Mulâtre." *La Revue des Colonies* 3 (1837), 376–92.

Sharpe, Christina. *Monstrous Intimacies: Making Post-Slavery Subjects*. Durham, NC: Duke University Press, 2010.

Silva Gruesz, Kirsten. *Ambassadors of Culture: The Transamerican Origins of Latino Writing*. Princeton, NJ: Princeton University Press, 2001.

Small, Audrey. "Tierno Monénembo: Morality, Mockery and the Rwandan Genocide." *Forum for Modern Language Studies*. 42 no. 2 (2006): 200–211.

Smith, Faith. *Sex and the Citizen: Interrogating the Caribbean*. Charlottesville: University of Virginia Press, 2011.

Smith, Jon. "Hot Bodies and 'Barbaric Tropics': The U.S. South and New World Natures." *Southern Literary Journal* 36 no. 1 (Fall 2003): 104–120.

Smith, Jon, and Deborah Cohn, eds., *Look Away! The US South in New World Studies*. Durham, NC: Duke University Press, 2004.

Smith, Raymond T. "Hierarchy and the Dual Marriage System in West Indian Society." In *Gender and Kinship: Essays Toward a Unified Analysis*, edited by Jane Fishburne Collier and Sylvia Junko Yanag-isako, 163–96. Stanford, CA: Stanford University Press, 1987.

Snead, James. "The 'Joint' of Racism: Withholding the Black in *Absalom, Absalom!*" In *Modern Critical Interpretations: William Faulkner's* Absalom, Absalom! edited by Harold Bloom, 129–42. New York: Chelsea House Publishers, 1987.

Socolovsky, Maya. "Patriotism, Nationalism, and the Fiction of History in Julia Álvarez's *In the Time of the Butterflies* and *In the Name of Salomé*." *Latin American Literary Review* 34 no. 68 (July–December 2006): 5–24.

Sollors, Werner. *Neither Black nor White yet Both: Thematic Explorations of Interracial Literature*. Oxford: Oxford University Press, 1997.

Somerville, Siobhan B. *Queering the Color Line: Race and the Invention of Homosexuality in American Culture*. Durham, NC: Duke University Press, 2000.

Sontag, Susan. *Regarding the Pain of Others*. New York: Farrar, Straus and Giroux, 2003.

Spear, Thomas C. "Marie Chauvet: The Fortress Still Stands." *Yale French Studies* 128 (2015): 9–24.

Stoler, Ann Laura. "Intimidation of Empire: Predicaments of the Tactile and Unseen." In *Haunted by Empire: Geographies of Intimacy in North American History*, edited by Ann Laura Stoler, 1–22. Durham, NC: Duke University Press, 2006.

Stringer, Dorothy. *Not Even Past: Race, Historical Trauma, and Subjectivity in Faulkner, Larsen, and Van Vechten*. New York: Fordham University Press, 2010.

Suárez, Lucía M. *The Tears of Hispaniola: Haitian and Dominican Diaspora Memory*. Gainesville: University Press of Florida, 2006.

Sublette, Ned. *The World That Made New Orleans: From Spanish Silver to Congo Square.* Chicago: Lawrence Hill Books, 2009.

Sullivan-González, Douglass, and Charles Reagan Wilson, eds. *South and the Caribbean.* Jackson: University Press of Mississippi, 2007.

Sweet, Frank W. *Legal History of the Color Line: The Rise and Triumph of the One-drop Rule.* Palm Coast, FL: Backintyme Publishing, 2013.

Taylor-Grover, Leslie, Eric Horent, Juarod Cal, and Vernard Sterling Jr. "Private Detention Centers: Implications for Policy." In *Prison Privatization: The Many Facets of a Controversial Industry.* Vol. 1, edited by Byron Eugene Price and John Charles Morris, 183–98. Santa Barbara, CA: Praeger, 2012.

Teutsch, Matthew. "'They Want Us to Be Creoles. . . . There Is No In-Between': Creole Representations in Ernest J. Gaines's 'Catherine Carmier' and Lyle Saxon's 'Children of Strangers.'" *Studies in the Literary Imagination* 1 (2016):113–28.

Teutsch, Matthew, and Katharine Henry. "'Memories Wasn't a Place, Memories Was in the Mind': The Gothic in Ernest J. Gaines's the Autobiography of Miss Jane Pittman." *Mississippi Quarterly* 3 no. 4 (2015): 511–30.

Thompson, Shirley Elizabeth. *Exiles at Home: The Struggle to Become American in Creole New Orleans.* Cambridge, MA: Harvard University Press, 2009.

Tolnay, Stewart, and E. M. Beck. *A Festival of Violence: An Analysis of Southern Lynchings, 1882–1930.* Champaign: University of Illinois Press, 1995.

Torres-Saillant, Silvio. "Dominican Americans." In *Multiculturalism in the United States: A Comparative Guide to Acculturation and Ethnicity,* edited by John D. Buenker and Lorman A. Ratner, 99–116. Westport, CT: Greenwood Press, 2005.

Towner, Theresa M. *Faulkner on the Color Line: The Later Novels.* Jackson: University Press of Mississippi, 2007.

Trefzer, Annette, and Ann J. Abadie. *Global Faulkner.* Jackson: University Press of Mississippi, 2009.

Trouillot, Michel-Rolph. *Haiti State Against Nation: The Origins and Legacy of Duvalierism.* New York: Monthly Review Press, 1990.

Tryon, Thomas. "Friendly Advice to the Gentlemen-Planters of the East and West Indies" (1684). In *Caribbeana: An Anthology of English Literature of the West Indies, 1657–1777,* edited by Thomas W. Krise, 51–77. Chicago: University of Chicago Press, 1999.

Turits, Richard Lee. *Foundations of Despotism: Peasants, The Trujillo Regime, and Modernity in Dominican History.* Stanford, CA: Stanford University Press, 2003.

Turits, Richard Lee. "A World Destroyed, A Nation Imposed: The 1937 Haitian Massacre in the Dominican Republic." *Hispanic American Historical Review* 82 no. 3 (August 2002): 589–635.

Vargas, Jose Antonio. *Dear America: Notes of an Undocumented Citizen.* New York: Dey Street Books, 2018.

Vargas Llosa, Mario. *The Feast of the Goat.* Translated by Edith Grossman. New York: Farrar, Straus and Giroux, 2001.

Vargas Llosa, Mario. *La fiesta del chivo.* Madrid: Alfaguara, 2000.

Vieux-Chauvet, Marie. *Amour, Colère et Folie.* Paris: Éditions Zellige, 2015. First published in 2005.

Vieux-Chauvet, Marie. *Love, Anger, Madness: A Haitian Triptych*. Translated by Rose-Myriam Réjouis and Val Vinokur. New York: Modern Library, 2010.
Walcott-Hackshaw, Elizabeth. "My Love is Like a Rose: Terror, *Territoire*, and the Poetics of Marie Chauvet." *Small Axe* 18 (2005): 40–51.
Wallenstein, Peter. *Tell the Court I Love My Wife: Race, Marriage, and Law—An American History*. New York: Palgrave Macmillan, 2002.
Wallerstein, Immanuel. *The Modern World System*. 3 vols. New York: Academic, 1980.
Ward, Jesmyn. *Salvage the Bones*. New York: Bloomsbury, 2012.
Ward, Jesmyn. *Sing Unburied Sing*. New York: Scribner, 2018.
White, Hayden. "The Burden of History." *History and Theory* 5 no. 2 (1966): 111–34.
White, Hayden. *Metahistory: The Historical Imagination in Nineteenth-Century Europe*. Baltimore: Johns Hopkins University Press, 1975.
White, Hayden. "The Politics of Historical Interpretation: Discipline and De-Sublimation." *Critical Inquiry* 9 no. 1 (September 1983): 113–37.
Wiarda, Howard J. *Dictatorship and Development: The Methods of Control in Trujillo's Dominican Republic*. Gainesville: University of Florida Press, 1968.
Wideman, John. *Brothers and Keepers: A Memoir*. New York: Holt, Rinehart, Winston, 1984.
Wideman, John. "*Of Love and Dust*: A Reconsideration." *Callaloo* 3 (May 1978): 76–84.
Wiegman, Robyn. *American Anatomies: Theorizing Race and Gender*. Durham, NC: Duke University Press, 1995.
Williams, Eric. *From Columbus to Castro: The History of the Caribbean 1492–1969*. New York: Vintage Books, 1984.
Williamson, Joel. *William Faulkner and Southern History*. New York: Oxford University Press, 1995.
Winters, Ben. *Underground Airlines*. New York: Mulholland Books, 2016.
Wong, Tom K. *Rights, Deportation, and Detention in the Age of Immigration Control*. Stanford, CA: Stanford University Press, 2015.
Wucker, Michele. *Why the Cocks Fight: Dominicans, Haitians, and the Struggle for Hispaniola*. New York: Hill and Wang, 1999.
Yancy, George. *Black Bodies, White Gazes: The Continuing Significance of Race in America*. Lanham, MD: Rowman & Littlefield, 2016.
Young, Robert J.C. *Postcolonialism: An Historical Introduction*. Oxford: Wiley Blackwell, 2001.

INDEX

References to figures appear in **bold**.

Abdur-Rahman, Aliyyah, 30
Aboul-Ela, Hosam, 177n11
Abraham, Nicolas, 163, 204n6
absent-presence, 19, 136, 139, 153, 159–63, 165
Adams, Jessica, 68, 188n1
Alexander, Michelle, 170–71, 182n2
Aljoe, Nicole, 104, 182n46, 187n47, 196n12
Alvarez, Julia, 4, 6, 13, 15–16, 18, 20, 99, 134–40, 144–46, 148–49, 151, 158–60, 164–66, 169, 181n43, 204n11, 205n15, 206n26, 208nn33–35, 210n48, 211n64; *In the Time of the Butterflies*, 15–16, 135, 137–40, 144–46, 148–51, 158–60, 169, 204n11, 206n26, 208n34; Papers, Harry Ransom Center, 138, 181n43
American studies, 7, 176n7, 178n17, 178n19
Ángel, José N., 215n12
Aslakson, Kenneth, 49, 54
Ayuso, Monica, 211n56

Babb, Valerie, 192n5
Beavers, Herman, 95–96
Bell, Madison Smartt, 200n42, 201n50
Bhabha, Homi, 67, 191n24
Bibler, Michael, 31–32, 83, 89, 176n5
blanqueamiento, 143–44
body, bodies, 3, 5–6, 11–12, 29, 32, 34–35, 38–39, 43, 62, 82–83, 85, 88–89, 92–93, 114, 116, 147–48, 151–52, 154, 163, 167, 169–70, 172–73, 184n24, 185n28, 186n41, 191n27, 198n25, 198n27, 213n73
Brooks, David, 100

Brown, Isabel Zakrzewski, 159, 211n64
Brown, Kimberly Juanita, 37
Brown, Sterling, 189n9
Butler, Judith, 178n16

Carastathis, Anna, 8
Cashin, Sheryll, 176n5
circum-Caribbean, Greater Caribbean, 4–7, 13–14, 23, 49, 78, 80, 99–100, 113, 118, 120, 136, 140, 152, 157, 172, 176n6
Carroll, Charles, 33
Chak, Tings, *Undocumented: The Architecture of Migrant Detention*, 175
Chancy, Myriam, 15, 140, 177n12, 199n31, 207n27, 208n34
Chauvet, Marie, 3–4, 6, 13, 15–16, 20, 57, 99–133, 143, 166, 168–69, 176n1, 178n22, 180n38, 181n39, 181n43, 184n19, 195n4, 196n11, 197n19, 200n42; *Anger*, 115, 131; *Love*, 3, 6, 16–17, 99–106, 109–33, 148–49, 164, 198n24; *Love, Anger, Madness*, 6, 15, 99, 168, 181n43, 195n4, 201n47
civil rights, 55, 74–76, 162
Civil War (US), 5, 22–24, 27, 39, 41, 55, 68, 72, 182n4, 183n11, 185n25, 186n36, 188n50
Clark, Emily, 127, 184n23, 189n13
class, 3–4, 8, 10, 14, 16, 21–23, 27, 29, 31–32, 40–50, 54–56, 59, 62, 64, 66, 71, 78–79, 83, 85–86, 91, 95, 97, 100–101, 104–6, 109–10, 113–15, 118–34, 137, 141–42, 146–47, 150, 167, 173, 176n3, 178n16, 178n22, 182n2, 184n21, 184n24, 187n48, 190n20, 194n25, 197n23, 198nn24–25, 199n37, 200nn38–39, 200n41, 203n3

INDEX

Code Noir. *See* legislation
Collazo, Julie Schwietert, *The Book of Rosy*, 175
Collins, Patricia Hill, 8
colonialism, 4, 7, 9–10, 12, 14, 16–17, 21–25, 27, 29, 20, 32–33, 37, 39, 42, 44–54, 56, 61, 78, 80, 99, 105, 109, 114, 118, 122, 124, 133–34, 141, 166, 169–70, 177n13, 179n26, 196n9, 198n27, 202nn55–56. *See also* hierarchy: colonialism; post-/neocolonialism
color line, 4, 7, 8, 11, 13, 21, 22, 23, 28, 31, 32, 37, 39, 44, 47, 48, 66, 67, 68, 77, 78, 177n9, 179n29, 183n9, 183n11, 185n27. *See also* racial construction
convict lease system, 23, 182n4, 196n15
Cooper, Brittney C., 8, 197n23
Costello, Brannon, 187n48
Crassweller, Robert, 159
Crenshaw, Kimberlé, 8, 177n15, 180n32
Creole of Color, 8–10, 13, 16, 31–32, 47–49, 54–61, 66–68, 72, 78–79, 82–83, 100, 120, 184n17, 188n5, 189n7; *Gens des Couleur Libres*, 48, 54; White Creole, 31–32, 184n21. See also *Mulâtres-Aristocrates*
Criniti, Steve, 204n11, 211n64
critical mixed race studies, 6–8, 177n14, 178n19
Cruz, Rosayra Pablo, *The Book of Rosy*, 175
Cult of Southern Womanhood, 28

Danticat, Edwidge, 4, 6, 13, 15, 20, 99–100, 109, 113, 116–24, 153, 166, 168–69, 175, 181n40, 207n27, 208n35; *Breath, Eyes, Memory*, 15, 117–18, 153–54, 157, 163, 168–69, 198n29, 211n62; *Brother, I'm Dying*, 175; "Children of the Sea," 116–17; *The Farming of Bones*, 153, 181n40; "Nineteen Thirty-Seven," 211n56, 212n71
Daut, Marlene, 27, 118–19, 177n12, 195nn2–3
Davis, Adrienne, 29
Davis, Angela, 185n28, 198n26
Davis, Thadious, 48, 189n7, 193n17
Dayan, Colin, 131, 181n39, 195n4, 202n57
de Alva, J. Jorge, 140

Derby, Lauren, 140, 148, 150, 204n10, 206n22, 207n28, 207n31, 210nn49–50
Díaz, Junot, 4, 6, 13, 15, 20, 99, 134–40, 145–55, 158–61, 164–66, 169, 199n35, 203n5, 204n11, 205nn12–13, 205n15, 206n26, 208n33, 208n35, 210n47, 211n63, 212n66; *The Brief Wondrous Life of Oscar Wao*, 15, 80, 135, 137–40, 145–55, 157–63, 169; *Drown*, 15
Dominican Republic, 4, 6–8, 13, 15, 48, 99, 134–64, 166, 169–70, 173–74, 181n40, 204n11, 205n14, 206n20, 206n23
Du Bois, W. E. B., 177n9
Duvalier, François, 4, 6, 13–15, 99–101, 105–6, 113–17, 123, 133–34, 140, 143, 146, 168, 172–73, 195n1, 197nn18–19, 198n29, 199n31, 200nn41–42, 203n3, 204n9, 207nn27–28

El Akkad, Omar, *American War*, 175
Emancipation, 5, 23, 34, 68, 90, 180n34, 182n3, 182n5, 185n25, 186n34, 196n15

family, family formation, 4, 11, 17–18, 22–27, 29, 31, 33–44, 53–54, 58, 66, 75, 77, 79, 109, 113, 116–18, 120–22, 127–29, 139, 141, 146–58, 179n29, 185n29, 185n31, 189n11, 201n53, 215n9. *See also* marriage
Faulkner, William, 4, 5, 9, 12, 14, 16, 18, 20, 21–46, 57, 59–60, 64, 81, 100, 103, 109, 113, 122, 136, 143, 159, 166–67, 169, 179n27, 180n37, 181n39, 181n43, 183n14, 184n21, 184n23, 185n26, 185n30, 186n37; *Absalom, Absalom!*, 5, 9–12, 17, 21–34, 37, 44–46, 84, 96, 133, 153, 163–64, 179n26, 182n1, 183n8, 183n10, 186n37, 188n50, 198n24, 209n46, 213n75; *Go Down, Moses*, 5, 16, 22–27, 34–41, 44–46, 113, 148, 164, 182n1, 191n24, 194n22; *Intruder in the Dust*, 34; *Light in August*, 34–35, 184n21; *Requiem for a Nun*, 5, 22–23, 41–46, 186n39, 187n46; *Sanctuary*, 34, 42–43; *The Sound and the Fury*, 188n50, 194n29
Felski, Rita, 164

Ferreras, Ramón Alberto, 159
Fitzgerald, F. Scott, *The Great Gatsby*, 81
Foster, Francis Smith, 176n5, 193n16
Foucault, Michel, 61, 111, 140, 190n15. *See also* Panopticon; surveillance
Fowler, Doreen, 43, 186n39, 187n44, 187n46
Fumagalli, Cristina, 174

Gaines, Ernest, 4–6, 12, 14, 16, 18, 20, 47–100, 103, 106, 109, 111, 113, 122, 127, 135, 140, 143, 166–67, 169, 176n3, 180n37, 192nn5–6, 192n8, 193n18; *The Autobiography of Miss Jane Pittman*, 16, 47–49, 54–56, 58–73, 78, 81, 94, 164, 180n37; *The Autobiography of Miss Jane Pittman*, drafts, 64–66, 69–72, 191n21, 191n28; *Catherine Carmier*, 47–49, 54–60, 72, 78, 81–83, 127, 167, 189n7, 189n10; *Of Love and Dust*, 17–18, 47, 59, 74–98, 113, 133, 135, 148, 151, 153, 167–68, 176n3, 193n18; *Of Love and Dust*, drafts, 74, 76, 193n18; Papers, 18, 64–66, 69–70, 72, 74, 91, 94, 181n42, 191n21, 191n28, 192n6, 193n18, 194n23
Galván, William, 159
gaze, looking, 14, 60–64, 80–83, 86–94, 97, 99, 168, 191n25. *See also* surveillance
gender, 4, 8, 11–14, 16, 21–22, 27–32, 34–35, 44–46, 78, 81–93, 95, 97, 100, 106, 109–10, 113, 115–16, 119, 126, 139, 146–47, 150, 155, 167, 170, 172–73, 176n3, 177n15, 178n16, 178n21, 180n32, 197n23, 199n32, 207n31, 208n38, 209n40, 214n1
Gens des Couleur Libres. *See* Creole of Color
Gerend, Sara, 177n11
Giddens, Anthony, 77, 98, 176n5
Gilman, Sander, 197n21
Gilman, Susan, 178n18
Gilmore, Ruth Wilson, 214n2, 214n5
Gleijeses, Piero, 159
Glissant, Édouard, 32, 45, 177n11, 187n49
Global North, 157, 173, 177n11
Global South, 157, 177n11, 215n11
Glover, Kaima L., 102, 195n8
Godden, Richard, 179n27, 184n18

Hagood, Taylor, 179n11
Haiti, 3–4, 6–10, 12–13, 15, 25, 30–31, 48–49, 80, 99–134, 140–46, 166, 169–70, 173–74, 176n8, 178n22, 181nn39–40, 188n2, 195n3, 196n9, 196nn13–15, 197nn16–18, 198n25, 199n37, 200n42
Haitian genocide, massacre, 144–46, 153, 156–59, 162–63, 199n35, 207n29, 208n36, 208n38, 212n71
Hale, Grace Elizabeth, 35
Hall, Gwendolyn Midlo, 188n3, 188n5
Hall, Jacquelyn Dowd, 35
Hamid, Mohsin, *Exit West*, 175
Handley, George, 177n11
Haney López, Ian, 12, 54, 141, 179n30
Harford Vargas, Jennifer, 160, 203n1, 203n5, 208n37, 211n58, 211n60, 212n66
Hartman, Sadiya, 19, 181n45, 182n46
Hebert-Leiter, Maria, 76, 79, 86, 95, 189n11
hemispheric, 4, 6–10, 31, 48–49, 104, 109–10, 136–39, 155, 157, 163, 178n17, 178n19, 196n15, 203n1, 205n11
hemispheric Americas, 3–4, 6, 12–14, 78, 105, 141, 177n13, 196n13, 199n30, 206n19, 209n45
hemispheric south, 4, 6–7, 9, 16, 29, 78, 166, 170
heteronormativity, 11–12, 17, 30, 180n31, 198n24
heterosexism, 146, 168
hierarchy, 3–6, 8, 16–17, 41–42, 48, 60–62, 64–65, 70, 83–86, 89–90, 92–97, 105–6, 109, 113, 115, 129–30, 133, 137, 140, 146, 149, 151, 153, 166–70, 173, 176n3, 197n23; colonial, 12, 16–17, 21–24, 25, 27, 31–32, 39, 44, 46, 49, 56, 66–67, 71, 100, 103–4, 113, 122, 124, 128, 132, 134, 141, 143, 167, 178n23, 183n9; gender, 83, 88–93, 95, 115, 207n31; plantation, 22–24, 28, 32, 35–36, 39, 45, 58, 61, 75, 77–80, 84–86, 89–90, 95, 167; racial, 32–33, 38–40, 48, 58, 67, 79, 89, 92, 105, 115, 125, 167–68; sexual, 28, 33, 83, 95, 115
Higginbotham, Evelyn Brooks, 110, 197n22
Hiraldo, Carlos, 177n12, 178n23

INDEX

Hispaniola, 4, 14, 99, 134, 141–43, 174, 205n17, 206n24. *See also* Dominican Republic; Haiti; Saint-Domingue; Santo Domingo
history vs. History (capital-H-History), literature and history, 16, 19–20, 24, 68, 75, 135–48, 152–65, 181nn44–45, 182n46, 191n23, 203n4, 204n11
Hodes, Martha, 120–21, 180n35
homosexuality, homosocial, 11–12, 31–32, 83–85, 113, 193n16, 198n24, 209n46
hooks, bell, 8, 35
Hutcheon, Linda, 181n44, 203n4
hypermasculinity, 146–47, 150–55, 169, 210n47, 210nn52–53

immigration industrial complex, 170–74, 214n6, 215n9
incest, **26**, 27, 32, 36–37, 39, 45, 58, 116–17, 179n29, 183n10, 187n49, 213n77
infanticide, 41, 43–44, 46, 186n39, 187n46
inheritance, property, 4, 11, 17–18, 21–23, 26–27, 35–37, 41, 45, 58, 150, 179n29, 189n11
Ink, Lynn Chun, 139, 204n11, 211n64
intersectionality, 5, 8, 22, 24, 27, 41, 45, 60, 65, 79, 82, 85, 89, 97, 104, 119, 125, 133, 136–37, 141, 168, 170, 174, 177n15, 180n32, 187n48, 194n25, 197n23

Jacobs, Harriet, 37–38
Jean-Charles, Régine Michelle, 176n1, 195n4
Jim Crow, 13, 23, 55, 68, 109, 170, 173, 176n3, 182n5, 183n6, 214n2
Jing, Yijia, 171
Jones, Gayl, *Corregidora*, 164, 213n77
Jones, Suzanne, 89, 192n12

Kalisa, Marie-Chantal, 198n27, 202n58
Kennedy, Randall, 22, 176n5
Kushner, Rachel, *The Mars Room*, 175

LaCapra, Dominick, 136, 138, 204n6
Lee-Keller, Hellen, 104, 130, 178n22, 202n55
legislation: 1685 Code Noir, Haiti, French Antilles, 9, 13–14, 50–55, 99, 105–9, 112–13, 115, 118, 125, 142, 197n21, 205nn17–18; 1724 Code Noir, Louisiana, 9, 13–14, 47, 50–54, 56, 78, 170, 205n18; 1784 Código Negro Carolino, Santo Domingo, 13–14, 141–42, 205n17; 1808 Digest, Louisiana, 50, 53–54, 189n11; 1825 Civil Code of Louisiana, 50, 53–54, 78; 1826 Code Rural, Haiti, 104, 196n10, 196n15; 1865 Black Code, Mississippi, 9, 13–14, 21–24, 28, 170, 182n1, 182n5; 1908 concubinage bill, Louisiana, 53–54; antimiscegenation laws, 13, 17, 27–28, 36, 75, 180n36, 183n13, 186n32; *Las Siete Partidas*, 50, 205n17; Naturalization Law 169-14, Dominican Republic, 174; Racial Integrity Act, Virginia, 75; Roman law, 50, 205n17. *See also* Jim Crow
Levander, Caroline Field, 177n12
Levine, Robert S., 177n12
liminality, 54, 60, 189n10
Lindskoog, Carl, 173
literature and history. *See* history vs. History (capital-H-History), literature and history
Loichot, Valérie, 32, 178n21, 184n21
Loomba, Ania, 140
Louisiana, 3–10, 13, 16–18, 31, 47–73, 76, 78–79, 85, 99–100, 103, 111, 105, 118, 120, 127, 146, 167, 170, 175, 179n24, 183n13, 188nn2–5, 189n6, 189n11, 192n6
Louisiana Purchase, 5, 10, 48, 50, 67, 118, 179n24, 188n2, 188n4
love, boundary-crossing, as resistance, revolutionary, 5, 16–18, 37, 39, 58, 63, 75–78, 80, 84–85, 87, 89, 94–95, 97–98
Loving v. Virginia, 74–75, 167, 186n32
Lowe, John Wharton, 61, 80, 177n12, 181n41, 191n1, 192n8
lynching, 22–23, 34–35, 41, 90–94, 167, 185n25, 185n28, 185n30, 191n21

Machado Sáez, Elena, 147, 205n15, 209n46
marriage, 3, 17, 21–22, 25, 27–28, 30, 52–54, 58, 66, 68, 75, 77, 89, 109, 115, 179n29, 183n11, 189n11, 189n13, 210n50

Matthews, John T., 177n11, 186n33
Mayes, April, 206n23
Menakem, Resmaa, 163, 213n73
métis, métissage, 10, 32, 84, 178n21, 184nn20–21, 184n24
Miranda, Katherine, 135
Mississippi, 4–5, 7–14, 17, 21–23, 28, 30–32, 36, 48, 99–100, 103, 105, 146, 170, 175, 179n25, 182n1, 182n5, 183nn11–14, 186n32
Mohammed, Patricia, 120
Molina, Rafael Leónidas Trujillo. *See* Trujillo, Rafael
Mootoo, Shani, *Cereus Blooms at Night*, 157, 211n61
Moran, Rachel, 28, 176n5
Morgan, Jennifer, 29
Morgan, Paula, 136
Morrison, Toni, *Beloved*, 43, 186n39, 187n46
Muhammad, Khalil Gibran, 201n49
Mulâtres-Aristocrates, 8, 10, 15, 31, 100, 101–4, 110–15, 118–25, 129–32, 148, 168, 178n22, 184n17, 184n19, 200n38. *See also* Creole of color
Mulvey, Laura, 63, 92–93
Murphy, Gretchen, 177n12

natal alienation, 43, 187n45
neocolonialism. *See* post-/neocolonialism
New Orleans, 31–32, 49–50, 54–55, 57, 60, 64, 184n17, 184n21, 184n23, 188nn1–3, 189n13
Nicholls, David, 119, 197n16
noirisme, noiriste, 123, 143, 200nn41–42, 207n27

O'Callaghan, Evelyn, 202n56
one-drop rule, **26**, 28, 30–31, 36, 38, 179n25, 200n38. *See also* racial construction: as binary
Other, 11, 22, 45, 58, 67

Padgett, John B., **25–26**
palimpsest, 101, 135, 140, 153, 162–63, 179n26, 199n35, 212n69
pan-Africanism, 103, 123, 200n45

Panopticon, 61–62, 80, 93, 97, 99, 110–11, 140, 190n15. *See also* Foucault, Michel; surveillance
passing, 8, 10, 31–32, 54, 57, 60, 67, 179n24, 194n25
patriarchy, 60, 73, 80, 95, 97, 105, 186n39, 187n48, 209n43
Paulino, Edward, 140, 206nn23–24
plaçage, 60, 184n21, 184n23, 189n13
plantocracy, 25, 27, 36, 39, 41, 122, 180n34
polyvocality, 15, 19, 26, 64–65, 139, 162–63, 167, 169, 205n15
post-/neocolonialism, 4, 7, 10, 13, 16, 22–23, 33–35, 37, 45–46, 54, 105–6, 115, 119, 122–23, 131, 137, 140, 146–47, 174, 176n2, 177n11, 178n19, 179n26, 180n34, 182n3, 185n25, 191n27, 196n15, 197n17, 198n28, 199n35, 202n56. *See also* colonialism
prison industrial complex, 6, 170–72, 214nn2–5
privilege, 4, 7–10, 17, 22, 32, 38, 47, 54, 57, 66, 85–86, 90–94, 100, 102, 104, 135, 182n2, 188n4, 195n4

queer, queerness, 5, 12, 31–32, 63, 85, 113, 146, 180n31, 209n44, 209n46

racial construction, 4, 7–13, 21–22, 28, 31, 53–56, 68, 79, 95, 109–10, 118–30, 141–42, 177n15, 178n23, 179n25, 183n6, 184n17, 192n9, 197n22, 199n36, 206n22, 214n1; as binary, 10, 12–13, 21, 26, 28, 30–32, 36, 48, 54–57, 59, 68, 70, 72–73, 78–79, 119, 131, 178n23, 179n25, 179n30, 184n20, 214n1; three-tiered system, 10, 13, 49–50, 54–57, 59, 68, 72, 78, 110, 118, 214n1. *See also* legislation; one-drop rule
racialization, 5–6, 12, 14, 16, 22, 32, 34, 85, 92, 95, 99, 116, 118, 134, 142, 156, 166, 170–73, 199n30, 207n32, 213n73
Rand, Nicholas, 163
Reconstruction, 5, 24, 28, 30, 34, 40, 54–55, 58, 90, 180n34, 183n11
Renk, Kathleen, 130

resistance, 5, 16–17, 24, 31, 38, 41, 44, 46, 63, 71, 78, 87, 92–93, 96, 112, 115, 133, 137, 139, 151, 156, 160, 163, 166–70, 175, 180n31, 186n33. *See also* love

Rich, Charlotte, 205n15, 211n64

Ricourt, Milagros, 140, 208n38

Rodríguez, Jenny, 215n12

Rodríguez, Juana María, 180n31

Rosario, Nelly, 4, 6, 13, 15–16, 20, 99, 134–46, 155–56, 158–59, 164–66, 169, 204n11, 208n33, 211n56; *Song of the Water Saints*, 15–16, 135, 137, 139–40, 142–43, 145–46, 155–60, 163, 169

Roy, Arundhati, *The God of Small Things*, 165, 214n78

Saint-Domingue, 49, 103, 126, 141–42, 188n3. *See also* Haiti

Santo Domingo, 13, 141–42, 178n23, 206n26. *See also* Dominican Republic

Sedgwick, Eve Kosofsky, 11, 31

segregation, 5, 12, 21, 23, 37, 39, 48, 67–68, 179n24, 180n36, 182n2, 183n6

sexual fluidity, 10–12, 16, 32–33, 37, 46, 84, 167, 170

sexuality, 3–14, 17–18, 21–22, 24, 28–38, 42–47, 51, 54, 56, 58–60, 76, 78, 81–85, 90, 94–95, 97, 100–103, 109–10, 112–13, 115, 117, 125–34, 137–41, 146–51, 156–57, 166–70, 176n3, 180nn31–32, 185n25, 194n24, 197n21, 198n24, 203n61, 205n18, 209nn40–42, 209n44, 209n46, 215n9. *See also* heteronormativity; homosexuality; hypermasculinity; sexual fluidity

sexual violence, rape, 6, 9–10, 12–13, 22–24, 29–30, 33–35, 37–38, 42–43, 68–71, 86–88, 90–92, 100, 105–6, 110, 113–18, 125, 128, 139, 146–59, 163, 167, 169, 172, 185n25, 187n42, 191n28, 198nn25–27, 198–99nn28–31, 199n34, 201n46, 201n50, 208n38, 210n47, 211n61

sharecropping, 6, 14, 23, 55–56, 78, 90, 166, 182n3, 189n7

Sharpe, Christina, 176n5

Silva Gruesz, Kirsten, 177n12

slavery, 3–4, 6–7, 9–10, 13–14, 17, 22–23, 27–30, 35–40, 42–45, 48–55, 61, 69, 71–72, 75, 80, 90, 96, 103–9, 114, 120, 122–24, 134, 138, 141–42, 153, 171, 173, 175, 179n24, 181n45, 182nn3–4, 183n8, 184n18, 187nn45–47, 187n49, 188nn2–5, 191nn23–24, 191n27, 194n21, 196nn9–10, 196n15, 197nn20–21, 198n26, 199n35, 200n39, 205nn16–18, 210n50, 213n77

Small, Audrey, 136

Smith, Jon, 177n11

Sollors, Werner, 29, 104

Somerville, Siobhan, 11

status quo, 4–5, 12, 16–18, 24, 39, 40, 46, 61, 63, 67, 77, 80, 86, 94–95, 100, 106, 110, 113, 115, 153, 167–69, 175, 176n3, 193n13

stereotype, myth (racial/sexual), 10, 13, 22, 29, 33–35, 57, 60, 63, 82, 90, 94, 100, 110, 113, 123, 125–28, 133, 144, 167–69, 184n23, 185n25, 185nn27–28, 187n47, 197n22, 199n30, 201n49, 201nn51–53, 202n58; tragic mulatto, 57, 60, 83, 127–28, 167–69, 189nn9–10, 189n13, 193n20, 201n52

Stoler, Ann Laura, 5, 12, 176n5

Suárez, Lucía M., 177n12, 199n34

surveillance, 3, 13–14, 60–61, 66, 86, 88, 93, 99–100, 105–6, 109, 111, 118, 140, 162, 190n15, 201n49, 203n3. *See also* Foucault, Michel; gaze; Panopticon

tonton macoutes, 114, 116–18, 149, 168, 198n25, 198n29, 211n57

Torok, Maria, 163, 204n6

transgenerational phantom, 163–64, 213n74

trauma, 19, 34, 42, 71, 114, 116–17, 135–39, 152–58, 162–64, 168–69, 186n41, 204n6, 210n47, 211n54, 211nn56–57, 213nn73–74, 213n77

Trujillo, Rafael (Rafael Leónidas Trujillo Molina), 4, 6, 13–15, 99, 116, 134–35, 137–55, 160–64, 172, 181n43, 198n25, 203n3, 204n9, 205n15, 206n24, 206n26, 207nn28–32, 208n34, 208n36, 208nn38–39, 209nn40–41, 209n45, 210n49

Vargas, Jose Antonio, 215n12
Vargas Llosa, Mario, *La Fiesta del Chivo*, 146, 203n5, 209n42
Vincent, Sténio, 101
Vodou, 123, 131, 200n44, 202n54, 203n62

Walcott-Hackshaw, Elizabeth, 131, 197n19, 202n60
Wallenstein, Peter, 75
Ward, Jesmyn, 175, 183n14
White, Hayden, 181n44, 203n4
Whiteness, 4, 6, 11–12, 17, 22, 24, 26, 29–30, 35, 40–41, 55, 62, 79, 85, 86, 90–93, 104, 120, 124, 126, 140, 143–44, 152, 194n25, 198n25, 208n32; as protected capital, 4, 11, 17, 24, 30, 79, 91, 121, 143
White supremacy, 4, 23, 45, 68, 123–24
Wideman, John Edgar, 175, 194n28; *Brothers and Keepers*, 175
Williams, Eric, 196n10, 196n15
Williamson, Joel, 28, 183n7, 186n34
Winters, Ben, *Underground Airlines*, 175
Wong, Tom, 171, 214n7
Wucker, Michele, 140, 146, 177n12, 199n37

Yancy, George, 92
Young, Robert J. C., 140
Youssef, Valerie, 136

ABOUT THE AUTHOR

Jenna Grace Sciuto is an associate professor of English at the Massachusetts College of Liberal Arts. Her work has appeared in *ARIEL*, the *Journal of Commonwealth and Postcolonial Studies*, *The Global South*, *Faulkner and the Black Literatures of the Americas* (University Press of Mississippi), and *Southern Comforts: Drinking & the US South* (Louisiana State University Press).

www.ingramcontent.com/pod-product-compliance
Lightning Source LLC
Chambersburg PA
CBHW030618230426
43661CB00053B/2050